**WITHDRAWN
UTSA LIBRARIES**

Colección Támesis
SERIE A: MONOGRAFÍAS, 313

THE FABRIC OF MARIAN DEVOTION IN ISABEL DE VILLENA'S *VITA CHRISTI*

Tamesis

Founding Editors
† J. E. Varey
† Alan Deyermond

General Editor
Stephen M. Hart

Series Editor of
Fuentes para la historia del teatro en España
Charles Davis

Advisory Board
Rolena Adorno
John Beverley
Efraín Kristal
Jo Labanyi
Alison Sinclair
Isabel Torres
Julian Weiss

LESLEY K. TWOMEY

THE FABRIC OF MARIAN DEVOTION IN ISABEL DE VILLENA'S *VITA CHRISTI*

TAMESIS

© Lesley K. Twomey 2013

All Rights Reserved. Except as permitted under current legislation
no part of this work may be photocopied, stored in a retrieval system,
published, performed in public, adapted, broadcast,
transmitted, recorded or reproduced in any form or by any means,
without the prior permission of the copyright owner

The right of Lesley K. Twomey to be identified as
the author of this work has been asserted in accordance with
sections 77 and 78 of the Copyright, Designs and Patents Act 1988

First published 2013 by Tamesis, Woodbridge

ISBN 978 1 85566 248 3

Tamesis is an imprint of Boydell & Brewer Ltd
PO Box 9, Woodbridge, Suffolk IP12 3DF, UK
and of Boydell & Brewer Inc.
668 Mt Hope Avenue, Rochester, NY 14620–2731, USA
website: www.boydellandbrewer.com

A CIP catalogue record for this book is available
from the British Library

The publisher has no responsibility for the continued existence or accuracy of
URLs for external or third-party internet websites referred to in this book,
and does not guarantee that any content on such websites is,
or will remain, accurate or appropriate

Papers used by Boydell & Brewer Ltd are natural, recyclable products
made from wood grown in sustainable forests

Printed and bound in the United States of America

**Library
University of Texas
at San Antonio**

In memory of Professor Alan Deyermond,
without whose support
this book would never have been written

CONTENTS

Illustrations		viii
Acknowledgements		xi
Abbreviations		xiii
Foreword, Rosanna Cantavella		xv
Introduction: Isabel de Villena: Her Life and Times		1
1	Reading the *Vita Christi*	21
2	Pure Bodies: Feeding the Soul in the *Vita Christi*	42
3	Veiled Bodies	63
4	Reading Red: Deepening Understanding of Red in the *Vita Christi*	85
5	For Richer, for Poorer: Redrawing the Boundaries in the *Vita Christi*	108
6	The Fabric of Society: Dressing, Undressing, and Gifting in Sor Isabel's Writing	133
7	Shoes, Shoes, Shoes: Stepping out in Style	153
8	The Crown of Stars and Franciscan Rosary Devotions	179
9	Literary Liturgy: Sor Isabel's Processions and Prayers	204
10	Conclusion	230
Appendix, selected chapters translated from the *Vita Christi*		235
Works Cited		255
Index		281

ILLUSTRATIONS

1. Convent of the Santa Trinitat, Valencia.   10
   Photograph by Lesley Twomey.
2. Woodcut of Isabel de Villena, *Vita Christi de la Abbadessa del*   28
   monestir de les monges de la Trinitat (Barcelona: Jorge
   Costilla 1513), fol. 232v; Biblioteca de l'Universitat de València,
   R-1/148. Reproduced with permission of the Biblioteca Històrica,
   Universitat de València.
3. Miniature of St Clare, *Breviarium franciscanum*, Biblioteca   32
   Nacional de España, MS Vitrina 21–6, fol. 349v.
   Reproduced with permission of the Biblioteca Nacional, Madrid.
4. Damià Forment, *Naixement de la Verge*, Museu Nacional d'Art   64
   de Catalunya, Barcelona, cat. 064141. Reproduced with
   permission of the Generalitat.
5. Master of Cinctorres, *Naixement de la Verge i la Presentació al*   65
   Temple, Museu Nacional d'Art de Catalunya, Barcelona,
   cat. 015853. Reproduced with permission of the Generalitat.
6. Nicolau Falcó, *Retablo de la Puríisma Concepción*, Museo de   66
   Bellas Artes, Valencia, cat. 287. Reproduced with permission
   of the Generalitat Valenciana.
7. *Taula de Sant Miquel*, Museu de Lleida Diocesà i Comarcal,   70
   cat. 83. Reproduced with permission of the Museu de Lleida.
8. Gonçal Perís Sarrià, Eucharist panel, *Retablo de San Martín,*   71
   con Santa Úrsula y San Antonio Abad, Museo de Bellas Artes,
   Valencia, cat. 250. Reproduced with permission of the
   Generalitat Valenciana.
9. Nicolau Falcó, *Tríptico de la Virgen de la Leche*, Museo de Bellas   72
   Artes, Valencia, cat. 294. Reproduced with permission of the
   Generalitat Valenciana.
10. Woodcut of the Nativity, *Vita Christi* (Valencia: Jorge Costilla,   73
    1513), fol. 56r. Reproduced with permission of the Biblioteca
    Històrica, Universitat de València.
11. Gherardo Starnina, panel representing the Sacrament of Marriage,   98
    Retablo de Fray Bonifacio Ferrer, Museo de Bellas Artes,

Valencia, cat. 246. Reproduced with permission of the
Generalitat Valenciana.
12. Jacomart, *Anunciación*, Museo de Bellas Artes, Valencia, cat. 241. 100
Reproduced with permission of the Generalitat Valenciana.
13. Nicolau Falcó, Annunciation panel, *Retablo de la Purísma* 101
Concepción, Museo de Bellas Artes, Valencia, cat. 287.
Reproduced with permission of the Generalitat Valenciana.
14. Master of Perea, *Adoración de los Reyes*, Museo de Bellas Artes, 102
Valencia, cat. 292. Reproduced with permission of the Generalitat
Valenciana.
15. Miquel Alcanyís, Annunciation panel, *Retablo de la Santa Cruz*, 114
Museo de Bellas Artes, Valencia, cat. 254. Reproduced with
permission of the Generalitat Valenciana.
16. Chopines dating from the fifteenth and sixteenth centuries, Museu 154
Textil i d'Indumentària, Barcelona, cat. 88.426, 430, 434, 435.
17. Tomb of Beatriu Cornell, Museu de Lleida Diocesà i Comarcal, 162
cat. 128. Reproduced with permission of the Museu de Lleida.
18 *Retaule dels Goigs de la Verge*, Hispanic Society of America, A13. 164
Reproduced with permission of the Hispanic Society of America,
New York.
19. *Retaule de Santa Maria del Roser*, Museu de Lleida Diocesà i 165
Comarcal, cat. 94. Reproduced with permission of the Museu de
Lleida.
20. Nicolau Falcó, detail from the panel of St Anne, *Retablo de la* 166
Purísma Concepción, Museo de Bellas Artes, Valencia, cat. 287.
Reproduced with permission of the Generalitat Valenciana.
21. Leonardo de Vinci, *Virgin of the Rocks*, National Gallery, cat. 1093. 186
Reproduced with permission of the National Gallery, London.
22. Abdón Castañeda, *Virgen de los Ángeles*, Museo de Bellas Artes, 188
Valencia, cat. 3860. Reproduced with permission of the Generalitat
Valenciana.
23. Jan van Eyck and workshop, *Virgin and Child with Saints and* 190
Donor, Frick Collection, New York. Copyright the
Frick Collection.
24. Vicenç Castelló, *Coronación de la Virgen*, Museo de Bellas Artes, 193
Valencia, cat. 464. Reproduced with permission of the Generalitat
Valenciana.
25. Michael Sittow, *Couronnement de la Vierge par les anges en* 195
présence de la Trinité, Musée du Louvre, cat. 1966–11.
Reproduced with permission of the Musée du Louvre, Paris.
26. Lluís Borrassà, *Retaule d'Advocació Franciscana*, Museu 208
Episcopal de Vic, cat. 714–19. Reproduced with permission
of the Museu Episcopal de Vic.

27. Throne of Prioress Blanca of Aragon and Anjou, Museu de Lleida 211
    Diocesà i Comarcal, cat. 19.
28. Pere Nicolau, Ascension panel, *Retablo de los Siete Gozos*, 214
    Museo de Bellas Artes, Valencia, cat. 2263–69. Reproduced
    with permission of the Generalitat Valenciana.
29. Artist unknown, Ascension panel, *Retaule dels Goigs de la Verge*, 215
    Museo de Bellas Artes, Valencia, cat. 278. Reproduced with
    permission of the Generalitat Valenciana.
30. Woodcut of the Ascension, *Vita Christi de la Abbadessa del* 216
    monestir de les monges de la Trinitat (Valencia: Jorge Costilla,
    1513), fol. 170v; Biblioteca de l'Universitat de València, R-1/148.
    Reproduced with permission of the Biblioteca Històrica,
    Universitat de València.
31. Woodcut of the Ascension, *Vita Christi d[e] la Reuerent* 216
    Abbadessa dela Trinitat corregit ab les cotacions nouame[n]t
    tretes en los marges (Barcelona: Carles Amorós, 1527), fol. 201r;
    Biblioteca de l'Universitat de València, R-1/107. Reproduced with
    permission of the Biblioteca Històrica, Universitat de València.
32. Pere Nicolau, Pentecost panel, *Retablo de los Siete Gozos*, 218
    Museo de Bellas Artes, Valencia, cat. 2263–69. Reproduced with
    permission of the Generalitat Valenciana.
33. Llorenç Saragossà, *Escenas de la vida de San Lucas: San Lucas* 219
    escribiendo su Evangelio al dictado de la Virgen, Museo de Bellas
    Artes, Valencia, cat. 248. Reproduced with permission of the
    Generalitat Valenciana.

ACKNOWLEDGEMENTS

I am grateful for the support of the Spanish Ministerio de Asuntos Exteriores which permitted me to undertake research in the Arxiu del Regne de València and access the records of the Puritat convent. This research underpins Chapters 1 and 2. Chapter 8 includes archive work undertaken as part of a research project entitled 'The Immaculate Conception in Hispanic Hymnody', supported by the Arts and Humanities Research Board and the British Academy. Research into the Guild of the *Tapiners* and the presence of *tapins* in Valencian archives was undertaken in 2009 with support from the Pasold Research Institute.

A number of the chapters included in this volume have been tested out as conference or seminar papers over the years. The early part of Chapter 2 was presented as a paper at the 38th International Medieval Congress at the University of Western Michigan, Kalamazoo, 8–11 May 2003. A refined version of the same chapter was presented as a seminar paper with the title 'Pure Bodies in the Writing of Isabel de Villena' at the Medieval Hispanic Research Seminar on 5 March 2004 at Queen Mary and Westfield College, University of London. A shorter version of Chapter 2 was published in *La Corónica* with the title 'Sor Isabel de Villena, her *Vita Christi* and an Example of Gendered Immaculist Writing in the Fifteenth Century'. It is reproduced here with permission of *La Corónica*. A shorter version of Chapter 4, 'Reading Red', was presented as a paper at the 'Metamorphoses of Allegory: Discourse and Power in Spain from Medieval to Modern Times' conference, held at Manchester University in September 2003; it was subsequently published in *Las metamorfosis de la alegoría: discurso y sociedad en la Península Ibérica desde la Edad Media hasta la edad contemporánea* under the title 'Relectura del color rojo: la alegoría en la *Vita Christi* de Isabel de Villena' (Twomey 2005). This chapter appears here in English for the first time, with the permission of the publisher. A first version of the chapter 'For Richer, For Poorer' was presented at the 38th International Congress for Medieval Studies at Kalamazoo, Western Michigan University, in May 2005. The section of the chapter relating to jewellery was presented at the Congreso Internacional e Interdisciplinario 'Avanzando hacia la igualdad' at Malaga University, 2–4 November 2005. This paper was subsequently published in Spanish as 'María: joya entre joyas' (2007c). It is published here in English for the first time and its scope is much extended.

A partial version of Chapter 8 was given as a paper at the XV Congreso Internacional de la Asociación Internacional de Hispanistas, Monterrey, Mexico, 19–24 July 2004. It was published in Spanish in the proceedings of the conference under the title 'La corona de doce estrellas: devoción y desarrollo' (2007a). This version of the article which appeared in Spanish has now been extended and its scope much developed. It appears here in English for the first time. Another section of this chapter was presented as a paper entitled 'Crowning the Virgin in Fifteenth Century Spain', at the 'Power' conference, held in the Centre for Medieval and Renaissance Studies, University of Durham, 13–16 July 2007. A paper entitled 'Cloth and its Function in Isabel de Villena's *Vita* Christi' was presented at the XIII Col·loqui of the North American Catalan Society, held at Temple University, Philadelphia, 6–8 May 2010.

I wish also to record my thanks to Professor Rafael Alemany at the University of Alicante for making available to me a copy of the digitized concordance to the text based on Miquel i Planas's edition of the *Vita Christi*, which I have used throughout for study of the text.

I also wish to acknowledge the painstaking comments on style and bibliography made by Professor Alan Deyermond on an early draft of the book, which greatly assisted in preparing the manuscript for publication. I am also grateful to Dr Jane Whetnall for her invaluable suggestions and comments on content, which have enriched the final stages of completing the book. I am grateful to all the colleagues at each conference who listened to and commented on the work in progress. Their ideas have invariably assisted me in bringing this project to fruition in its present form.

All the translations, unless otherwise stated, are the author's own. The English translation of the Bible used, unless otherwise stated, is *The Jerusalem Bible*. It is the standard Catholic scholarly edition, translated from Hebrew and Greek, and combines scholarly philology with Catholic theology.

The author and publishers are grateful to all the institutions and individuals listed for permission to reproduce the materials in which they hold copyright. Every effort has been made to trace the copyright holders; apologies are offered for any omission, and the publishers will be pleased to add any necessary acknowledgement in subsequent editions.

ABBREVIATIONS

ACG	Arxiu de la Catedral de Girona
ACSU	Arxiu Capitular de La Seu d'Urgell
ADG	Arxiu Diocesà de Girona
ARV	Arxiu del Regne de València
BC	Biblioteca de Catalunya, Barcelona
BHS	*Bulletin of Hispanic Studies*
BL	British Library, London
BNE	Biblioteca Nacional de España, Madrid
BNF	Bibliothèque Nationale de France, Paris
BRAE	*Boletín de la Real Academia Española*
CSIC	Consejo Superior de Investigaciones Científicas
CUP	Cambridge University Press
DRAE	*Diccionario de la Real Academia Española*
MBAV	Museo de Bellas Artes San Pio V, Valencia
MEV	Museu Episcopal de Vic
MLDC	Museu de Lleida Diocesà i Comarcal
MNAC	Museu Nacional d'Art de Catalunya, Barcelona
MVC	*Meditationes vita Christi*
OUP	Oxford University Press
PL	*Patrologia Latina* (*Patrologiae cursus completus: series Latina*, ed. J.-P. Migne)
RAE	Real Academia Española

FOREWORD

When Alan Deyermond in 1983 suggested I prepare a critical edition of Isabel de Villena's *Vita Christi* as the subject of my Ph.D thesis, it was one of the least-known medieval texts, even in Sor Isabel's home town of Valencia.

I started by reading the *Vita Christi* in the only readily available edition by Ramon Miquel i Planas (1916) and it was a most revealing experience. Here was a female author who was not inferior to Francesc Eiximenis, Bernat Metge, or even to her highbrow contemporary, Joan Roís de Corella, 'mestre en sacra teologia' [Master of Theology]. I discovered a style of writing that was moving and intellectually stimulating at the same time. Villena's form of expression, though distinctly feminine, did not pretend to be humble, nor did she ask to be forgiven for her womanly daring in taking up the quill. Hers was an ambitious, straightforward discourse, which was self-affirming in its intellectual approach, and emotionally effective. Later on I would discover the writing of Hroswitha of Gandesheim, and then the special quality of Hildegard of Bingen's learned works. But at that time, in my early twenties, I had found only one female author with a similar degree of certainty about her intellectual views, and that was Susan Sontag.

Although there is of course a world of difference between a twentieth-century woman writer of the avant garde, such as Simone de Beauvoir or Julia Kristeva, and a fifteenth-century Franciscan nun, we must not forget that any woman from a past age would have faced similar challenges when expressing her views as a writer. She would find herself trespassing into a world run by men, whether they were clerics or vanguard intellectuals. The level of confidence demonstrated by Isabel de Villena in her own theological views and in her interpretation of Scripture was, therefore, most admirable, as self-doubt may often prevent a woman from writing.

Eventually, although I still included a survey of her work in my Ph.D thesis, I had to abandon my edition of Villena's *Vita Christi*. Thirty years on, Isabel de Villena's *Vita Christi* still has no complete modern edition, even though such an edition is long overdue.

It is because of the absence of a good critical annotated text that current Villena studies possess a special merit, as researchers still have to make do with Miquel i Planas's classic edition and the 1497 incunable – now fortunately available through the Biblioteca Virtual Joan Lluís Vives.[1] The University of Alicante research group which has digitized the Miquel i Planas text under the direction of Rafael Alemany is also responsible for a most useful CD-Rom, *Concordança de la 'Vita Christi' de Sor Isabel de Villena* (Alemany et al. 1996).

In the last few decades, Isabel de Villena has finally found a place within modern surveys on Hispanic women writers. She was first made known to the English reader in *Women Writers of Spain: An Annotated Bio-Bibliographical Guide* (Galerstein 1986), as well as in *Double Minorities of Spain: A Bio-Bibliographical Guide to Women Writers of the Catalan, Galician, and Basque Countries* (McNerney & Enríquez 1994). Wolfram Aichinger (2003) has introduced Isabel de Villena's work to the German-speaking area, and Dominique de Courcelles (2000) to the French. Other scholars who have devoted their efforts to the study of Isabel de Villena in recent years include Roxana Recio (1993), Jean Dangler (1998), Montserrat Piera (2003), David Barnett (2006), and Lesley Twomey, who has written on her more frequently than the rest.

Unfortunately, there are still researchers who overlook Isabel de Villena in their overview of medieval women writers, even t hough she is probably the most prominent medieval Hispanic woman writer. I consider her one of the most important western European women writers of the later Middle Ages, because of the subtlety of her learned discourse as well as the sensitivity and refinement of her narrative. She is also, along with Christine de Pizan, one of a very small number of late-medieval female writers to champion her sex. She does this by using her religious work to emphasize the good points and virtues of women and to suggest that they are favoured by God.

Isabel de Villena, however, deserves attention not only as a woman writing in a world of men, but also because of the inherent quality of her writing. She must have her place not only in the ranks of women writers, but also within a more general history of medieval literature.

It is in this context that Dr Twomey's approach to her research should be placed. There is so much about Isabel de Villena's work that still needs to be made known and Dr Twomey has addressed the task with commendable vigour and perseverance.

The present book is the first complete monograph on Isabel de Villena and it is also the first on her for the English-speaking reader. Furthermore, it focuses on important aspects of the *Vita Christi* which have never been considered before, namely, the material and symbolic worlds which underpin references in Isabel de Villena's work. Clothes, ornaments, and footwear in the *Vita Christi* are interwoven with symbols of medieval Christian theology,

---

[1] <http://www.lluisvives.com/FichaAutor.html?Ref=1404&portal=1>.

such as those associated with the Immaculate Conception. Many have a particularly Franciscan focus; others are explored by Twomey in order to cast light on how they should be understood as conscious choices by Isabel de Villena. Her intentions can then be set in their contemporary context.

Lesley Twomey has succeeded in presenting a groundbreaking and much-needed piece of research, which should open the way for other scholars to undertake further studies of Isabel de Villena, her life and her work.

Rosanna Cantavella
University of Valencia

Introduction

Isabel de Villena: Her Life and Times

The contribution Franciscan women have made to medieval religious life through their writing has been little understood and neglected in comparison with that of the friars until relatively recently. For example, Jill R. Webster apologizes for the tentative nature of her conclusions about the Poor Clares in the realms of Aragon (1993: 220). There has been an upsurge of interest in little-known Franciscan women writers in the new millennium. Lezlie S. Knox points to the way in which literary production flourished in Poor Clare convents and presents the work of a selection of little-known Italian writers, including Caterina Vigri (1413–63) and Battista Alfani (2008: 157–90).[1] Caterina Vigri or de Bologna is given a brief study also in E. Ann Matter's study of Italian religious women writers (2010: 538–9). Bert Roest's study of Franciscan literature (2004) gives a balanced overview of male and female Franciscans, including works for and by women. He divides his study into works for preaching, religious instruction – which incorporates works of edification and rules –, catechisms, and liturgies. Even though he examines the genre of the *Vita Christi* (488) and gives a brief introduction to the *Vida de Jesuchrist* by the Franciscan moralist, Francesc Eiximenis (1327–35?–1409), he does not mention Sor Isabel de Villena. A recent publication, *Medieval Holy Women in the Christian Tradition c.1100–c.1500* includes a short study of Isabel de Villena (Surtz 2010: 516–20, 522) which is incorporated into a chapter on Iberian religious women writers.

Across other Orders, the picture is the same. A few convent writers have made acknowledged contributions to medieval spirituality or liturgy, such as Hildegard of Bingen (1098–1179), yet those whose writing has been placed in its rightful position in the genre are few. Similarly, there has been interest in the writings of a few lay religious women, such as Angela of Foligno (1248–1309), from the Franciscan Third Order (1993), and Julian of Norwich (1342–1416), but much of the writing by women has not been thought important enough to be critically examined or even to preserve.

Ronald E. Surtz's 1995 study, *Writing Women in Late Medieval and Early Modern Spain: The Mothers of Saint Teresa of Avila*, brings together the

---

[1] I have referred to the Franciscan Second Order throughout as the Poor Clares.

writing of previously unconnected Spanish medieval women, most of them religious. These women, probably a minority of those whose work may have preceded St Teresa of Avila's, all wrote devotional, liturgical, and theological literature.

It was puzzling that Sor Isabel (1430–90), the most important woman author in late medieval Spain, was not included among their number, even though the book she wrote is longer than other women's texts. To be fair to Surtz, all the other writers he studied wrote in Castilian and her book was written in Catalan.

My work on the contemporary context in which Sor Isabel lived and worked in Valencia has been directed at making her work better known to an English-speaking public and setting her in her rightful place within Franciscan literature of the Middle Ages. Her book stands out because of its length, because of its devotional content, because of her erudition, and because of the fact it was written from start to finish in her own hand. I address the importance of these elements in Chapter 1.

Sor Isabel was born Elionor de Villena into a high-ranking family which moved in court circles in both Castile and Aragon.[2] She was the illegitimate daughter of Enrique of Aragon and Castile (1384–1434), son of Pere d'Aragó i Arenós. Sor Isabel's father continued to style himself Marqués de Villena, but he lost the right to the title (Cátedra 1985: 63), one among many vagaries which dogged his life. He died when Isabel was very young and she grew up at the court in Valencia under the tutelage of María of Castile (1401–58).

Her father was connected to the royal families in both Castile and Aragon. He was a grandson of Enrique II of Castile (†1379) through his mother, Juana, the King's illegitimate daughter. Sor Isabel was connected to the Portuguese royal family through Juana's second marriage to Prince Dinis of Portugal. Her paternal great-grandfather, Alfons d'Aragó i Foix (1336–1442), was first Marqués de Villena. Alfons was Constable of Castile, Count of Ribagorza, and Duke of Gandia. He was descended from King Jaume II of Aragon (1267–1327), grandson of Jaume the Conqueror (1208–76), who took Valencia and the area to the north and south of the city from the Moors. His wife was Violant d'Arenós († 1431).

Enrique de Villena grew up in Gandia, an important urban centre south of Valencia, under the tutelage of his grandfather. Derek C. Carr and Pedro M. Cátedra point to the flourishing of a Valencian literary circle, including

---

[2] In this section of the introduction, I follow the outline of Villena's life which Albert Hauf provides in his critical introductions, written in one case in Catalan and in the other in Castilian, to his editions of the *Vita Christi* (Villena 1995 and 2006).

leading poets and authors, around the young Villena (1983: 296–7). These included members of the March family, as well as Francesc Eiximenis.³

Sor Isabel's relationship to the reigning monarchs of her day in both kingdoms was close enough for them to recognize and take an interest in her. She was second cousin of Juan II of Castile (1405–54) and of María of Castile, his sister. María, born in Segovia, came to Aragon in 1415 as a young girl to marry her cousin, Alfons the Magnanimous (1396–1458), son of Fernando de Antequera (1380–1416). Shortly after her marriage, she became queen. Like his wife, Alfons was Sor Isabel's second cousin, as was his successor, Joan II of Aragon (1398–1479).

Sor Isabel's connections to the crowns of Castile and Aragon are apparent in her coat of arms on the frontispiece of the first edition of the *Vita Christi*. The castles of Castile and the lions rampant of Leon are present, as well as the red-and-yellow bars of the coat of arms of Aragon. There is also a label with fleur-de-lys, which Sor Isabel's grandfather, Pere, inherited from his mother, Blanche of Anjou (1280–1310), wife of Jaume the Just of Aragon and Sicily.

Little is known about Sor Isabel's mother, except that it is thought she was from Valencia, where Sor Isabel lived most of her life. She was orphaned at four years of age and was taken to María of Castile's court, where she lived as a member of the Queen's household. It could have been at court that the young Elionor became familiar with novels of chivalry, such as *Tirant lo Blanc* [Tirant the White Knight], which was written by Joannot Martorell in the mid fifteenth century and circulated in manuscript form before it was printed in 1490 (Martorell 1990; 2008).

María was not only pious and upright but she was a redoubtable woman. From 1432, she was frequently left in charge of the Kingdom, while her husband was away fighting wars in Naples. The young Elionor was almost certainly influenced by the exemplary life of the Queen. She may have followed her counsel when she entered the Poor Clare convent at the age of fifteen.

---

3 Ausiàs March (1400–59) was one of the principal poets of his day, enjoying the favour of the court in the 1420s. He was born in Gandia and spent most of his life between Valencia, Gandia, and Beniarjó, where the March family had a manor house (Archer 1992: 9–10). The literary merits of the March family were well known outside the Valencia region. Two of them were mentioned in the eulogy of Valencian, Aragonese, and Catalan poets in the *Proemio y carta* of Íñigo López de Mendoza, the Marqués de Santillana (1398–1458). Pere, 'el Viejo' [the Elder] (1336–1413), is honoured as 'valiente e honorable cavallero, fizo asaz gentiles cosas' [courageous and honourable knight, who composed noble works], whilst Ausiàs is given higher praise: 'Mosén Ausiàs March, el qual aún vive, es gran trobador e omne de asaz elevado spíritu' [Mosén Ausiàs March, who still lives, is a great poet and a man of quite the highest inspiration] (Santillana 2003: 653).

The life and writings of Sor Isabel's father

Elionor de Villena's father was a colourful character as well as a prolific writer. A brief understanding of his status, both political and literary, will provide a dynastic context for his daughter's life and work. Enrique of Aragon and Castile, or, as he is most frequently known, de Villena, was important enough at the court of his cousin Enrique III of Castile (1379–1406) to be among those nobles included in the *Generaciones y semblanzas* [Generations and Appearances] by Fernán Pérez de Guzmán (1965), Lord of Batres (1376–1460?). Fernán Pérez was a scion of the Guzmán family, one of the principal ones in Castile. Thanks to Fernán Pérez, Villena goes down in history as a glutton, a man whose face was blotchy, someone constantly embroiled in lawsuits, a womanizer, a man driven by ambition, but one whose ambitions never paid off. This vitriolic pen-portrait, written at first hand, has irrevocably coloured the way in which Villena has been regarded over the centuries.

Villena was a courtier and a man of letters. He was thought erudite by Fernán Pérez: 'tan sotil e alto engenio avía, que ligeramente aprendía cualquier çiençia e arte a que se dava' [he had such a clever and outstanding wit that he learnt any art or science he tackled] but the compliment has a sting in the tail, for his practical skills left a great deal to be desired. Fernán Pérez writes that Villena 'sabía mucho en el çielo e poco en la tierra' [he had his head in the clouds and did not often come down to earth]. What is more, his love of books led him into dangerous practices: 'dexóse corer a algunas viles e rahezes artes de adevinar e intrepetrar sueños e estornudos e señales e otras cosas tales' [he allowed himself to be led into the vile and evil arts of divination and into interpreting dreams, sneezes, signs, and other such matters] (1965: 32–3).

Villena was both favoured and deceived by Enrique III, who married him off in 1399 to María de Albornoz, a rich noblewoman. María was one of the King's paramours. Some of the humorous treatment meted out to Villena may have sprung from the common knowledge that he was being cuckolded.

Fernán Pérez's description of Villena is testimony to the scant regard in which many of his fellow nobles held him. Fernán Pérez records that Villena was a disappointment to his grandfather, who tried in vain to train him as a knight: 'que lo quisiera para cauallero' [for he wanted him to be a knight] (1965: 32). For Nicholas Round, this is evidence of the different attitudes to learning between the older and younger generations of the nobility (1962: 207). Perhaps it has more to say about Fernán Pérez's own views that 'este amor a las escripturas', or bookishness, was allowable in noblemen but only when it was circumscribed by other abilities and balanced by military acumen. His criticism of Villena may also spring from family loyalties. Round points out how, when Fernán Pérez discusses his uncle, Pero López de Ayala (1332–1407), his love of learning is contrasted with his military ability (Pérez de Guzmán 1965: 15–16). According to Round, it is despite his aptitude for war and matters of state that López de Ayala spent time reading (1962: 206). Unlike Villena, who 'fue avido en pequeña reputaçión de los reyes de su tienpo' [was held in little regard by the kings of his day] (1965: 33), López de Ayala 'ovo grant lugar açerca de los reyes en cuyo tienpo fue' [he was held in high regard by the kings of his day]; 'Amó mucho la çiençia, dióse mucho a los libros e estorias, tanto que como quier que él fue asaz cavallero e de gran discriçión en la plática del mundo' [he loved science, was much given to reading books and histories, in so much as possible being a knight and of very gifted in worldly discourse] (15). López de Ayala's ability to judge character was also valued: 'él era onbre que fablava cuerda e razonablemente e avía conocimiento de los onbres para entender quál fablava mejor e más atentado e más graçioso' [he was a man who spoke with sense and reason and knew how to understand those men who spoke better and more courteously, and with wit] (1965: 39). Such courtly attributes are in contrast to what is said about Villena.

A different view of Enrique de Villena, however, can be glimpsed through contemporary documents. He was called upon to be an arbiter in a dispute between two noblemen over how the 1411 *Ordenanzas*, which had been established to prevent public affray, should be interpreted. At the time, Villena was acting as adviser to Fernando de Antequera, King of Aragon, and was constantly in his company. Cátedra considers that he might have been called upon to revise a section of the *Ordenanzas* because of his legal expertise (1985: 61). The letter sent in response to the town council of Cuenca reveals that Villena had been asked to settle a dispute between the council and some of his own vassals and that he was able to act reasonably, approve the appointment of a panel of judges, and act upon the respect for his authority (Cátedra & Carr 2001: 48–50). Another positive perspective is presented by Santillana in his *Defunsión de Enrique de Villena, señor doctor e de exçellente ingenio* [Death of Enrique de Villena, a Man of Learning and Excellent Wit] (2003: 285–94). Santillana praises Villena as 'mayor de los sabios del tiempo presente' [the greatest learned man of the present age] (294, line 170). His eulogy follows a lament for the loss of great poets and writers of the past, classical poets and historians, including Homer, Ovid, Livy, Virgil, Valerius Maximus, Lucan, Cicero, Terence, and Quintilian, and a smaller number of Christian poets and Fathers of the Church: Petrarch, Dante, Fulgentius, Macrobius, and Alain de l'Isle. Although Santillana's desire to praise a fellow noble on his deathbed needs to be taken into account, his eulogy is not lessened by any caveat.

In 1405, Enrique III appointed Villena Commander of the Order of Calatrava, exempting him from completing his novitiate. In order to become Commander, Villena had to request that his marriage be dissolved on the grounds of impotence and to give up his right to be Count of Cangas and Tineo (Cátedra & Carr 2001: 14). After the death of the King, the knights rejected their new Commander, sending a complaint to the Avignon Pope, Pedro de Luna or Benedict XIII (1328–1423). Unlike his daughter's, Villena's vocation seems to have had more of a financial than a spiritual motivation.

Villena fell out of favour at the court of Juan II of Castile and of his favourite, Álvaro de Luna (1390–1453) (Cátedra 1985: 59) and he took refuge at the court of his cousin, Martí the Humane of Aragon (1356–1409).[4] It was Álvaro de Luna who inherited all the lands which Villena had held as dowry from the Albornoz family.[5] Villena's reputation at the court is unclear. Martí de Riquer argues he was held in high regard there because he continued to be styled Master of Calatrava (1961: 721). There were some negative opinions of him at the Aragonese court. According to Hauf, Martí the Humane was concerned that some of the personal disrepute in which Villena was held might damage the Aragonese royal family and he proposed that Villena should be appointed Commander of the Order of Santiago (2006: 9). Unfortunately for Villena, Martí died before that happened. Villena was in dire financial straits, as the begging letter in 1416 to Martí's successor reveals (Cátedra & Carr 2001: 40).

Villena stayed in Aragon, first at the court of Fernando de Antequera and then at that of Alfons the Magnanimous. He retired to Iniesta, today a quiet backwater in Cuenca province, where he established a library.[6] Jeremy Lawrance argues (1985: 83) that his library may have been even finer than Santillana's and that it probably contained Italian books. R. B. Tate itemizes Fernán Pérez's library at Batres (Pérez de Guzmán 1965: 99–101) with its collection of histories by both classical and Castilian authors. His insights show how noblemen's taste in reading matter developed. Courtly taste in reading can be discerned also from what Fernán Pérez has to say about the reading interests of King Juan II of Castile: 'sabía fablar e entender latín, leía muy bien, plazíanle mucho libros e estorias, oía muy de grado los dizires rimados' [he knew how to speak and write Latin, he read well, he enjoyed books and histories, he was keen on verse] (1965: 39), but they do not go beyond what Fernán Pérez deemed suitable for a monarch. It is likely that the scant regard in which her father was held would have affected the young Elionor, although at court she was no doubt protected by her youth and by her relationship to the Queen.

---

[4] Pedro Cátedra and Derek Carr (2001: 23–38) edit the letters from the period of Villena's leadership of the Order (1404–6).

[5] For the changes in wealth and power among the nobility in the fifteenth century and the rewards accorded by kings to their favourites, see Marino 2006.

[6] Cátedra follows Franco Silva in indicating that the concession of Iniesta, formerly part of his wife's lands, was probably brokered by Álvaro de Luna (1985: 60, n. 25).

Sor Isabel did not inherit her father's library. Nothing of Villena's collection remains. After his death, Bishop Lope de Barrientos (1382–1469), the Dominican tutor of the young Prince Enrique, was dispatched to examine its contents and many of the books were burnt, ostensibly because of Villena's fame as a necromancer (Cotarelo y Mori 1896: 108–17; Pérez de Guzmán 1965: 33; Gascón Vera 1979: 317–19; Torres-Alcalà 1983; Hauf 2006: 8). Enrique de Villena was certainly interested in astrology, although the critical consensus is that he was not the author of the *Tratado de astrología* [Treatise on Astrology] (1983; 1994–2000: I, 397–557). His reputation as a practitioner of the dark arts may be because of what Elena Gascón Vera calls his eclectic interest in study (1979: 318), but, in any case, it would have had a negative impact on his daughter, until her own exemplary conduct put such memories to rest. Her father's interest in magic was indisputable, for he was author of the *Tratado de la fascinación o de aojamiento* [Treatise on Bewitching or the Evil Eye] (1994–2000: I, 325–41; 2004). His fame as a necromancer may also spring from hostile political propaganda (Round 1969: 801).[7]

Villena's interest in science is displayed in two treatises, the *Arte cisoria* [Art of Carving] (1994–2000: I, 133–218), and the *Tratado de la lepra* [Treatise on Leprosy] (113–30). He also wrote philosophical works, like the *Arte de consolaçión* [Art of Consolation] (223–99).

Manuscripts of Villena's many works circulated in both kingdoms. For some, the range of subjects that interests him makes him a Renaissance scholar (Gascón Vera 1979: 318; Torres-Alcalá 1984: 26). For others, his approach to his subjects was more akin to the deference to *auctoritas* displayed by medieval scholars (Santiago Lacuesta 1979: 13). Donald Gilbert-Santamaría contends that Villena, although foreshadowing Renaissance humanism, remains unable to 'transcend his medieval context' and that the vernacular was always second to Latin for him, a 'traditional medieval attitude' (2005: 426, 428; see also Recio 1991). However, Étienne Dolet's *La manière de bien traduire d'une langue en aultre* of 1540 clearly shows that the vernacular continues to be second to Latin for many years after the end of the medieval period (see Lloyd-Jones 1989: 348–9). Villena's most widely disseminated work, the *Doce trabajos de Hércules* [Twelve Labours of Hercules], published in 1499, was translated from the Catalan, *Dotze treballs de Hèrcules*, completed in 1417.[8] The Labours of Hercules are given a typically medieval interpretation:

---

[7] Round indicates that Santillana was called a necromancer too, but that in his case the label did not stick; he suggests that, in a period when learning was suspect, 'anyone learned enough to be an author was also subtle enough to be a magician' (1969: 795, 804–5).

[8] The original is now lost and the Catalan version survives only in an edition of 1514 (Cátedra 1985: 55).

> En la ejemplaridad humana universal de Hércules […] injerta otra ejemplaridad más específica, la del caballero medieval, socorro de los débiles y afligidos, protector de la Iglesia, defensor de la justicia.
>
> (Morreale 1954: 32).
>
> [Into the concept of Hercules as a universal example of humanity, he inserts the symbolism of the medieval knight, another more specific exemplary type who acts to succour the weak, protect the Church, and defend justice.]

Villena's translation of classical authors, such as his Castilian version of the *Aeneid*, shows that he was interested in epic history. In this, he was like other members of the high-ranking nobility (Lawrance 1985: 87–9), and his interest in translation was inherited by his daughter.[9] Critical opinion has not valued Villena's translation skills because of his lack of serious understanding of Latin, his failure to take sufficient care with linguistic choices, and his misguided decision to divide the *Aeneid* into 366 glosses.[10] Julian Weiss, however, attempts to redress the balance by outlining how Villena redefines the status of poetry by advertising its 'claims as a worthy means of educating a noble elite' (1990: 17). He shows how Villena's amplification of Virgil's text enables a theory of reading to be reconstructed, and postulates that reading was thought to be a means of enabling the nobility to emulate the warrior-statesman of ancient times (1990: 21).

He was the author of one of the principal medieval poetics, the *Arte de trovar* [Art of Poetry-Writing], which he completed between 1427 and 1428 (Sánchez Cantón 1919; Enrique de Villena 1923; 1994–2000: I: 351–79).[11] His prose translation of the *Aeneid* is, paradoxically, the sole textual testimony to Villena's understanding of poetry.[12]

---

[9] For a critical overview of medieval translation studies to 2005, see Conde 2006.

[10] Enrique de Villena 1994–2000: II & III. See, for example, Santiago Lacuesta 1979: 12–14; Russell 1985: 47; Lawrance 1985: 83. Cátedra (Enrique de Villena 1989) examines the etymologies and sources for Villena's translation errors. José Francisco Ruiz Casanova (2000: 101) offers a reminder of the haste under which the translation was carried out, as well as of Villena's awareness of possible criticism from erudite readers. For a study of Villena's translation of the *Aeneid*, see also Miguel Prendes 1998.

[11] Despite the numerous eulogies of Villena's poetic skills or poetic theories, his poetry has fared less well than some of his other works: 'en lugar del rico acervo de poemas originales que prometen [los elogios], no nos han llegado sino trozos dispersos de una producción esporádica y heterodoxa' [instead of the rich cluster of original poems which are promised, nothing has reached us except scattered fragments of a poetic production which is of a widely differing nature written at different moments in his career] (Walsh & Deyermond 1979: 84–5).

[12] John K. Walsh and Alan Deyermond point out that the titles of any poems he wrote have been lost (1979: 83). The argument that political reasons kept Villena's poetry out of the *cancionero* collections of his day rings hollow (Cátedra 1985: 54).

Sor Isabel's prolific output is a single work on a religious topic but her father's religious works are few, with just one commentary on Scripture, *Exposición del salmo 'Quoniam videbo'* [Commentary on the Psalm 'Whatsoever I see'] (1994–2000: I, 301–24). In his *Exposición*, he adopts a bilingual approach, combining phrases in Latin with commentary in Castilian. Sor Isabel's *Vita Christi* incorporates Latin texts too, blending them with translation and commentary (Recio 1993).

Nevertheless, Villena's prolific authorial output sets Sor Isabel in a literary dynasty. Her father died when she was very young, which means that she was unlikely to have any memory of him at work. She may have possessed and read some of her father's works before entering the convent, but it is indubitable that her decision to enter the convent had a far more important impact on her literary output than anything her father wrote.

Isabel de Villena and the religious life

Sor Isabel joined the Poor Clares at the age of fifteen. Despite there being several established Poor Clare convents in the city of Valencia, she chose to enter the new foundation of the Santa Trinitat (Fig. 1). The older Poor Clare convents were founded shortly after 1250, the first being those of St Elizabeth and St Clare. Lands were given to the Franciscans immediately after the Christian conquest in 1238. As in other areas of the Peninsula, convents were originally established in the city but later began to be situated outside the city walls. The convent of St Clare transferred outside the city walls in 1326. There was a surge in Poor Clare foundations in the area in the fifteenth century: the Santa Trinitat was founded in 1445, and the Jerusalem convent in 1495. The Santa Trinitat occupied a position just across the river from the city in the fertile *huerta* [plain]. It was linked to the city by the Trinitat bridge.

Both foundations correspond to the interest in founding monasteries and convents in the late medieval period (Moorman 1983: 679; McKendrick 1987: 31–7; 202). Legacies, concession of lands, donations, and other privileges were granted to the Franciscans by the Aragonese royal family (Webster 1993: 311–12, 314–16, 329–31, 336–7, 339, 352–4, Silleras-Fernández 2008: 123–5). Geraldine McKendrick argues that the 'royal "monopoly" of Franciscan patronage' was probably a way of strengthening authority for the monarchy, with spiritual reasons likely to have outweighed political ones (1987: 36–7). Nuria Silleras-Fernández also considers that the Aragonese royal families' piety 'had a clear political dimension'. Their programme of almsgiving both expanded the monarchy's influence and enhanced their image as devout rulers (2008: 135).

McKendrick discusses the reasons for the high number of noblewomen

1. Convent of the Santa Trinitat, Valencia.

entering religious orders, particularly the Poor Clares, from the mid fifteenth century onwards. In particular, she notes the close correlation between founding convents and the entry of female family members, which she sees as underpinning noble families' spiritual credentials and as instrumental in building dynastic prestige. There were female Second Order houses in the region around Valencia, at Jativa (founded 1326) and at Gandia (founded 1428).

María of Castile was instrumental in the transfer of the Poor Clare convent from Gandia to Valencia and she was the principal patron of the Santa Trinitat convent in its early days. In the various noble Castilian families which McKendrick investigated there was a desire to ensure eternal security for their souls by endowing monasteries and convents and by funding family pantheons in them, and this was very much the pattern adopted by María, Castilian by birth, when she endowed the Santa Trinitat convent. Even though there was already a Poor Clare convent within the city walls, Maria donated funds for the transformation of the Santa Trinitat and she also left a sum in her will for the construction of her tomb within its cloisters. María's actions mirrored those of her kinswoman, Isabel la Católica of Castile, who left 34,000 *maravedís* in her will to the Franciscans for two thousand Masses to be said (McKendrick 1987: 48), as well as endowing numerous Franciscan convents, and providing alms and donations to others.

Sor Isabel's vocation has been the subject of some speculation, but there can be no doubt that her choice of the Santa Trinitat as the place where her vocation was to be lived out was stimulated by the support it had from the Queen. Although she is discussing Castile, McKendrick's conclusions about the patronage of convents assist in determining some of the reasons which must have influenced her entry. Young women from the founding family were always among the first to enter the convent: 'the patron supplied property, money, and goods in the form of dowries and alms; inmates were recruited from the immediate and extended family' (1987: 213). María's patronage would have recommended not only entry to the convent but also put Sor Isabel in a position to advance within the convent (1987: 202).

To argue that Sor Isabel was urged to take the veil by her kinswoman, or to indicate that it was a period in Peninsular history when wars had vastly reduced the number of possible suitors, is to 'fail to take account of the possibility that for many aristocratic and patrician women the adoption of a religious habit was a positive rather than a negative choice' (McKendrick 1987: 184). Donald E. Queller and Thomas F. Madden also make the point that there was no saving to be made for families whose daughter entered a convent (1993: 708), and that, on top of the dowry, families had to provide girls with a pension for life.

The Santa Trinitat monastery had been established by the monks of the Trinitarian Order in 1256. The monks began to administer and run the hospital and convent of that name, founded by Guillem Escrivà shortly after the conquest of Valencia. Because the Trinitarians were approved by Pope Innocent II in December 1198 to ransom Christians held captive under the Moors, Guillem's family, on his death, decided to hand over the convent and hospital to them. By 1444, however, two Dominicans who had moved into the monastery had caused scandal among the townspeople with their dissolute and disorderly conduct. The monastery, according to reports of the day, had become little more than a bordello (Villena 1995: 15; Benito Goerlich 1998: 33–44). Queen María wrote to Pope Eugene IV (1388–1431), requesting permission to expel them.

The Pope instructed Alfons de Borja (1378–1458), Bishop of Valencia, to expel the friars on 11 July 1444 and to give possession of the convent and all its goods to the nuns of the convent of St Clare. María of Castile had been educated by the Poor Clares in Tordesillas (Benito Goerlich 1998: 45) and that influenced her decision to found a new Poor Clare convent.

In January 1445, seventeen nuns from the convent in Gandia moved to Valencia to occupy the former Trinitarian monastery. The reaction of the city to the new convent was positive from the first. Many new nuns professed and there were many generous donations. Sor Isabel entered the convent on the last day of February in 1445, just a month after it opened. She made her profession one year later, on 25 March, the Feast of the Annunciation. The abbess at the time was Violant del Puig, who had come from Gandia, where she had also been abbess. When Violant died, she was succeeded by Isabel de Solsona. On Isabel de Solsona's death in 1462, Sor Isabel's name was put forward for election as abbess. She was thirty-three years old. The candidacy of Sor Isabel followed the custom in many Castilian convents for the nun most closely related to the founder to be elected.

> Promoted posts within the convent, although theoretically subject to election by vote, became in practice the preserve of nuns from a privileged background. […] These nuns […] were often blood relatives of the convent's patron. (McKendrick 1987: 193)

Although a blood relative of the patron, there was a major problem preventing Sor Isabel's advancement. Normally, illegitimate women could not hold the office of abbess and electing her was not straightforward, even with the support of the Queen. Sor Isabel was granted a papal dispensation and presided over the convent until her death twenty-nine years later.

She was held in high regard by Valencians of her day and there are a number of contemporary eulogies of her. Bernat Fenollar (1438–1516) dedicated his *Passi en cobles* [Verse Passion] to Sor Isabel: 'A la molt illustre e deuotissima senyora dona Ysabel de Villena, digna abadessa dela Sancta Trinitat' [To the most illustrious and highly devout lady, Isabel de Villena, worthy abbess of the Holy Trinity] (cited in Hauf 2006: 7; Garcia Sempere 2002: 225). Similarly, Fray Jaume Péreç mentions her encouragement to write his commentary on the Magnificat, *Canticum virginis*. Péreç shows that her lineage was known in the city: 'Regia ex yspanorum et illustri propagine filie et dilectissime domine' [Illustrious scion of the kings of Spain and well-loved lady] (1485: unnumbered folios; fol. 91v, cited in Villena 1992: 149).

Sor Isabel's period of office had a great influence on the Santa Trinitat. There was a contemporary impact because of the respect in which she was held during her lifetime and there was a longer-term one because of her authorial legacy (Hauf 2006: 25).

Sor Isabel de Villena and the *Vita Christi* tradition

Sor Isabel chose to write a *Vita Christi* in the vernacular for her nuns. The printing of religious works in the vernacular, whether religious poetry or other works, was a major element of the output of the Valencian presses at the end of the fifteenth century and at the start of the sixteenth (Berg Sobré 1979: 303). Sor Isabel was opting to write in a genre which was beginning to capture a reading public at the turn of the century. At the end of the fifteenth century, various *Vitae Christi* were being written, translated, and published in Castile, Valencia, and Portugal. She chose to write her own, even though Eiximenis had already written a Franciscan *Vida de Jesucrist*, which her nuns could have read.

The tradition of the *Vita Christi* was an important one, as the number of copies of the *Meditationes vitae Christi* (*MVC*) shows (Fischer 1932). It was thought to be by St Bonaventure (†1274) and was copied and conserved in cathedral and royal libraries in most European countries.[13] It is now known that the *MVC*, which gained pride of place in so many libraries and book collections, was by John of Caulibus, a Tuscan Franciscan. The *MVC* was written for a Poor Clare nun, and in this has some similarity to the *Vita Christi*, which Sor Isabel wrote for the nuns in her charge. Like Sor Isabel's *Vita Christi*, it begins with a scene set in heaven, prior to the birth of Christ, in which two heavenly beings plead with God for humanity's redemption (John of Caulibus 1997: 11–12). Sor Isabel amplifies the debate between Mercy and Truth, two female allegorical figures, at chapter 15, from a short scene (John of Caulibus 1997: 12–14) to a much longer one (Villena 1497:

[13] This attribution continued well into the seventeenth century. See, for example, John Heigham's English translation, which was also dedicated to the Poor Clares, specifically to the 'Reverend and religious Mother, Clara Mariana, Right worthie Abbesse of the poor Clares of Graveling: and to all her devout and Religious daughters' (1622: 3).

fols 23v–26v; 1916: I, 86–96).[14] At the end of their debate, Mercy and Truth plead with God for the redemption of humanity (fols 26v–27r; I, 97–9). The life of Mary prior to the Incarnation is covered in the third chapter of the *MVC*, 'De vita Marie virginis ante incarnationem filii' [On the Life of the Virgin Mary before the Incarnation of her Son] (John of Caulibus 1997: 15–18), whereas in the *Vita Christi* the Annunciation begins at chapter 20 (fols 30r–31r; I, 113). In the *MVC* there is a passing reference at the Ascension to the adoration of the Virgin by the hosts of heaven, which seems to have stimulated Isabel de Villena's three scenes of obeisance to the Virgin at the Ascension. John of Caulibus ends his life of Christ, as St Luke's Gospel does, with the Ascension. Sor Isabel continues her life of Christ after his death, ending with the Dormition, Assumption, and Coronation of Mary.

Ludolph of Saxony (1295–1377) wrote the best-known *Vita Christi* of the late Middle Ages. It was translated into French, Castilian, and Catalan, as well as Portuguese, Italian, Dutch, and German (Conway 1976: 2; for a study of the Valencian version, see Romero Lucas 2003. Sor Isabel knew Joan Roís de Corella (1433/43–97) and his family, as they were benefactors of the convent, and she would have been aware of his translation of Ludolph's *Vita Christi* (Courcelles 2000: 107) as the manuscript would have been in circulation prior to its going to press. Roís de Corella had the last part, *Lo quart del Cartoxà*, printed first, in 1495, by Lope de Roca, five years after Isabel de Villena's death. *Lo terç del Cartoxà* appeared in print next, also in 1495, with *Lo primer del Cartoxà* in 1496. The final volume, *Lo segon del Cartoxà*, was printed by Cristóbal Cofman in 1500 (Romero Lucas 2003: 300, 307). *Lo quart*, the Passion of Christ, was reprinted just fourteen months after its first print run, marking its 'gran éxito editorial' (2003: 302).

Ludolph's *Vita Christi* begins with the 'eternal Godhood of Christ, the Fall, and the divine plan regarding the redemption of the world' (Conway 1976: 19). Sor Isabel begins her *Vita Christi* with the prescient vision of God planning for the redemption of humankind. Sor Isabel, like Ludolph, opens with words from Scripture. He begins 'In principio erat Verbum' [In the beginning was the Word] from the opening of St John's Gospel. She begins '*Ecce jam venit plenitudo temporis*' [Behold now the fullness of time has come] (fol. 2r; I, 9) with its echo of Galations 4. 4. Ludolph opens with an account of the birth and espousal of the Virgin, Sor Isabel begins with the

---

[14] All citations from Isabel de Villena's *Vita Christi* are given with folio numbers from the 1497 edition. Although the numbering is not consistent, this version is now the most readily available following the publication of Hauf's facsimile and critical study (Villena 2006). The first modern edition was published in 1916. All references to the *Vita Christi* give the volume and page number from this edition.

conception, birth, and childhood of the Virgin. Ludolph bases the events of the life of Christ closely on Gospel events, whereas Sor Isabel spends a considerable proportion of her book describing events which occur before the birth of Christ. Ludolph and his Catalan translator explicitly avoid the Apocryphal Gospel stories, whereas Sor Isabel gives them a central place in the *Vita Christi,* taking from them a wealth of details including the stories of the annunciation to Anne and Joachim, and their meeting at the Golden Gate, the story of Mary and Joseph's meeting with the thieves (ch. 85, fols 104r–105r; I, 343), and her stories of Mary's work to support the family in exile (ch. 94, fol. 99v–100r; II, 17). Some of the elements of the apocryphal stories she uses have their parallel in the *Legenda aurea* [Golden Legend] by Jacobus de Voragine (1993), a Dominican friar (1230–98). His book was second only to the Bible in its diffusion in the Middle Ages. Voragine's accounts of the saints, which follows the calendar, includes theological commentary, legend, and miracles.

Sor Isabel's work is structured very differently, but the extensive coverage she gives to the Nativity of the Virgin, to her Presentation in the Temple, and to her Assumption reflects the importance given to those feasts in the *Legenda.* Their treatment by Voragine is very different. As an example, when Voragine presents the Assumption, he describes the death and burial of the Virgin, giving St Peter centre stage, as he takes charge of organizing events. When Sor Isabel describes the moment of the Virgin's 'passament' [passing] there is a very delicate transition from farewells to the apostles, St Paul, and Mary Magdalene, among others, to the Virgin's arrival in heaven, accompanied by Christ and St Gabriel.

Eiximenis's *Vida de Jesucrist* dedicates a vast number of chapters to the life of the Virgin but has a very different structure to Sor Isabel's. It is written as ten *tractats* or treatises, which contain the main points the friar considers worthy of teaching to the faithful. Each point made is supported by the teaching of a holy doctor. The division given to the *Vita Christi* gives it a very different feel to Sor Isabel's, in which the events of the story take precedence and there are no references to authoritative sources. Because of its didactic purpose, among the most frequent words used in Eiximenis's treatises are 'punts' [points], 'enscnya' [teaches], and 'mostra' [reveals]. Hauf considers that Eiximenis's *Vida de Jesuchrist* exemplifies how written sermon technique was closely aligned to oral technique (2004: 286; see also Hauf 1978).

Among Eiximenis's techniques is the use of miracle stories. He adds a number of miracles, such as the one involving Angela of Foligno (Barcelona, BC, MS 299, fols 64v–65r) at the tomb of St Dominic, which are extraneous to the life of Christ, or ones which involve the Virgin engaged in struggle against the devil (fol. 59v). Sor Isabel does not incorporate contemporary miracles of the Virgin or of other saints. She does, however, mention that the

Virgin should be praised for her 'virtuts e miracles' (fol. 60v; I, 219), which suggests that she was aware of the miracle stories in Eiximenis's version.

The emphasis Eiximenis gives to the events in the story of Christ's life keeps his audience in mind. Because he is writing for a noble, court audience he does, for example, emphasize the sacrament of marriage, taking advantage of the Virgin's marriage to Joseph to include two chapters arguing in its favour.

Eiximenis's *Vida de Jesucrist* has a strong focus on Christ, unlike Sor Isabel's. For example, in Eiximenis's version, the body of Christ is adorned with a series of gifts to mark his reception into heaven. In Sor Isabel's *Vita Christi*, it is the Virgin who receives a royal robe and a triple crown on her Assumption. The Ascension of Christ causes homage to be paid to the Virgin and there is immediate focus on her after the Ascension of her Son (fol. 276r; III, 227). However, Eiximenis's third treatise, which contains the Incarnation and is the longest, is an exception, and includes many chapters about the Virgin. It is here that Eiximenis incorporates the twelve dignities of the Virgin, a section which takes up sixty-one folios in MS 299. Sor Isabel is inspired to include the twelve dignities of the Virgin in her *Vita Christi* but does so as part of the crown gifted her at the Annunciation, as I will show in Chapter 8 (see Hauf 1987). He also dedicates several chapters of the treatise on the Incarnation to praising the Virgin's prayerful life whilst she lived in the temple.

Eiximenis's *Vita Christi* ends with a series of brief treatises on the Resurrection, Ascension, and the reception of Christ into heaven. He also includes a chapter on the Last Judgement, which is similar to the way in which Ludolph of Saxony ends his *Vita Christi*.

Ubertino da Casale wrote his *Arbor vite crucifixae Iesus* (*Arbor*) in 1305 and it went to print in 1485. There are a number of points of similarity between the *Arbor* and Sor Isabel's *Vita Christi*, particularly in the representation of the Passion. Ubertino begins his *Arbor* with the origins of God's grace (1961: 7) and then the creation of Wisdom together with other Old Testament prefigurations of the Virgin, such as the rod of Aaron, the burning bush, Gideon's fleece, and the throne of Solomon (18–19). After a lengthy chapter on the prefiguration of the Virgin, Ubertino moves directly to the Annunciation of Christ's birth in chapter 9 (22–33). The longest chapter in the first section is the one which deals with the birth of Christ (52–80). The final book of the *Arbor* is a series of disquisitions on different aspects of Christ glorified: 'Iesus seraph alatus' [Jesus the winged seraph] (434–43), 'Iesus resuscitatus' [Jesus resurrected], 'Iesus victor magnificus' [Jesus the magnificent victor] (473–6, 'Iesus sponsus ornatus' [Jesus the bridegroom adorned] (493–95). In this fifth book the generation of St Francis in Christ's mould is also accorded importance (421–34). The fourth book concludes the life of Christ, however, and ends on the Assumption of the Virgin (397–402) and her Coronation (404–5).

Vitae Christi continued to be popular reading for the faithful after Isabel de Villena's period. The first book of Eiximenis's *Vita Christi*, the *Vida de Jesucrist* (1496), translated into Castilian, updated, and printed by the Archbishop of Granada, begins by selecting the chapters which show how the Incarnation was revealed to the prophets (fols 2–4v). Its second, longer, book begins with the Incarnation. The final, eighth, book ends with the public ministry of Jesus and a sermon on forgiveness. The reading public's interest in the genre meant that Eiximenis's *Vida de Jesucrist* was translated and printed a hundred years after it was written. Sor Isabel's version was reprinted twice.

Despite the marked differences between Sor Isabel's *Vita Christi* and the others, she had access to both Ludolph of Saxony's *Vita Christi* and to Eiximenis's *Vida de Jesucrist*. Copies of both were among the possessions of María of Castile, and Jaume Exarch gifted them to the convent (Benito Goerlich 1998: 71).

There were also a number of shorter works which coincided with some parts of Sor Isabel's *Vita Christi*, such as Roís de Corella's *Vida de Santa Anna*, written before 1463. Roís de Corella also wrote a *Història de la Magdalena,* finished before 1489, and, as the end of his life approached, 'es va dedicar a la tasca de hagiògraf' [he devoted himself to being a hagiographer] (Cingolani 1998: 56, 72).[15] Roís de Corella's positive presentation of the female characters has much in common with the way female saints like St Anne and Mary Magdalene are depicted by Sor Isabel in the *Vita Christi*.

There are also many versions of the Passion of Christ written in Catalan. These include the *Contemplació de la passió de Nostre Senyor Jesucrist,* which begins with an exhortation to contemplation with a clear focus on its benefits:

> Qui en la passió e creu sancta de Jesús gloriar-se desija, ab diligent meditació de son cor deu pençar en ella. Los misteris de la qual mort e passió, e les coses que en ella foren fetes, si ab la vista de nostra pença ffossen contemplades, crech que reduirien al nou estat al qui de aquesta manera meditàs en ella; per quant al qui ab profondo cor e ab tota pietat de ses entranyes las escodrinya, mots passos devots se li presenten, ab los quals nova compassion, nova amor, noves consolacions, per consegüent nou estat vindrà quasi a rebre, qui li sera com un denunciador e participació de la esdevenidora glòria. (Hauf 1982: 29)

---

[15] For Roís de Corella's other writing, see the editions of 1913 and 1973.

[He who longs to boast in the Passion and Holy Cross of Jesus, should think on it in his heart with diligent meditation. Believe that if the mysteries of that Death and Passion, and the events which were part of it, were contemplated with the eyes of our reflection, they would bring the person who so meditated on them to a new state, in so far as he who examines them in the depths of his heart and with every piety deep within will take many steps in devotion and will in this way receive new compassion, new love, new consolations which will be to him as a sign and share in future glory.]

The emphasis in this text, as can be seen from this short excerpt, is on interior reflection, with the author emphasizing 'la vista de nostra pença' [the eyes of our reflection] and the engagement of the emotions. It is structured as a series of short contemplations to fit around the monastic hours, beginning with matins. The events of the Passion begin with the Garden of Jericho at the Thursday vigil and end on the Virgin Mary's vigil before the tomb, accompanied by the women and St John. Hauf considers that both versions A and B of the text, held respectively in the Arxiu de la Corona de Aragó (MS 78) and in the Biblioteca de Catalunya (MS 451), date from the fifteenth century; a copy was made in the sixteenth century (Hauf 1982: 7–8). Other Passions in Catalan include the *Contemplació a Jesús crucificat* by Joan Scrivà and Bernat Fenollar (Garcia Sempere 2002: 419–46).

Roís de Corella also chose to begin by publishing the final section of the *Vita Christi*, *Lo quart*, which begins with the Passion. It follows the monastic hours and begins with an exhortation to contemplation couched in very similar words to the *Contemplació de la passió*: 'Qui donchs en la creu e passio de Jesus desija gloriar-se, ab continu studi stiga ferm en lo recort e contemplació de aquella' [He who longs to boast in the Cross and Passion of Jesus, should be diligent with continual study in recourse and contemplation of the same] (1495: fol. 2r). Roís de Corella's *Vita Christi* moves from the Ascension of Christ (fol. 145v), to Pentecost (fol. 166r), to the Assumption of the Virgin (fol. 169v–174v), and finally the Last Judgement (fol. 174^v).

Sor Isabel's *Vita Christi* has many similarities with Ludolph of Saxony's *Vita Christi* and ends with the Assumption and Coronation of the Virgin; it is possible that, were her endeavours not interrupted by her death, she would also have included the Last Judgement. However, Sor Isabel's *Vita Christi* devotes more chapters to each of these events, particularly to the Virgin's preparation for her Assumption and to the events surrounding her arrival in heaven.

Sor Isabel's writing

The *Vita Christi* is Sor Isabel's only attributed work, although for some years it was believed she was author of the *Speculum animae* or Mirror of the Soul (Sales 1761: 90–1; Hauf 1997 and 2006: 25–30). The immediate popularity of the *Vita Christi* is shown by the variety of editions which survive from the period.[16] It is a long, unfinished piece, which begins the life of Christ from the moment of God's visualization of the conception of his mother, Mary, through to scenes of her Assumption into Heaven. It was written in the vernacular for the nuns in Sor Isabel's charge. After her death, supposedly at the instigation of Queen Isabel la Católica, the book was prepared for publication by Sor Aldonça de Montsoriu, Sor Isabel's successor as abbess of the convent (see Chapter 1) and was printed in 1497 by the German Lope de Roca.[17]

Sor Isabel's *Vita Christi* is long, it is not yet fully available in a critical edition, and it would be difficult to cover every aspect of it in a preliminary study.[18] I have therefore chosen to centre my investigation on two intersecting themes, the Immaculate Conception, the doctrine which declares that the Virgin was conceived free from original sin, and Sor Isabel's use of the material world which surrounded her – the colours, the fabrics, the enamels, the styles of female dress, the jewels, and the embroideries and paintings of the Virgin. Such elements provide valuable insight into her purpose in writing, her treatment of her subject, and her response to her Franciscan heritage. Wolfram Aichinger indicates that further exploration is required into what he calls 'las secuencias circulares […] entre texto, imaginación, memoria y comportamiento social' [interconnections between text, imagination, memory, and how people operate within society] (2003: 61).

In Chapter 1, I focus on the context in which she worked, examining how her writing exemplifies the Rule by which she lived her life. The purpose of Chapter 2 is to explore the nature of Sor Isabel's writing and how she fitted within the bounds normally established for female writers. Chapter 3 addresses Sor Isabel's eucharistic devotion and the way in which she brings convent devotion to the body of Christ into her *Vita Christi*.

A cluster of chapters pinpoints aspects of the colour and texture of Sor Isabel's world. The colours which surrounded her in the convent, and the contemporary use of the colours crimson and scarlet, are the subject of Chapter 4. Chapter 5 continues the theme of opulence, as it sets Sor Isabel's descriptions of embroidery, blazons, and jewels in the context of the work of Valencian broiderers and goldsmiths. This chapter also examines the impor-

---

[16] See Villena 1497, 1513, and 1527.

[17] For discussion of Villena and the issue of her status as a female writer, see Riquer 1972; Fuster 1975a and 1975b; Hauf 1987, 1991 and 2006; Cantavella 2000, 2005, and 2011; Aichinger 2003; and Twomey 2003a; on the exclusion of female authors from the literary canon, see Piera 2003.

[18] There are edited selections of the text by Hauf (1995) and, focusing on female characters in the text, by Cantavella & Parra (1987).

tance of radiance and, with reference to other contemporary texts, explores how it was understood in the late fifteenth century. Chapter 6 examines the fabrics which Sor Isabel thought appropriate to clothe the Virgin. The richness of the fabric and the preponderance of gold thread make them fit for the Queen of Heaven. The chapter also addresses medieval understanding of nuptial gifts. The importance of decorating, clothing, and adorning the female body contributes to deepening awareness of the nature of the Virgin.

Chapter 7 explores the gift of six pairs of silk shoes. They mark the six estates of man but also point to how the Virgin's feet were to be revered. Descriptions of fifteenth-century fashion in shoes, diatribes against them, and the battle over making them which marked fifteenth- and sixteenth-century Valencia, enhance understanding of Sor Isabel's choice of adornment.

Chapters 8 and 9 explore different aspects of religious devotions, with the first of the two showing how the rosary influenced Sor Isabel's descriptions of the crown of the Virgin, and the second framing Sor Isabel's life of Christ in the various liturgies of the Immaculate Conception.

1

Reading the *Vita Christi*

A medieval book written for, about, and by women

Isabel de Villena's *Vita Christi* holds a central place in Valencian letters, since it is not only one of the earliest books published in Catalan, in 1497, but also the only substantial piece of medieval Catalan writing by a woman. Martí de Riquer's overview of Catalan prose has termed her 'l'única figura femenina important de la literatura catalana medieval' [the only significant female figure in Catalan medieval literature] (1972: 70). She is also one of the few examples of Hispanic female authorship, since literature by women from other parts of the Iberian Peninsula is also uncommon.[1] Alan Deyermond (1995: 31) deplores his omission of Villena in his earlier article about Hispanic women writers, and Ronald Surtz inexplicably omits her from his roll call of writing women in late medieval and early modern Spain (1995). Surtz later makes amends by including her among the 'Iberian Holy Women' about whom he writes in 2010. The very existence of the *Vita Christi* leaves the modern critic with a conundrum: is the text perceived as unique merely because it was preserved, or has the text been deliberately preserved because it was considered to have a unique perspective to offer to the reader? Lola Luna in her historical study of female authorship (1995: 127) contends that this uniqueness may have been due to the systematic silencing of other female writers, in deliberate antifeminist action by the masculine hierarchy. Certainly the survival of the printed edition of the *Vita Christi* may be due in no small measure to the royal approval granted to the text from the time of its publication. Sor Aldonça, Sor Isabel's successor, claims that Isabel la Católica requested a copy of Sor Isabel's *Vita Christi* and that, in order to comply, she decided to have the text printed.[2] Female readership thus had a vital impact on the text in that it preserved it.

Luna offers the alternative proposition that women lacked the necessary

---

[1] See, for example, Deyermond 1978, 1983, 1995; Whetnall 1984, 1992–93, 2006, 2007; López Estrada 1986; Luna 1995; Constance L. Wilkins 1998; Piera 2003; Twomey 2003a.

[2] The request by Isabel la Católica may have been incorporated by Sor Aldonça to emphasize Sor Isabel's relationship to the Queen.

thinking to enable them to write, although she does not intend her reader to opt for that suggestion and, rather, seeks to highlight the way in which society has always valued masculine authors over female ones. However, a possible explanation is women's lack of time and energy to dedicate themselves to writing. Lesley Smith raises the same question in her evaluation of why there are so few women scribes depicted in manuscripts, arguing that women may have preferred to dedicate their time to more social and collaborative activities, such as needlework, making vestments, or tapestry (1996: 35). Many women in the medieval period also lacked the educational tools for writing. María Milagros Rivera Garretas (1990: 21) highlights the problems women writers had to overcome.

Rosanna Cantavella and Lluïsa Parra in their partial edition of the *Vita Christi* have emphasized a different aspect of its uniqueness. The text is certainly unusual in having female ownership of the intellectual process. Since it was written by a female writer, prepared for printing by another woman, and made public at the request of a queen, and since the subject-matter of the book focuses on the female characters of the Gospels, Mary, her mother, Anna, and Mary Magdalene, Cantavella and Parra consider that the *Vita Christi* is the feminist text *par excellence* (1987: vii). It could be added to the feminist credentials of the book that the original, pre-publication, readers of the book were female, because it was written for the sisters of the convent where the writer was abbess. Whatever the reason for the uniqueness attributed by critics to the *Vita Christi*, it provides a supreme example of gendered literature in the fifteenth century in so far as it is possible to consider that literature may be gendered. The very concept of whether female writing can be said to exist in a male-dominated culture is called into question by Paul Julian Smith's study of St Teresa of Ávila and María de Zayas. Smith argues that the '"feminine soul" is defined and delimited by both the material restrictions of a male culture and the psychological constraints of a received female consciousness' (1987: 230).

Eileen Power's contention that convents 'offered to the main body of nuns opportunities for education, organization, and responsibility, not easy for women to find elsewhere' (1975: 90) is true in the case of Sor Isabel. Although her education took place outside the walls of the convent, she was able to deepen her studies within it. She entered the convent at fifteen, after a court education, and she gained considerable responsibility, once she was elected abbess, taking office in 1463 at the age of thirty-three (Benito Goerlich 1998: 15, 62). Entry into the convent provided her with another essential benefit by giving her access to a well-stocked library (71), which facilitated her personal development and her work as an erudite writer.[3]

---

[3] Cátedra indicates that books for reading at table and books for use in choir (2005:

The 'espacio propio' [personal space] which María del Carmen García de la Herrán identifies as being proper to convent life had a deeper meaning in the case of the Santa Trinitat (1995: 183). The convent even afforded her a central place in Valencian literary society, since cultured society gathered to debate and write there: 'Así el patio de la Trinidad en tiempos de sor Isabel se constituirá en un espacio privilegiado, un lugar de coloquio e incluso de redacción de documentos' [So the courtyard of the Holy Trinity in the time of Sor Isabel was to become a forum where debate and even document writing took place] (Benito Goerlich 1998: 68–9).

There are two ways of determining the author's purpose in writing the *Vita Christi*. The first is to explore the views on her reasons for writing, laid out in the letter-prologue written by her successor, Sor Aldonça de Monsoriu. The second is to examine the clues embedded in Sor Isabel's writing. Her treatment of the conception and birth of the Virgin Mary in the early chapters of the *Vita Christi* will provide initial insight into the rationale underlying the narrative, as well as into how she deals with doctrinal matters such as the Immaculate Conception.

Writing the *Vita Christi*

The text of the *Vita Christi* is framed by two short texts written by another woman, Sor Aldonça. The first serves as a prologue, leading the reader into the opening chapter of the text.[4] The second acts as an endnote to the *Vita Christi* and marks the point at which Sor Isabel's writing was interrupted by her death.

The prologue to the 1497 edition is in the form of a letter, addressed to Isabel la Católica and written by one of the earliest readers of the *Vita Christi*, Sor Aldonça. Her concept of the nature of authorship and her view of the text provide vital contemporary clues as to what was expected from female writers, and also as to how the *Vita Christi* was viewed by its reading public at the time, since she seeks to remedy what she sees as aspects of the text which differentiate it from other examples of female authorship.

It is striking that Sor Isabel, unlike her female contemporaries, includes no reference to how she was inspired to begin her life of Christ, nor does she indicate her reason for writing. Surtz has shown how her Castilian counterparts Teresa de Cartagena (b. 1415–35), probably a Franciscan nun at Santa Clara convent in Burgos, and Constanza de Castilla, prioress of the Dominican convent of Santo Domingo el Real in Madrid from 1416

---

89) were listed in some Franciscan convent inventories. The Santa Trinitat is likely to have possessed similar books.

[4] On prologues to didactic works of the period, see Machado 1995.

to 1465, claim authority from spiritual inspiration.[5] He notes how frequent the humility topos is found in female religious writing (1995: 23; see also Jantzen 1995). His views on Teresa de Cartagena are supported by the commentary of Dayle Seidenspinner-Núñez (1997: 8). Surtz argues that Teresa de Cartagena 'invokes tactics that had become rhetorical commonplaces for medieval women writers' (1995: 21–2). Teresa refers to her own weakness and unworthiness and she combines this with the topos of divine inspiration, suggesting that God will inspire her. The *Arboleda de los enfermos* [The Grove of the Infirm], her first extant work, contains references to the author's poor sense and her little discretion, and she hopes that, because her intentions are good, her book will be pleasing in the eyes of God (Seidenspinner-Núñez 1998: 25). Despite Surtz's confident assertion about humility being a literary commonplace in female writing, no trace of authorial humility is found in Sor Isabel's work.

Other convent writers, such as Constanza de Castilla, take great pains to emphasize their feminine weaknesses.[6] Constanza begins her devotions with a prayer: 'Esta oración que se sigue compuso una soror de la orden de Sancto Domingo de los Predicadores, la qual es grant pecadora' [This prayer was written by a sister of the Preaching Order of Saint Dominic, and she was a great sinner] (1998: 3). Constanza refers to her 'simpleza' [simplicity] and 'grosería' [coarseness], even though she, like Sor Isabel, was a noblewoman, and granddaughter to King Pedro of Castile. She points out other faults such as her laziness, and the fact she is 'sin virtud' [without worth]. She considers her handiwork to be 'defectuosas' [flawed] (1998: 9, 90).[7]

In many senses, Sor Isabel's determination to approach the task in hand without delay, recalls some of the phrases in the letters of Hildegard of Bingen. Hildegard was frequently praised by her correspondents as 'mistress of singular merit', 'lady, beloved and blessed of God as it is believed', 'mirror of divine contemplation', or 'the beautiful olive tree' (1998: II, 94, 98, 118, 131). Their letters begin with fulsome praise and emphasis on their own humility. The abbess Sophia writes: 'Sophia called abbess in Kitzingen but deficient in herself' (1998: II, 94). Similarly, the abbess of Neuss calls herself 'unworthy' (138). Hildegard's replies frequently begin without a greeting, going straight to the matter raised in each letter: 'O Sophia I

---

[5] Surtz (1995: 21) follows Cantera Burgos in placing Teresa's birth between 1420 and 1435. Seidenspinner-Núñez (1997: 9) places it as 1415–20.

[6] Constanza's life and writings are studied by Ángela Muñoz Fernández (1995: 123–55), who concentrates on documentary evidence about her; Surtz provides a valuable introduction to her writing (1995: 41–67); Seidenspinner-Núñez compares her with Teresa de Cartagena (1997: 1–14). A valuable study of Constanza's life and writing is Constance L. Wilkins's introduction to the edition of her *Book of Devotions* (Constanza de Castilla 1998: vii–xviii), and she also provides an overview of Constanza's contribution to liturgy (2002).

[7] See 'Constanza de Castilla and the Gynaeceum of Compassion' (Surtz 1995: 41–67).

say this to you according to a mystic vision' (95) or 'in the True Light I saw a fiery sphere like a wheel turning inside you' (96). To the unnamed abbess, she begins 'O servant of God, run in the circle of the sun' (138). Hildegard cloaks herself in the authority accorded by her visions which she expounds. Her eagerness to advise and recount spills from the words which tumble from her pen. Yet, even Hildegard, refers to herself as 'poor little woman that I am' (169). Like Teresa of Cartegena, Hildegard also refers to her own weakness: 'Poor little form of a woman that I am, I was weighed down heavily with sickness' (165). Interestingly Hildegard claimed papal validation for her writing, although no independent record of such a blessing survives (Kerby-Fulton 2010: 350). Male authority, whether real or invented, framed her writing, giving her permission to write.

Other women writers take up the pen at the instigation of their confessor, although this is generally because of divine inspiration, which gives them the authority to write. Mechthild of Magdeburg (1208–82) says that it is her confessor Henry of Halle who encourages her to write the book 'out of God's heart and mouth' (1998: 144).[8] In the case of Margaret Ebner (1290–1351), a Dominican nun, it was a combination of divine voices and the encouragement of her confessor which caused her to write her revelations (Koch 2010: 405).

In the *Vita Christi,* Sor Isabel cloaks herself in the mantle of scriptural authority, she calls on no male authority, whether papal or confessorial, and even dares to move into the area of glossing texts into the vernacular, an area dominated by male scholars. Glossing, or translation with critical commentary, was the archetypal male activity, since it involved engaging in a critical capacity with the source material, a task for which women's education did not readily equip them. Indeed, on occasion, Sor Isabel goes so far as to speak with authority, for example, to castigate those who do not accept the doctrine of the Immaculate Conception (fol. 5r; I, 20). If it is the case, as Seidenspinner-Núñez argues, that all acts of signifying, such as writing, glossing, or allegorizing are in themselves gendered and associated with the masculine (1998: 21), Sor Isabel's achievement is all the more striking.

Sor Aldonça's letter also serves as a fount of information about the process of writing. Synonyms for the act of writing abound: 'scriure' [write], 'compondre' [compose], 'ordenar' [order], 'fer' [made] (fol. 1r; I, 6). She uses an agricultural image 'sembrar' [sow], paralleling production of food with the production of the text.

Seidenspinner-Núñez has explained, in relation to the writing of Teresa de Cartagena, that writing itself was seen as a masculine act, with the passive, receptive paper construed as representing the feminine (1998: 21).

---

[8] For Mechthild as a mystic, see Cirlot & Garí 2008: 127–50; for Mechthild's view of herself as an author, see Anderson 2000: 104–25.

Following the sowing, the seed will come to fruition, allowing the reader to pick the fruit. The interplay between the productive act, writing, and the receptive act, reading, centres on the picking of fruit, which represents the utility of the subject matter for the reader. Writing is thought to equate to the sowing of seed on the white paper.

In Sor Aldonça's letter, the reader is offered a picture of the female author labouring at production as the agricultural image is extended. The hard work Sor Isabel has to put in, 'que volgué ab afanyós treball compondre aquest tant gran volum' [so that she laboured to compose this weighty tome] (fol. 1v; I, 6), has been observed at close quarters by Sor Aldonça. She underlines an aspect of the reformed Rule of St Clare in which contemplation was to be allied with work, and she places such emphasis on writing as a gruelling activity to emphasize the fact that Sor Isabel's work was not physical but mental (*Reglas* 1988: 28).

Besides the labour-intensive production of the volume, Sor Aldonça is keen, on behalf of Sor Isabel, to publicize the profound knowledge which her predecessor possessed. She refers to Isabel's 'luminosa intel·ligència' [radiant intellect], and says she works on her writing 'ab la lum del seu clar enteniment' [with the light of her bright understanding] (fol. 1v; I, 5). Her assessment of Sor Isabel's skills clearly springs from pride in an important member of the Order, as well as from pride in her achievements in the masculine world of authorship.

It is therefore significant that Sor Aldonça feels the need to use the humility topos. Her prologue provides the missing humility bridge to the text and palliates its absence from Sor Isabel's writing. With a clear sense of closing the gap between expectation and the absence of any apologetic material provided by the author, Sor Aldonça repeatedly appropriates the humility topos. She even claims that her predecessor's decision not to put her name to the text is evidence of her humility, even though the *Vita Christi* is unfinished, and it is uncertain how the author might have presented her final text had she ever decided to make it more widely available than the confines of the convent. Sor Isabel might have written her own *captatio benevolentiae*. Nevertheless, Aldonça argues: 'en tan baix centre de humilitat era devallada, que no volgué scriure lo seu nom en alguna part de aquest libre' [she was so steeped in the depths of humility that she did not wish to put her name in any part of the book] (fol. 1v; I, 5). Sor Aldonça does not extend the humility topos to envisaging Sor Isabel as a receptive author, who did nothing more than respond to the impulses of divine grace, but, by describing her labours, sets her firmly in a context which mirrors masculine production. In addition to these introductory insights, Aldonça finds the need to underline the authority of the text and to bolster its status in three ways. She claims divine inspiration for it, she underlines the high social standing of the author, and she draws on posthumous patronage for the text.

She claims divine inspiration on behalf of Sor Isabel when she points to the communication between the Sun of Justice, a title frequently accorded to Christ, and Sor Isabel's understanding:

> hý los raigs del clar sol de justícia, entrant per les finestres de la sua luminosa intel·ligència, axí en encesa caritat la scalfaren, que volgué ab afanyós treball compondre aquest tant gran volum e libre. (fol. 1r; I, 6)

> [and the rays of the bright Sun of Justice, shining through the windows of her radiant intellect, so set her ablaze with ardent charity, that she might labour long to compose this weighty tome and book.]

Sor Aldonça's emphasis on the illumination of the Spirit as a necessary element of Sor Isabel's authorial efforts is not dissimilar to Teresa de Cartagena's in the *Admiraçión operum Dey*:

> E sy yo no era digna ni lo soy de conosçer tanto bien [...] e aquello que a mi entendimiento mugeril se fazía escuro e difficultoso, púdolo fazer claro e ligero Aquél que es verdadera Luz e Sol de justiçia.
> (Hutton 1967: 129, lines 27–32)

> [And if I were not worthy to know such important treasure, and I am not, and those things that were obscure and difficult for my female understanding, He, who is true Light and Sun of Justice, could make it clear and easy.][9]

Sor Aldonça's emphasis on the humility of Isabel de Villena is a double-edged strategy with a number of motivating factors. For example, Aldonça refers to her former abbess as an 'humil religiosa' [lowly nun], whilst in the same sentence she takes the opportunity to emphasize her royal lineage: 'la claredat de son il·lustrissim linatge' (fol. 1v; I, 6). She also ensures that Sor Isabel's anonymity as a Poor Clare sister is dispelled by giving her former name, 'il·lustre dona Elionor' (fol. 1v; I, 5) and suggests that her humility is even more worthy because it required a greater sacrifice of worldly recognition of her family background and noble lineage. The mixture of pride and humility displayed in the introductory letter reflects a need to bolster the authority of the text through the evidence of its noble provenance. Both the humility topos and the boast about royal lineage are sides of the same coin.

---

[9] Teresa's wrestling with difficult subject-matter and the inspirational clarity afforded by the Sun of Justice has many similarities with the way Sor Aldonça describes Sor Isabel in her preface. Hilary Pearson discussed the passage from the *Admiraçión operum Dey* in her paper 'Was Teresa de Cartagena an Author?', presented at the 21st Colloquium of the Medieval Hispanic Research Seminar, Queen Mary, University of London, 25–6 June 2010.

2. Woodcut of Isabel de Villena, *Vita Christi de la Abbadessa del monestir de les monges de la Trinitat.*

The letter serves a final purpose in conjunction with the text which it accompanies, and that is to provide it with a royal patron. The centrality of patronage to medieval authorial endeavour is emphasized by George Whalen in his discussion of engendered patronage (1995: 123–36), and, since Isabel de Villena had no patron, Sor Aldonça provides her with an illustrious one in the person of Queen Isabel la Católica.

Sor Aldonça is not averse to turning the humility topos to her own benefit, wishing to gain some of the merit in associating herself with such a spiritual text. She seeks divine favour by naming Isabel, moving her out of the private, conventual sphere, and returning her to the public domain: 'yo·n crech atténver no poch mèrit davant Déu en publicar lo nom de tant singular mare' [I believe I will attain no little merit in the face of God by making the name of such a singular mother public knowledge] (fol. 1v; I, 6). She chooses a tripartite formula to do so: 'Sor Ysabel de Billena lo ha fet; Sor Ysabel de Billena l'à compost; Sor Ysabel de Billena ab elegant ý dolç stil l'à ordenat' [Sor Isabel de Villena wrote it, Sor Isabel de Villena composed it, Sor Isabel de Villena with sweet and elegant style set it in order] (fol. 1v; I, 6).

The readership

The woodcut placed at the end (fol. 232v) of the 1513 edition provides a sixteenth-century view of how the original all-female readership might have looked (Fig. 2). It depicts two books, one held by Sor Isabel, and one on a lectern behind the gathering of nuns. The presence of the lectern indicates that texts were read aloud in the convent and the tome, perhaps a Bible, perhaps the Rule of the Poor Clares, is set there because it is read to the gathered community. It shows that books formed an important element of instruction in convent life, and that even the nuns who could not read would have access to them.[10] However, there is a need to distinguish between those sisters, like Isabel herself, capable of reading and studying scripture and doctrine in the original Latin, and those who were able to read but were not literate in Latin, and who needed to be provided with a translation (McSheffrey 1995: 158–9).[11] The readership of the *Vita Christi* played

---

[10] Shannon McSheffrey (1995) addresses the difficulties posed by investigating which members of the Lollard community were able to read and what is meant by literacy in the late medieval period, whilst Wybren Scheepsma argues that female literacy and the *devotio moderna* movement were inextricably linked, and emphasizes the connections between the production of manuscripts and religious zeal (1995: 34).

[11] For a study of the use of the vernacular in Dominican convents, albeit with focus on southern Germany, see Ehrenschwendtner 1996 and 1997.

a central role in the way the text was developed, given that the audience determined 'the genesis, the meanings, and the fortunes of texts'. The *Vita Christi* was shaped around the readers' needs (see Gill 1994: 65).

The rubric, added at the time of printing, indicates that the *Vita Christi* was written 'en romanç, perquè los simples e ignorants puguen saber e contemplar la vida e mort del nostre redemptor e senyor Jesús, amador nostre' [in the vernacular, so that simple and ignorant people could find out about and meditate on the life and death of our Redeemer and Lord Jesus, our beloved] (fol. 2r). Its aim was two-fold. It was written so that simple people might come to knowledge, 'saber', but, more importantly, it was written to promote meditation, 'contemplar'.

Several points can be made about the early readers. They were not so simple or ignorant as the rubric implies, since they were well enough educated to read, even though they might not read Latin with ease. They were also of sufficient means to purchase the book. Finally, the book was published at the request of Queen Isabel, and this meant that among the simple folk for whom it was intended were members of the royal household.[12] Even though the words 'simples e ignorants' are written in the masculine plural, referring to both male and female readers, it is possible that the writer of the rubric had a largely female readership in mind, since women formed an important market for devotional works. Annette Grisé shows how many of the Middle English devotional treatises addressed women, either implicitly or explicitly, and found an eager market in female religious readers (2002: 210). At the Aragonese court, queens and their ladies read devotional books, as Eiximenis's *Scala Dei* (1985), a devotional tract written for the wife of Martí the Humane, proves. Joan Roís de Corella's lives of St Anne and Mary Magdalene were each dedicated to noble women, Na Montpalau de Castellví and Flors de Vallbona (Cingolani 1998: 127). Isabel de Riquer (1994), in her study of the reading habits of Violant de Bar, Duchess of Girona and, later, Queen of Aragon, shows that noblewomen were capable of reading. Sandra Penketh outlines women's relationship with the books of hours they commissioned and read (1996). Jeremy Lawrance argues from a reference in the *Corbacho* that women regularly owned a copy, as well as having a number of other books in their possession, such as devotional works, copies of the Seven Penitential Psalms, and a translation of the psalter, and that they read them (1986: 79). Isabel la Católica had a wide-ranging book collection included in the list of her other important possessions (Sánchez Cantón 1950).

The woodcut has several additional functions, the first of which is apparent when it is compared with a manuscript miniature adorning the

---

[12] Cristina Segura Graíño, writing about the educated noblewomen at the court of Isabel la Católica, provides an insight into the levels of female education in the medieval courts of Spain (1994). See also Beceiro Pita 2003.

initial letter 'F' in the prayer for the Office of St Clare (BNE, MS Vitrina 21–6, fol. 349v) (Fig. 3). St Clare is seated on a throne with an open book on her lap, her Rule, which she fought throughout her life to have adopted and which the pope recognized only on her deathbed in 1253. Around the seated figure, at the right-hand side, the sisters of the Order are clustered. There are striking similarities between the pose of Clare and that of Sor Isabel, which suggests that it was a standard one for female spiritual leaders. The throne is similar to those used by bishops in cathedral churches, and thus sets the authority of the abbess on an equal footing to the episcopacy. The woodcut publicizes the didactic nature of the *Vita Christi*, serving also to enhance the standing of the text. Whilst the reformed Rule does not include any reference to instruction of the nuns by the abbess, the original Rule refers to them as the 'grey' [flock], for whom account must be given in the sight of God (*Reglas* 1988: 24). The tradition of women's instruction by women has long been represented in religious art, and has been addressed by Pamela Sheingorn in connection with St Anne teaching the Virgin (2003). The Virgin is also often depicted reading with the Child in medieval art and the book she reads is traditionally the Book of Wisdom, marking her out as Mater Sapientiae (James Hall 1974: 329). Once the book was published, Sor Isabel's writing would serve to teach men as well, and she would model herself on the Virgin, disseminating wisdom to others.

Secondly, the woodcut intends to give pride of place to the *Vita Christi*, embedding its use in convent life. It is around the *Vita Christi*, rather than the tome on the lectern, that the members of the community cluster. The first readers were of prime importance to the printer as a marketing tool. It was written for a community whose reputation for holy living was high in Valencia. He wished to underline the sanctity and authority of the text by setting its original purpose in picture form before potential readers.

The woodcut also serves to promote the subject matter of the *Vita Christi*. From the book in Sor Isabel's lap there descend three small cameos: the meeting of the Virgin Mary's parents, Joachim and Anne, at the Golden Gate, the Annunciation of Christ's birth, and his Nativity. These scenes place importance on Mary's genealogy, as well as projecting her future role in the economy of salvation. The *Liber de generatione* from St Matthew's Gospel was one of the most commonly used readings in fourteenth and fifteenth-century Conception offices. It was also used at the Nativity of the Virgin. The cameo thus provides a visual link to both offices.

Sor Aldonça's epilogue (fols 306r–306v *bis*; III, 365), as well as noting the date of Sor Isabel's death, provides an insight into how the readers of the *Vita Christi* were to respond to the book. The devotion and usefulness which result from reading it will serve to enhance the merit of Sor Isabel: 'Que la utilitat e devoció que los que ·l legiran ne reportaran sia augment de la accidental glòria de aquella singular dona qui ·l ha ordenat' [May the

3. Miniature of St Clare, *Breviarium franciscanum*.

devotion and usefulness that those who read it display lead to an increase in the glory of that singular lady who compiled it] (fol. 306v *bis*; III, 365). Sor Aldonça's comments provide further contemporary views of the relationship between readers and writer, in which the response of the readers enhances the status of the author, and they may indicate a desire to see Isabel de Villena canonized.

Sor Isabel's purpose in writing

Critical consensus has considered that Sor Isabel was responding to the misogynist currents rife in Valencia in the late fifteenth century.[13] Hauf, in the introduction to his edition (Villena 1995), and Cantavella and Parra in theirs, accept that Sor Isabel intended to intervene in the 'debat pro i antifeminista' (1987: xxi). Cantavella compares her to Christine de Pisan (2000: 43). Martí de Riquer notes the misogynist diatribe directed against religious women in the *Espill*, and its author's connection with the convent (1972: 71). Jaume Roig's daughter Violant was professed in the Santa Trinitat, he was a benefactor, and also the convent doctor. However, although Sor Isabel nowhere makes any claim to be responding to debate about the nature of women, she presents a positive view of women and allows women to occupy a greater proportion of the narrative than they do in other writers.

Contributing to public debate would have been daring for women writers because one of the principal aims of women's education was to encourage women to stay silent. Silence was equivalent to chaste behaviour, as is shown by the advice to princes on the education of their daughters by Eiximenis in his *Dotzè del crestià* (1986–8: I, 217, lines 35–51).[14] Eiximenis's instruction about women's education was based on St Paul's injunction (Timothy 2. 13), mediated by the doctors of the Church, that women should keep silent. Women writers also had to deal with the perceived negative consequences

---

[13] See Cantavella 1992, a study of Jaume Roig's *Espill* which traces many of the key elements of the antifeminist debate, setting Roig's deployment of them in the context of that of other authors, such as Matheolus, Boccaccio, Juan Ruíz, Bernat Metge, and the Archpriest of Talavera, and providing a useful index of motifs of the antifeminist debate. See also Archer 2001, an anthology which includes both Latin and vernacular contributions, and Solomon 1997, which focuses on two Hispanic misogynists, the Archpriest of Talavera and Jaume Roig. With reference to certain female professions, see Macpherson & MacKay 1994. Archer in his recent book on misogyny denies its existence and argues that those who discussed it were merely citing authorities and were not respondents in a debate (2005).

[14] The nature of women's education is discussed in Rivera Garretas's study (1994) of Christine de Pizan's *Livre des trois vertus* [Book of the Three Virtues] and the *Castigos e dotrinas que vn sabio daua a sus hijas* [Chastisements and Teaching that a Wise Man Gave his Daughters], and also in María del Mar Graña Cid's study (1994b) of female colleges.

of committing thoughts to paper (Weber 1993: 486–7; Seidenspinner-Núñez 1997: 13). The authoritative dissemination of women's speech was discouraged, since, as daughters of Eve, they were considered to be in direct association with the devil (Blamires et al. 1992: 83–98). The impact of both theology and education on cloistered female authors has been drawn out, among others, by Surtz (1995: 5) and Seidenspinner-Núñez (1998: 18–19; see also Weber 1993: 487).

Despite this, female authors were able to escape from the cultural limitations placed on them, and one enabling factor was responsibility for the spiritual direction of the readers. Both Isabel de Villena and Constanza de Castilla began writing for a circumscribed readership. Constanza's task of transcribing and formulating devotions led her into the male-dominated territory of liturgical authority, whilst Sor Isabel's took her into that of reworking the Scriptures in the vernacular. Neither mentions the need to seek permission for what was essentially a piece of writing for private purposes. Both differ from religious women obliged to submit their experiences to the judgement of others because of their illiteracy. In Angela de Foligno's case, her male scribe takes it upon himself to vouch for the authority of the book by only writing down her words after he had been to confession to ensure his conscience was clear (1993: 138). It is clear that Brother A filtered Angela's words as he transposed them into his own (see Mooney 1994: 39, 41–2). Similarly, Elizabeth of Schönau's words were written by Ekbert and, according to Anne L. Clark, 'it is difficult to know the extent of Ekbert's suppression of Elizabeth's words (2010: 374). Margery Kempe was another woman obliged to dictate her religious experiences to a priest (Goodman 2010: 223). Literacy gave both Constanza and Isabel the opportunity to escape masculine control of the process.

The closed female readership of the *Vita Christi* also provides an important fund of knowledge for the modern scholar because it makes the relationship between author and reader visible. In line with Kathryn Shevelow's discussion of how female readers are 'imaged' by the author, a term she uses for the way in which early women's journals 'defined and organized the readers' social reality' (1989: 195), I will draw on examples taken from the Marian conception and birth narratives to show how Sor Isabel uses her writing in the same way.

Observing observance in the *Vita Christi*

Critics have gone to great lengths to emphasize the feminine style of Sor Isabel's writing. Joan Fuster (1975a) and Riquer (1972) emphasize the domesticity of the scenes in the *Vita Christi*. Hauf considers that Sor Isabel's interest in narrating Bible events is to show their human angle (1987: 122).

Yet critics who have approached the *Vita Christi* by pointing to its human touches are, consciously or subconsciously, responding to what they consider a suitable text for a woman to write or to read. This is also the case when they emphasize the non-conceptual nature of the *Vita*, as opposed to the more conceptual approach taken by other authors of *Vitae Christi* (Hauf 1987: 112). They are assuming that a female author is only able or willing to recount what was familiar. Such critical evaluation of the *Vita Christi* only deals with textual events at one level, because ostensibly simple scenes perform a variety of functions.

Scenes such as the one where the neighbours congratulate St Anne after the birth of the Virgin Mary certainly have a family focus: 'alegraren-se molt ab ella los vehïns ý parents, car conexien que nostre Senyor Déu havia exalçada e magnificada la sua misericòrdia e gràtia en ella' (fol. 5v; I, 21) [They rejoiced greatly with the neighbours and members of the family, for they knew that Our Lord God had exalted and magnified his mercy and grace in her]. At a birth, women were always prime agents, whether as parturient mother or as midwife. Familiarity with, if not personal experience of, birth would have drawn the sisters to the scene unfolding in the *Vita*. Births take place in the home, the principal female sphere, and one familiar to them before they entered the convent.

It could be argued that observing is an archetypal female role. In many public events, women would have taken this role, since their involvement in acts of government or in holding public office was limited. Coronations of queens were a notable exception to the exclusion of women from public events, since women took centre stage (Twomey 2007b). Contemporaries of Sor Isabel include Isabel la Católica (Weissberger 2004) and María, Queen of Aragon, a small but powerful group of women rulers. Abbesses like Isabel de Villena also wielded power, but the ceremonials in which they took part were largely behind closed doors. The majority of women did not hold public office and their domain was the private sphere.

Observing is a prerequisite of contemplation. Beth Mulvaney (2005: 186) points to the way in which the beholder is an important element in Franciscan devotional exercises, as instructed by manuals such as John of Caulibus's *MVC*. At the manger, the contemplative-observer is encouraged to touch the child, pick him up, and then hand him back to his mother:

> accipias eum, et inter brachia tuas retine. Intuere faciem ejus. Diligenter ac reuerenter deosculare, et delectare in co confidenter. Hec facere potes quia ipse ad peccatores uenit pro eorum salute [...] Postea redde ipsum matri; et conspice diligenter quam studiose et sapienter gubernat eum, lactate. (John of Caulibus 1997: 35)

[take him and hold him fast in your arms; gaze on his face. Kiss him with loving reverence and delight confidently in him. You can do this for he came to sinners for their salvation. (…) Afterwards hand him back to his mother, and carefully note how devotedly and tenderly, she minds him, nurses him, and so forth.] (John of Caulibus 2000: 48)

In Franciscan art too, there are depictions of observers. Beth Mulvaney points to the *Retable of the Crib* at Grecchio, with Francis and some of his friars in front of an altar at the foot of which stands the crib. A group of observers, all women, stand in the doorway of the rood screen. In Mulvaney's view, they are denied visual access to the events taking place, and their position in the scene is akin to that of the reader of the *Meditations* or of any Life of Christ: physically absent and imagining him or herself present (2005: 174, 184–7).

Thomas of Celano describes the scene at the manger, emphasizing the presence of the witnesses to the birth of Christ: 'The night is lit up like day, delighting both man and beast. The people arrive, ecstatic at this mystery of new joy' (Thomas of Celano 1999: I, 255–6). According to Mulvaney, Celano repeatedly points to the importance of witnesses in the scene he is describing to provide 'a practical guide to meditation' (2005: 181), and Mulvaney claims there are constant exhortations to the reader to imagine being present. Celano is careful to create visually appealing scenes with detailed descriptions of those present, but he never directly exhorts his readers. Celano's inclusiveness of age and type of observer can be appreciated in a chapter about people's eagerness to see Francis:

> Men ran, women also ran,
> clerics hurried,
> and religious rushed to see the holy one of God […].
> People of all ages and both sexes rushed to behold the wonders
> which the Lord worked anew in the world through his servant.
> (Thomas of Celano 1999: I, 215)

Whilst Celano's emphasis on witness is more developed than Sor Isabel's, she is working within the same tradition. It is a simple step in meditation for the beginner to be encouraged to imagine observing scenes from the life of Christ (Cross 1958: 882). In so doing, a cloistered woman meditating deepens her faith and her response to the actions of God. Sor Isabel indicates that the observer is to experience the joy felt by the onlookers: 'e molts en la nativitat sua se alegraran, fahent singular festa cascun any en semblant jornada!' [and many rejoiced in her Nativity, celebrating a special feast every year on the same day!] (fol. 5v; I, 21).

Sor Isabel is also developing a response to faith which points to the importance of celebrating biblical events: 'fahent […] cascun any' [celebrating

(…) every year] (fol. 5v; I, 21). She is recreating the tradition stretching back to the day of the Virgin's birth, which enabled St Bernard to support the presence of her Nativity in the calendar. Sor Isabel's allusion to the argument from tradition is one which is also used about the Feast of the Immaculate Conception, which had shared a liturgy with the Nativity until the Franciscan Pope Sixtus IV approved the writing of dedicated Conception liturgies during his papacy, in 1477 and 1484. When she presents the Conception of Mary, she promotes it in a similar way to the Nativity. First, St Anne is vouchsafed the privilege of celebrating it: 'feu gran goig e festa' [she celebrated with great joy] (fol. 4v; I, 20). Although there is only one witness to this very private event, the joy evinced is to be imitated in meditation. Then Sor Isabel steps aside from the narrative to exhort the reader: 'Aquesta festa gloriosa de la Concepció deu ésser per tots los crestians ab gran devoció festivada' [This glorious Feast of the Conception ought to be celebrated by all Christians with great devotion] (fol. 5r; I, 20). The change of tone, unusual in the *Vita Christi*, indicates that she is aware of some doubt over whether to include the feast in the calendar.

Archives from the Puritat convent in Valencia show that the Feast of the Immaculate Conception was being celebrated by the Poor Clares as early as 1460. I have examined all available manuscripts in cathedral and public archives across the Peninsula and discovered that all Franciscan breviaries, books of hours, missals, and offices of saints include the Conception feast in their calendar in manuscripts dating from the late fourteenth century onwards. Other Orders vary much more in their practice.

Sor Isabel's exhortation echoes the one in the 1486 *certamen* dedicated to the Immaculate Conception. Its *Introit* refers to those who refuse to celebrate the feast instituted by Sixtus IV: 'mas huy los nostres capellans / seguir no ·l volen' [but our chaplains do not want to follow him] (Ferrando Francés 1983: 436), and several poems denounce the Dominican Order for their lack of acceptance (Twomey 1997: 30–3). The institution of a series of *certàmens* honouring the Immaculate Conception in Valencia and the presence there of a copy of the Conception office of Leonardo Nogarola, dating from 1533 (Valencia, Biblioteca de l'Universitat, R2–219, p. 422), is indicative of a measure of municipal and ecclesiastical support for it in Valencia. Sor Isabel, in pointing to tradition, subtly supports the Franciscan stance on the Immaculate Conception, but she also supports what she wishes to claim as Valencian orthodoxy.

Building the community of the Santa Trinitat

The way in which Sor Isabel presents the doctrine of the Conception is an example of her intent to build a sense of community. When she writes of the annunciation to Joachim, she follows the Apocryphal Gospel of Pseudo-Matthew in portraying the Virgin's father as exiled for his infertility at the moment of meeting with the angel. God speaks to Joachim through the angel, instructing him 'fabriquen la casa mia' [build my house] and adding 'en la qual per excel·lència yo vull posar la primera pedra del fonament' [in which by excellence I wish to place the first foundation stone] (fol. 2v; I, 10). The symbolism of the Virgin Mary as a house prepared for the Infant Christ is found in the *Annotationes in cognitione baptismi* [Notes on Understanding Baptism] of St Ildephonse, who writes 'a Domino quidam erat mundata' [for by God she was cleansed] (Solano 1954: 146–8). Sor Isabel may have been influenced by the Archpriest of Talavera's translation of Ildephonse's 'mundata' as 'fundata' [founded].

She may also have been influenced by Ludolph of Saxony's description of Mary as a castle which Christ entered:

> Hoc castellum quod intravit Jesus singulariter intemeratam Virginem, ejusdem Jesu genitricem Mariam per similitudinem accipimus. Castellum enim dicitur qualibet turris et murus in circuitu ejus, quae due sese invicem defendunt, ita ut hostes per murum ab arce, et a muro per arcem arceantum.

> [This castle which Jesus entered we accept especially by analogy as Mary the unspotted mother of the same Jesus. For any tower with a wall around it is called a castle; and the two defend each other, so that the enemy is kept off from the tower by the wall and from the wall by the tower.]
> (Conway 1976: 89, translation from Conway)

The extended metaphor of the sacred dwelling, whether house, temple, or palace, is a regular element of literary defence of the Immaculate Conception in Valencia, being found, for example, in a number of entries to the 1486 *certamen*, such as Lluís Cathalà's 'posada condigne' [worthy dwelling] and 'digne palau de tanta noblea' [worthy palace of such nobility], or Jaume del Bosch's 'un bell palau' [a beautiful palace] (Ferrando Francés 1983: 478–80, 458). Such architectural images of Mary have their origin in St Francis's 'Salutation of the Blessed Virgin Mary':

> Hail, O Lady
> Holy Queen,
> Mary, holy Mother of God [...]
> Hail his Palace!
> Hail his Tabernacle!
> Hail his Dwelling
> Hail his Robe! Hail his Servant!
> Hail his Mother! (cited in Boss 2003: 70–1)

The metaphor of Mary as a home is found on several occasions in Franciscan Conception liturgy, with Nogarola's office using it repeatedly. The house of God is a response at third night prayer, as a response after the ninth lesson, and also an antiphon: 'Domus quam cupio edificare magna est [...] et inclita' [The house which I wish to build is great and renowned], 'Hec est domus dei' [This is the house of the Lord], 'O Israel quam magna est domus dei et ingens' [O Israel, how great and mighty is the house of the Lord]. In the prayer at the vespers office there is a suggestion of the house being prepared for his Son by God, which could have provided Sor Isabel with the suggestion for her image: 'Deus qui per immaculatam Virginis conceptionem: dignum filio tuo habitaculum preparasti' [God who through the conception of the Immaculate Virgin prepared a worthy dwelling for your Son] (BC, MS 1043, *Officium immaculate conceptionis*, fols 16v, 18r, 22r, 13r).

Other holy containers and circumscribed places abound. Among these are the ark, the aumbray, and the sanctuary (in Ferrando Francés 1983: 511, 509, 465). The ninth lesson in Nogarola's Conception office also includes a number of prefigurations of Mary, many of them sacred vessels and enclosed spaces. Mary is a temple, the ark, the garden full of every scent, the most ornate of tabernacles holding the world's treasure. She is also the dwelling of the Holy Spirit and the tower with unbreachable walls (MS 1043, fol. 16v). The metaphor of a room within the temple is present in indigenous fifteenth-century Franciscan breviaries, such as one held in the Escorial: 'et spiritu sancto cepit hoc templum quod uerbum propheticum elegit se in habitaculum per speciali domicilio fabricare' [he took that temple through the Holy Spirit, which the words of the prophets had selected, to build for himself a room for a special dwelling].[15] The use of such metaphors places emphasis equally on the sacrality of the containing space as well as on the Godhead contained.

To make the Virgin Mary a sacred space, she must be preserved from original sin, and to conceptualize how, Sor Isabel uses the metaphor of a temple where no hammer sounds are heard: 'en la conceptió sua no vol sa magestat sia hoÿt colp de martell ni de ferro' [his Majesty wanted neither hammer sound nor the striking of iron to be heard at her conception] (fol. 2v; I, 12). The text is not found in Conception offices, and other biblical images used to symbolize the Immaculate Conception, like the burning bush or the rose without thorn, are ostensibly more appropriate to female sensibilities than the hammer blows. However, the building metaphor is applicable to the Santa Trinitat as I have demonstrated (Twomey 2003b).

---

[15] *Breviarum fratrum minorum secundum consuetudinem curiae romanae*, Biblioteca del Monasterio de El Escorial, MS A.III.14, fol. 433r.

To summarize, the hushed temple must have recalled the quiet periods in the convent to the cloistered reader. Second, the hammer blows, part of construction, were not outside the sisters' experience, since work on the half-ruined Trinitarian monastery continued even after their arrival in 1445. Sor Isabel initiated numerous building projects during her period as abbess. In the notes she made in the *Libro mayor de títulos* [Great Register], preserved in the archives of the Convent of the Santa Trinitat in Valencia (Benito Goerlich 1998: 49–50, 63–5), she lists the building of the new hospital, exterior doorways, and a dormitory. There was also the placing of the foundation stone of the new monastery by María of Castile in 1445. All could be drawn upon to reinforce the nuns' understanding of the Conception doctrine.

The association of the hammer blows with sin has another purpose, and that is to associate the beginning of the life of Christ with its end. As Christ is placed on the Cross, the hammer blows inflicted on his holy flesh by those crucifying him, 'ab un clau gros e despuntat clavaren-la stretament en la creu ab grans colps de martells' [with a large, blunt nail they nailed (his hand) to the Cross with great hammer blows] (fol. 210v II, 370), strike hammer blows in the soul of the Virgin: 'e, sentint los grans colps del martell, travessada per dolor, treballava per veure lo seu fill, e no podia per la multitut de la gent' [and feeling the great hammer blows, torn asunder by sorrow, she sought to see her Son, and could not because of the crowd of people] (fol. 211r II, 371). They are intended also to strike hammer blows into the souls of the listening nuns.

In some versions of the *Vita Christi*, there is no emphasis on the sound of the hammer blows. In John of Caulibus's *MVC* the narrative focuses rather on the actions of those carrying out the Crucifixion, describing how there is a person responsible for extending the hand and another for hammering: 'ille qui est ex latere sinistro accipit manum et trahit quantum potest et extendit' [the man on the left took the hand and pulled it as far as he could and stretched it out] and 'alium clauum intermittit et percutit et configit' [the other put in the nail, hit it, and fixed it to the Cross] (1997: 271). The sound of the hammer blows heard by the Virgin is no doubt suggested to Sor Isabel by her reading of Eiximenis's *Vida de Jesucrist*:

> Lo terç punt és pensar ací quant aquella sagrada mare sua oyera aquelles colps que daven tan grans ab los martells sobre los claus, tranchant los preciosos membres del seu fill, quanta dolor e compassió travassava la sua ànima. (BC, MS 460, fol. 216r)

> [The third point is to think how his sacred mother heard those blows that they gave with the hammers on the nails piercing his precious limbs and how much pain and compassion pierced her soul.]

Eiximenis includes 'oya' [heard], 'grans colps' [great blows], and 'travessava' [pierced]. However, in Eiximenis's version the hammer blows is one of series of points relevant to meditation at sext. It is only in Sor Isabel's version that the image of the hammer blows and original sin and the Crucifixion which redeems it are connected.

Sor Isabel describes at length the alliance of the Virgin Mary with grace to equip her for the Incarnation. She describes the first chamber, the Virgin's Memory, in her head, adorned by a carbuncle, which is where God is to dwell. The second chamber is the Virgin's Understanding, where God the Son is to dwell. The third chamber is her Will and it is here that the Holy Spirit will dwell. Hauf points to the fusion of genres: biblical, patristic, allegorical, christological, apocryphal, and liturgical (Villena 1995), a tactic typical of defence of the Immaculate Conception (Twomey 2008). Yet Sor Isabel also meshes the world of the nuns in the convent, in the process of being built, with the holy dwelling-place, the Virgin Mary, constructed by God. The three-chambered temple, associated with the building works at the convent, is the dwelling-place of the Trinity, just as the convent is named after it. Sor Isabel then recalls it in the hammer blows of suffering at the death on the Cross and draws the sisters into the suffering humanity of Christ, as similar hammer blows punctuate their day inside the Santa Trinitat.

The nuns were, however, not only to relate the metaphor to their own experience, they were to become engaged in it. The different realities in the narrative empower the readers, recreating them as participants in the events, showing them the value of observance, reinforcing their sense of being a community, and creating a female space within which they can deepen spiritual growth. Contemporary reality is simply another strand to add to Sor Isabel's skein.

2

Pure Bodies: Feeding the Soul in the *Vita Christi*

> There is a voice crying in the wilderness, Hélène Cixous and Catherine Clément say – the voice of a body dancing, laughing, shrieking, crying. Whose is it? It is, they say, the voice of a woman newborn and yet archaic, a voice of milk and blood, a voice silenced but savage.
>
> (Cixous & Clément 1986: ix)

Sor Isabel begins to create a community of readers from the opening pages of the *Vita Christi*. The way in which she presents the female body also provides insights into the nature and purpose of the work. Her depiction of the female body will be set in the context of how women's bodies were understood in the medieval period, taking into account three important societal spheres of influence: the Church, the medical profession, and literary convention. I shall also explore the body in the context of Sor Isabel's desire to draw the experiences of her own Poor Clare community into the life of Christ.

Women in theology, medicine, and literature

By the late medieval period, theologians and philosophers had developed a long tradition of depicting the female body as the embodiment of evil, closely allied to the Fall and, therefore, a site of temptation. Not only were women more likely to sin but their bodies were also, as Giles of Rome (1243–1316) taught at the University of Paris, less perfect and less divine than the male body (Allen 1997–2002: I, 434).[1] Theologians maintained that man was symbolized by the head, capable of rational thought, whilst the female was represented as the body, subject to the head, and incapable of reason. In this they followed the precepts of early Christian writers like St Paul, who had differentiated men and women in the early Christian community (Ephesians 5. 23–33; I Corinthians 11. 7–10). Classification of women's

---

[1] Caroline Walker Bynum terms the categorization misogynistic and distinguishes the following binaries: intellect/body, active/passive, rational/irrational, reason/emotion, self-control/lust, judgement/mercy, order/disorder (1991: 151).

bodies as less than perfect had its origins in the creation story (Genesis 2. 19), in which Adam's body was created first, whilst the female body was formed to be a companion, suggesting secondary status. The female body was formed indirectly out of the male body rather than directly from the creative matter, the earth. St Paul's teaching, in combination with the Genesis creation story, led theologians to argue that women's bodies were merely a reflection of men's. Theologians also absorbed the philosophy of Aristotle into their academic treatises (Allen 1997–2002: II, 65–171), believing that women's bodies were earthbound and belonged to the material world (Robertson 1993: 148).

Medical treatises, as well as other philosophical texts, provide another important set of criteria against which Sor Isabel's depiction of the female body should be set. Women's contribution to reproduction was thought to be limited and passive, because of Aristotle's views on reproduction and physionomy.[2] Women were thought to provide matter in the form of blood to nourish the developing foetus, whilst the man provided the seed, which developed into the child (Price 1998: 123; Allen 1997–2002: I, 91–3).

In the medieval period, physical and spiritual health were inextricably linked because both derive from the Latin *salus* [health; salvation]. Michael Solomon's study (1997) of two important medieval texts, the *Corbacho* and the *Spill,* addresses how sexual love, *amor hereos*, was associated with disease. However, the evidence he considers is directed at the well-being of male patients. Elizabeth Robertson, on the other hand, in her short study of Julian of Norwich and Margery Kempe, has drawn on medieval biological views of women to address how medical ideology 'shapes the […] representation of the feminine in mystical works' (1993: 142). Although she formulates her theories on the basis of studying two English mystics, her views will provide valuable insights into how such beliefs must have informed Sor Isabel's view of the female body.

A further important context into which the *Vita* must be set was the vein of misogynist literature in fifteenth-century Aragon (Cantavella & Parra 1987; Cantavella 1987, 1992, 2003: 45–56; Archer 2001 and 2005). Sister Prudence Allen traces the philosophical roots of such texts back to Roman satire (1997–2002: II, 181–222); such commonplaces were firmly embedded in accepted literary tradition by the late medieval period. I have argued elsewhere that the purpose of the *Vita Christi* might be in danger of being undervalued by being cast as a response to Valencian misogyny (Twomey 2003a). Sor Isabel was, of course, aware of secular literary trends. The convent was at the heart of Valencian literary life, so we can be sure that when she took

---

[2] For a study of Aristotelian thought in the teachings of the main Western theologians and how it was developed in an academic context from 1250 to 1500, see Allen 1997–2002: II, 65–179.

up the pen she did so in the knowledge of the way women and their bodies had been described.

The three male hierarchies (ecclesiastical, medical, and authorial) coincided in their categorization of woman as more dangerous, more unstable, and more likely to corrupt than man. Isabel de Villena had imbibed such belief during her life at court, where she may have read Eiximenis's *Dotzè llibre del crestià* [Twelfth Book of the Christian] with its views on women's unsuitability to rule and its advice to princes on the way to educate women and keep them subservient (1986–88: II, 14, 245–7). She had learned from her reading of theology that she, like others of her sex, inhabited an imperfect female body. How she describes the perfect, uncorrupted body will reveal the relationship between it and the imperfect ones which made up the reading community.

In the theological and anatomical climate of negative views of the female, there could be no possibility of a sinful body contributing imperfect matter to the formation of the Saviour. Sor Isabel, therefore, begins her story of the life of Christ by establishing how his mother was conceived. Like the rest of the Franciscan Order in fifteenth-century Valencia, Sor Isabel was an ardent supporter of the doctrine of the Immaculate Conception (Papa 1994: 213–23; Cantavella & Parra 1987: xii; Twomey 2003a and 2003b). This doctrine, which underpins the opening chapters of the *Vita Christi*, celebrates Mary's body, unstained by actual or original sin (O'Connor 1958; De Fiores & Meo 1988: 611–37; Lamy 2000). Study of the female body in Sor Isabel's writing must begin by examining a perfect one.

The constructed body

The first chapter of the *Vita Christi* reveals how Mary was prepared for her role in salvation. Sor Isabel first affirms the role of God the Father in the planned construction of the temple, which is to be a dwelling-place for the Son. The typological interpretation of the Bible, in which elements of the Old Testament, both people and objects, are believed to imperfectly figure those in the New, underpins her method (Auerbach 1984: 28–49). Sor Isabel depicts God the Father as a noble Lord decreeing that building work shall be carried out:

> Sabia molt cert que en tota la dita terra no y havia posada decent per a sa altesa reposar; per què li plagué manar e ordenar que fos fabricada huna tal posada com a sa Majestat pertanyia, obrada de tan excel·lent e singular obra, que semblant jamés no fos trobada, en tant que los miradors hajen a dir, admirats de la bellea d'aquesta casa: *Non est hic aliud nisi domus Dei et porta celi*. (fol. 2r; I, 9)

[He truly knew that in that land there was no suitable dwelling for his highness to rest in, and so he wished to ordain and decree that such a dwelling be built as might belong to his majesty, constructed in such a magnificent and wondrous way that never was there one like it to the extent that those who looked on it were bound to say, in their amazement at such a work: *This is none other than the house of God and the door of heaven.*]

The body of the Virgin becomes a geographical location, a 'posada' [dwelling-place] for the King. In this, it parallels the Ark of the Covenant, which contained the covenant with Yahweh, or the temple, which is the earthly place where God is present (II Kings 8. 14–21).

Sor Isabel provides some details about the temple, indicating it is to be 'obrada de tan excel·lent e singular obra' [constructed in such a magnificent and wondrous way]. Hauf, in the introduction to his edition of the *Vita Christi*, indicates that 'Non est aliud nisi domus Dei' is taken from the office for the dedication of a church (Villena 1995: 49). However, Sor Isabel could have taken it from the new Conception office written by Leonardo Nogarola at the request of Pope Sixtus IV (1414–84). It is likely that Nogarola's office would have been used in the Santa Trinitat convent for the Conception octave.³ Nogarola employs 'Nisi domus' [Unless the house], as an antiphon, as a response, and as a canticle.

In the office, as well as in Sor Isabel's work, the bricks-and-mortar sanctuary of the Old Testament Holiest of Holies prefigures the construction of a new and more intimate one, the construction of Mary's body. Her pure body is a new creation and is contrasted with bodies like Adam's, Eve's, and their descendants', created under the Old Law. Sor Isabel intertwines sanctity and regality in her description of Mary's body. Her choice of image of the temple to represent the Virgin's body is not unusual in Marian writing, being found in the writing of the early Church Fathers, such as St Ildephonse (†667). It is also to be found in among Eiximenis's chapters about the twelve dignities of the Virgin:

> e a axò respon la sancta scriptura en l'article de la sancta fe cathòlica dient que és estada feta en lo ventre virginal qui és appellat per los sancts temple de Déu, oit conclus del general monarcha, sala del Rey eternal, cambra del sobiran mestre, cadira imperial, archa dels tresors divinals, secretari

---

³ I have examined copies of Nogarola's office in the Biblioteca Nacional de España (MS 4437), in the Biblioteca de Catalunya (MS 1043), in the Universidad de Zaragoza (Incunable 60), in the Biblioteca Colombina, Seville (MS Vitrina s/s), in the Escorial Library (MS Vitrina 8), and in the Archivo Capitular de Toledo (MS 33.13 and MS 9.8). Nogarola wrote the first officially accepted Conception office in 1478.

dels consells eternals, jardí dels delits de glòria, refugi de tots los tribulats. (*Vida de Jesucrist*, BC, MS 299, fol. 37v)

[and to this Holy Scripture responds according to the articles of the holy Catholic faith, saying he was made in the womb of the Virgin, which the saints call temple of God, enclosed place of the monarch, hall of the King, eternal chamber of the sovereign Master, chair of the Emperor, ark of God's treasure, chest of everlasting counsel, garden of glory's delights, refuge of all those in tribulation.]

Nevertheless, its use in a narrative, rather than a theological, context proves startling. Sor Isabel distinguishes Mary from other members of the human race, 'fills d'Adam' [sons of Adam], in marked contrast to Jaume Roig's parallel between Mary and the daughters of Eve in his *Espill* (1978: 154).

The Virgin's physical body: hands, feet, and eyes

To provide an insight into Sor Isabel's vision of the body, I shall first examine the parts unspecified by gender, followed by specifically female ones. In the *Vita Christi*, the Virgin's eyes, hands, and knees are defeminized, except for an occasional use of 'bella' [beautiful].

The Virgin is found, even from her childhood, with her hands folded in prayer: 'sovint la trobava la sua mare ab les mans plegades, los ulls levats al cel' [often her mother found her with her hands folded and her eyes raised heavenward] (fol. 7v; I, 25). The holy posture is repeated throughout the *Vita*:

E la Senyora humilíssima, vehent la sua cosina germana, axí plena del Sanct Sperit, parlar coses tan altes en glòria e lahor sua, volent referir e tornar tota aquella lahor e magnificència a la magestat divina, ficà los genolls en terra ab los ulls al cel e les mans junctes. (fols 69v–70v; I, 254)

[And the very humble Lady, seeing her cousin, full of the Holy Spirit, praising and glorifying her in such noble words, sought to turn all that praise and magnificence towards God's majesty, bent her knee to the ground and with eyes turned to heaven and her hands clasped.]

Sor Isabel does not believe the perfect body of the Virgin is untouched by human hand, for she shows her engaging with others to touch and be touched. Touching can be part of an informal gesture but it can also be part of a formal greeting. It is expressed in an informal manner when she is taken by the arm by her attendants: 'portant-la per lo braç Humilitat e Pobrea' [with Humility and Poverty leading her] (fol. 69v; I, 252), or by her son. Greetings are expressed formally when the hands of the Virgin

Mary are kissed in obeisance: 'aquella gentil donzella Sperança besà la mà a la Senyora' [and the gentle lady Hope kissed the Lady's hand] (fol. 38r; I, 140). The Virgin engages in human embraces in the scene where she takes the child John the Baptist in her arms: 'prenint sa senyoria lo gloriós Johan dels braços de Elizabeth, sa mare, e abraçant-lo estretament ab molta amor' [her Ladyship took the glorious John from his mother Elizabeth's arms, and hugging him tightly with great love] (fol. 70v; I, 258).

Knees are equally important. Mary kneels at the manger, with her hands folded and her eyes turned heavenward: 'sa senyoria stava enmig agenollada, ab les mans plegades, los ulls al cel' [her Ladyship was kneeling in the midst, with her hands folded, and her eyes heavenward] (fol. 73r; I, 268); she kneels also at the Annunciation and she kneels before her Son during the journey to Egypt: 'e la Senyora e Joseph agenollaren-se davant la magestat sua' [and the Lady and Joseph knelt before his Majesty] (fol. 94v; I, 339). Each of these gestures focuses on devotion to the Saviour and serves to show Mary's reaction to important moments in her life. They are an important witness of devotion to the body of Christ. The Incarnation, God made manifest in flesh, is one of the two principal focuses of Franciscan devotion (Rubin 2009: 201) and is visible to the reader through the Virgin's devotional posture.

Eiximenis also writes of the Virgin kneeling at the Nativity, mentioning her eyes and hands:

> Qui lavors, axí com dit és, estava en terra agenollada, tenint los hulls e les mans esteses envers lo cel, e axí com la gloriosa tench aquell gloriós fill en les mans guarda-lo ferm en la cara ab sobiran delit.
>
> (*Vida de Jesucrist*, BC, MS 299, fol. 170v)
>
> [For, as it is written, she was kneeling on the ground with her eyes and hands raised to heaven and, as the Glorious Lady had that glorious Son in her arms, she held her gaze on his face with great delight.]

Sor Isabel includes a scene of adoration of the Virgin by St Anne with clear antecedents in Eiximenis's version. Eiximenis places the incident in the context of a revelation to a saintly hermit, using it as a sign of the Virgin's humility:

> Diu aquest doctor que estech revelat a un sanct hermità appellat Fèlix en l'ermitaje de Tebaida que en aquell temps de sa poquea ensenya de si gran humilitat. Car sabent la sua mare ella qui era ne a què era deputada, e veent en ella tants senyals de virtut, sovint li volia besar los peus e les mans e estar-li davant agenollada e la sobre humil creatura, no podent axò sofferir per res, dava a la mare tan grans senyals de avorriment de aytals honors que la mare despuix no u gosava fer altra vegada.
>
> (MS 299, fol. 50r–v)

[That doctor said that it was revealed to a hermit named Felix, in the hermitage in Thebes, that during her early days she displayed great humility. For her mother, aware who she was and what she was sent to do, and seeing in her such great signs of virtue, often wished to kiss her feet and hands and kneel in front of her. The extremely humble child could not bear that at all and gave her mother such clear signals of abhorring such great reverence that the mother afterwards did not do it any more.]

The Virgin's body, exempt from sin, can also be an object of devotion. Sor Isabel writes of St Anne's adoration of the Virgin as a child, after she had been to the temple, when she was instructed about the great things her daughter would achieve: 'E ella stave-li davant, agenollada, besant-li los peuets e manetes ab goig no recomptable' [and she was before her, kissing her little feet and hands with indescribable joy' (fol. 7v; I, 24). She places greater emphasis on the mutual relationship between the two central characters, the Virgin and St Anne, although she does refer to the Virgin as 'humilíssima' [most humble]:

> E la humilíssima Senyora, no podent comportar que la sua mare li fes tals servirs, ab tot no parlàs, mostrava en la sua careta no li plahyien semblants coses. E la virtuosa mare, que en rés no pensava més sinó en complaure aquella excel·lent filla, conexent la voluntat sua, posà fi en lo seu propri plaer per contentar a ella; e de aqui avant no li besava peus ni mans, sinó solament la boqueta, frontet et galtetes, ab grandíssima amor et reverència.
> (fol. 7v; I, 24–5)

> [And the most humble Lady, unable to bear that her mother should pay homage to her in that manner, did not speak, but showed in her little face that she was not happy with such things. And the virtuous mother who thought of nothing but pleasing her excellent daughter, once she knew her will, put an end to her own pleasure to content her; and from then on she kissed neither feet nor hands but merely her mouth, her forehead, and her little cheeks with the greatest love and reverence.]

Even though it is possible to see that Sor Isabel included ideas present in Eiximenis's *Vita Christi*, in her version kneeling is emphasized to a far greater degree and is present with greater frequency. The movements made by knees, hands, and eyes are closely aligned to ones common in the nuns' lives. They spent regular hours of the day kneeling, they frequently turned their eyes to heaven, and, during their prayers, their hands were placed in a folded or clasped position. Like the Virgin Mary, stopping for a time of devotion on her journey to Egypt, they too would have set aside parts of their day for contemplation.

Sor Isabel then moves her consideration of the female body to the sacramental level: 'E de la vostra [boca], Senyora, no solament exiran paraules celestials, ans ab vostre dolç parlar fareu obrir lo cel' [And from your mouth, Lady, not only do heavenly words issue forth, but with your sweet speech you open heaven's door] (fol. 38r; I, 141). The Virgin's hands are given a salvific function: 'car en la mà vostra stà la salut e vida nostra' [for your hand holds our salvation and our life] (fol. 12v; I, 43). Sacralization of the female body presents the female reader with an opportunity to see their own bodies as more sacred than the current theological climate allowed.[4]

The Virgin's body: inside and out

Sor Isabel depicts the Virgin's inner parts softening or melting with compassion, associating her with the sufferings of her Son. When the Virgin is faced with flight into Egypt, her emotion is expressed through inner turmoil: 'Joseph, spos meu, totes les entràmenes mies són stades regirades e han tremolat' [Joseph, my husband, all my innermost being is stirred up and trembling] (fol. 99v; I, 326). Similarly, at the departure of her Son to begin his ministry, interior changes can be noted: 'O, quant se alteraren les entràmenes de la Senyora excel·lent hoint que lo senyor fill seu de ella se havia a partir, la companyia del qual no volguera perdre sols per un moment!' [O how the innermost being of the noble Lady was moved when she learned her Son was to depart, since she did not want to lose his company even for a moment] (fol. 109v; II, 56).

Even though the *Vita Christi* begins with the conception of the Virgin, many figures from the Old Testament make their appearance, mostly to honour Mary or, even, in the case of Eve, to admit her culpability for sin coming into the world. Eve is another female figure who takes part in Sor Isabel's narrative and who experiences a similar interior softening to the Virgin's, when she considers the pain and suffering her action has caused:

> E la mare Eva, que véu lo seu marit e fills en tanta dolor e pena, atendrien-se les entràmenes de aquella, com a mare piadosa, e dix: 'O, Adam senyor! aquesta dolor mia és principalment, car yo he lançat a vós ý als fills meus en tanta dolor e pena, e en cascú de vosaltres yo só turmentada.'
> (fol. 17v; I, 64)

> [And the innermost being of mother Eve, who saw her sons and husband in such suffering and travail, softened just like a compassionate mother's, and she said: 'O, Lord Adam, this pain is principally mine own, since I

---

[4] Sarah Jane Boss points to the way in which the Middle Ages could be 'characterized as strongly sacramental'. She notes that the medieval world 'tends to focus on the potential for sanctity rather than on its distance from that which is divine or sacred' (2000: 93). See also Boureau 1994.

have cast you and my sons into such pain and suffering and in each of you I am tormented.']

Eve's emotive response is to be interpreted in two ways. First, it is depicted as proper to the female body. Without falling into the commonplace of associating female writing with emotion, which Caroline Walker Bynum decries in the case of the nuns of Helfta (1982), Sor Isabel is seeking to demonstrate women characters' bodily rather than rational response to sorrow. In this, she does not counter the views of male theologians and philosophers but works within their expectations. Stephen Haliczer notes that the idea that emotion, rather than reason, predominated in women's psyche was deep-rooted in medieval culture (2002: 48). Bynum's study *Fragmentation and Redemption* (1991: 153–4) makes the point that women do not seek to challenge the male hierarchy through their religious experience by creating a 'religious subculture'. Secondly, the emotive response of Eve, far from being a result of the Fall, is shown as a redemptive feature, because, through it, she is able to demonstrate compassion and penitence.

Reinterpreting tradition also applies to the *Vita Christi*'s emphasis on the Virgin's tears. Robertson argues that behind the emotive response lay a belief that the female body was allied to cold and wet humours, and therefore, had a propensity to release moisture, whether blood, milk, or tears, in order to purge the organism (1993: 142). She indicates that emphasis on female liquids in works for and about women reveals knowledge of contemporary medical philosophy about the way in which their bodies required constant letting of liquids in order to keep them in balance. Sor Isabel depicts the female body responding with curative liquefaction.

However, more important for an understanding of the emphasis on tears is Robertson's view that female spirituality is expressed through the body. Sor Isabel's focus on bodily response to life events in the *Vita Christi* provides further evidence in support of Robertson's thesis (1993: 149). The Virgin's bodily response to sorrow sets her, the perfect woman, within the confines of her gender. She gives visibility and value to female bodily responses, so that, when they occur in the convent, they will be recognized as valuable too.

Tears are also part of the Franciscan response to God. The early documents written about Francis's life showed how tears were cleansing and had a salvific function:

> Truly, even though he had attained purity of heart and body and in some manner was approaching the height of sanctification, he did not cease to cleanse the eyes of his soul with a continuous flood of tears. He longed for the sheer brilliance of the heavenly light and disregarded the loss of his bodily eyes […]. He asserted that he preferred to lose sight rather than repress the devotion of the spirit and impede the tears which cleansed his

inner vision so that he could see God. [...] He was a man devoted to God, who drenched in spiritual tears, displayed serenity in both mind and face.
(Armstrong, Hellmann, & Short 2001: 695)

Tears and their assuaging thus indicate how the perfect body is to respond. The Virgin dissolves into tears at the circumcision of her Son and her tears are stopped by the Infant Christ, who covers her eyes:

> ab les sues dolçes manetes tocava-li lo cap e la cara, posant-li los dites sobre la boca, volent-li mostrar que tenia gran compassió de la sua dolor e quasi pregant-la que cessàs de plorar per amor sua. (fol. 98v; I, 322)

> [with his sweet little hands he touched her head and her face, putting his hands over her mouth, wishing to show her that he had great compassion for her sorrow and almost pleading with her to desist from crying for the love he bore her.]

The primary narrative purpose is served when the tears of someone so closely related to and so loved by Christ are deepening the sorrow and pain he is feeling, and, for this reason, they must be stemmed. The purpose, on a second level, is recognition of the change to the Virgin's state from impure body to pure one. If the female body is made perfect and ceases to require purgation through release of humours, does Sor Isabel intend to show it moving closer to the model of male perfection?

The contemplative body

It is not new to suggest that contemplation is central to the *Vita Christi*, because it was the raison d'être of the genre.[5] Hauf, in the introduction to his edition of the *Vita Christi,* underscores its importance to the development of the narrative, pointing to both the Virgin Mary and Mary Magdalene as 'models pràctics de vida contemplativa' (Villena 1995: 44). Hauf does not address, however, the function of the female body in contemplation, nor the way in which the female body and spirit can be shown to interact. Isabel de Villena follows Franciscan tradition in placing contemplation at the heart of the *Vita Christi*. John of Caulibus's *MVC* breaks the story to insert a theological discussion on contemplation in chapters 46 to 58 (2000: 158–204).

---

[5] John of Caulibus refers to the high level of contemplation which will be induced in the practitioner in the prologue to the Poor Clare nun: 'Vides ergo ad quam excelsum gradum meditacio uite Christi perducit' (1997: 9) [You see, then, to what an exalted height meditation on the life of Christ leads] (2000: 3). On Sor Isabel, see, for example, Aichinger 2003: 58–9.

Her approach is different. Any teaching on contemplation is embedded in the narrative.

Hauf points elsewhere to the 'efusión contemplativa' in the pages of the *Vita Christi* (1987: 112), but he does not address the intimate and two-way relationship between Mary and the Poor Clares. As Miri Rubin shows, Mary became the 'core of Clare's legacy'. Clare was thought to be the 'footprint of Mary' and Clare, like her followers, was 'the person chosen by Mary for the renewal of her "virginal purity and humility"'. Rubin parallels the return of Christ in the Eucharist with the embodiment of Mary in the 'pure bodies of chaste, enclosed nuns' (2009: 200).

Sor Isabel develops bodily responses to contemplation, beginning with the scenes of the Virgin's childhood:

> En les hores de matí e de vespre se exercitava sa senyoria en la pus alta contemplació, seguint lo consell del seu devot avi David, que diu: *Ad vesperum demorabitur fletus, et ad matutinum leticia.* (fol. 8r; I, 26)
>
> [At the hours of matins and vespers she engaged in the highest contemplation, following the counsel of her forefather David, who said: *In the evening come tears, and in the morning, joy.*]

Sor Isabel focuses on the engagement of the child Virgin in praying the liturgical hours, particularly the principal offices, in which she follows the tradition in many of the *Vitae Christi*. John of Caulibus depicts the Virgin praying the hours. Eiximenis shows how her day was marked by the hours although he does not mention that she prayed them:

> Segonament, fet lo sacrifici en lo temple, ella estava en oració vocal, ço és en aquella qui per los bisbes e sacerdots era ordenada que·s faes per les donzelles a Déu consagrades o deputades a estar en lo temple de Déu al seu servey e en aquesta sancta oració ella occupava lo temps qui era aprés lo dit sacrifici fins a terça. (*Vida de Jesucrist*, MS 299, fol. 81v)
>
> [Secondly, once she had completed the sacrifice in the temple, she engaged in oral prayer, which is the prayer set aside for priests and bishops and made by the young girls whose lives are dedicated to God in the service of his temple. In this holy prayer she spent the time between the sacrifice of the Mass and the third hour.]

He then instructs his reader as to how she occupied her time in sewing and weaving between the hours of terce and none (MS 299, fol. 81v). However, in Sor Isabel's version, it is her role in turning aside God's anger from his people which is emphasized. She alludes to Psalm 30. 5, which gives a scriptural basis to the use of tears and joy in prayer:

> En aquesta caritativa pregària stava la Senyora la major part de la nit, ab contínues làgrimes secretes e molt amagades, havent ferma fe de obtenir lo que demanava; e açò li feya convertir les sues làgrimes en grandíssim delit e dolçor de la divinal bonea. (fol. 8r; I, 26)
>
> [In that charitable prayer the Lady spent most of the night, with constant secret and bitter tears, with firm hope of being granted what she asked and this made her tears turn into the greatest delight and sweetness for God's goodness.]

In the *Vita Christi*, the Virgin's contemplation leads to extremes of emotional response: tears and delight. Cantavella and Parra have termed the type of emotional response in the *Vita Christi*: 'l'emotivitat en la recerca de la puresa' [sensibility seeking out purity] (1987: x). Sor Isabel wishes to show that Mary's tears are not a result of having an imperfect body, nor of the Fall. Emotional reactions are to be celebrated, since they occur in a perfect body. She suggests that female bodily reactions are sanctified.

The Virgin's physical body: a mother's matrix

The most identifiably female organ, the womb, and the way it is presented in the *Vita Christi*, point to deeper levels of spirituality. It is depicted as a sacred vessel contained within the edifice of the body. Bynum discusses the way in which the Cistercians associated the Virgin's womb with the tabernacle and shows how their devotion to the womb as a eucharistic vessel causes them to commission vessels in the shape of Mary, with Mary tabernacles found in Cistercian monasteries and a Mary pyx found at Cîteaux (1988: 81). A Spanish standing pyx in copper-gilt, with Mary represented as the Pietà, is held in the Victoria and Albert Museum (M459–1956). It dates from the 1520s.

Sor Isabel illustrates the transmutation of the womb into sacred object in the *Vita Christi*. It then becomes worthy of veneration:

> E coneixent sa senyoria que ja era mare verdadera de un fill tan excel·lent, hagué goig infinit, e, baixant los ulls, mirà lo seu propri ventre, adorant aquell com a tabernacle divinal. (fol. 44v; I, 164)
>
> [And her Ladyship realizing she was mother of such an excellent Son, was filled with joy and, lowering her eyes, gazed on her own belly, venerating it as a divine tabernacle.]

Eucharistic symbolism becomes apparent just after the Annunciation. Bynum points to the association between the reservation of the sacrament and the Annunciation as part of late medieval eucharistic devotion. In the

Vita Christi, after her conception of the Infant Christ, the Virgin adores her own womb and its sacred contents, which is almost independent of her body. Sor Isabel's purpose is to draw the events of the *Vita Christi* into close union with everyday events in the convent.

The interplay between body and mind provides further insight into how Sor Isabel envisages the contemplative state. The Virgin Mary's contemplation takes her into a transcendent state in which the body and the corporal senses are left behind. It is important to note that in medieval concepts of female spirituality, the female was thought to be able to experience union with Christ only through her body, but Sor Isabel shows the female body in a different way. She shows the Virgin so completely enraptured in contemplation, after hearing Gabriel's words, that she does not answer: 'E havent dit lo missatger totes les sobredits rahons a la Senyora, e vehent que sa mercé no responia, ans stava tota elevada en contemplació divina' [The angel having given all the above reasons to the Lady and seeing that her Ladyship did not reply, but was rather completely swept up into divine contemplation] (fol. 35r; I, 131). At this important turning-point in the *Vita*, to which she dedicates five chapters, Sor Isabel is pointing to the type of contemplation which engages women so utterly that they are no longer aware of the material world.

Contemplation is not experienced solely by the Virgin Mary. Elizabeth is so caught up in a trance-like state at the sight of her cousin arriving to visit her that she is unable to move her body: 'fon así recomplida de gran alegria e consolació, que no·s pogué moure de allà hon era' [she was so filled with great joy and consolation that she could not move from where she was] (fol. 69v; I, 252–3). Also the Virgin and St John are caught up in a rapturous contemplative state before the consecration of the Eucharist (fol. 297v; III, 304): 'parlaven ab tanta fervor e devoció que ja paria fossen fora de la mortal vida' [they spoke with such fervour and devotion that it seemed they were not part of mortal life.] It is the Virgin, however, who is styled 'la vera contemplativa' [the true contemplative] (fol. 7r; I, 31) at the point where she enters the temple.

Feeding the body

Whilst dedication to contemplative prayer is one of the key values of the Poor Clare Rule, the vows also place central focus on self-denial. Bynum has sought to argue that fasting and food are major themes in female spirituality, whereas they are less important in male spirituality (1988: 95), although her study takes no account of Spain. For the purpose of this section of the chapter, I focus on the concept of fasting in the *Vita Christi*, not because I consider it a feminine trait but because abstinence is part of the Rule.

Sor Isabel follows a tradition present in Eiximenis's *Vida de Jescrist* (Hauf 1987: 107) when she describes infant ascetiscm. The Virgin suckled only once a day on certain days of the week:

> Car la dita penitència és salut de la ànima, restauració e conservació de les virtuts, camí real dels justs, refectió e confort de tot bé; e per ço la nostra Senyora la ha presa e amada en lo començ de la vida sua, per donar exemple als servents seus que seguissen la via sua, si pervenir volran al repòs seu. (fol. 7v; I, 25)

> [For such penitence is salvation for the soul, restoration and preservation of virtue, true path of the just, refreshment and comfort of all good and for that reason Our Lady adopted penitence and loved it from the start of her life so as to give an example to her servants who followed in her footsteps if they wished to attain the rest she affords.][6]

Mary's ascetic suckling is closely allied to the reality of life for the nuns. The Santa Trinitat nuns, like their Franciscan Conceptionist counterparts, whose Rule laid down the days on which fasting should take place, followed strict guidelines. They were to fast in Lent and on other days of abstinence laid down by the Church, as well as the days between the Presentation of the Virgin (18 November) and Christmas (25 December).[7]

Fasting in the *Vita Christi* provides a model to the sisters in terms of their own ascetic practice (*Reglas* 1988: 22, 53). Bynum points to the fact that food abstinence was central to Clare's Rule, noting that the nuns were to take only one meal a day (1988: 100), and contrasting the focus on food with St Francis's emphasis on possessions. In the Rule, fasting was considered a community activity and a purification of the communal and individual body prior to a given day. In the *Vita Christi,* the emphasis on food abstinence is to promote it as a form of penitence to embrace and love. Alain de l'Isle (1128–1203) indicates that 'fast is a medicine to soul and body. It preserves the body from disease, the soul from sin. About its medicinal effects, earthly and heavenly philosophy agree' (cited in Bynum 1988: 44). Sor Isabel takes the same approach. It will affect both their souls and their bodies, which it will confirm in virtuous behaviour.

Fasting and feasting were important in Valencian convent life. At the Puritat convent fifteenth-century convent records give an insight into the way in which the sisters took care of their earthly bodies. They show which foods were purchased, and in what quantities. Fresh eggs, fruit, vegetables, rice, and bread were staples of their diet. Prior to major feast days, special

---

[6] The Protoevangelium of James does not include this tradition (Schneemelcher 1990: I, 428), nor does Jacobus de Voragine (1993: II, 149–58).

[7] *Regla de la orden de la Concepción de Nuestra Señora de la ciudad de Toledo*, BNE, MS 1111: fol. 8r.

purchases were made.[8] On 14 December, chestnuts as well as walnuts were bought, in preparation for the Christmas menu (Clero, Libro 956, fol. 124r). The nuns' diets were varied on occasion with snails (Clero, Libro 946, fol. 108r). Chickens and capons were bought just before Christmas annually (Clero, Libro 956, fols 187r, 124v). During the Christmas period in 1495, the nuns had *neules*, a sweet pastry, as well as the traditional almond sweet, *turrón* [nougat]. According to Antoni Maria Alcover, *neules* are 'full de pasta prima de farina, generalment barrejada amb sucre i alguna essència, caragolat formant com un canó' [sheet of high-quality pastry, usually coated in sugar and a flavouring, rolled into a tube shape]. He has evidence from both Empordà, in the Pyrenees area of the Kingdom of Aragon, and Majorca that they were typical of Christmas, citing a Majorcan refrain 'cada cosa a son temps i a Nadales les neules' (1988: VII, 745) [there is a time for everything, and at Christmas it is time for wafers].

Fasting is, however, quite clearly recognizable from the orders they placed for foodstuffs. During March 1441, at a period corresponding to the Lenten fast, the purchases were limited to green vegetables, including spinach (Clero, Libro 946, fol. 25v), and on Monday 14 August 1441 the nuns had a diet of bread and water in preparation for the Feast of the Assumption (fol. 29v). Food hardship was clearly part of the annual cycle of the liturgical year, but the nuns did not appear to be adulterating food to destroy the flavours, which Bynum indicates was frequent practice: 'Both men and women fasted or adulterated any food they ate in order to destroy any pleasure they might experience in it' (1988: 73). Spices such as pepper, ginger (Clero, Libro 956, fol. 184r; Clero, Libro 946, fols 86v, 106r), and saffron (Clero, Libro 946, fols 21r, 89r) were regularly purchased. They could have been used to flavour foods, assuming that a certain amount of expense was acceptable. Pepper, ginger, cinnamon, and cloves, among foodstuffs bought, are found in the accounts of the Marchioness of Gandia for 11 November, and the listing among vegetables and eggs appears to confirm that the spices were bought for the kitchen:

> Item rebi cols.
> Item rebi canella.
> Item rebi pebre.
> Item rebi gingebre.
> Item rebi clavels.

---

[8] These accounts are found in two manuscripts in Valencia, in the Arxiu del Regne de València, Clero, Libro 946, *Libro de recibos y gastos del convento siendo procuradora Sor Antonieta Ceriol y abadessas Sor Margarita Tolsa y Sor Damiata de Mompalau* (1439–99), and Clero, Libro 956, *Libro de dades y rebudes fetes per la reuerent Sor Beatriz de Soler abbadessa del monestir de Santa Clara de la ciutat de Valencia* (1454–60, 1492).

> [...] Item rebi eus.
> Item rebi mel.   (ARV, Maestre Racional, Libros, 12560, Marquesat de
> Villena, *Comptes de la Senyora Marquesa*, fol. 2r)

> [Also I received cabbages
> I received cinnamon.
> I received pepper.
> I received ginger.
> I received eggs.
> I received honey.]

On the other hand, ginger and saffron were also included among a fascinating list of medicines on a loose folio in the accounts of the Marquesat de Villena, dated 1390:

> Medicines del mes d'octubre
> item per camomilla per la senyora l ii.
> item per cafra per la senyora l ii.
> item per i quart de gengebre sech per la senyora l ii.
> item per cafra per obs de dona Leonor l ii.   (ARV, Maestre Racional,
> Libros, 12538, Marquesat de Villena,
> *Comptes del Comprador*)

> [Medicines for the month of October
> Also for camomile for her Ladyship, 2 pounds.
> Also for saffron for her Ladyship, 2 pounds.
> Also for one quarter of dry ginger for her Ladyship, 2 pounds.
> Also for saffron for Lady Leonor, 2 pounds.]

This points to the fact that both the ginger and saffron purchased could also have been used in the infirmary in the Puritat, although the abbess does not specify. It might be that the combination of rice (Clero, Libro 946, fol. 121r) and saffron in the Puritat convent accounts means that fifteenth-century paella was being prepared in the convent, and the nuns certainly bought 'fideus' [noodles] (fol. 111r), probably for making soup. Abstinence meant denying the body meat, and reliance on vegetables, but it did not mean such levels of denial that the body was unable to function.

Renouncing the desires of the body

The third aspect of the Virgin's life style is renunciation of possessions. Sor Isabel applies the spirit of the Rule to the life style of the Virgin to show how it can be lived out in a perfect way. She emphasizes the fact that the Virgin must leave behind the things of the world to enter the temple. The Virgin declares she is to be an example to others when she separates herself from possessions:

> Aquesta és la voluntat de nostre Senyor Déu que yo vaja hí.m separe de vosaltres, per donar exemple als esdevenidors qui perfetament volran Déu servir, que de necessitat coneguen que s'han a separar e voluntàriament apartar de les coses pus cares que en aquesta present vida tendran
> (fol. 9r; I, 30).
>
> [This is the will of our Lord God that I go and leave you to give an example to those coming behind me, who want to serve God perfectly, and who know that, of necessity, they have to make a break with, and, of their own free will, leave behind the things that they hold dearest in this world.]

Letting go of possessions has been interpreted in the Franciscan Order as a way of mirroring Christ's Incarnation and, because of the christological understanding, it becomes more than just a 'penitential practice' (Short 1999: 61). The Virgin Mary's self-dedication links poverty and salvation, and also acts as a support to the Santa Trinitat sisters, as they seek to renounce the things of the world and embrace their life of poverty.

The narrative of the Protoevangelium of James, which Sor Isabel follows closely, does not suggest that Mary's parents were living in poverty. Joachim is described as owning a herd, 'seu ganado' (fol. 2v; I, 10), and, when he goes out into the wilderness, it is to live among the shepherds, his employees: 'los simples pastors ajudaven a plànyer a son senyor la congoxa sua' [The simple shepherds helped their lord to bewail his sorrow] (fol. 2r; I, 10). Sor Isabel wishes to show that being born into poverty is of less value than taking it up through an act of will, since such an act of will once again implies control of bodily instincts, as well as foregrounding of the spiritual. The case of the Virgin Mary provides a pointer to the situation of the nuns, many of them of wealthy backgrounds; they could identify closely with Mary's renunciation of comfort to seek holiness and, thus, bring their earthly bodies closer to hers.

Poverty is one of the allegorical figures that come to serve the newborn Virgin, but she is only the second to arrive, the first being Benignitat [Kind Nature]. Poverty declares, 'fins a huy no he trobat jamés persona qui de bon cor ne voluntàriament m'aja receptat' [up to now I have never found anyone who has willingly taken me in with a good heart] (fol. 5v; I, 22). Sor Isabel emphasizes the difficulty of renouncing the things of the world, recognizing that poverty is not an easy part of the Rule to accept. It is probable that for Elionor de Villena, illegitimate descendant of the Castilian and Aragonese royal family, it proved hard. The early folios of BNE MS 1111 include details on the hardships to be faced as a member of the Franciscan Conceptionist Order: 'No sea reciuida alguna que aya menos de doce años ni tanta edad que no pueda sin graueça llevar la aspereça desta vida y Regla' [Let none be received who is younger than twelve years old nor so old that she cannot support the harshness of this life and Rule] (fol. 2r). The reformed Rule of Urban IV also refers to the hardship of living it (*Reglas* 1988: 43).

Emphasis on renunciation of the things of the world, as a sign of sanctity, is a common feature in Franciscan art and history. Both Francis and Clare stripped off their rich garments to adopt the Rule and their followers did the same. A retable in the chapel of St Clare in Barcelona Cathedral shows Clare in a rich velvet dress. Her renunciation is marked by the shearing of her hair. In a description of Sor María González de la Fuente, the first abbess of the St Anthony of Padua convent, which belonged to the Franciscan Third Order, there is the same need to divest herself of rich outer garments: 'acompañada de algunas virtuosas doncellas y matrones determino dexar la pompa y vanidad de el mundo [...] desnudando las galas de que según la calidad de su sangre andaba vestida' [accompanied by a few virtuous ladies and matrons, she decided to leave the pomp and vanity of the world (...), stripping herself of the rich garments in which in virtue of her noble rank she was attired].[9] The pure body of this abbess was found incorruptible even after death, a sure sign of the sanctity her conduct had brought. According to the author, renunciation of the things of the world led holy Franciscans to bodily purity and incorruptibility.

The working body

The final way in which the Virgin Mary is shown employing her body as a precursor of the Rule is in work. Work is described as an accompaniment to prayer in the reformed Rule which the Santa Trinitat Poor Clares followed: 'Mas las hermanas [...] ocúpense en trabajos útiles y honestos, teniendo en cuenta que, desechado el ocio, enemigo del alma, no apaguen el espíritu de la santa oración' [But the sisters (...) should occupy themselves in useful and honest tasks, bearing in mind that, casting aside leisure, the enemy of the soul, they must not let the spirit of holy prayer wither away] (*Reglas* 1988: 50).

When the Virgin's life in the Christian community in Jerusalem is described by Sor Isabel, she is seen to be working for the good of the community, from midday to vespers: 'sa senyoria feya faena fins a hora de vespres per ajudar a la comunitat' [her Ladyship worked until the time for vespers, to assist the community] (fol. 297r; III, 303). The Virgin's work time would correspond to the period of work carried out by the nuns in the Santa Trinitat. At the

---

[9] BNE, MS 3840, *Documentos relativos a la historia de la provincial franciscana de Castilla*, fol. 88r. For a history of the Order, see Oma Echevarría 1973.

same time, the *Vita Christi* allies work and prayer, emphasizing that any work carried out by the Virgin Mary is also a prayer:

> E la vida de vostra senyoria no solament ha de ésser entesa en contemplar, ans encara en les altres obres virtuoses […]. E lo legir de vostra mercé, e la faena de mans, e les altres obres, tot és una pura oració qui puja dret al cel, *sicut incensum in conspectu Dei*. (fol. 9v; I, 32)

> [And the life of your Ladyship not only has to be fully contemplative but also rich in other virtuous works (...) and your Ladyship's reading, and the work of your hands and the other tasks all comprise a pure prayer which rises straight up to heaven, *just like incense in God's sight*.]

Work under the Rule was not necessarily manual. In Valencia, there were 'seruiçiales' [serving sisters], undertaking the heavy work in the kitchen. They also did the shopping, as they were allowed out of the convent, as long as they were respectably attired. In the records of the Puritat convent, in the *Libro de dades i rebudes (1454 a 1460)* [The Book of Income and Expenditure] (ARV, Clero, Libro 956), there are entries for payments made in the 1450s to Ana Violant and in the same year to Ana Maria. Ana Maria is designated 'seruiçial del conuent' (fol. 152r). Some folios later, an entry indicates 'auem presa huna fadrina per seruir la cuyna e la mesa' [we have taken on a girl to work in the kitchen and serve at table] (fol. 156r). The women also served the sisters, confirming the fact that these noblewomen preserved at least one aspect of their privileges from outside the convent.

For fifteenth-century Poor Clares, rank was maintained: the abbess of the Santa Clara convent in Toledo, an illegitimate infanta, continued to be addressed by her title (Pérez de Tudela y Bueso 1994: 492). There is no reason to suppose that the Santa Trinitat convent would have been very different. The noble nuns there would, thus, be spared the heaviest of menial tasks. They could, therefore, concentrate their efforts on the more spiritually improving and less corporal tasks, like reading.

It is clear from the Rule that reading and study were work, and Sor Isabel includes reading in the work carried out by the Virgin Mary. The Rule, under the paragraph on work, allows for instruction of those sisters who are capable of it:

> Si algunas jóvenes o mayores fueren de ingenio y capacidad, la Abadesa, si le pareciere convenir, hágalas instruir, señalándoles una maestra idónea y discreta, la cual les instruirá tanto en cantos como en oficio divino.
> (*Reglas* 1988: 50)

> [If any young women or older women were of sufficient wit and capacity for it, the Abbess, if she thought fit, should have them instructed by a suit-

able and discreet teacher. Such a teacher would instruct them to sing the office and other sacred song.]

In the case of Sor Isabel, her work was quite clearly her writing, described as an agricultural task in the letter by Sor Aldonça, as discussed in Chapter 1.

There is one further connection between the work carried out by the Virgin Mary in the *Vita Christi* and that carried out by the nuns. In the *Vita Christi*, the Virgin makes cloth, using a loom which Joseph has made for her: 'E la Senyora, vehent que lo guany de la filosa era molt poch, dix a Joseph que li fes un teler que pogués texir' [And the Lady, seeing that the income from the distaff was very low, instructed Joseph to make her a loom so that she could weave] (fol. 99v; II, 17). She follows the *Vita Christi* tradition in which the Virgin supports the Holy Family by her weaving. Eiximenis includes a lesson about the Virgin weaving and teaching the women of Egypt about the dangers of fine cloth for women's bodies.

The depiction of the Virgin weaving has a long tradition in Christian art, and Alan Deyermond, in a study relating text and textiles in the *chansons de toile*, has discussed the tradition of the Virgin weaving in depictions of the Annunciation (1999: 74, n. 6), believing that images of the Virgin spinning were replaced by ones of her reading.

However, the Virgin continued to be depicted spinning, in, for example, an early fifteenth-century French breviary from the library of the Duque de Osuña (BNE, MS Vitr. 24.7, fol. 17v), because of her connection with the good wife of Proverbs. The Virgin spinning was no longer usual at the Annunciation scene, but in the French breviary there is no other miniature depicting the Annunciation and the Virgin spinning is placed where an Annunciation miniature might be found.

However, Sor Isabel may have had reasons other than tradition for including the Virgin spinning. From the records of the Puritat convent there is evidence that the nuns undertook silk work. In 1496, the convent records describe the purchase of frames for twisting silk 'dos dotsenes de fusos i sis torçers pera torse seda dos sous' [two dozen wooden beams and six spindles for twisting silk at two *sous*] (Clero, Libro 946, fol. 108r). Twisting silk was an important outsourced industry often carried out by women in Valencia (Navarro Espinach 1999: 97–8). There was a guild of *torcedors* [twisters] to undertake the spinning of silk, but there is evidence that, at times of heavy demand, the majority of the population was involved. It is possible, given the evidence from the sister convent in Valencia, that the Santa Trinitat nuns were also involved in the process. The link between the Santa Trinitat convent and silk production provides a pointer to yet another way in which Sor Isabel linked the life of the Santa Trinitat community with the life of Mary.

Conclusion

The starting point for this chapter was three interrelated frames, the theological, the medical, and the misogynistic view of the body. All point to the female body as imperfect and secondary. Sor Isabel uses the theology of the body to show that the female body is perfectible and redeemable if the Virgin is imitated. Whether or not this constitutes being a respondent in the *querelle des femmes*, Sor Isabel links convent life with the life of Mary, indicating that the Virgin took these steps 'per donar exemple als servents seus que seguissen la via sua' [to give a good example to all her servants who should follow her way] (fol. 9r; I, 25). In the words 'la via sua' [her way], the Virgin usurps the role of Christ, and the Way of the Gospels (John 14. 6). Sor Isabel is creating a female way to sanctity.

But there is more to the *Vita* than providing a way to holiness. As I have argued (2003a), the reality of the convent is relived in the pages of the *Vita Christi*. Jocelyn Wogan-Browne contends that every Rule constructs an ideal body, which all members of the community accept as a template (1994: 27). By using the Poor Clare Rule to construct a template personified by the Virgin Mary, Sor Isabel is able to display the Rule embodied to perfection, but also show how a body of women can attain perfection.

The contemplative prayers put into the mouth of the Virgin Mary can provide an inspiration for the nuns. Through the association Sor Isabel creates between their lives and that of the Virgin Mary, the sisters are encouraged to develop in their contemplative and regular practices. Far from being a preliminary to the main events of the *Vita Christi*, 'un magne preludi' (Hauf in Villena 1995: 48), the life of Mary is central to the purpose of the *Vita Christi*, which moves from the constructed female body to the building of a pure body, the community of nuns at Santa Trinitat convent.

Sor Isabel offers her *Vita Christi* as a way of affirming women's physical bodies in relation to God. Through it we glimpse a very real body, a group of women who, even as they read and contemplated, were providing a sign that women were redeemable and could become purer in body and in spirit. The nuns living within the convent walls are within God's body ('en la santa Trinitat') at the same time, and are God's body.

3

Veiled Bodies

The pure flesh which makes the Virgin fitting to bear Christ is at the heart of the *Vita Christi*. In the previous chapter, I discussed the veneration of the Virgin's own body following the Incarnation, when it became a eucharistic tabernacle, or vessel holding the sacred body of Christ. In this chapter I will examine ways in which the Virgin covers her Son, protecting his human body from the consequences of sin. The veiling and shrouding of Christ's body can also be shown to fit within Franciscan traditions of devotion to the Eucharist.

Covering the Christ Child in the Vita Christi tradition

As in the Gospel of St Luke, where swaddling clothes are wrapped around the newborn baby, in Sor Isabel's *Vita Christi* cloths are brought to wrap the child. First, at the angelic revelation of the birth to the shepherds, the angels announce the child is 'embolicat en pobrellets draps' [wrapped in poor cloths] (fol. 74v; I, 273). A few pages earlier, at the time of the birth of the baby, one of the Virgin's handmaids, Pietat [Piety], 'portava un drap que li fos posat damunt lo cap' [carried a cloth which was put over his head] (fol. 73v; I, 270). The purpose of the cloth is to keep the child warm and it is a way of emphasizing the humanity and frailty of the suffering Christ from the beginning of his life.

Post-birth depictions of fifteenth-century newborn babies often show them wearing a cap or head covering. The birth of the Virgin is depicted almost as frequently as that of Christ, and in the homely scene she is often shown wearing cloth to cover her head. In Damià Forment's sculpture of the *Nativity of the Virgin* (MNAC 064141), the wrap and cap the Virgin wears show that the baby's head was kept warm with a protective covering.[1] Forment (fl. 1499–1540) was a Valencian sculptor, although active in

---

[1] Similarly, in the *Naixement de la Mare de Déu* [Nativity of the Mother of God] by Pere Garcia de Benavarre (active 1450s to 1470s), dated 1475, which is from northern Aragon (Ribagorça, Huesca) (MNAC 114750), the Virgin is wrapped in red with bands shown laced around and her cap is of white cloth.

4. Damià Forment, *Naixement de la Verge*.

5. Master of Cinctorres, *Naixement de la Verge i la Presentació al Temple*.

different parts of the Kingdom (Fig. 4). The Master of Cinctorres (active 1400) shows the Virgin wearing a little cloth cap in his *Naixement de la Mare de Déu i la Presentació al Temple* [Nativity of the Mother of God and her Presentation in the Temple] (MNAC 015853) (Fig. 5). He was working for the Bishop of Tortosa from 1390 to1420.[2] In the panel depicting the Virgin's birth in his *Retablo de la Purísima Concepción* [Altarpiece of the Most Pure Conception] (MBAV 287) (Fig. 6), Nicolau Falcó (active in the

---

[2] See also the Flemish painting *Alegoría* (Museo Municipal de Vigo), in which a male child wearing a head covering, tucked over his head and longer at the back, is suckling (reproduced in Ríos Lloret & Vilaplana Sánchis 2006: 182–3).

6. Nicolau Falcó, *Retablo de la Puríssma Concepción*.

late fifteenth and early sixteenth centuries) presents the Virgin wrapped in a red cloth trimmed with white. Cloths are being warmed by St Anne's attendants to put over her.[3] Warming cloth over a brazier, like covering a newborn's head, is indicative of the importance of keeping a newborn infant warm in the draughty surroundings of a medieval home.

Following the birth of the Infant Christ in Sor Isabel's *Vita Christi*, the

---

[3] Not all babies have their heads covered in birth panels. In the *Naixement de San Eloi* [Birth of St Eligius] (MNAC 024254), in which the little Eligius is wrapped in a white cloth, his head is bare. Pere Nunyes, who painted the Eligius panel, was a Portuguese artist documented in Catalonia and Aragon from 1513. The preparation of cloth and warming of cloths to cover the infant is being carried out by two attendant women.

Virgin approaches her Son in what appears at first sight to be a simple Nativity scene, and she lifts the cloth the angels had placed on his head:

> E sa mercé, levant-se de peus e acostant-se al Senyor, qui jayia en lo pesebre, ab molta reverència levà-li un drap ab què tenia cubert lo cap e la careta, e mostrà aquella faç divina del seu sagrat fill als devots pastors.
> (fol. 75r; I, 274)
>
> [And her Ladyship, rising to her feet and going close to the Lord in the manger, with great reverence lifted away the cloth that was covering his face and head and showed that divine countenance of her sacred Son to the devout shepherds.]

The Virgin's movement to uncover the Child is, however, striking, since mothers do not generally keep their child's face covered. Her removal of the 'drap' over Christ's head for the watching shepherds transforms the Child into a Host, so that the Adoration of the Shepherds becomes another moment of eucharistic veneration, which complements that of the veneration of the womb-tabernacle (discussed in Chapter 2), a time of exposition of the Blessed Sacrament. Sor Isabel merely reverses the numerous miracle stories in which the Host changes into the body of an Infant Christ (Bynum 1988: 60; Rubin 1991: 135, 137–9). This second example of how Sor Isabel's narration slips towards depicting paraliturgical rituals provides further indications of why she effects this parallelling of realities.

Two reasons why Sor Isabel might choose to include this detail can be suggested. First, as Anabel Thomas argues, generally the moment of consecration of the Host was an extremely important moment in nun's lives. As I will show, it was also a moment with which Sor Isabel identified. Thomas considers that consecration brought together the outer world otherwise unseen by the cloistered nuns and the world with which they were familiar inside the convent walls:

> It was only after this moment that a connecting door or window between the outer and inner spaces of the conventual complex was opened, thus effecting a physical union of the two worlds. It was through this aperture that the enclosed women [...] received the consecrated wafer. Clearly, this was a moment of heightened tension and sensation. The elevation of the wafer was a moment that had significance for the entire body of worshippers in both outer and inner space. For cloistered women, the opening of the grille that separated them from the conventual church and the ingestion of the consecrated wafer were also moments of personal, and even mystical experience. (Thomas 2003: 292)

For Thomas it was the physical reality of the connecting door which was all important.

The surprising description by Sor Isabel of the adoration of the Infant Christ provides a Valencian example of the experiential importance Thomas discerned in the moment of reception of the Host. It is a moment when the world outside the convent walls, the city of Valencia, and the female space inside the Santa Trinitat collide, with the nuns' world momentarily penetrated by the dramatic events taking place on the altar.

In the second place, St Francis's veneration of the manger initiated a tradition of spirituality within the Order which used the Child in the crib as a focus to awaken the sluggish faith of those with whom he came in contact (see Chapter 1). St Francis's story, recounted in St Bonaventure's *Legenda maior*, describes how Francis took the Child in the manger into his arms, 'and seemed to wake it from sleep' (Mulvaney 2005: 172–3). In the tradition established by St Francis, Sor Isabel also seeks to awaken the sluggish faith of the nuns in her charge.

Sor Isabel's narrativization of the manifestation of the Infant Christ-Host provides evidence that, whilst communion was an important moment, seeing the consecrated Host was too. In this she appears to provide support to Thomas's argument. For Franciscans, like Sor Isabel, nothing is more certain than that the spiritual intensity of exposition, bringing the nuns face-to-face with the Child in the crib, or with the sacrificial Saviour, was a glorious moment in the calendar.

Both Rubin (1991: 288) and Victor M. Schmidt (2007: 203–4) discuss the exposition of the Eucharist and its growing presence in Church ritual in the late medieval period. Exposition occurred at Corpus Christi processions, following the introduction of the feast by Pope Urban IV (†1264) in 1264. Display of the Host was also common on Thursdays, in commemoration of the institution of the Eucharist at the Last Supper. Liturgically speaking, Corpus Christi was one of the principal feasts in the Kingdom of Aragon by the fifteenth century:

> Redoble mayor es quando se dizen las an[tiphon]as todas ante et post psalmos et las de magnificat et ben[edictu]s tres uegadas […]. E son las que se siguen. Natiuitas d[omi]ni, Epiphania, Resurrectio d[omi]ni, Pentecostes, Ascensio, Corpus, et Transfiguratio d[omi]ni, Assumpcio b[ea]te Marie, Uisitatio b[ea]te Marie.
> Redoble menor es quando doblan las an[tiphon]as de magnificat et b[e]n[edictu]s ad modum de redoble e no las otras an[tiphon]as.
> (Huesca, Archivo de la Catedral, MS 21, fol. 88r)

> [A major feast is when the antiphons are said before and after the Psalms and at the Magnificat and Benedictus three times. The feasts which follow are major feasts: Nativity of the Lord, Epiphany, Resurrection of the Lord, Pentecost, Ascension, Corpus, Transfiguration of the Lord, Assumption of the Blessed Virgin, and Visitation of the Blessed Virgin.

A minor feast is when the antiphons are said before and after the Magnificat and Benedictus, as at major feasts, and not at the other psalms.]

Displaying the Host in public places was common in the late medieval period. Rubin points to the presence of monstrances for the public display of the Host in inventories, in bequests, and in Church documents from the 1380s onward across Europe. She mentions monstrances from England, Germany, the Low Countries, Italy, and Ireland, but there are examples from Valencia too. A beautiful *custodia mayor* (architectural structure to hold a monstrance), dating from the period just after Sor Isabel's death, is held in the Collegiate Church of St Mary in Játiva, commissioned by the Borja family (Generalitat Valenciana 2007: 10). *Custodias* were also part of the patrimony of ordinary parish churches by the late fifteenth century, a processional one was held in the church of San Antonio in the city and another at El Salvador parish church, Burriana, in Castellón province (Català Gorgues 1982: 48–50). Panels showing Corpus Christi processions regularly incorporate monstrances. One such is the retable from Sant Miquel [St Michael] in Montmagastre in Noguera province in the Crown of Aragon (MLDC 83) (Fig. 7).

The lifting of the cloth with which the angels cover the Child in the Adoration scene in the *Vita Christi* is to be associated with the removal of the covering cloth, the corporal, which covers the Host from view at the moment of exposition. Corporals were being used in fifteenth-century Valencia. They are present on the altar in a Eucharist panel in a fifteenth-century Valencian painting by Gonçal Perís Sarrià (Valencia 1380–1431), the *Retablo de San Martín, con Santa Úrsula y San Antonio Abad* [Retable of St Martin, with St Ursula and St Anthony Abbot] (Fig. 8) (MBAV 250; see Benito Domenech & Gómez Frechina 2009: 143).

Sor Isabel has not taken the scene she describes from artistic representation of the Adoration. I have not found altarpieces of the Nativity in which the Child has his head covered, because there is a different tradition taking precedence. It is customary for the Christ Child to be displayed naked to the observer, and that is in order to promote the teaching that Christ was truly human, reflecting the doctrine of the Incarnation. For example, in the Valencian altarpiece by the Master of Artés (thought to be Pere Cabanyes active in Valencia 1472–1538), the naked Child is laid on a piece of red brocade, which is an extension to the skirts of the Virgin.[4] Such paintings of Christ's Nativity make a deliberate connection between the clothing of the Virgin and the Christ Child in order to symbolize how the Child was clothed in flesh in the Virgin's womb. Frequently, as in the Cabanyes painting, the Child is displayed on her skirts, or the artist may subtly connect the Virgin's

---

[4] Panel from the private collection of Juan Abelló, seen in the Edad de Oro exhibition (Benito Domenech & Gómez Frechina 2009: 197).

7. *Taula de Sant Miquel.*

8. Gonçal Perís Sarrià, Eucharist panel, *Retablo de San Martín, con Santa Úrsula y San Antonio Abad*.

encircling cloak and the Child. For example, the Valencian Nicolau Falcó depicts the *Virgen de la Leche* [Virgin with Child Jesus at the Breast] (Fig. 9) with her cloak wrapped loosely around the body of her Son. The positioning of the Child in Falcó's painting is echoed in the woodcuts of the Nativity from the 1513 (Fig. 10) and 1527 editions of the *Vita Christi*. In neither woodcut is the Child depicted with his head covered.

However, elsewhere, particularly in the *Vita Christi* tradition, there developed a tradition of covering the Child. In John of Caulibus's *MVC*, the Virgin Mary 'inuoluit eum in uelo capitis sui et posuit eum in presepio' [wrapped him in her veil and laid him in the manger] (1997: 31; 2000: 25). Whilst there is no mention of the 'drap de cap' [head cloth] in Eiximenis's *Vida de Jesucrist*, he also has the Virgin Mary wrap the Child in a 'velet' [little veil]: 'e cobrí'l lo cap ab un velet' [she covered his head with a little veil] (BC, MS 299, fol. 170r). He does not explicitly say whether the veil was the Virgin's. Voragine (1993: 37–43) does not refer to the veil in his account of the Nativity. Ubertino da Casale follows a discourse on the

9. Nicolau Falcó, *Tríptico de la Virgen de la Leche*.

10. Woodcut of the Nativity, *Vita Christi*.

poverty of Christ with the detail that he was wrapped in his mother's veil: 'facta fascia de capitis sui uelo' [a swaddling band was made from the veil from her head] (1961: 63).

The presence of Sor Isabel's 'drap' was more than likely suggested by the word for 'veil' in one or other of the *Vitae Christi* with which she worked, the *MVC*, the *Arbor*, or the *Vida de Jesucrist*, but, rather than using 'veil', Sor Isabel has chosen a different expression, 'drap ab que tenia cubert lo cap' [cloth with which she kept his head covered], in her narration of the scene.

In doing so, she has chosen one relevant to her day. According to Alcover, 'drap de cap' is documented from 1445 (1988: IV, 593), less than fifty years before Sor Isabel's death. In *Tirant lo Blanc*, the headdress is one element of the trick played on Tirant: 'La Viuda s'acostà a la donzella, donà-li un drap de cap' [The Widow approached the young woman and gave her a headdress] (Martorell 2008: 283). The headdress is placed under the skirts of the innocent princess, following the scene where Plaerdemavida disguised as the Moorish gardener touches her breasts and private parts. Tirant is watching through cleverly placed mirrors.

Sor Isabel and adoration of the sacred body

The nature of Sor Isabel's devotion to the Eucharist is further explained in the two chapters she dedicates to the Virgin and the way she prepares to receive it. The Virgin's communion takes place after Sor Isabel has recounted how the apostles have to depart from Jerusalem because of being persecuted by the Jews (fols 295v–296v; III, 301–3), leaving behind the Virgin and St John, and just before the Virgin makes a visit to three holy places, Calvary, the Holy Sepulchre, and Mount Olivet (fols 298r-299r; III, 307–10).

The narration begins with the Virgin's self-preparation the day before the Eucharist is to be consecrated. The Virgin 'despenia aquella nit en preparació' [spent the night in preparation]. She spends the time alone in her 'cel·la' [cell] (fol. 297v; III, 304), with the choice of the word *cel·la* already drawing the Virgin Mary and her devotion behind the grille of the Santa Trinitat. Then she makes her confession to St John, who has already robed.

Adoration of the Eucharist requires time spent in front of the Host, and the Virgin deliberately requests the Host to be held 'una gran estona' [a long while] before her eyes:

> lo dia ans deya al seu amat secretari, sanct Joan, que li tingués aquella sagrada hòstia una gran estona davant, ans que·l rebés quant deya missa, perquè, contemplant e mirant en aquell excel·lent e amorós sagrament, pogués largament sentir los delits e tresors en aquell amagats.
> (fol. 297v; III, 304)
>
> [the day before, she said to her much-loved secretary, St John, that, when he said Mass, he should keep the Host a long while in front of her before she received it, so that, contemplating and gazing on that excellent and beloved sacrament, she might sense the delights and treasures which it contained.]

Eventually the moment of consecration and adoration provides Sor Isabel with an opportunity to include a time of prostration before the Host, as the Virgin adores it with her eyes:

> venint la hora que sanct Joan se girava ab aquell tresor impreciable per comunicar-lo a la Senyora, sa senyoria se prostrava en terra, adorant

aquella alta magestat ab profunda humilitat e reverència, com aquella que sabia quina reverència se devia fer a tan immensa excel·lència e senyoria; e, dreçant-se, mirava de fit ab los ulls corporals aquella hòstia sagrada.
(fol. 297v; III, 305)

[when the time came for St John to turn with that priceless treasure to give her Ladyship communion, she prostrated herself on the ground, adoring that great majesty with deep humility and reverence like someone who knew how much homage should be done to such an Excellency and Lord; and, standing up, she looked with her bodily eyes fixed on the sacred Host.]

Following reception of the Host, the Virgin retires to her cell and spends the rest of the day in contemplation:

aprés dita la missa, la Senyora se tancava en la cel·la sua, passant aquell dia sens menjar, ne veure ni sentir res corporal, adelitant-se de cor e de ànima ab aquell divinal hoste que rebut havia. (fol. 298r; III, 306)

[after Mass was ended, the Lady shut herself in her cell, spending the day fasting, not seeing or feeling anything of the bodily world, delighting in heart and soul in the divine Host which she had received.]

The description of the Virgin's devotion to the Eucharist provides insights into convent life. It is very likely that the nuns would have spent the night before they were to receive the Eucharist in a similar manner to the Virgin, each in her cell; no doubt Sor Isabel sought to promote the same devout self-preparation modelled by the Virgin. They too would await the moment when the priest attending them was robed and ready to celebrate. Their reception of the sacrament, like the Virgin's, would regularly be preceded by confession. They too would have been likely to have prostrated themselves to adore the Host, perhaps at the Eucharist but more probably at times when exposition took place in the convent. As in other scenes of the *Vita Christi*, convent life and its rituals are immortalized in the story of Christ and his mother and the scenes of eucharistic veneration provide a window on the world of the convent. At the very least they provide an insight into the way the abbess would have liked it to be.

Covering and shrouding the body of Christ

The frailty of the Child and the need to cover his head to protect him from the cold is also a feature of the Flight into Egypt. In this scene, the Child has his head covered with a double cloth, with which his mother partially covers his face, 'tant com podia' [in so far as she could]:

> La Senyora vestí lo seu fill e bolcà·l, posant-li tota la robeta que tenia, ab tot fos tan poca e tan pobreta que no·l podia molt calfar ni guardar del fret, e posà-li un drap doble al cap cobrint-li la careta tant com podia, car la fredor de la nit era gran e lo Senyor tan delicat que sentia les penalitats humanes pus vivament que nengun altre home. (fols 100ᵛ–101ʳ; I, 331)

> [The Lady dressed her Son and wrapped him, putting on all the little clothes she had, even though they were so few and so poor that they could not protect him from the cold, and she put on his head a double cloth covering his face as much as she could, for the cold of the night was great and the Lord so delicate that he felt all human suffering more keenly than any other man.]

Christ's double head-covering might be a simple folded cloth in the style of the 'tocas' [headdresses] which women wore, which often were a simply cut, folded piece of cloth, of a variety of types (Sigüenza Pelarda 2000: 47–8). Ruth Matilda Anderson describes a veil 'turned back from the head in a double fold' (1979: 173), over which a hood is worn. Anderson found evidence of both sexes wearing draped cloth on their heads, *tocas de camino*, in the Moorish style, especially for travelling, as of course the Holy Family did (1979: 44).[5] Juan Martínez Ruiz (1967) documents a range of Moorish headdresses, from the period just after the conquest of Granada, made of different cloths, including 'tocas de lienço' [canvas headdresses], 'tocas de seda' [silk headdresses], 'tocas de calicud' [calico headdresses], 'tocas de azache' [rough silk headdresses]. He also documents Moorish veils.

In the *Vita Christi*, the tender maternal covering of Christ to keep him from the cold is deliberately contrasted with the dirty and rough cloth used by the soldiers who cover Christ's head at the scourging, making the journey to Egypt a foreshadowing of the journey to the Cross: 'E cobriren la sua excel·lent cara ab un sútzeu e gros drap, e daven en aquella de grans bufets' [and they covered his excellent face with a rough, dirty cloth and struck it with great blows] (fol. 194v; II, 303). In John of Caulibus's version, the soldiers blindfold him, covering his eyes, not his head (2000: 244) and the *Pasión trobada* follows the tradition of the blindfolding of Christ (San Pedro 1973).

Placing a cloth or veil over Christ's head is found in other accounts of the Passion, including Voragine's *Golden Legend* (1993: I, 206). Ubertino da Casale also has Christ's face veiled, 'uultu uelatus' [with his face covered],

---

[5] I am grateful to Gemma Avenoza for drawing to my attention the practice of covering babies' heads in rural Catalonia as they are taken to baptism. This may have been a custom which Sor Isabel knew and which she reflects here. In rural Valencia, it is still the custom to put on a white cap, longer at the back to cover the shoulders, after the child is baptized (personal communication, 25 August 2011).

at the scourging (1961: 313), although he does not mention the dirty cloth about which Sor Isabel writes. Ubertino's words might have suggested to Sor Isabel the presence of the rough cloth at the scourging, as might Voragine's: 'vultum tuum, bone Jesu, desiderabilem [...] velo pro delusione operuerunt' [your lovely face, good Lord Jesus, they covered with a veil to mock you] (1850: 226; see also 1993: I, 206).

Sor Isabel's version diverges from artistic tradition in Valencia, where representations of the scourging do not represent Christ with his eyes covered or with his head covered.[6] Joan Reixach (c. 1411–c. 1484), a contemporary of Sor Isabel, in his depiction of Christ at the pillar shows his face unveiled but with a light cloth covering his manhood. As at the Nativity, artistic and *Vita Christi* traditions diverge, and Sor Isabel follows the written tradition.

The theme of Christ's head covered and uncovered, with different classes of cloth for different purposes and provided by different people, resurfaces again in Sor Isabel's *Vita Christi* after his death on the Cross. When he is taken down from the Cross and prepared for burial, the cloth brought by the disciples to enfold the body is 'prima e molt neta' [fine and very clean], in marked contrast to the one used at the scourging:

> Untat lo Senyor, embolicaren lo seu cors en aquella tela prima e molt neta, dexant-li la cara descuberta per contentar la mare, qui ab tanta dolor totes estes coses mirava; e, del drap que restava, feren unes benes largues e embenaren tot aquell divinal cors a la manera judayca. E tenien un sudari, a manera de tovallola larga, per a cobrir-li lo cap e la cara, e staven així de peus sperant que la dolorosa mare los licenciàs de cobrir-li la cara.
> (fols 246v–247r; III, 115).

> [Once the Lord was anointed, they wrapped his body in that very clean and fine cloth, leaving his face uncovered for his mother. She was looking on these things with great sorrow; and from the remaining cloth they made long bandages and bandaged all his divine body in the Jewish manner. And they had a shroud, like a long sheet, to cover his head and his face and they stood there waiting for the sorrowful mother to give them permission to cover his face.]

In Rois de Corella's translation of Ludolph in the *Lo quart del Cartoxà*, the disciples purchase clean linen cloths for the shrouding of the body: 'Compra Joseff teles de li blanques mundes e netes' [Joseph bought fresh, clean white linen cloths] (1495: fol. 85v). Unlike Rois de Corella, Sor Isabel narrates how Joseph of Arimathea and Nicodemus wait for permission from Christ's mother before completing their wrapping of the body. This seems to follow

---

[6] Perís Sarrià (1380–1451) depicts Christ looking down sadly as he is scourged (Benito Domenech & Gómez Frechina 2009: 123).

the *MVC*, where the wrapping of Christ's body is a task reserved for the Virgin:

> Tunc Iohannes et Nicodemo et alii ceperunt inuoluere corpus, et aptare cum lintheaminibus ut mos erat Iudeis. Domina tamen semper tenebat capud ipsius in gremio suo quod sibi reseruauit aptandum.
> (John of Caulibus 1997: 281)

> [Then John and Nicodemus and the others began to wrap the body and fit it with the burial cloths, as was customary with the Jews. Our Lady, however, throughout held his head on her lap, and reserved for herself its wrapping.] (2000: 261)

Sor Isabel's emphasis on the covering of Christ's face differs from Valencian representations of the burial of Christ, and it is not found in such specific detail in other *Vitae Christi*.[7]

Veiling Christ at the Crucifixion

Sor Isabel depicts the Virgin covering her Son with her headdress during his Passion, and in this her version follows the other *Vitae Christi*. The inclusion of the scene enables her to link the Nativity and the Passion. She had already incorporated the scene in which the soldiers strip Christ naked. At this point Sor Isabel has the Virgin take her head-covering and cover his naked body: 'E, levant-se una tovallola que portava al cap lançada sobre l'altre ligaça, cenyia ab molt amor al seu fill, pus ab aldre no podia cubrir la sua nuditat' (fol. 212r; II, 368) [And taking off a cloth she had on her head loosely over another holding it in place, she girded her Son with much love, for in no other manner could she cover his nakedness]. The use of 'tovallola' as a head-covering is found also in the *Espill*, where the beguine and the priest meet at Mass to carry on together; Roig notes that the sinful priest wore his stole and the woman wore a veil: 'portava's ella / sa tovallola' [she wore her veil]. 'Ligaça' or 'lligassa' is listed in contemporary works among the useless ornaments which women wear. 'Ligaces' are mentioned in the *Espill*: 'Tu no adores ses alcandores / ni les ligasses per ses carasses' [you do not adore her shifts nor the bindings for her masks] (Roig 1978: 149).

Sor Isabel takes her lead from her antecedents in the *Vita Christi* tradition, although her version does not follow them exactly. When Christ is stripped

---

[7] Contemporary images such as Perís Sarrià's *Entombment of Christ* (Seville, Museo de Bellas Artes), for example, depict the body loosely covered in a shroud. Christ's face and all of his upper body are uncovered as he is placed in the tomb.

naked in the *MVC*, the Virgin is embarrassed, 'cum rubore quod eum uidet totaliter nudum' [with embarrassment, for she saw him completely naked]. She then rushes forward and 'amplexatur et cingit eum velo capitis sui' [she embraces him and girds him with the veil from her head] (John of Caulibus 1997: 271). In Eiximenis's version, she rushed forward, with the shame of the situation paramount: 'e levant-se lo vel del cap, cobrí les sues parts vergonyoses' (*Vida de Jesucrist*, BC, MS 460, fol. 215v) [and taking the veil from her head, she covered his shameful parts]. Shamefulness also features in Roís de Corella's *Lo quart del Cartoxà*, where the Jews strip Christ with a plan to increase the impropriety and shame of the events: 'despullen li per augment de improperi e vergonya les vestidures. Tenen lo tot nu al fret e ayre' [they strip his clothes off him to increase the impropriety and shame. They have him quite naked to the cold and winds] (1495, fol. 58r). Sor Isabel's version, on the other hand, emphasizes the Virgin's love as the reason why she covers her Son's body: 'ab molta amor' [with great love].

Ubertino da Casale's version of the scene takes account of the difficulty the Virgin would have had in placing her veil on Christ on the Cross. Ubertino describes the miracle of the veil thrown by the Virgin and the way it sticks to the body on the Cross. He rejects such tales, preceding the scene with 'in aliquibus historiis non autenticis legitur' [it is read in some made-up tales]. Ubertino uses Christ's nakedness following the stripping for the Cross to link it to his nakedness when he came out of his mother's womb. In both instances, he is covered with her veil:

> mater videns eum sic nudum: uelum capitis sui a seipsa amouens ad filii renes proiecit: quod aliqualem consolationem uirginis illis locis corporis sui miraculose adhesit: que semoralia in ceteris contegunt ad pudenda celanda. (1961: 317)

> [his mother seeing him thus naked took the veil from her head and, going forward, threw the veil at the kidneys of her Son; it stuck miraculously in that place on his body, affording some measure of consolation to the Virgin, for it covered his shameful parts.]

Despite Ubertino's misgivings, the covering of Christ's nakedness at the Crucifixion by the veil of the Virgin is widespread in the Kingdom of Aragon. It is found also in the *Passi en cobles*, although there is no mention of the Virgin's shame:

> Lavòs acostà's sa mare molt santa
> levant-se del cap lo seu vel sagrat,
> y aquell prest cobrí sentint pena tanta
> que sols lo recort en mort nos tresplanta.
> (Garcia Sempere 2002: 363)

> [Then his most holy mother approached
> and, taking the sacred veil from her head,
> she covered him swiftly feeling such sorrow
> that its memory was only taken away in death.]

In the *Passi en cobles*, the Virgin feels 'pena' [sorrow], rather than shame, and the veil with which she covers Christ on the Cross is 'sagrat' [sacred].

If Martha Bayless is correct, then merely displaying the lower body was enough to suggest the presence of sinfulness. Bayless discusses the ripped clothing and exposed flesh of those involved in different stages of the Crucifixion, such as the scourging: 'To unveil the shameful body is to expose human sin and corruption: it is humiliating and hence laughable at best, and sinful and impious at worst.' She is here describing the unattractive and ripped clothing of the other actors in the Passion, the soldiers and the torturers, which often reveals naked parts, such as their buttocks. She then goes on to show that the upper body was proper to God and the lower to the devil (2007: 289, 295). For the authors of *Vitae Christi*, exposing Christ's lower body would have been suggestive of sin, and for this reason, the sinless Virgin is depicted as hastening to cover it.

There are, however, subtle differences in Sor Isabel's version. In most other *Vitae Christi*, the Virgin takes her veil. However, in Sor Isabel's *Vita Christi*, the Virgin takes a 'touallola' [head-covering, veil] from her head. Only in Roís de Corella does the Virgin use a 'touallola' to cover her Son's nakedness: 'hi levant-se del cap vna touallola cobrí aquestes parts de son fill: que·ls primers nostres pares aprés de auer peccat se cobriren' [and, taking a head-covering (veil) from her head, she covered those parts of her Son that Adam and Eve covered after they had sinned] (1495: fol. 58r). The presence of the 'touallola' in two related Valencian versions of the *Vita Christi* could indicate either that Roís de Corella knew the *Vita Christi* and was influenced by it or that Sor Isabel knew a manuscript version of Roís de Corella's translation. Sor Isabel's choice of 'touallola' is significant because to have used 'veil' might have seemed more appropriate and, in line with her usual practice, would have brought the text close to the nuns because they too wore veils. She no doubt preferred 'touallola' for another reason, whether or not she saw it first in Roiç de Corella's translation.[8]

Using 'touallola' enables Sor Isabel to make another link between coverings of the body of Christ at different points in the *Vita Christi*. The 'touallola' is the 'sudari' [shroud] which, as noted above, covers the body of Christ at his Entombment: 'tenien un sudari, a manera de tovallola larga' [they had a shroud in the style of a long sheet] (fol. 47r; III, 115).

---

[8] It seems more likely that he knew it from her *Vita Christi* and chose it for his translation of the veil in Ludolph of Saxony.

Sor Isabel's choice of 'touallola' rather than veil may have liturgical significance. Among the vestments in the inventory in Valencia cathedral there are several liturgical 'toballolas' or 'toballala'. Listed among the red vestments is found 'huna toballola de vellut vermell, forrada de tela vermella, ab flocadura blancua e blava, brodada tota' [a towel (or cloth) of red velvet, lined with red cloth, flocked with white and blue, all in embroidery] and 'altra tobollala de vellut vermell, forrada de tela verda ab flocadura de vert scur e vert gay, ab sengles ymatges al cap de profetes, tota brodada' [another towel, or cloth, of red velvet, lined with green cloth flocked with dark and light green with pictures of prophets at the top, all in embroidery] (Sanchis y Sivera 1933: 6). A black one belongs to a full set of vestments:

> Item una casulla e dues dalmatiques, hun gremial, huna tovalola, tres maniples e dues stoles de domasqui negre, nou [...] e la tovalola ab flocadura negra, tot forrat de cendat vermell. (Sanchis y Sivera 1933: 12)
>
> [Also a chasuble and two dalmatics, a gremial, a veil (or cloth), three maniples, and two stoles of black damask, new, and the veil flocked with black, lined with slubbed red silk.]

The liturgical 'tovalola' [veil] was a eucharistic cloth used before and after the consecration of the Host to cover the chalice and patten. The ritual of covering the eucharistic vessels follows consecration and simulates the tomb. By using it Sor Isabel is again drawing her nuns' attention to connections between the symbolic veiling which takes place during the celebration of the Eucharist and her narrative.

Roís de Corella provides an interpretation of the two sets of cloths used at the Entombment, 'hi en teles mundes e netes dins lo sepulcre de la sua consciencia lo enbolica' [and (the Christian) wraps it in clean and fresh cloths in the sepulchre of his conscience], and, again, of the linen cloth: 'en lo drap de li munde pobretat e castedat se entenen' [and in the linen cloth are understood poverty and chastity] (1495: fol. 85r). Sor Isabel does not provide an interpretation of the cloths she uses.

Veiling the Virgin

Before the body of Christ is shrouded, in many versions of the *Vita Christi* the Virgin is brought clothes to dress her for mourning. Sor Isabel has St John's mother and sister bring the black veil and cloak for the Virgin to wear:

> E, elles venint, donaren-los lo vel e mantell de dol que portassen a la trista mare; e aquestes ab molta amargor e plor, acostaren-se a sa senyoria

e digueren-li: 'Senyora germana, aquests senyors tenen per bo que vós
vistau de dol, e totes nosaltres, per a la sepultura de del vostre tan amat
fill, seguint lo costum de les altres dones. (fol. 240v; II, 88)

[And the women came and gave them the veil and mourning cloak to take
to the sad mother with great sorrow and weeping. They approached her
Ladyship: 'Sister, Lady, these gentlemen think it would be best for you,
and all of us, to dress in mourning for the burial of your beloved Son, as
other women are accustomed to do.]

The black cloak and veil placed on the Virgin's head would have a resonance for the sisters in the Santa Trinitat who daily wore the black veil and cloak of the Franciscan Second Order, particularly because the Virgin here is called 'germana' [sister].

The veiling of the Virgin is not found in the *MVC*.

Shrouding the body in the Santa Trinitat

Ritual display and the veneration of the Host was part of the public Corpus Christi procession, as discussed above. One of the main consequences of devotion to the Host, and the growing culture of devotion through seeing, was that private veneration of the Host became more frequent, and where no consecrated Host was present devotional objects served in its place and could be used for devotion. Rubin provides evidence from elsewhere in Europe for the presence of a covered pyx, sometimes suspended above the altar (1991: 47). It is more than probable that the nuns in the Santa Trinitat followed the custom of adoration of devotional objects, like the *agnus Dei*, or of the pyx, if not of the Host itself.

Part of the ritual of preparing for devotion was the unveiling of the sacred object. Schmidt shows how unveiling was part of the performance of Gospel scenes and he does this with reference to both art and liturgical objects. He indicates that a panel of the Madonna and Child would be unveiled to the congregation at the moment of the presentation of the Child to the shepherds in the Christmas play in Padua (2007: 199–200). He also points to the veiling of tabernacles (201), sometimes by shutters and sometimes by curtains. He links this veiling to many uses of curtains, through which the divine mystery of the Incarnation can be glimpsed, in paintings of the Virgin and Child (206–8).

Veiling or covering of the Host was also common. These sacred objects had their own special protective covering, often a jewelled bag or one of cloth-of-gold. For example, Saurina, the widow of Guillem de Salas, Lord of Duocastella, had an inventory made of her husband's possessions on his death, and among these was a silver *agnus Dei* with its own pouch: 'Item una bossa de pel d'or ab floquadura blaua, Item un agnus dei d'argent' [Next, a gold leather bag with blue pattern. Next, a silver *agnus Dei*].[9] The pouch has value apart from its contents and is listed separately. Significantly, it precedes the *agnus Dei* in the inventory. Each time the sacred object was to be adored, there would be a moment of revelation, as in order to begin the act of devotion, the devout owner had take it out of its pouch. For the nuns of the Santa Trinitat, there would be a tension and expectancy just before the time when the sacred object was unveiled and then displayed for them to adore.

Conclusion

Franciscans wrote many religious works instructing both religious and the faithful about the Eucharist (Roest 2004: 356–73), and in her eucharistic scenes Sor Isabel shows that she is versed in that tradition. For Franciscans like Sor Isabel and her sisters the spiritual intensity of the consecration and elevation of the Host would have been powerful. Sor Isabel's nuns would have paid attention to the position of the cloth over the Child's face, and noted how, as contemplatives or observers at the scene, they were to mirror the maternal relationship of the Virgin with her Son. As Cantavella says, they identify with the actions of Mary.

The Virgin's actions are repeated within the convent walls by the nun whose duty it is to expose the sacrament. She becomes a player in a drama, taking the role of the Virgin Mary, through the act of removing the cloth or corporal covering the pyx, *agnus Dei*, or monstrance. At the end of the devotion the nun responsible for replacing the corporal or the veil performs the scene from the Deposition with the covering of his face. Whenever they undertake the paraliturgical act of venerating the Blessed Sacrament, their actions are given value because they are caught up in the narrative.

Wrapping and veiling Christ's sacred body using the Virgin's hands links key scenes in the *Vita Christi*, and interpreting these provides a glimpse into the construction of the *Vita Christi*. Through unveiling, the Incarnate body of the Nativity is displayed for the visiting shepherds and, through veiling on the Cross, the pure body of the Saviour is saved from shameful and inappropriate display. The presence of the Child-Host and the Sacrificial Victim-Host are both intended to emphasize the seamless union between the Child's birth and his Passion, between the renunciation of his heavenly privilege, his final sacrifice on the Cross, and the institution of the Eucharist. As Rubin notes, the image [of the Child] brought together 'two strains in eucharistic

---

[9] BC, Registre 313, Perg. 5, *Inventari de bens de Guillem de Sala, senyor de Duocastella*.

symbolism, one which stresses the presence of a real human suffering body and the other, which stresses redemption through sacrifice' (1991: 136). The movement from the concept of a distant God to the Incarnate Christ is a key aspect of Franciscan spirituality (Fleming 1977: 18), and one which is ever-present in the *Vita Christi*.

As I have argued in this chapter, the nuns' experience of venerating the Blessed Sacrament is subsumed into events in the narrative, so that the two fuse. The nuns are to take on the maternal relationship of the Virgin, whom they imitate, as they venerate the sacrament. Conversely, because of Sor Isabel's narrativization of convent ritual, the sisters at the same time become bystanders in the exposition of Christ at the Adoration, at the veiling of the sacrificial body on the Cross, and also at the scene of the Entombment of Christ, with all three events deepening their relationship with Christ Incarnate, crucified for them.

4

Reading Red: Deepening Understanding of Red in the *Vita Christi*

Sor Isabel's *Vita Christi* belongs to the extensive collection of allegorical meditations on the life of Christ, for the most part written by Franciscan authors. Such meditations were widely read after early printing made them more readily available. They were by far the most important genre of lay devotional works, especially for women.

I will focus on the crimson colour of the tunic given to the Virgin by God, brought by the Archangel Michael, after she accepted her role in salvation history as Mother of God, in order to examine the allegorical use of crimson and also to assess whether crimsons were known in Valencia in the period. The angel presents the tunic to Mary as one of a number of allegorical gifts, including five strings of pearls (ch. 40, fol. 49r–v; I, 179–81), a tunic or 'gonella de carmesí' (ch. 51, fols 49v–50r; I, 182), a mantle of blue brocade (ch. 48, fol. 50r–v; I, 185), twelve pairs of differently coloured gloves (chs 45–6, fols 57r–57r *bis*; I, 193–208), a necklace of precious stones (ch. 44, fols 50v–57r; I, 185–93), 'tapins' [high-soled shoes] (ch. 47, fols 57v *bis*–59r *bis*; I, 208–13), and a crown (ch. 48, fol. 59r–v *bis*; I, 214–16).

Each of the gifts has a symbolic or prophetic meaning for the life or cult of the Virgin, clearly enunciated in each case in the chapter rubric. The pure white oriental pearls are the 'cinc graus de puritat' [five degrees of purity] (fol. 49r; I, 179), the silk chemise embellished with gold is 'visceral pietat ab guarniment de perseverança' [deep-rooted piety with a decoration of perseverance] (fol. 49v; I, 181), the blue cloak with green damask lining symbolizes her 'gran misericòrdia' [great mercy] (fol. 50r; I, 185), and the necklace with its sixty-two pearls, eight diamonds, and seven rubies represents each year of her life, the eight beatitudes, and the seven spiritual works of mercy (fol. 50v; I, 185). The twelve pairs of gloves 'en les sues precioses mans, guarria per sol tocament dotze spirituals mals' (fol. 57v; I, 193) [when she wore them, healed twelve spiritual ills by mere touch]; the six pairs of shoes (see Chapter 7) are to put on when she hears the pleas of the six states of humanity; the crown (see Chapter 8) 'de dotze murons o esteles, ço és les dotze dignitats sues' [of twelve crenellations or stars, that is to say her twelve dignities] has seven jewels 'ço és los set dons del sant Esperit' (fol.

59v; I, 214–15) [that is the seven gifts of the Holy Spirit]. The brocade tunic described by Sor Isabel is marked in its contrast to the emphasis on poverty in other *Vitae Christi*. For example, in the scene of the Nativity in Ubertino da Casale's *Arbor*, the Virgin possesses only one tunic: 'Mater Christi non habuit nisi unam tunicam: et qualem habere carpentarii uxor' [The Mother of Christ had just one tunic, such as the wife of a carpenter might have] (1961: 63).

Allegory and medieval writing

The allegorical scenes containing the gifting of the tunic to the Virgin are an intercalation set within the Gospel events of Luke 1. 26–38. This technique is characteristic of the *Vita Christi* (Hauf 1990: 312; Riquer 1972: 70–1). The 'preponderància que té l'element al·legòric i fantàstic' (Fuster 1975a: 159) is part of the didactic purpose of Sor Isabel's life of Christ and differentiates it from other contemporary lives of Christ. According to Hauf, 'el ritmo de los tres libros [Villena's, Eiximenis's, and Roiç de Corella's *Vitae Christi*] es muy distinto' [the pace of the three books is very different] (1987: 153). Surtz also refers to the 'unusual structure' of the *Vita Christi* considering it is also a 'life of the Blessed Virgin, for Christ's life is framed by that of his mother' (2010: 517). Ubertino da Casale's *Arbor* is a life of Christ framed by the story of the Fall and the Assumption and Coronation of the Virgin, not dissimilar in structure to the final chapter of the *Vita Christi*, except that in his version the focus never strays from Christ. For example, at the Coronation of the Virgin, which ends the *Arbor* (1485: 405), it is Christ's actions in the crowning which takes centre stage. Critics also differentiate Sor Isabel's *Vita Christi* from other types of medieval allegory where the allegory is the principal technique. Her use of allegory is always a technique for embellishment rather than the main thread of the narrative.[1]

The use of allegory to typify Mary and provide greater understanding of her relationship with the Trinity is fundamental to mariology (Jiménez Hernández 1999: 13–17). Jehuda Feliks, discussing the origins of Jewish allegory, argues that 'in rabbinic tradition, the Song of Songs is an allegory of the chronicles of the Jewish people, the relationship between God and his children, between Israel and the nations of the world' (1983: 9). The relationship between God and the most privileged daughter of Israel, Mary, is also prefigured by the Song of Songs. By the time of the Fathers of the Church, a range of objects and locations from the natural world prefigure

---

[1] See Raabe 1990 for the way in which allegory becomes the story of faith in another medieval work, *Piers Plowman*.

Mary. These are often drawn from the Song of Songs but also from other Old Testament books (Levi d'Ancona 1957: 65). In the writings of Peter Abelard, Bernard of Clairvaux, and Richard of Saint Laurent the figures most often used include the rose garden (Ecclesiasticus 24. 13), the enclosed garden (Song of Songs 4. 12), the star of Jacob (Numbers 24. 17), and the star of the morning (Revelation 22. 16), all of which can be traced in fifteenth-century Hispanic poetry. The Song of Songs had an impact on courtly poetry (Hunt 1981), but Valencian poets also used its symbolism to signify the Immaculate Conception (Twomey 2008: 160–73).

The use of allegory was not just embedded in Christian tradition but was also a method of imitating Scripture (Barney 1979: 191), which had always modelled New Testament personae on their Old Testament counterparts. The Fathers of the Church adopted a technique already present in St Paul's letters, following a tradition already present in Christian theology from its earliest days (Auerbach 1984: 28–49). Typological interpretations of the Song of Songs as the love of the Christian soul for God, or of the relationship between the Church and Christ, or of the Virgin with the three persons of the Trinity, permitted it to take its place in the canon. In the same way the vision of the woman and her defeat of the dragon from Revelation 12. 1 was interpreted as the beginning of the Church but could also figure the birth of Christ, who defeated every evil (Pelikan 1996: 32).

By the thirteenth and fourteenth centuries, according to John V. Fleming, Scripture and its narrative techniques were at the heart of how Franciscans thought and wrote (1977: 22). For, as C. S. Lewis argues (1936: 45), the value of allegory in religious writing is that it enables the writer to present spiritual truths in a visible or 'picture' form. For this reason, Sor Isabel's allegories should never be regarded as flights of fancy subordinate to the narrative (Fuster 1975a: 159). They were rather a way of recreating Scripture in a contemporary text, which took the Gospel narrative of the life of Christ as its starting point.

Sor Isabel combines allegorical details with elements drawn from the Apocryphal Gospels (Hauf 1987: 107–9). Like most religious writers in the medieval period, she saw typology as the perfect way to amplify the limited details provided by the Gospels about Mary. She did not make any distinction between Gospel, Apocryphal Gospel, and allegory because she considered all pointed the way to human salvation.

My study of the Virgin's crimson tunic in the *Vita Christi* takes as its starting point one by Hauf, in which he traces parallels between the tunic gifted to the Virgin in the *Vita Christi* and that of Carmesina in *Tirant*. He considers the tunic and the name of its wearer could have inspired Sor Isabel's choice of colour and the nature of the garments: 'qui se era devisada en la següent forma, ço és, de gonella de brocat carmesí de fil d'or tirat, ab la cortapisa lavorada per subtil artefici de perles orientals molt grosses' [she was adorned in the following way, a tunic of scarlet brocade with drawn-gold thread, with the border delicately decorated with very large oriental pearls] (Martorell 1990: II, 865). Hauf places the antecedents of the *Vita Christi* in the developing medieval chivalry novel, much read by women and considered frivolous. To prove Sor Isabel's debt to Martorell's descriptive art, Hauf fixes on the colour of the Virgin's tunic: 'd'un excel·lent carmesí, significant la ardent caritat vostra' [of an excellent crimson, signifying your ardent charity] (fol. 49v; I, 182). Her explanation of the meaning of 'carmesí' even enables him to interpret Carmesina's name (Hauf 1991: 123).

For Hauf the *Vita Christi* is 'un llibre de cavalleries celestiales que resultàs útil i assequible a les seues monges' [a chivalric novel which is useful and accessible to the nuns] (1991: 124). The interrelationship goes even deeper, since the allegories in chivalry novels are known for being of a religious nature. One example is that given by Dominique de Courcelles, who indicates that the white of the gowns of the ladies of the court symbolizes the Joys of the Virgin (1997: 115).

Hauf's linking of the crimson tunic with Princess Carmesina is far from providing a full understanding of Sor Isabel's choice of colour. It is true that descriptions of regal and highly ornate clothing are a key element in chivalry novels, but they were not the only literary source to describe dress. There are descriptions of the garments worn by the Virgin in contemporary poems, submitted to the *certàmens*, or poetry competitions, celebrated in Valencia throughout the fifteenth century. In a poem presented to the 1474 competition held in honour of the Virgin, Lluís Cathalà describes Mary as:

> Sola, sens par, dels cels la més insigne,
> de puritat teniu ornat vestir
> al que valeu la corona condigne,
> lo loch pus alt, la cadira més digne,
> que maternal se pogués elegir.
> De castedat teniu blanca divisa,
> daurat cinyel de luminosa fe,
> y de set goigs brodada cortapisa.
> (cited in Ferrando Francés 1983: 309, lines 41–8)

[Alone, incomparable, the most worthy in heaven,
you had garments decorated with purity
meriting a most honourable crown,
in the most honoured place, the most worthy seat,
that could be chosen for you as mother.
You have a white pennant of chastity,
a golden belt of luminous faith,
and the border of your gown embroidered with Seven Joys.]

Although the garments and the allegorizing of them are different from

Sor Isabel's, and they are not as minutely described or as luxurious as hers, the aim of Cathalà is also to laud the Virgin for her purity. In 'daurada' [golden] and 'luminosa' [luminous], Cathalà is probably alluding to the light of the sun which encircles and clothes the Woman of the Apocalypse. Both Cathalà's poem and the *Vita Christi* emphasize the richness of the garments (golden, embroidered) and, in each case, the allegorical interpretation does not refer merely to characteristics of the Virgin but also to events in her life as a decorative feature: the *cortapisa* [border] of joys or sorrows.[2]

The holy chemise which the Virgin wore at the Annunciation was the object of veneration in the medieval Church. By the twelfth century the number of pilgrims going to Chartres to venerate Le Sainte Voile, considered to have been presented by Charles the Bald, traditionally believed to be the chemise or tunic of the Virgin, was so great that a new and bigger place of worship was built, the present cathedral. The tunic of the Virgin was thought to have assisted in the defeat of the marauding Vikings. It is probable that Sor Isabel would have known about the veneration of the garment from the *Miracles de Nostre Dame* of Gautier de Coincy (1970).

Interest in the Virgin's clothing has as its inverse the way in which the Virgin clothed the Christ Child in her womb, as noted in Chapter 3. St Ephraem of Syria (d. 373) described the Virgin's body as a 'shining unspotted garment' (Graef 1963–65: I, 58). The topos of the Virgin clothing Christ is found in the writings of St Bernard. His *Sermon on the Octave of the Assumption* points to the clothing of Christ as a reciprocal gesture:

> Thou clothest Him with the substance of your virginal flesh and He clothes thee in return with the glory of His majesty. Thou clothest the Sun with a cloud and art clothed by the Sun with His splendour. (1984: 213)

Donna Spivey Ellington translates an example of the metaphor of the garment woven to clothe Christ's body from her flesh from Johannes of Verden's *Sermons*:

> Mary 'made him a white tunic to put on from her very pure virginal flesh [...]. But that white garment of his most holy body was, for us, reddened by his pure blood during his pilgrimage' (2001: 50–1)

The tradition of describing human flesh as clothing is also found in the Poor Clare investiture of novices:

---

[2] Cathalà could have been inspired by sight of a manuscript version of the *Vita Christi*; conversely, Sor Isabel might have been inspired by Cathalà's poem.

> Domine Iesu Christe Seminator et Inspirator Religiosi, […] qui indumentum nostre carnis, pro salute humani generis misericorditer suscipere uoluisti et precepio villibus pannis inuolui non horruisti.
> (BC, MS 865, *Ritual per a l'ús de un convent de clarisses*, fol. 1v)

> [Lord Jesus Christ, root and inspiration of monks and nuns, […] who wished to put on the garment of our flesh, for the salvation of human kind, you compassionately wished to take it and did not reject being wrapped in lowly swaddling clothes in the manger.]

Valencian *certamen* entries, such as that of Lluís Roíç, symbolize the Incarnation as an action of clothing by the Virgin: 'vestint lo Verb de carn humana' [dressing the Word in human flesh] (Ferrando Francés 1983: 492, line 31).

Behind the first level of allegory, which Sor Isabel helpfully expounds for the reader, there lie other allegorical resonances to be grasped at a deeper level. If some details may appear well worn, others challenge the reader's expectations revealing that there are possible secondary or double allegorical meanings (Barney 1979: 17). Stephen A. Barney may be thinking of the double entendres apparent in works like the *Roman de la Rose*, but his premise holds good. Although Sor Isabel is not intending to challenge in the same way as the authors of the *Roman*, she leaves additional meanings unexplained.

Colours and their value

Marisa Astor Landete (1999: 78–9) emphasizes the importance of colour symbolism in medieval dress, 'el lenguaje, expresión y simbolismo del color' [the language of colour, how it is expressed and what it symbolizes], as well as its communicative power, noting the careful way colour is itemized in medieval inventories. Carmen Bernis, in her classic study of medieval clothing and fabrics, notes that crimson was one of the most highly prized of colours because of its rarity and because of its high price. According to Bernis:

> este color hacía subir el precio de terciopelos, rasos y ceties a más del doble. Si el precio de terciopelo de otros colores oscilaba entre 800 y 900 maravedís la vara, los terciopelos carmesíes se pagaban desde 2.000 a 2.800 maravedís. (1978–9: I, 22)

> [this colour (crimson) more than doubled the price of velvets, silks, and satins. If the price of velvets in different colours was around 800 or 900 the bale, crimson velvets cost between 2000 and 2800 *maravedis*.]

Françoise Piponnier's work on the court of Anjou shows a similar variance.

Figured satin in black cost 16 or 17 francs a foot, whilst crimson cost 23 francs. In velvets the differential was even higher. Black velvets ranged between 9 and 18 francs and crimson cost 30 francs a foot. Crimson satin, between the dates of 1472 and 1481 at least, was also more costly than other colours. Crimson ranged from 30 to 36 francs a foot, whilst pink or red satins cost 18 francs a foot. However, Piponnier's research reveals that, at the lower end of the price bracket up until 1459, crimson was equalled in cost by other colours: crimson satin cost over 8 francs the foot, whilst black satin was the same price. More expensive crimson satin could cost as much as 18 francs per foot (1970: 307–9). Ordinary reds were cheaper.

Luca Mola devotes a chapter to dyeing in his study of the silk industry in Renaissance Venice. Artisans had several means at their disposal for dyeing silk thread red. The dyes included madder (*rubia tinctoria*), orchil (*rocella tinctoria*), and brazilwood (*Caesalpinia sapan*). All were vegetable dyes. Lac, or shellac, was extracted from insects. Grain and kermes were both extracted from insects and 'were of higher value'. The word grain derives from the Latin term *granum*, since the insects when dried for selling look like grains of wheat. Mola indicates that:

> Kermes derives from the Sanskrit word *krmi*, that is worm, which indicates the insect from which the dye was obtained; in Persia this term was transformed into *kirmiz*, from which came the European *kermes, chermes, chermisis, carmesí*. (2000: 109)

Kermes gained primacy among the dyes for silk, becoming synonymous with princely luxury. Dyeing silk cost about twice as much if kermes was used as grain, and this explains the high price of the finished bales of crimsons. The pigment had to be soaked for several days, before it was filtered and ground. Finally, the thread had to be immersed in it two or three times to obtain the desired colour. Grain took just one bath and was immediately ready after being crumbled.

The whole process of dyeing with kermes added value to the finished product. It produced a finish that was more shiny and wear-resistant than dyeing with vegetable dyes (2000: 110–12). Mola shows that dyeing with crimson was little known in Venice in 1393 but had become widespread by the first decades of the fifteenth century (110).

Because of the sheer expense of kermes, a number of unscrupulous dyers sought to mix it with cheaper red dyes and, in Venice at least, a number of decrees forbade the practice (Mola 2000: 114–19). The Guild of Dyers in Barcelona also sought to legislate against unscrupulous members: 'tot tintorer que tenÿra llana de tenat per a draps no li sia llicit ne permés metre en lo dit tenÿr algun aposit o altre qualsevol mestura de mal tint' [any dyer dyeing wool dark red for pieces of cloth is not allowed or permitted to put any additive or other mixture of poor dye].³ Sor Isabel may have been aware of the value accorded to unadulterated kermes and she probably thought that pure crimson was attractive because the colour to clothe the Virgin should be unadulterated. It would certainly fit well with the early chapters of the *Vita Christi* in which Sor Isabel shows the preparation of Mary for her role as God's mother through her immaculate nature. It was connotations such as crimson's rarity and expense which made it an appropriate choice for the tunic of the Virgin.

Shades of red

Crimson, scarlet, or purple were the colours to designate high office. John H. Munro argues that the 'most highly esteemed, most regal colour in medieval Europe, especially during the fourteenth and early fifteenth centuries, was that shade of brilliant or vivid red known as scarlet' (2007: 56). The noble ladies who attended the coronation of Queen Elizabeth I wore scarlet (Arnold 1978: 730, n. 38). The cost of scarlet, effective in excluding the poor from its purchase, made it appropriate to denote high rank or nobility. Munro's research shows a shift to black in the eighty-year period from 1471 to 1550, with black accounting for over 75% of purchases in volume and close to 82% in value (2007: 55). In Castile, black also gradually took precedence at court. Noblemen present at the wedding of Princess Margaret, daughter of the Emperor Maximilian, to the son of the Catholic Monarchs, Prince Juan, were dressed '*a la francesa*'. Nancy Marino indicates that the term referred both to the black colour, made popular by Philip the Good of Burgundy, but also to the wide-shouldered cut and narrow-waisted cut. Black was thought to be the colour of authority and virtue (2008: 48).

Scholarly opinion on the origin of the word scarlet has taken two routes. It has often been thought to have derived from the Persian term *iškirlâta*, itself deriving from *siklat* or *siklatun*. Siklatun was 'indisputably a [...] rich, heavy damask silk, usually ornately brocades and often brocaded in gold'. *Siklat* was borrowed from Graeco-Latin *cyclas*, a circular mantle with a border of purple or gold embroidery (Munro 1983: 24). Munro repeats a potential problem in associating *siklatun* with the origin of scarlet, since it is a silk rather than a woollen cloth and he is particularly concerned with its use in Flemish woollen manufacture and purchase. In Northern Europe, another possible origin for the word scarlet has been thought to be in the Flemish term 'scarlaeken', to shear. Maria Hayward traces its origin to a

---

³ BC, MS 3422, *Llibre registre de exàmens, Gremi dels Tintorers de Llana de Barcelona*, fol. 57r.

Persian word meaning broadcloth, *saglan*. She notes scarlet can refer either to colour or to the cloth (2007: 141). In Philip Stubbes's diatribe against women's fine clothing written in the sixteenth-century England, in which he refers to the character of the fabric used, he mentions 'scarlet' among the different types of cloth:

> Than have they petticoats of the best cloth that can be bought, and of the fairest dye that can be made. And sometimes they are not of clothe neither, for that is thought to base but of scarlet, grosgrain, taffatie, silk and suche like, fringed about the skirts with silk fringe of chaungable coloure. (1877–82: I, 78)

There is no such problem in Spain, where the presence of Moorish silk-makers in the trade is documented (Navarro Espinach 1992: 88). The *DRAE* indicates that the origin of 'escarlata' is in the Arabic *iskirlâta*, which is defined as a 'tejido de seda brocado de oro' [gold silk brocade], and does not consider it could be a woollen cloth (1999: I, 872). The main definitions of 'escarlata' are as a 'color carmesí fino menos subido que la grana' [a fine crimson colour lighter than deep red] or as a 'tela de este color' [cloth in that colour]. By the sixteenth century Covarrubias gives a clear definition of 'escarlata' with reference to its colour: 'Es la color subida y fina del carmesí, o grana fina; y desta seda o paño se vestían los grandes príncipes y hoy día es la color del hábito de los cardenales' [It is the deep and fine colour of crimson or fine deep red; and the greatest princes used to dress in this silk or cloth and nowadays it is the colour of cardinals' habits] (2006: 809).

Çiclaton is documented in the vernacular in one of the earliest prose works in Castile, the thirteenth-century epic poem, *Poema de mío Cid*, in which the Cid wears 'sobr'ella un brial primo de çiclaton' [and over it a fine tunic of silk woven with gold] (Colin Smith 1972: 94, line 3090). 'Çiclaton' cannot be used as a circular cape since it describes the Cid's tunic and could be either a colour or type of cloth. It was considered exceptional and particularly appropriate to clothe the mighty Cid, who had just defeated the Moors. Smith considers it was silk woven with gold (145).

Munro, in his earlier writing on the subject of scarlet, concluded that the origin of scarlet probably drew on a mix of the Arabic and the Flemish use of the term (1983: 29). In a later study, he considers that the Arabic origin is more likely (2007: 63). He argues that 'all medieval scarlets, without exception, were luxury-quality woollens that were dyed, wholly or partially, "in grain" – in kermes' (2007: 66); except, of course, when they were luxury silks, as Munro acknowledges.

Examples of the use of *escarlata* from medieval Spain do not specify whether it is a colour or a method of fabrication. However, in two cases *escarlata* might be read as the colour. In Bernat Desclot's recounting of the conquest of Valencia, for example, one of the Saracens met with King Jaume the Conqueror, and his dress is described as follows:

> Vénc en un cavall liar [de color barrejat] molt bell, e la sella e·l petrel obrat ab fulla d'aur de son senyal, e·l fre e les regnes de seda ab platons [làmines] d'argent ab obra entallada de péres [pedres] e ab perles encastades; e fo vestit d'escarlata ab fresadures d'aur e no aportà negunes armes mas una espaa pendent en son coll, molt rica ab ric guarniment.
>
> (cited in Riquer, Comas, & Molas 1984: 447)

> [He came on a beautiful dun-coloured horse, and the saddle and the breast-piece were worked in gold leaf, and the bridle and the reins of silk with plaques of silver encrusted with precious stones, and with pearls mounted on them; and he was dressed in scarlet with gold fringing, and carried no arms except for a sword hanging around his neck, which was much decorated with rich ornament.]

The chronicler wished to emphasize the magnificence and unusual nature of the Moor's appearance, as he details the impressive ornamentation of his accoutrements and his sword. His clothing, it is to be presumed, is also intended to impress. He is clothed in 'escarlata' [scarlet or silk cloth] fringed with gold, and the word could refer to either colour or cloth. Similarly, when the Archpriest of Talavera wishes to describe the costly and ostentatious garments worn by the woman attending Mass, he says she wears 'buenos paños de escarlata con forraduras de marta' [good scarlet or woollen cloth with marten fur lining] (Martínez de Toledo 1985: 130). The cloth she wears might be in scarlet, but it might also refer to fine wool or even to silk. On balance, because of the fur lining, it might be assumed that it is either scarlet-coloured or Flanders wool.

Who wore reds?

Hayward discusses how various shades of red were chosen by Henry VIII in the sixteenth century for his wardrobe, listing scarlet, crimson, murrey, carnation, incarnate, and tawny. Shades of red were worn both for ceremonial and for everyday wear (2007: 141). Some of the finest garments in Henry VIII's wardrobe book for 1516–20 were crimson, such as 'a riche gowne of crimosyn cloth of gold tissewe with wide slyues damask gold furred with pouderd ermynes' (141). In the Kingdom of Aragon, crimson was already being used in 1349. King Pere the Ceremonious orders a piece of crimson satin to make cushions for the residence of his third queen, Eleanor of Sicily (Martínez y Martínez 2004: 559). As a descendant of King David, the Virgin was of royal descent, so regal crimson or scarlet was appropriate to her tunic.

Crimson was also the colour of choice for members of noble families.

The catalogue for an exhibition of silks in 1957 listed a 'capa masculina de satén carmesí, con adornos radiales de cordoncillo' [a man's cape of crimson satin with radiating adornments of plaited rope] (*La seda* 1957: 21, no. 2).

Crimson could be used for either the cloth or the colour (*DRAE* 1999: I, 417). In the *Cantar que fizo el Marqués a sus fijas loando la fermosura de ellas* [Poem the Marqués Wrote to his Daughters, Praising their Beauty], to be discussed also in Chapters 5 and 6, Santillana refers to one of the fabrics his daughters were wearing as 'carmiso'. Maxim P. A. M. Kerkhof and Ángel Gómez Moreno note that 'carmiso' or 'carmeso' is a 'tela de color carmesí' [crimson-coloured cloth] but do not explain how crimson cloth can then be 'blanco y liso' [white and smooth]: 'Carmiso blanco e liso / cada qual en los sus pechos' [each has the finest of smooth white silk on her breast] (Santillana 2003: 102, lines 21–2). Crimson, like scarlet, is synonymous with rich fabric, and therefore can be of other colours.

Crimson for cloth or colour is also found in another *cancionero* poem, referring to a gift requested from the king by his majordomo. The rubric describes the cloth as 'tres varas de carmesí' [three rolls of (crimson?) fabric] (Labrador, Zorita, & Di Franco 1994: 131).

Reds or scarlet, as Judith H. Hofenk-De Graaff concludes, were also the colour of choice for 'Flemish aldermen, to whom we owe so many medieval cloth prices' (1983: 70). Jane Schneider, in her study of the advance of black with particular reference to its entry into favour as the colour of the elite in early modern Europe, indicates that the same was true of late medieval Italy, where 'reds and purples surfaced to mark off not only courtiers and royalty from the less prestigious social ranks, but the merchant elite as well' (1978: 427). At the ceremonial entry of the new queen into Valencia in 1415, City Councillors and magistrates were to be dressed in red as two pieces of 'drap de Mellines de grana' [Mechelen wool cloth, dyed in the grain] were to be bought to make robes for them (Carreres Zacarés 1997: 115–16) (for Mellines, see Astor Landete 1999: 174). The cloth, crimson or scarlet, dyed in the grain, is similar to that described for the civic dignitaries of Flanders. Wearing red, normally crimson, was usual for town councillors in the Kingdom of Aragon, as a reproduction of a painting of the four Valencia *jurats* shows (Ferrando Badía 1995: 64). Just a short time after the death of Sor Isabel, the Valencia city councillors took part in the entry of Fernando el Católico (1452–1516) and Germana de Foix (1488–1536):

> Y los dits Jurats estaven vestits ab gramalles de vellut carmesí, ab un pali de brocat ras, rich forrat de seti carmesi. Y portaven dit pali quatre Jurats y los Officials Reals de la ciutat y Regne de València ab alguns nobles i cavallers. (Ríos Lloret & Vilaplana Sánchis 2006: 151)

> [And the aforementioned councillors were dressed in robes of crimson velvet, with a canopy of velvet satin, lined with crimson satin. And the

canopy was carried by four councillors together with some knights and nobles from the city and Kingdom of Valencia.]

Another well-known representation of city dignitaries wearing red is depicted in *La Verge dels Consellers* [The Virgin of the City Councillors] by Lluís Dalmau (1428–61) (MNAC 9774).

In the medieval Church, the use of shades of red to delineate rank was more widespread than today. Egerton Beck notes how in the See of Canterbury, Archbishops Arundel and Warham, in the late fifteenth and early sixteenth centuries, wore red. In the northern dioceses of the Kingdom of Aragon, bishops and canons wore red, whilst in cathedrals in the provinces of Valencia, Aragon, and Catalonia, canons wore a 'dark red cappa, *morado* or mulberry colour' (1905: 373). Among the entries in the inventory for the cathedral is a cope of 'vermell de grana' [red dyed in the grain] (Sanchis y Sivera 1933: 6):

> Item huna capa de vellut vermell de grana, tota brodada de hor e de seda ab ymatges, ay perles menudes, ab fresadura de ymatges ab perles […]: fon del bisbe en Vidal.
>
> [Also a cope of a red velvet dyed in the grain, all embroidered with gold and silk with images, and there are small pearls, with a border of images with pearls. […] It belonged to Bishop Vidal.]

All the liturgical vestments listed are headed 'vermell'. However, this cope is particularly luxurious because of its decoration with pearls. It has been dyed in the grain.

Spain's museums, such as the Museu Episcopal de Vic, preserve some fabulously ornate brocade copes. A number of pairs of bishop's gloves from the Kingdom of Aragon are crimson, all of Italian origin (*La seda* 1957: nos 14–16). The first two are of crimson silk with gold embroidery and the third pair is decorated with gold ropework. The same exhibition reveals that abbesses followed bishops in the wearing of crimson: 'par de zapatos de abadesa, de terciopelo carmesí, bordados en hilo de oro y seda negra con emblema heráldica [a pair of abbess's shoes in crimson velvet, embroidered in thread of gold and with black silk with a heraldic emblem] (1957: 22, no. 8). Sor Isabel may have possessed a pair like these.

Scarlet and crimson were the colour of luxury, of regal and ecclesiastical status, but they had a number of other connotations in the fifteenth century. They were used for the garments worn by bride and bridegroom in the *Retablo de Fray Bonifacio Ferrer, o de los Sacramentos* [Retable of Friar Boniface Ferrer, or of the Sacraments] (c. 1396–98).[4] The central panel

---

4 Bonifaci Ferrer (1350–1417) was a brother of St Vincent Ferrer. He founded the Carthu-

represents the seven sacraments as rivulets of blood from the seven wounds of Christ. The sacrament of matrimony is one of seven small panels and in it both bride and groom are clothed in crimson (Fig. 11). It is possible that Sor Isabel might have known similar paintings of the seven sacraments.[5] A third example of the sacrament of marriage is depicted in the *Très riches heures du Duc de Berry* (BNF, nouv. acq. [Lat.], MS 3073), in which the bride is dressed in red.

Representations of the marriage of the Virgin, at least those from Southern Europe, regularly depict her dressed in a red gown with a blue cloak. *Marriages of the Virgin* from other parts of Europe often depict the Virgin in blue. Clothing the Virgin in a red tunic is traditional in Spanish art (Twomey 2005), whilst in Northern Europe blue is the colour of preference.[6]

It is also possible that royal weddings could have been a source of inspiration for Sor Isabel. Where the sacramental or biblical aspect is not emphasized, miniaturists use a range of bridal colours, among which, on occasion, red figures.[7]

---

sian monastery at Vall de Crist, in Valencia province, and reputedly translated the Bible into Valencian. The retable, originally in the Carthusian Monastery of Vall de Crist, is now MBAV 246.

[5] It is unlikely she visited the monastery of Vall de Crist, even though the Ferrers were well known in Valencia itself. It is in a very isolated position, in a mountain valley, and difficult to reach even today. Another representation of the seven sacraments is that of Rogier van der Weyden (1400–64), painted some fifty years after the Valencian one (c. 1453–55). In the *Sacrament of Matrimony*, the bride is dressed in scarlet. Her husband wears a gown of the same hue and both are dashingly dressed. The bride's dress is trimmed with miniver and she wears 'a coronet, a token that she is a bride' (Scott 1980: 137–8).

[6] Pietro Perugino's (1446–1515) *Marriage of the Virgin* was painted in the first years of the sixteenth century. Domenico Ghirlandaio in his *Marriage of the Virgin* depicts her in red with a traditional blue cloak, as does Raphael (1483–1520) in his (Pinacoteca de Brera), and Luca Signorelli (1440–1523) in his. Northern European miniatures in books of hours depicting the Virgin in blue include a book of hours copied in Flanders by a Spanish copyist (BC, MS 1852), a book of hours from Burgundy (BC, MS 54), the *Annunciation* of the Master of James IV of Scotland (active 1485–1530) (Los Angeles Getty Centre, MS Ludwig IX.18, fol. 92v), and the Salisbury Book of Hours (BC, MS 1855, fol. 46r). Northern European retables follow the same pattern. She is depicted in blue in the *Annunciation* of Rogier van der Weyden (1400–64) (MBAV 427), as well as in his *Descent from the Cross* (Prado, PO 01894), and Albrecht Dürer's (1471–1528) *Madonna of the Pear* (Uffizi 1171). Robert Campin's *Marriage of the Virgin*, painted in 1425, shows her crowned with a bridal coronet and attired in a gown of deepest blue (Prado, PO1887).

[7] For example, Tristan and Isolt, in the *Tristan de Léonois* manuscript (BNF, fonds fr., MS 102, fol. 73), are both attired in dark gold. The miniature depicting the marriage of Bohemond I, Prince of Antioch, and Constance, daughter of King Philip of France, shows both in gold with the bride with a blue cloak, and a coronet, and the groom with red visible through the slashes in his robe (BL, MS Royal 15E1, fol. 170). The miniaturist illustrating Henry V and Catherine of France's wedding from the *Chroniques de France ou St Denis* (BL, MS Royal 20E VI, fol. 9v), in 1420, chooses gold. Illustrators of chronicles sometimes

11. Gherardo Starnina, panel representing the Sacrament of Marriage, *Retablo de Fray Bonifacio Ferrer*.

Chronicles of royal weddings provide another source of information on bridal colours. Anderson notes that for the second marriage of Margaret, daughter of the Emperor Maximilian, widow of Prince Juan of Castile, to the proxy of Duke Philibert of Saxony, the bride went to the marriage bed in a 'dress or coat (*robe*) of gold cloth over gold cloth made in the Spanish style and lined with crimson satin, the skirt slit (*fendue*)' (1979: 141). For the marriage of Lucrecia and Alfonso de Aragón, crimson was a colour of choice. It was used mainly for decorative touches, whilst the robe was gold brocade and the tunic, white silk camlet:

selected reds as appropriate for royal marriages. For example, at their marriage, Mélusine and Raymond both wear red (*Roman de Mélusine*, BL, MS Harley 4418, fol. 36), as do Princess Sybil and King Alfour (BL, MS Harley 326, fol. 9).

Iba la señora Lucrecia vestida de aquesta manera: una camisa de cambray de mangas ricas, unas faldillas de pompa de raso carmesí, un brial de camelote de seda blanco con trepas de terciopelo negro; traía una ropa francesa de brocado de oro tirado de negro con trepas de brocado carmesi, las mangas del brial eran todas llenas de joyeles.
(cited in Borja 2008: 122)

[Lady Lucrecia was dressed in this manner: a chemise of cambray with rich sleeves, fine overskirt of crimson satin, a camlet tunic of white silk with frills of black velvet; she wore a gold brocade robe with frills of crimson brocade; the tunic sleeves were covered in large jewels.]

Princess Juana is dressed in scarlet and crimson to receive the ambassadors of Archduke Philip in the royal poem *El casamiento*, and, although it is not on her wedding day, the colours are thought to display her to best advantage as a woman with potential to become a suitable wife:

Vos diré como la vi
con una ropa colorada
d'escarlata muy preçiada,
forrada de carmesí. (Marino 2008: 20)

[I will tell you how she looked
with blush-coloured dress
of most precious scarlet
slashed with crimson.]

The crimson and scarlet gown and the ruby the Princess wore are depicted in the portrait commissioned for the occasion by the Catholic Monarchs, which was painted by the Flemish artist Michael Sittow (1469–1525). Marino considers that the poet may have been Pedro de Gracia Dei (2008: 20).

Judith Berg Sobré (1979), Hauf (1991: 111–12), and Ferran Muñoz (2002) have pointed to links between the plastic arts and Sor Isabel's writing. In Valencia, artists like Pere Nicolau (active c. 1390–1408), Joan Reixach, Joan de Joanes (1505–79), Vicent Macip (1475–1550), Jacomart (1411–61) (Fig. 12), Nicolau Falcó (Fig. 13), and the Master of Perea (active 1490–1510) (Fig. 14), choose red for the Virgin's overdress in their retables. In paintings of the Virgin in the Museo de Bellas Artes de Valencia (MBAV), of twenty-five representations of the Virgin at various points in her life, nine artists select red; most of those who do not choose gold. Only rarely do Valencian artists choose blue for the Virgin, such as Gonçal Perís Sarrià (1380–1451) for his *Veronica* of the Virgin (MBAV 406), although he uses red for her tunic at the *Annunciation* on the reverse.[8]

---

[8] Other Iberian artists also prefer red, with occasional use of blue. For example, Nicolau Francés (active 1445–60), in his *Retablo de la Virgen de la Vida y de San Francisco* [Retable

12. Jacomart, *Anunciación*.

The tradition of dress for the Virgin in sculpture was another important source of inspiration for Sor Isabel (see Graef 1963–65: I, 271–2). Statues such as that of Santa Maria del Puig from the Church of Sant Pere in Játiva, Valencia, reveal traces of bright scarlet on the lining of the Virgin's cloak and possibly on her overdress (Generalitat Valenciana 2007: 24).

of the Virgin of Life and St Francis] (Prado, PO 7878), chooses blue for the Virgin's robe. His name may of course indicate that his origins were Northern European.

13. Nicolau Falcó, Annunciation panel, *Retablo de la Purísma Concepción*.

14. Master of Perea, *Adoración de los Reyes*.

Reds in the Church

Sor Isabel was surrounded by colour in the convent. Observance of the liturgical calendar brought changes in the colour of the vestments, altar frontals, and other hangings. Red is one of the liturgical colours, marking the stages of the Christian year for the readers and author of the *Vita Christi*. Sor Isabel paid 3000 *sueldos* [silver pieces] for some crimson brocade to make hangings for the main altar as well as for a pulpit hanging (Benito Goerlich 1998: 90). Hayward's study of Henry VIII's court has also shown that courtiers observed liturgical days for the wearing of red (2007: 146).

In the convent, the production of these liturgical vestments and hangings would have been in the hands of Sor Isabel, and it is to the women's work of needlecraft that Bernat Fenollar seems to allude in his dedication of the *Passi en cobles*, 'a la molt il·lustre e devotíssima senyora dona Ysabel de Billena, digna abadessa de la Sancta Trinitat en Valentia' [to the most illustrious and devout Lady Isabel de Villena, worthy Abbess of the Santa Trinitat in Valencia], as he compares her prose to a 'fin drap' [fine cloth] covered in 'grans pedres y joyes […] ben engastades' [large stones and jewels (which have been) well set] (see Garcia Sempere 2002: 225).

Red is the colour for Pentecost, symbolizing the flames which burned on the heads of the apostles when they received the gift of the Holy Spirit. Embedded here are further allusions in the colour of the tunic. When she writes about the 'excel·lent carmesí' [fine crimson], of the tunic, Sor Isabel indicates it symbolizes holy charity, which she describes as 'fervent' and 'ardent' (fol. 50r; I, 182–3). 'Ardent' [burning] suggests the crimson flames which mark the presence of the Holy Spirit. In traditional symbolism of the four elements, red corresponds to fire (Astor Landete 1999: 79), and in ancient Middle Eastern colour symbolism red is the colour of life (MacKenzie 1922: 162). In Sor Isabel's narrative the Virgin puts on the crimson tunic after accepting the angel's greeting and after giving her assent to becoming Mother of Christ, and just before she is overshadowed by the Holy Spirit, often represented by fire symbolism, as the new life grows within her: '*Spiritus Sanctus superveniet in te et virtus altissimi hobumbrabit tibi*); car lo Sperit Sanct sobrevendrà en vostre senyoria e la virtut del Altisime vos abrigarà tota' [the Holy Spirit will overshadow you and the virtue of the Most High will be upon you] (fol. 33r; I, 125).

At the moment of her reception of the Holy Spirit the Virgin dresses in his colour. Association of the Virgin Mary at the Incarnation with the fire of the Spirit can be seen in a contemporary painting, that of *The Virgin and Child before a Firescreen* (London, National Gallery, 2609). Beth Williamson argues that the flames licking the top of the Virgin's head signify her overshadowing by the Spirit at the moment of the Incarnation (2004: 392).

In Conception hymns from across the Peninsula the Holy Spirit is termed *ignis* as he overshadows the Virgin with grace at the conception: 'Cuius ignis aceditur / sanctificare gracia' [whose fire came close to sanctify her with grace] (BNE, MS 8902, *Breviarium toletanum,* fol. 327v). The same hymn is found in several Castilian breviaries, including one in El Burgo de Osma (Archivo de la Catedral, MS 2B, fol. 382r), on the frontier with the Kingdom of Aragon.

The presence of the Holy Spirit in one of the poems submitted to the 1486 *certamen*, dedicated to the Immaculate Conception, is represented by crimson. Baltasar Joan Balaguer's poem constructs a retable on which the image of the Woman of the Apocalypse is being painted. Stanza by stanza the colours are added to the painting, as the Immaculate Virgin is formed by the Creator. At the painting of the crimson tunic, Balaguer notes that it was the Holy Spirit who painted it:

> Lavors primer ab vermell lo Paraclit
> donà color, pintant Ell la gonella
> d'un carmesí cubert de riqua porpra;
> car ffós per Ell de gràcia fecunda
> dins en l'instant que us concebé sent·Anna.
>   (cited in Ferrando Francés 1983: 518–19, lines 25–9)

> [For first the Paraclete
> added colour, painting the tunic
> in crimson covered with rich purple;
> for you were fecund by him through grace
> at the instant when St Anne conceived you.]

Balaguer's explanation of crimson assists in interpreting Sor Isabel's. Both dress the Virgin in crimson to mark her reception of the Holy Spirit, with Balaguer emphasizing reception of the Holy Spirit at her Immaculate Conception.

A final pointer to Sor Isabel's intention in selecting crimson for the tunic of the Virgin is to be found in the chapter title: 'Com fon presentada a la senyora una humana gonella de carmesí, significant fervent caritat brodada y embellida de honestat e paciència' (fol. 50r; I, 182) [How the Lady was presented with a human tunic of crimson, signifying fervent charity, embroidered and embellished with honesty and purity]. Crimson also represents humanity, in other words, blood.[9]

According to Aristotle and his theory of human generation, which was adopted by medieval theologians, a mother's contribution to the generation of a human being was her blood to nourish the foetus. This can be seen in Eiximenis's description of the formation of Christ from the blood and matter in the body of the Virgin:

> per sola virtut de Déu lo preciós cors de Ihesu Christ estech complidament format de la pus pura sanch et matèria qui era en lo cors de la Gloriosa et posat per sol Déu en lo loch hon les dones naturalment conceben.
> (*Vida de Jesucrist*, BC, MS 299, fol. 98r)

> [By the virtue of God alone the precious body of Jesus was fully formed of the most pure blood and matter which was in the body of the Virgin and set by God alone in the place where ladies naturally conceive.]

The crimson tunic symbolizes the blood of the Virgin, the human being chosen to hold the Child in her womb for the period of gestation. Blood was her contribution to the Child's development, and blood links mother and child. Josep Guia i Marin traces the origin of the name of *Tirant lo Blanc*'s heroine to an 'irreverent duplicat' [irreverent parallel] with the 'color *carmesina* de la sang de Crist en la *Història de Santa Magdalena*' [crimson colour of the blood of Christ in the *History of Mary Magdalene*] (1996: 276). Breast milk, depicted many times in medieval altarpieces of

---

[9] See Bynum 2007 for an overview of blood and its importance in medieval theology.

the Virgin, flowing from mother to child, feeding the saints, and sprinkling over the faithful, was also believed to contain nourishing blood and to transmit characteristics and lineage from mother to child (Bergmann 2002: 92). Ellington, in her chapter 'From the Very Pure Blood', comments on the glorification of the shared flesh of Mary and Christ by linking it to the whole edifice of the sacramental system (2001: 47).

Sor Isabel does not, however, merely follow medical theory: she uses it to strengthen a theological point. The gift of the human tunic underlines that Mary's humanity and the contribution she made through it both to the conception of Christ and also to his nourishment, achieved with her blood, was God's gift. She has already made this theme explicit when discussing the Virgin as the dwelling-place for the Christ Child: 'e·l vestirà d'aquell carmesí singular de les sues preciosíssimes sanchs, e li farà una vestidura de tanta excel·lència que en bellea e valor no·s trobarà ja més semblant en natura' [and she will dress him in that singular crimson of her most precious blood, and will make him a garment of such excellence that in beauty and value it had no equal in nature] (fol. 27r; I, 103).

Both crimson and scarlet mark the wearer out for his or her singularity but also have connotations of sinfulness in the Old Testament. Jeremiah exhorts Jerusalem to recognize her weakness and her dependence on God but, in her ruined state, she covers herself in scarlet: 'You may dress yourself in scarlet, put on ornaments of gold [...] but you make yourself pretty in vain' (Jeremiah 4. 30). However, the King James Bible translates the Hebrew word *šānî* as 'crimson'. Underpinning the gifting of the crimson tunic must be the contrast between two female figures so dressed. Jerusalem, despoiled and ruined and clothed in scarlet, symbolizes the wantonness of unredeemed humanity.

Both crimson and scarlet are associated with sinfulness by Isaiah:

> Though your sins are like scarlet,
> they shall be white as snow;
> though they are red as crimson,
> they shall be like wool. (Isaiah 1. 18)

The gift of the crimson tunic to the Virgin may also resonate with the crimson colour appropriate to sinful humanity and the moment at which God chooses to forgive humanity their sins. Later in the story, humanity is to be redeemed by the blood of Christ, another crimson. At the Crucifixion, his blood and his humanity, received from his mother, are to be poured out.[10] In Isaiah's prophecy about the time of judgement the Messiah comes

---

[10] For a study of the shedding of Christ's blood at the Passion in the *Vita Christi*, see Courcelles 2000: 114–19.

in crimson garments which are linked both to wine and the sacrificial shedding of blood:

> Who is this coming from Edom,
> From Bozra in crimson garments,
> So magnificently dressed [...]
> Marching so full of strength?
> Why are your garments red,
> Your clothes like someone treading the winepress?
> [...] Their blood squirted over my garments. (Isaiah 63.1–3)

In the prophecy the magnificent garments are worn by the Messiah and the gifting of similar crimson garments to the Virgin associates her with the Messianic coming which Isaiah prophesied.

The association of adornments, jewels, scarlet, and purple with fallen women is present in the New Testament, where it is part of the vision in Revelation:

> The woman was dressed in purple and scarlet and glittered with gold and jewels and pearls, and she was holding a gold wine-cup filled with the disgusting filth of her prostitution. (Revelation 17. 4)

Sor Isabel's choice of crimson clothing for the Virgin is, therefore, a deliberate antithesis of the whore of Babylon and of the fallen Jerusalem, as it is re-appropriated for holiness, reversing God's attitude to the colour. God selects crimson garments for the Virgin and, in her case, crimson honours and is no longer a sign of sinfulness. The re-clothing of the Virgin in crimson, at the direction of God, is intended to mark the parallel between the new creation and the old. The garment foreshadows the crimson ones prophesied for the Messiah, her Son, and heralds the regal robe put on Christ, as part of the scourging before his Crucifixion.

Sor Isabel's choice of regal red may also echo the regal pearl and purple which, with an allegorical meaning, clothes the Virgin in Leonardo Nogarola's Conception office, written after Sixtus IV's decree of 1476: 'fortitudo et decor indumentum eius: byssus et purpura uestis illius' [strength and beauty are her clothing: pearl and purple her raiment] (BC, MS 1043, fol. 13v).

Conclusion

Study of the colour red, an apparently minor detail, part of the allegorical clothing gifted to the Virgin in the *Vita Christi*, provides an insight into the difficulties in making distinctions between colour and fine cloth. Sor Isabel clothes the Virgin in crimson in the *Vita Christi*. I have shown that, despite the many precedents in chivalry novels, it is most likely that Sor Isabel took her inspiration from the colours in paintings she saw around her, from the hangings which decorated the altars and chapels in the convent, from the colours used for ecclesiastical vestments, and also from its presence in Scripture. She also reversed biblical uses of crimson garments to point to the Virgin as the New Eve.

Many different levels of allegory can be discerned in Sor Isabel's description of the presenting of the crimson tunic to the Virgin. On one level, the only one clearly signalled by the author, the tunic signifies the ardent love which causes the Virgin to assent to her role in the history of salvation. However, the colour crimson suggests greater depths. It symbolizes her collaboration with the Holy Spirit in the salvation of the world and it echoes the liturgical colour accorded to Pentecost; it symbolizes her crimson blood which nourished the Christ foetus within the confines of her womb; finally, because it is one of a series of gifts brought by the archangel, it emphasizes her place within God's lineage and points to her role as mediatrix between God and humanity, which she accepts at the same time as the tunic.

In this chapter I have sought to demonstrate that Sor Isabel did not wish her readers to be distracted by the outer shell of her allegory, by the medieval gifting scenes, by the fine clothing, or by the bright colours. She invites the reader to plumb the depths, like disciples, and to tease out the many truths disguised under the allegorical surface. Sor Isabel's 'ternura femenina' [feminine tenderness] (Hauf 1987: 153) and the critical tendency to benevolently skim the pages of the *Vita Christi* should be resisted, for Sor Isabel's narrative reveals a mind capable of great subtlety. It has been tempting for critics to classify her as a female writer, for whom intuition was all-important. To read her text, a detailed knowledge of Old Testament prefiguration and powerful reasoning are required.

Her desire to awaken faith in the nuns in her charge operates on various levels but, at all times, it has a strong rationale and a deliberate purpose. Sor Isabel believed that writing a book in which allegory was centre stage was to imitate a tradition from New Testament times. She sought to use every human faculty, from imagination to reason, to lead Christian souls to lose themselves in the contemplation of the Creator.

5

For Richer, for Poorer:
Redrawing the Boundaries in the *Vita Christi*

> He has wrapped me in a cloak of saving justice,
> […] like a bride adorned in her jewels. (Isaiah 61. 10)

In this chapter I will set Sor Isabel's interest in jewelled and embroidered decoration in the context of adornment of medieval textiles. I will at the same time seek to establish how far an interest in adornment is related to women's writing.

Sor Isabel's constant description of beautifully decorated clothing in her *Vita Christi* has been remarked upon by a number of critics. In one of his studies of the *Vita Christi*, Hauf shows how Sor Isabel follows the dress protocols she observed at court and how she provides an 'explicació del vestuari que portaren els protagonistes en cadascuna d'aquestes celebracions protocolàries' [explanation of the garments which each one of the characters is wearing in each of these celebrations where protocol is all-important] (1991: 123). Berg Sobré also considers that Sor Isabel sets her life of Christ into a courtly context. She describes the *Vita Christi* as 'an extravagant rambling tapestry' (1979: 303). Elsewhere, Hauf emphasizes the 'pleitesías y galas cortesanas' [courtesies and courtly finery], which mark the spiritual nuptials of Mary in the *Vita Christi* (1987: 113). Surtz too equates the gloves gifted to the Virgin with the gloves worn by noblewomen at court (2010: 517, n. 41). Because of the way in which Sor Isabel's use of courtly dress appears to reflect the display of court finery described in *Tirant*, Hauf concluded that her interest was to write a chivalry novel *a lo divino* [in the sacred style] for the delight of her nuns (1991: 124).

Scholars have highlighted the relationship between the austerity of the cloister and Sor Isabel's imagination and memories of court life which blend in the *Vita Christi* so that 'la vistositat de l'espectacle mundà, aristocràtic s'insereix, "contrafet a l'espiritual"' [the showiness of the worldly, aristocratic spectacle is put in, 'reworked on a spiritual level'] (Hauf 1991: 123). Those commenting on the *Vita Christi* have seen in Sor Isabel's detailed descriptions of clothing and courtly ceremony, as well as the way in which they occupy centre stage, evidence of the courtly qualities of her writing and an indication that she misses, 'enyora', as Fuster terms it, the court life she once knew (1975a: 166). The underlying suggestion is that such emphasis on the world of the court is unsuited to the convent writer.

In *Tirant*, colour, fabric, and decoration of clothing are described in minute detail. Harriet Goldberg examines some of the scenes in which clothing and fabrics feature in *Tirant* and she believes that 'Martorell's gift was to create a complete, totally credible world using the raw material of the real world which he observed around him' (1984: 392).

Studies of medieval female writers have emphasized their interest in adornment. Focus on dress is evident from Laura Rinaldi Dufresne's study of how Christine de Pizan took the trouble to commission miniatures, which she personally supervised, to illustrate her *Treasury of the City of Ladies*. One of the illustrators Pizan used was Anastaise, 'learned and skilled in painting manuscript borders and miniature backgrounds', who, exceptionally for the period, was a craftswoman (Dufresne 1995–96: 29). Since the *Treasury* was dedicated to a noble patron, Margaret of Burgundy, Christine's care with the illustration of her little book of instruction is also witness to Margaret's perceived interest in seeing images of female dress.

Embroidery and adornment of the female body

Mary's archetypal female body is adorned with jewellery and by fine garments by Sor Isabel in the scenes following the Annunciation by the ambassador-angel, Gabriel. In chapters 39–48, the Virgin is presented with several gifts fitted to her royal status by the Archangel Michael. In chapter 49, she is adorned with the betrothal gifts and in the chapters immediately following (50–8), takes part in a courtly reception of the representatives of heaven's hierarchy and of her forefathers, Adam, Eve, and Abel. Sor Isabel returns to Gospel events only in chapter 61.

She describes the presentation of garments, which are beautifully embellished with embroideries, jewelled borders, and gold thread work. One of the first gifts is a silk 'camisa' [chemise or shift], embellished with gold work:

> Veus açí una camisa molt special que tramet a vostra mercè nostre Senyor Déu omnipotent, la qual és tota de seda singular, guarnida de maravellosa obra d'or. [...] lo guarniment qui per excel·lencia lo embelleix és la perseverança contínua de vostres caritatives obres. (fol. 49v; I, 183)[1]

---

[1] I discuss the silk chemise in Twomey 2007b and summarize the key arguments in this part of the chapter.

[Here you behold a very special chemise, which Our Lord God Almighty sends to you. It is of singular silk, decorated with marvellous gold work; (…) the ornamentation, which most excellently embellishes it, is continuous perseverance in your good works.]

The silk undergarment in the *Vita Christi* has three similarities to the one belonging to Carmesina in *Tirant*: its fabric, its embroidery, and its interpretation. The Virgin's silk shift is embellished with gold, which Sor Isabel interprets as the Virgin's perseverance in good works. Carmesina's is also silk and is embroidered with red stripes on which there are ships' anchors, also a symbol of constancy. The embroidery with appliquéd objects described by Martorell and Villena became known as Spanish style by the early seventeenth century (Bernis 2001: 281). Anderson comments that stripes like the ones which Martorell describes were the most accepted form of chemise embroidery, particularly on the sleeves. Patterns embroidered on a chemise were frequently from the natural world and in this they 'showed Moorish influence' (Anderson 1979: 187–9).

Embroidery was valued because of its expense. Just fifty years after Villena's death the authorities were condemning the cost of embroidery on women's undergarments:

> En 1544 los procuradores del reino, en las cortes de Valladolid, acusaban a sastres, jubeteros y calceteros de haber 'inventado muchas maneras de guarniciones, que cuestan más las hechuras que las sedas'.
> (Bernis 2001: 281, citing Alonso de Santa Cruz)
>
> [In 1544 the king's procurators, in the Valladolid courts, accused tailors, doublet-makers, and breeches-makers of having 'made up many types of decorations, which cost more to make than the silk'.]

By the seventeenth century, chemises embroidered with silver and gold thread had become part of ordinary women's dress (Bernis 2001: 209) but their cost was prohibitive, as Lope de Vega notes in one of his plays, 'agora en solas guarniciones un dote de otro tiempo va cifrado' [now just in decorative work there is spent a whole dowry from previous times] (cited in Bernis 2001: 281). Bernis notes that silk shifts were relatively rare in medieval Iberia, although queens and princesses did have them: 'Queen Isabel (la Católica) and Queen Juana each owned a chemise of silk' (1978–79: 183).

Embroideries incorporating plants or herbs feature on a number of Sor Isabel's gifted garments, including the red tunic discussed in Chapter 4. The tunic is 'sembrada de liris e de brots de *agnus castus*' [sprinkled with lilies and knots of *agnus castus*] (fol. 50r; I, 183). I have noted elsewhere how the tunic evolved from a liturgical garment, the dalmatic, which the Virgin wears in many paintings. I have also discussed how it is related to the garment used in the Kingdom of Aragon for robing queens for their coronation (2007b: 130). Dalmatics gradually evolved into the *gonella* (in Catalan) or *brial* (in Castilian), the tunic or overdress, normal wear for noble ladies of the court (Trens 1947: 360; Astor Landete 1999: 45).

Gradually, as the fourteenth and fifteenth centuries progressed, paintings depict the Virgin in garments ornamented with the accoutrements of wealth and privilege: ermine, jewels, and pure gold lace being the most common. The magnificent garments given to the Virgin have many features in common with artistic representations from convents and churches in Valencia and its provinces.

There are also records of similarly richly embroidered garments worn by nobles for state occasions. At a tournament held for Charles V, Pedro Girón wore cloth of drawn gold on which were applied chevrons of silver tissue interlaced and laden with roses and pomegranates (Anderson 1979: 100–1).

In her discussion of coronation garments, Astor Landete emphasizes how they are decorated with insignia embroidered on the brocades and velvets (1999: 100–1).[2] They are part of how the royal personage, the relationship between king and queen, and the alliance between nations are to be constructed. Barbara Weissberger's discussion of the royal coat of arms designed for the Catholic Monarchs is also indicative of how a ruling narrative was constructed through text and symbol (2004: 64–8). The embroidery of *agnus castus* and lilies on the Virgin's tunic serves the same purpose. It is ostensibly decorative but also fashions a narrative about her purpose in the economy of salvation.

Lily embroidery

Lily embroidery can be found on several liturgical vestments included in the 1418 inventory for Valencia Cathedral:

> Item huna capa, casula e dues dalmatiques de drap de seda verda e holra menuda, forrades de cendat groch ab fresadures de savastre, ab senyals de flos de lis, en camp vermell. (Sanchis y Sivera 1933: 9)

> [Next, a cope, chasuble, and two dalmatics in green silk cloth with fine linen, lined with yellow silk and linen mix, with borders of rich cloth, with fleur-de-lys insignia on a red background.][3]

Another, a cope for major feast days, is also embroidered with lilies: 'una

---

[2] For a study of insignia and how they were used at court, see Macpherson 1997.
[3] 'Savastre' is an expensive but unknown cloth, used for prestige items, together with silks and brocades.

capa de vellut vermell de grana brodada de flors de lir de hor' [a dark red velvet cope embroidered with fleur-de-lys in gold] (1933: 7). The fleur-de-lys insignia may be intended to suggest a royal coat of arms but it is worth remembering that it also had a place on Sor Isabel's own coat of arms because of her connection to the French royal family (see Introduction). In his discussion of the fleur-de-lys on Castilian coats of arms, Martí de Riquer recalls that its symbolism is Trinitarian (1986: 199), and at the supreme moment of salvation history, when the Virgin enters into relationship with each member of the Trinity, Sor Isabel wished to emphasize that relationship by emblazoning the Virgin's clothing with it. The presence of lily embroidery on church vestments indicates that, whilst Sor Isabel may have sought to copy the emblems and embroideries from noble insignia, she was also inspired by the symbolism present at High Masses and feast days.

Symbolism of lilies was a constant feature of litanies and offices of the Virgin, and for that reason it takes its place in Sor Isabel's ritual to celebrate the Annunciation. Lilies, with their pure white colour, were age-old symbols of purity (James Hall 1974: 330). Lilies represent the Virgin's purity, established in her conception, heralded in her Annunciation, and enshrined in her perpetual virginity, recalling Song of Songs 2. 2, 'sicut lilium inter spinas' [like a lily among thorns], used by medieval commentators to emphasize the difference between this birth and other births and between this woman and other women. The lily had an important role in Nogarola's Conception office because it featured in the opening antiphon at first vespers: 'Sicut lilium inter spinas, sic amica mea inter filias Ade' (BC, MS 1043, fol. 13v) [Like a lily among thorns, so my beloved among the daughters of Adam]. The same antiphon precedes the hymn *Ave maris stella* at first vespers. The lily was beginning to develop into an emblem which could signify the Immaculate Conception by the end of the fifteenth century, when it became part of the *Tota pulchra es* in art and literature (Twomey 2008: 162–73).[4] When the Song of Songs text about the lily among thorns became associated with Mary's conception without sin, the 'spinas' represented Mary's relationship to sin, whether venial, mortal, or original. The 'spinas' could also represent other, sinful, women, providing a differentiation of the pure Virgin from the stock of humankind.

Lilies frequently symbolize female beauty and, in Marian poetry, the Virgin's purity. There is an early fourteenth-century *certamen* entry where lilies are associated with the Immaculate Conception, *Lirs virginals* (Ferrando Francés 1983: 75–6). The association is also found in the *Aureola mona-*

---

[4] The *Tota pulchra es* (literally, 'You are wholly beautiful') was a representation of the Virgin with some of the accoutrements of the Woman of the Apocalypse. She is surrounded by Old Testament symbols, such as the enclosed garden or the fountain of the gardens from the Song of Songs.

corum vel dicta diuersum patrum que quiere dezir Corona de los monjes [Aureola monachorum or sayings of various fathers which means Crown of monks], copied in a late-fourteenth-century manuscript, where 'lirio entre spinas' [lily among thorns] is part of a litany of epithets in praise of the Virgin (Dutton 1990–91: II, 239, line 46).

The lily was the flower most frequently depicted either beside the Virgin or presented to her as a gift in contemporary Annunciation paintings. The angel holds lilies out to the Virgin in a mid-fifteenth-century *Annunciation* painted for the Dominican convent by Jacomart (MBAV 241) (Fig. 12), as well as in the Annunciation panels of the *Retablo de la Santa Cruz* [Altarpiece of the Holy Cross] (Fig. 15) by Miquel Alcanyís (active 1408–47), in a painting originally in the Carthusian monastery of Portaceli, Valencia (MBAV 254).[5]

Sor Isabel introduces lilies as a symbol at the moment when the Virgin is receiving gifts of jewels and finely decorated fabrics to adorn her for her betrothal. They provide a reminder that it is God's bounty which supplies all: 'Si ergo neque quod minimum es potestis solliciti estis? Considerate lilia quomodo crescunt, non laborant, neque nent: Dico autem vobis nec Salomon in omni gloria sua vestiebatur sicut unum de istis' (Luke 12. 27–8; see also Matthew 6. 28). The Vulgate text is beautifully rendered in the King James Authorized Version: 'If ye then be not able to do that thing which is least, why take ye thought for the rest? Consider the lilies, how they grow: they toil not, they spin not: and yet I say unto you, that Solomon in all his glory was not arrayed like one of these'. William Tyndale's first translation of the Bible rendered the first question as 'And why care ye then for raiment?'. The symbolism of the lily is a scriptural reminder of the Franciscan call to poverty.[6]

Embroidery and adornment of the female body: agnus castus

Knots of *agnus castus* embroidered on the Virgin's tunic are not common in iconography of the Virgin.[7] *Agnus castus*, or chasteberry, is associated with

---

[5] Jacomart's painting was previously believed to be by an unknown Master of Bonastre. There is a vase of lilies in the Virgin's chamber in the panel of the Annunciation in the *Retable of the Life of the Virgin*, which Pere Nicolau completed in 1404 (MBAV 2263-8). (See also fig. 13).

[6] I am grateful to Rosanna Cantavella for pointing out that the coat of arms of the University of Valencia was formerly a Virgin and Child, holding a lily. The University was founded in 1499. The coat of arms was later replaced by the city's coat of arms. See Kenneth Baxter Wolf's study of the tension between poverty and riches in the life of Francis and his followers (2003).

[7] I extend the discussion of *agnus castus* from 2007b, particularly in terms of the symbolism behind the embroidery.

15. Miquel Alcanyís, *Retablo de la Santa Cruz*.

treatments for the female reproductive system. It can be used for the regulation of heavy periods or for controlling changes in the female body at the menopause. It was also noted for its ability to preserve chastity: according to Pliny, leaves of this plant scattered on the marriage bed had this effect. Chasteberry was used to preserve chastity but it was also used to address all manner of women's problems. According to Arnau de Vilanova's *Tractatus de virtutibus herbarum* [Treatise on the Virtues of Herbs], *agnus castus* was efficacious for disposing the womb to conceive: 'Et ceptri galli et arthemesie in aq[ua] superfluitates matricis exiccat [...] et ad conceptionem disponit' [Both wild clary and mugwort in water dry excess liquid in the womb (...) and make it ready to conceive] (1499: fol. 22; see Herrera 1996: I, 763 and I, 154). The information Arnau de Vilanova provides is appropriate to Juno, as goddess of the moon and of marriage, but is also appropriate as a gift to the Virgin at the point of her conception of Christ. *Vitex agnus castus* grows in Mediterranean Spain and was likely to have been one of the remedies for female ailments grown by the nuns in the kitchen garden beside the convent.[8]

The properties of herbs and foodstuffs were particularly significant in the medieval period, when it was believed that people's bodies were affected by what they ate. Peppers and spices had the properties of counteracting cool, wet humours and they were held to have aphrodisiac qualities. *Agnus castus* was thought to be particularly appropriate in a monk's diet; St Anthony 'called it "monks' pepper tree", because it "makes men as chaste as lambs"' (Turner 2007: 227). It was appropriate both inwardly and outwardly as an emblem of female chastity for the Virgin, whose virginity was perpetual even though she bore a son.

It is possible that Sor Isabel's description of the *agnus castus* embroidery on the Virgin's tunic draws on the *agnus castus* emblazoned on Juno's mantle in Roís de Corella's *Visió del Judici de Paris* [Vision of the Judgement of Paris] (1913: 294): 'estaua lo real manto en rriqua orfebreria brodat de verts florits agnus castus, sobre los quals entresi des tortres planyien' [the royal mantle was in rich cloth-of-gold embroidered with green chasteberry on which turtledoves cooed sadly] (293). She may have known the description of Juno's robe in Roís de Corella's tale, because his daughter was a nun in the Santa Trinitat.

The *agnus castus* may also have a similar intent to the herb *amorval* (amor vale) [love suffices], embroidered on Carmesina's dress in *Tirant lo Blanc*. Martorell's love-token discourse is completed with the embroidery of the words 'mas no a mi' [but not for me] (1990: I, 234). The name of the herb, *agnus castus*, which Sor Isabel chooses, foreshadows what is to be the

---

[8] Joan Amades describes the custom of picking the 'hierba de la virtut' [herb of virtue] in Castellar and placing it under girls' pillows to preserve their chastity (1982–83: IV, 95).

outcome of the Virgin's assent at the Annunciation. *Agnus castus* commemorates the Child whom the Virgin is to bear who is to become the *agnus*, the Lamb of God, chaste because of his sinless nature, to be slaughtered in expiation of the sins of the whole world. The message of the *agnus castus* is not just a prefiguration of the Crucifixion but because in Revelation 5. 6 the Lamb is glorified, it foreshadows the glorious end of salvation history. Sor Isabel's herb embroidery must have been suggested by images of the Lamb of God as a eucharistic symbol, the New Testament equivalent of the Passover lamb of the Old Testament (Exodus 12. 21), which was sometimes depicted on devotional and ecclesiastical objects, processional crosses, and hangings.

Queen María of Castile possessed two *agnus Dei* as devotional objects, according to an inventory, as did other members of the aristocracy (see Chapter 3). One was the size of a doubloon and the other in a little silver pouch was in the shape of a Host, presumably of a similar size:

> Item un agnus d'argent blanch ab brescadures nielat de blau quasi tamany com una dobla.
> Item hun agnus Dei de la forma de una hostia guarnit d'argent daurat, smaltat en lo mig de blau, e en la una part al cap baix ha un crucifix ab una ymatge a cascuna part, e en lo mig Nostra Dona ab sis ymatges de cascuna part, a al cap dalt Déu lo Pare ab quatre angels, e a l'altra part un agnus Dei acompanyat dels quatre evangelistes. Sta conservat en hun stoig de seda blava ab flochs vermells, lo qual pesa a march de Valencia sis onzes e miga. (cited in Astor Landete 1999: 113)

> [Item an *agnus* in silver with edges in blue, the size almost of a doubloon. Item an *agnus Dei* in the shape of a Host, decorated with gold-plated silver, enamelled blue in the centre, and on one side there is a Crucifix with an image on each of the four cross pieces, and, in the centre the Virgin with six images on each cross piece, and, at the top, God the Father with four angels and on the other an *agnus Dei* with the four Evangelists. It is kept in a blue silk pouch with yellow flocking. It weighs six-and-a-half ounces in Valencian measure.]

Devotional *agnus Dei* such as Queen María's would have been familiar to Sor Isabel. Noble families possessed them, as recorded by Saurina's inventory of the goods of her husband, Guillem de Sala. He had 'un agnus dei d'argent' [a silver *agnus Dei*] among his possessions in 1382.[9]

There is a twelfth-century cross from Vic, an important See in the northeast of the Kingdom of Aragon, with an *agnus Dei* in the centre and the symbolic creatures representing the four Evangelists on each of its arms (MEV 1609). The same design was constant through the Middle Ages in the

---

[9] BC, Registre 313, Perg. 5, *Inventari de bens de Guillem de Sala, senyor de Duocastella*.

Kingdom, with a burnished silver processional cross (MNAC 37765) made by Juan Tol (active in Aragon in the second half of the fifteenth century), and another silver cross from Zaragoza (MNAC 122181), showing the Lamb with its pennant in the centre. The *agnus Dei* was found on embroidered altar frontals, such as the appliquéd one on an Epiphany frontal, which may have been embroidered on Valencian silk (MEV 1949).

Devotion to the Eucharist was central to Franciscan practice and that is why Sor Isabel chose to use it as an emblem of the Virgin. Rona Goffen illustrates how it links Christ and St Francis, who began his *Admonitions* with a reminder to his friars to venerate the Eucharist, linking it to Christ's descent to earth at the Nativity:

> It is the Most High himself who has told us, 'This is my Body and my Blood [...]'. Every day he humbles himself just as he did when he came from his 'heavenly throne' (Wisdom 18. 15) into the Virgin's womb; every day he comes to us and lets us see him in abjection, when he descends from the bosom of the Father into the hands of the priest at the altar. He shows himself to us in this sacred bread, just as he once appeared to his apostles in real flesh. [...] We too, with our own eyes, see only bread, but we must see further and firmly believe that this is his most holy Body and Blood, living and true.
> (Goffen 1986: 260; see St Francis 1999a: I, 52; 1999b: I, 129)

Goffen argues that Francis is referring to Christ's descent to earth at the Nativity. However, the descent to earth most frequently depicted in medieval art is the flying baby, descending towards the Virgin to enter her womb through her ear, and it is surely the moment of the Annunciation to which Francis refers in his association of different aspects of doctrine. Christ's descent at the Annunciation towards the ear of the Virgin is depicted by many Valencian artists, including Gonçal Perís Sarrià (MBAV 406).

The Franciscan tradition of linking the Eucharist and the moment of the Annunciation may inform Sor Isabel's choice of the *agnus castus* image for Mary's tunic. The tunic is a red colour to represent both the wine of the Eucharist and the blood supplied by the maternal womb to nourish the male seed (see Chapter 4).

The image of the lamb recalls other texts to readers well versed in daily readings from the scriptures. Although it is Christ who is most often called the Lamb, there are many instances in the Bible where his followers are called sheep or lambs, whilst Christ is the Good Shepherd. The nuns of the Santa Trinitat, part of their abbess's 'grey' [flock], are included among the sheep. Mary, as first of the flock to follow Christ, is occasionally called a lamb in medieval religious writing. In the Castilian cleric Gonzalo de Berceo's *Himnos a la Virgen*, she is a lamb because of her gentleness: 'plena de mansedumbre, plus simple que cordera' [full of gentleness, more guileless than a lamb] (1975: 63, line 5b).

The embroidery on the tunic of both the Virgin and Martorell's princess are intended to construct themes appropriate to the person wearing them. Both tell a story for the reader or observer, requiring little deciphering from the name of the herb. Carmesina's becomes a motto combining text and image to depict her love for Tirant, whilst the Virgin's evokes a biblical vision and hints at a dual narrative about her motherhood and virginity.

In this part of the chapter, I have sought to draw out the parallels between Sor Isabel's descriptions of embroideries and those in both *Tirant* and contemporary church vestments. Piponnier (1970) indicates that embroidery at the court of Anjou was used ever more infrequently for women's garments as the fifteenth century progressed. She argues that embroidery is found as decoration for men's garments and for jousts. She does not mention ecclesiastical garments, because she is focusing on courtly ones. In Valencia, evidence from *Tirant* points to its use in female garments for the nobility, but Martorell may have been inspired more by the colours and insignia of the joust than by reality for his descriptions. Astor Landete describes a number of embroidered garments for the nobility, but many are drawn from literary sources, either from Martorell, Eiximenis, or Roís de Corella (1999: 45–7), and the question must remain as to whether the authors concerned simply invented or embellished reality. Protocols for celebrating coronations indicate that garments for queens were embroidered with insignia (Astor Landete 1999: 100) (see Chapter 6). Sor Isabel could have been inspired by her memory of novels like *Tirant,* although the models she used directly for her descriptions bear much resemblance to ecclesiastical ones.

Hand-embroidered goods – women's work?

Both the embroidered lilies and the *agnus castus* were insignia of the type proper to royalty or the nobility. Hand-embroidered goods were luxury items and status symbols for those who owned them, because of the work involved and the cost of creating them. Stella Mary Newton notes how the 'highest dignitaries of the Church and the state have always chosen to appear on the most important and ceremoniously solemn occasions in clothing that has depended for its magnificence on embroidery' (1980: 21). The decorative embroidery would sometimes have been provided by nuns or by charitably minded noblewomen, and may correspond to needlework produced in Sor Isabel's convent.

Needlecraft was recognized as a suitable female 'labor' or labour, which medieval Churchmen thought signalled a virtuous woman. They took as a model the strong woman of Proverbs and the way she provided for her household with her needle (Proverbs 31. 10–13, 19, 24). In his *Vida de Jesucrist*, Eiximenis depicts the Virgin weaving, sewing, and working with silk whilst in the temple, seeing her as a perfect example of Christian womanhood:

> ja ella estant en lo temple infanta de cinch anys; car ja en aquell temps nos provoca fort a maravellar en la sua astucia et saber. Car en aquell temps com totes les donzelles deputades al servey de Déu en lo temple fossen comunament ocupades en cosir et obrar de seda e d'aur e ço que pertanyia als sacerdots et ministres del temple de Déu per lo servey del Senyor. Sàpie·s que Maria cosia et obrava pus altament et pus suptil et pus aguda que les majors que y fossen. (BC, MS 299, fol. 59r)
>
> [in the temple as a child of five, for even at that time we are given cause to marvel at her cleverness and knowledge. For at that time as all the girls given over to the service of God in the temple were jointly occupied in sewing and working silk and gold cloth, and materials that pertained to the priests and ministers of the temple of God for his service. Know that Mary sewed and worked the cloth more perfectly and more subtly and more cleverly than the older girls who were there.]

When Sor Isabel describes the Virgin in the temple she does not follow Eiximenis in his emphasis on the high quality of craftwork produced by the Virgin, the example of perfect womanhood. She mentions the crafts only briefly: 'de tèrcia fins a nona feya fahena de mans, ab les altres donzelles' [from terce to none she did craftwork with the other girls] (fol. 15v; I, 53).

Weissberger indicates that Isabel of Castile's prowess as a needlewoman was used as a means of enhancing her virtue, particularly in Fray Íñigo de Mendoza's *Dechado a* [...] *la reina Doña Isabel*, a poem which narrates the deeds of the Queen as though they were 'elegant stitchery' in a sampler. He describes the stitches and each colour of thread in careful detail. His purpose is to show how the Queen must develop masculine virtues if she is to rule successfully but that she must do so without straying from the pattern for female behaviour. The Queen must display perfect obedience and never depart from his instructions (2004: 61). The uneasy balance between masculine and feminine virtue in the body of the Queen is thus contained within the 'double-gendered' sense of *labrar* [plough]. Weissberger also shows how weaving was not merely a passive female task, but in the person of Arachne could pose a challenge to accepted authority, just as the Queen's claim to the throne did (2005: 413). Needlework, like those tasks deemed fitting for women in Proverbs, such as spinning or weaving, was associated with the sexual act because of the way the needle pierces the cloth (Macpherson & MacKay 1994: 200). Weissberger points to the way in which the Queen used her needle for political ends. She used sewing as a point of contact and, ultimately, as a way to establish power over wayward nuns, as, over the needle, she was able to extract information from them, enabling her to enclose them to preserve their virtue (2004: 62–3). Rosa E. Ríos Lloret notes how comparison with Isabel la Católica was used to discredit Fernando el Católico's second wife, Germana de Foix:

> aunque se haya dicho que Isabel hilaba y tejía todas las camisas que se ponía su marido, no puede comprobarse de modo absolute, porque las camisas, pañizuelos, tohallas y tocas, consta fueron hechas con lienzo casero, vizcaíno, tunecí, de Cambray y de Holanda. No ofrece duda, sin embargo, que la Reina realizaba algunos trabajos de costura. Tiene confirmación documental [...], el velo que hizo para cubrir el santo Sepulcro de Jerusalem, que entregó personalmente a los religiosos que vinieron con la embajada del Sultán de 1489. (2003: 73, citing José Ferrandis)

> [although it has been said that Isabel spun and wove all the shirts her husband wore, it cannot be definitively confirmed, because it is apparent that the shirts, neckerchiefs, veils, and headdresses were made with Spanish cotton cloth, cloth from the Basque region, from Tunisia, from Cambray, and from Holland. There can be no doubt however that the Queen did make some garments. It is confirmed by documentary evidence (...). There is the veil she made to cover the Holy Sepulchre in Jerusalem, which she passed in person to the monks who came over with the Sultan's embassy in 1489.]

Ríos Lloret comments how Germana had imbibed foreign customs, was keen on feasting and dancing, and left no record of her needlework (2003: 73–8).

Despite the association of embroidery with women's work, there were professional broiderers active in Valencia, and the presence of the Calle Bordadores [Broiderers' Street] in the present-day city, within the city's medieval boundaries, is testament to their activity (Sanchis y Sivera 1921: 201). It was in that street that members of the profession, part of the Armourers' Guild, lived and worked. It was, however, the male head of household who was registered with the guild. Sanchis y Sivera lists forty references to broiderers in testaments and other archival documents in the city (1921: 201; 1933: 3). Under the entry for Bartolomé Mariner, active in the city in 1401, there is a description of a complex piece of embroidery carried out:

> primo, ha de largaria lo senyal set palms, et de amplaria altres set palms, e en mig una donzella la qual ha de largaria una alna. – Item als peus de la donzella una muntanya, ab los squexos de les çoques e taylls, qui seran rexats dor e dargent, e lals de punt alçat de seda, de la collor ques pertanyera. – Item en la falda que roçega la donzella, deu haver una bestia [...] sobre alçada de punt, e perfilada dargent, e la corona que te en lo cap tota daur. (1921: 209)

[first, there are seven palms in length, and seven palms in width, and, in the middle, a lady who is one ell long. Also, at the feet of the lady, a mountain, with green shoots from trunks and branches, which will be barred in gold and silver, and the sides of raised silk stitch of the corresponding colour. Also, on the full-length skirt which the lady wears, there should be a beast (…) with a raised stitch, and threaded with silver, and the crown she has on her head is to be all of gold.]

The work was undertaken for Joana, wife of the merchant Pere Bou.

Sanchis y Sivera also notes that needlework was established pre-conquest in Játiva, where tapestries covered in the geometric images permitted by Islam were produced. By the fifteenth century there were many foreigners, both Italian and Flemish, active in Valencia (1921: 201). He considers this to be evidence that Valencia attracted foreign specialists because of its importance as a centre for the hand-decoration of garments. Bernis indicates that the broiderers enjoyed high esteem in Spain (2001: 282) and their work was considered equivalent to art:

> Es de notar por cosa admirable se labre con una aguja pequeña perfetísima un rostro, mezclando en él cincuenta géneros de sedas todas de una color y cada una diferente. Aventaja en esto a la pintura.
> (Bernis 2001: 282, citing Suárez de Figueroa)

[It is to be noted that a face is worked with a tiny perfect needle as a wonderful thing, mixing in it fifty types of silk, all of the selfsame colour and yet different. In this it has an advantage over art.]

The broiderers undertook work for the cathedral on vestments and altar frontals, with the Church still the principal customer for silk embroidery in the twentieth century (Vicente Conesa 1997: 20).

Enamelling, royal insignia, and the Sorrows of the Virgin

Sor Isabel's tunic has a *cortapisa* or decorative band at hem or cuff.[10] Such bands were often decorated with ermine or with jewels.[11] The *cortapisa* is decorated 'ab singulars esmalts' [with singular small blazons] (fol. 50r;

---

[10] Goldberg mistakenly identifies the *cortapisa* as an overskirt (1984: 384).

[11] See, for example, the *cortapisas* in retables of the Virgin. Bartolomé Bermejo (1440?-98) depicts the *Virgin of Montserrat* in crimson, with a broad ermine *cortapisa* (Acqua Terme, Cathedral of Santa Maria della Assunzione, Sacristy). The Master of Perea depicts the Virgin with a red dress, edged with a gold, red, and black *cortapisa*. The dress is also decorated with tiny pearls at neck and cuff (MBAV 211). His *Adoration of the Magi* has a similar *cortapisa* (Valencia, private collection). It was shown in the MBAV, 1 February-27 April 2009, as part

I, 183), which represented the Sorrows of the Virgin. Marina Warner sets the origins of the Sorrows of the Virgin for her dead Son in the East, with the Laments of Jacob of Sarug († 521). They were adopted in the eleventh century in the West and reached full fruition in the fourteenth century (Warner 1985: 209–10). Rubin details the development of the European Joys tradition and indicates how it developed with a new focus on Mary's distress. From the Central Italian confraternities promoted by the friars it spread to many parts of Europe (2009: 254).

Decoration of garments with enamels was fashionable from the fourteenth century onwards and was another means of establishing dialogue with the observer through clothing (Black 1974: 128). J. Anderson Black's discussion of royal garments indicates that small enamelled pictures also function as insignia (139). Enamelling could combine with embroidery to display either royal or religious coding. David A. Hinton argues that enamelling was particularly desirable for the nobility, since, because of its increasing complexity, it could not readily be imitated by the lower classes (2005: 261).

Literary examples of *smalts* or blazons appear in *Tirant* on the Princess's dress:

> La qual se era devisada en semblant forma: de un brial de domàs groch, les obres del qual eren perfilades per art de molt subtil artifici de robins, diamants, safirs e maragdes qui lançaven molt gran resplandor, e la ampla cortapisa stava sembrada de perles orientals, molt grosses, de fulles e flors de verts smalts qui admirar feyen als miradors.
>
> (Martorell 1990: II, 860)
>
> [A dress of yellow damask, the working of which was skilfully shot through with a very subtle confection of rubies, diamonds, sapphires, and emeralds, which reflected such great resplendence; and the broad decorative border was scattered with enormous oriental pearls with leaves and flowers in green enamels, which amazed all who saw them.]

Sor Isabel's enamel work is not intended to imitate the decorative style of Martorell's.[12] In the *Vita Christi*, at the joyous moment of the Annunciation, the purpose of the enamels is to provide a contrast: 'son pintades totes les dolors de vostra senyoria' [there are painted all the sorrows your Ladyship is to undergo] (fol. 50r; I, 183), for they focus on the sorrows inherent in the joys of the birth of Christ, and act as a *memento mori*. The Sorrows of the Virgin varied in number in the fifteenth century but included events from

---

of the Golden Age of Valencian Art exhibition (Benito Domenech & Gómez Frechina 2009: 192–3, no. 49).

[12] Josep Guia and Curt Wittlin note that *cortapisa* is one of the nine problem areas of *Tirant*, since it is not used in any of the descriptions of dress before ch. 448 (1999: 124).

the Passion and Death of Christ: the Agony in the Garden, the Scourging, the Crowning with Thorns, the *Via Crucis*, the Crucifixion, and the Death of Jesus.

Sanchis y Sivera's transcription of the 1418 inventory provides numerous examples of decorative 'imatges' [pictures] as part of the 'fresaduras' [borders] on church vestments. Listed, for example, are 'altra capa de drap de hor, ab fresadura de ymatges' [another cope in cloth of gold with a border of pictures] and 'una capa de drap de hor vermell, ab fresadura de ymatges' [a cope of red cloth-of-gold with a border of pictures] (1933: 7, 8).

Of 139 items included in the vestments inventory, there are 45 with a border of pictures. In one case, the images are specifically described as being scenes from the life of the Virgin: 'ab ystories de la Salutació, Nativitat, la Maria e son fill, e dos angels, los tres Reys, la Purificació' [with stories from the Annunciation, the Nativity, Mary and her Son with two angels, the Three Kings, and the Purification] (Sanchis y Sivera 1933: 10). The events listed are traditionally ones included in the Joys of the Virgin. Scenes on vestments similar to these could easily have suggested the scenes in Sor Isabel's enamels, even though the Valencia Cathedral copes are embroidered rather than decorated with blazons.

Valuable enamels from the Valencia region indicate that Sor Isabel's could have been inspired by church treasures. A chalice dating from the late fifteenth century and marked with a Valencia stamp, originating from the Parish Church of St John the Baptist at Alcalà de Xivert, has several enamels on the base. One of these shows Christ on the Cross with the Virgin and St John, together with the sun and moon; another is a Pentecost scene; another shows the Virgin with six apostles amid rays of the sun; and, finally, there is a Nativity scene. The enamels are 'champlevée' [raised]. They have lost the inlay but are coloured red, blue, sienna, and green. The chalice may have been commissioned by a royal person, perhaps even María of Castile (Català Gorgues 1982: 22). A magnificent chalice, with three enamels on the base, was manufactured for María de Luna (1357–1416) in Valencia between 1395 and 1406 (MNAC 40425).

Another important example of Valencian enamelwork is the Pere Bernés processional cross from the Colegiata in Jativa which has twelve enamels on the front and fifteen on the back (Català Gorgues 1982: 36). The twelve scenes on the front are from the Passion, such as Christ on the Cross and in Limbo. The fifteen enamels on the back relate to the Joys of the Virgin: the Annunciation, the Nativity, the Adoration of the Kings, and the Purification. This processional cross has been termed 'la más hermosa pieza de orfebrería esmaltada y pictórica del reino de Valencia y aun de todos los estados de Aragón' [the most beautiful piece of enamelled, pictorial gold work in the Kingdom of Valencia and all the lands under the jurisdiction of Aragon] (Tormo 1920: 193). The enamels are of a similar style to those made in important centres of production, such as Limoges or Cologne (Igual Úbeda 1956: 46).

According to Black, the technique of enamelling *en ronde bosse* was new in the fifteenth century and he depicts both a rosary and a brooch using this new raised enamelling technique (1974: 136–7, 143). In this type of enamelling, the figures stand out in relief. It is probable that Sor Isabel is describing inlaid enamels which feature different colours; hers are painted, 'pintades', and depict scenes from the life of Christ and of the Virgin, similar to those in a rosary.

The Sorrows of the Virgin

The Virgin's portrayal as Mater Dolorosa had been the subject of Christian poetry and art from the twelfth century. Artists depicted her as the suffering mother, the Pietà, holding the body of her dead Son in her arms. Poets represented her suffering in her cry of despair at the Cross, giving rise to the *Marienklage* tradition (Pelikan 1996: 125). Her compassion for the crucified Christ was such that she suffered internally what he suffered externally.

Berceo's *El duelo de la Virgen* (1975) is a mid thirteenth-century Hispanic *Marienklage*, with a distinctive canticle, 'Eya velar' [Arise, keep watch]. Pedro Cátedra studies the literary antecedents to Gómez de Ferrol's *cancionero* and its *Santa Pasión del nuestro Redentor e Salvador Ihesú Christo*, providing an overview of how the *planctus* developed between its earliest literary manifestation in Berceo's work through to the fifteenth century (2001; see also Tillier 1985). Richard Donovan discovered that the refrain '*Ay tan greus son nostras dolors*' [Alas, how great is our sorrow] was being used in the thirteenth century in the Kingdom of Aragon, in Majorca, as part of the Passion liturgy (1958: 136; Cátedra 2001: 197). Passions of Christ, such as the *Contemplació de la passió de Nostre Senyor Jesucrist* (Hauf 1982) the *Istòria de la Passió* (Garcia Sempere 2002: 225–416), or the *Contemplació a Jesús crucificat* (Garcia Sempere 2002: 419–46), as well as Roís de Corella's popular fourth volume, the *Lo quart del cartoxà* (1495), were read in Valencia. In her *Vita Christi* Sor Isabel incorporates a lengthy *planctus*, separated into several acts, each following one of the scenes from the Crucifixion, frequently punctuated by the swooning of the Virgin.[13]

Another manifestation of the Virgin of Sorrows was the iconography of the Virgin of the Seven Swords, which supposedly originated in Flanders. The iconography of the Seven Sorrows was being developed in Sor Isabel's

---

[13] See fols 209v–210r, 211r–v, 215v–216r, 216v–217r, 218r–v, 218v–219r, 218v *bis*–219r *bis*, 219r–v, 220r–v; II, 372–4; 377–8; 381–2; 387–8; 389–90; 391–2; 394–5; 396; 399–401.

period. Margaret of Austria founded a convent in Antwerp dedicated to the Virgin of the Seven Swords in 1509. According to Louis Réau, the iconography travelled south through France and the Rhineland from Flanders, where it was first represented at the end of the fifteenth century (1955–59: II, ii, 108–9). There is a representation of the Virgin of the Seven Sorrows by Juan de Juni in the early sixteenth century, that is, shortly after Sor Isabel's death. The Virgen de los Cuchillos [Virgin of the Daggers] is at the centre of a retable for the Church of the Angustias in Valladolid in 1509. However, Réau's theory is challenged by the existence of a poem by Gómez Manrique dedicated to the Virgin 'de los Siete Cuchillos' [of the Seven Daggers] in the mid fifteenth century (Dutton 1990–91: VII, 152, ID3368).

Enumeration of the Sorrows, as opposed to the fixed number of Hours, can range from five to seven, and the English poet John Lydgate has fifteen Sorrows of the Virgin. Rosemary Woolf differentiates between the Hours of the Compassion and the Sorrows of the Virgin, because the latter are drawn from the whole life of the Virgin and include, for example, Simeon's prophecy at the Presentation that the Virgin will be pierced by a sword, in whose words the Virgin assumes her destiny as a true Daughter of Zion. Woolf notes that Sorrows poems are relatively rare, indicating that their extravagant grief was rejected both by the Protestant reformers and by the Counter-Reformation (1968: 269, 272). Joys of the Virgin are much more commonly found in lyric and, as noted in Chapter 4, Lluís Cathalà's poem submitted to the 1474 *certamen* depicts the Virgin dressed in richly decorated garments, including one decorated with an embroidered *cortapisa*: 'y de set goigs brodada cortapisa' [and a border embroidered with Seven Joys] (Ferrando Francés 1983: 309, line 48). Like Sor Isabel's, Cathalà's *cortapisa* is embroidered and its use of the Seven Joys of the Virgin shows that the tradition of such garments and their description was familiar in religious writing.

The Sorrows of the Virgin on the *cortapisa* worn at the Annunciation are a pictorial foretaste of the Passion. Their depiction on the *cortapisa* also points to the way in which the tradition of the Sorrows of the Virgin was developing as a counterpoint to her Joys.

Jewellery as an enhancer of radiant beauty

Sor Isabel emphasizes the enhancement of the Virgin's body with richly decorated fabrics and she includes other jewelled items among the gifts given to the Virgin. Odile Blanc points out that 'there was sudden transformation in manners of dress from the mid fourteenth century', which the author of the *Chronicle of Limbourg* attributes to a sign of renewal after the ravages of the Black Death (2002: 157, 159).

Adornment with jewels and other ornaments is prevalent in earlier Iberian literatures too. In her study of clothing in *Tirant*, Goldberg provides an overview of the subject of dress in medieval Hispanic literature, mentioning scenes from the *Poema de mío Cid*, *Razón de amor*, *Caballero Zifar*, *Libro de Alexandre*, *Amadís de Gaula*, *Libro de buen amor*, and *El Conde Lucanor* (1984: 385–6).

According to J. Huizinga, splendour and adornment reached new heights in the fashion of the late medieval period (1924: 249). Goldberg argues in favour of evidence of the new aesthetic of light, drawing on the descriptions of beautiful adornments in *Tirant* (1984: 383). She cites Huizinga to indicate that a 'fondness for all that glitters reappears in the general gaudiness of dress, especially in the excessive number of precious stones sewed in the garments' (1924: 270). In her study of how medieval ideals of beauty were expressed, Sarah-Grace Heller comments that 'beyond the light-enhancing treatments that could be applied to skin and hair, clothing represents an important medium in this period, allowing light to be caught and reflected over an even larger personal surface area' (2001: 945). Even fabrics, as Margaret Scott shows, could have light-enhancing properties. Her description of the nature of damask (1980: 249) highlights that it is a 'form of satin weave, which uses the free-floating threads on the surface of the satin, alternating the floating threads along the length of the textile and across its width'. In the next chapter I discuss the use of damask in garments gifted to the Virgin. Suffice it to say here that damask proposes an interplay with light, and, for that reason, as well as for that of cost, would be considered appropriate as a fabric to clothe the nobility. Sor Isabel, and contemporary artists, thought it a suitable fabric to adorn the Virgin.

The beauty sought by women through adornment with jewels, gold, silver, enamels, and other light-emitting items often leads to anxiety in their husbands. The Mal Marié in the *Roman de la Rose* is enraged by the glittering hair ornaments his wife affects:

> Que me revalent ces gallandes,
> ces coifes a dorees bandes,
> et ces dïorees treçoërs,
> et ces yvorins miroërs,
> ces cercles d'or bien entailliez
> precieusement esmaillez,
> et ces corones de fin or,
> don enragier ne me fin or,
> tant sunt beles et bien polies,
> ou tant a beles perreries,
> safirs, rubiz et esmeraudes,
> qui si font les chieres baudes

ces fermauz d'or a pierres fines
a voz cous? (Lorris & Meun 1973–6: II, 32, lines 9241–54)

[What are they worth to me,
these headbands,
these gold-banded coifs,
these decorated braiding ribbons,
these ivory mirrors,
these carefully shaped circlets of gold
with precious enamelling,
these crowns of fine gold,
which never cease to enrage me,
so beautiful are they and so well-polished,
which have such rich stones,
sapphires, rubies, and emeralds,
which give your face such a bawdy look
those clasps of gold with fine gems
around your neck?] (partially translated by Heller 2001: 955)

Condemnation of women's glittering accoutrements is a regular element of the writing of male moralists in the fourteenth and fifteenth centuries. According to the Castilian writer Alfonso Martínez de Toledo, the Archpriest of Talavera, the gleaming apparel sought after by women has the double effect of leading observers astray and leading the woman so attired into sin. He displays a surprisingly detailed knowledge of female garments and ornamentation in his condemnation of the woman who dresses to the nines to go to church on Easter Sunday. Many of the features of her outfit are condemned for their high cost or for their excessive size or length, but others are condemned for their effect on the observer, such as the glittering array of jewels, gold work, and fabrics:

> las mangas de brocado; los paternostres de oro de doze en la honça; almanaca de aljófar – ¡de cuento eran los granos!– ; arrancadas de oro que pueblan todo el cuello; crespina de filetes de flor de açucena con mucha argentería la vista me quitavan, un partidor tan rico que es de flor de canell, de filo de oro fino con mucha perlería; los moños con temblantes de oro e de partido cambray, todo trepado de foja de figuera; argentería mucha colgada de lunetas e lenguas de páxaro e retronchetes, e con randas muy ricas [...], axorcas de alanbar engastonadas en oro, sortijas diez o doce, donde ay dos diamantes, un çafir, dos esmeraldas; lúas forradas de martas para dar con el alyendo luzor en la su cara e revenir los afeytes: reluzía como un espada con aquel agua destilada. [...] las cejas algaliadas, reluziendo como espada. (Martínez de Toledo 1985: 130)[14]

---

[14] See translation by Leslie Byrd Simpson (Martínez de Toledo 1959: 110).

[brocade sleeves; gold paternoster beads twelve pounds in weight; necklace of pearls – each one a precious stone of great value; gold chains wound around the neck from top to bottom; hairnets with bands of lilies in silver work so bright it blinds me, a comb so expensive that it is of cinnamon flower; with a snood of fine gold covered all over with pearls; hair clips with gold pins and with a cambray veil, topped with fig leaves;[15] silver jewellery with dangling half moons and birds' tongues, and slides, and with fine lace bands (…), bands of amber set in gold, ten or twelve rings, among them two set with diamonds, one with sapphire, and two with emeralds; leather gloves lined with marten to shine up her face and refresh her cosmetics: (her face) gleamed like a blade with the distilled water she uses. (…) Her brows slathered in musk, shining like a blade.]

Martínez de Toledo takes exception to the glittering array of jewellery and shiny fabrics, because he believes they counterfeit beauty. The light-emitting ornaments include all the woman's gold chains, rings, and necklaces, as well as her silver combs. In order to make herself more beautiful, the woman even polishes her skin; she rubs up her face, spritzing it with water to make her beauty all the more bright. On two occasions, he uses the dangerous metaphor of gleaming like a blade to describe her features. First, after spraying with distilled water, it is her face that is likened to a blade, and then her brows, when they have been moulded into shape with musk. In this way, he emphasizes the dangers posed for observers. He compares the woman's face to a sword with its phallic suggestiveness, as well as its ability to mesmerize and to kill. Martínez's emphasis on blades also points to the unnaturalness of excessive adornment and underpins the way in which the counterfeit luminescent beauty displayed by the object of his opprobrium has been achieved with the assistance of an excessive number of adornments and with cosmetic arts. The steps and lengths to which women go to achieve the luminescent look are decried.

He also remarks on the many dangling ornaments from the churchgoer's necklaces and headdress. Scott indicates that spangles or dangles hanging from headdresses were common in the mid fifteenth century, in Europe at least. She comments on the women in the La Tremoille family who had silver-gilt spangles (*paillettes*) hanging from their hoods with six double links per spangle (1980: 249).[16] The dangling half moons and tongues described by Guillaume de Lorris are similar to the ones displayed in French fashion of

---

[15] Translated as 'linen' by Simpson.

[16] Disappointingly, despite the title of her book, *Late Gothic Europe, 1400–1500*, Scott concentrates on France, England, Germany, and the Netherlands. Spanish dress is not mentioned or illustrated.

the period. Whilst the dangling charms may have been light-emitters, they would also have created sound as the wearer moved. Scott indicates that aural display was fashionable from the late fourteenth century onward. She notes that dress began clinking, as well as swishing, as early as 1389, when the Duke of Touraine acquired a *chayenne d'or à sonnettes* – a gold chain with bells – and in the following year the king and the duke went hunting in gowns (robes), to which twelve small gold and silver bells had been attached by gold ribbon. She associates the tinkling sounds with riding. She also cites from *Le dit de la pastoure* of 1403, in which the shepherdess is amazed by the tinkling sounds emitted by the sashes of the knight's attendants:

> escharpes qui bel et gent
> Leur estoient avenans,
> Dont les cliquetes sonnans
> Tout le boys retentissoient
> Pour les sons qui en yssoient.
>
> [sashes which were beautiful and became them, with the whole wood echoing to the noise which rang out from their tinkling trinketry.]

Scott also notes that bells were used on horse harnesses to 'enable the knight to spread terror'. She does not address the use of sound-emitters in female dress (1980: 83).

Martínez de Toledo's anxieties were replicated in the sumptuary laws which were brought in by the end of the fourteenth century to limit the use of glittering silks, brocades, jewellery, and embroideries (see also Chapter 6). Rosaries, unlike the one used by Martínez de Toledo's churchgoing beauty, should not be made of gold or of pearls (Astor Landete 1999: 89). A sumptuary law passed at the Corts of Morvedre in 1428 stipulated the penalties for using over-expensive rosary beads: 'que las mujeres usasen paternosters que valian mas de 500 sueldos so pena de 200 y de perder aquéllos' (Sanchis y Sivera 1922: 4).

Wearing jewellery was extremely fashionable in fifteenth-century Spain and, depending on the perspective of the observer, could be read positively. Goldberg does not refer to *cancionero* poetry among her examples of dress and jewels in her overview of Castilian literature, although in the *Poem the Marqués Wrote to his Daughters*, the poet, ostensibly the Marqués de Santillana, provides details of the beauty and dress of his daughters. Their gold, silver, and gleaming jewels are not dissimilar to those decried by his contemporary, Martínez de Toledo. He approvingly notes the gold and silver bracelets, which he considers appropriate adornments for a daughter of an important nobleman. In praising them, Santillana is indirectly promoting his own ability to adorn his daughters in such a magnificent manner:

> Blancas manos e pulidas
> [...]
> uñas de argén guarnidas:
> rubíes e margaridas,
> çafires e diamantes,
> axorcas ricas, sonantes
> todas de oro labradas. (Santillana 2003: 103, lines 29, 32–6)
>
> [Hands white and beautiful,
> nails decorated with silver:
> rubies and pearls,
> sapphires and diamonds,
> magnificent tinkling bracelets,
> all worked in gold.]

The shiny whiteness of his daughters' skin, 'pulidas'[beautiful, see Corominas and Pascual 1980–91: IV, 688), prized by Santillana, is what the churchgoing woman described by Martínez de Toledo is seeking to achieve with her marten-lined gloves which she uses to touch up her face. It is not only the proliferation of jewels which make the hands of the noble Mendoza girls catch the light, but their skin is so white and beautiful that it too is luminescent. The Mendozas are also surrounded by the fashionable tinkle of jewellery like Martínez de Toledo's young woman.

Goldberg notes that jewels are luminescent and contribute to the medieval ideal of beauty. Rubies, pearls, emeralds, sapphires, and diamonds decorate the clothing of Carmesina in *Tirant* (Goldberg 1984: 384). The jewellery presented to the Virgin incorporates the same stones: pearls, rubies, diamonds, and emeralds. Sapphires are only mentioned once in *Tirant* and not at all in the *Vita Christi*. Sor Isabel is aware of their light-emitting properties and she shows this through her interpretation. The five strings of pearls 'la puritat de vostra mundísima pensa ha clarejat e clareja continuament' [the purity of your pure, pure thinking has gleamed and continues to gleam] (fol. 49r; I, 179).[17]

Sor Isabel does not, however, refer to the fashionable tinkling of jewel-

---

[17] Luminescence is associated with the Virgin in many medieval devotional works. See, for example, the *Corona Beatissime Virginis* by Pseudo-Ildephonse, to be discussed in more detail in Chapter 8: 'Tu sapientie et virtutis candida luce radians, horridas temporum tenebras virtutum fulgore fugasti' [Radiating bright light of wisdom and virtue, you dispel the gloom of centuries with the brilliance of your virtue]. The theme recurs throughout the devotional work, so that the Virgin is hailed as 'purissima, tota splendida, tota candida, tota rutilans, tota mundissima' [most pure, all splendid, all bright, all gleaming, all spotless] (BNE, MS 17674, fols 9v, 14r).

lery. This is one indication that it is not feminine style which was her prime motive.

The Virgin's jewels are like the contemporary ones depicted in Valencian art, as I have shown previously, suggesting that Sor Isabel was also inspired by the representations of the Virgin she had seen. The Master of Perea in the *Adoration of the Kings* (MBAV 292) (fig. 14) depicts the Virgin wearing a dress with a gold *cortapisa* edged with pearls.[18] Reixach's *Triptych of the Virgin and Child* (MBAV 294) also shows a gold-embroidered *cortapisa* at the hem (fig. 9).

Whilst artists adorned the Virgin with finery which displayed the wealth of patrons, as well as the worthiness of the Virgin, devotional writers chose equally fine allegorical jewels. The *Corona Beatissime Virginis*, a meditation on the crown of the Virgin, to be examined in more detail in Chapter 8, is a good example of Franciscan focus on jewels, light symbolism, and the perfection of the Virgin in both body and soul.

Conclusion

The interest Sor Isabel displays in embroidery, jewellery, and adornment of the Virgin is present not because she wishes to set before her nuns a display of fashionable items for their delectation and to carry them in the imaginary finery back to their pre-convent days. Comparison of the embroideries and jewels displayed in contemporary art, inventories, and poetry with Sor Isabel's reveals that there is more at stake than an interest in fashion. Royal insignia on display at the nuptials of the kings and queens of Aragon are deliberately recalled by Sor Isabel in her description of the gifted items, but, in addition, many of the decorative items she describes bear a close relationship to ecclesiastical embroideries. Not only does she follow artistic tradition in her adornment of the Virgin but she is a keen observer of their colour and decoration.

The decorative emblems have important information to provide about the place of the Virgin in salvation history. The lily embeds the Virgin's betrothal in the aching expressions of love of the Song of Songs but also evokes the doctrine of the Immaculate Conception. The *agnus castus* embroidery has a message about the Virgin's virginity and also points to the vision of glory in Revelation.

I have shown how descriptions of contemporary jewellery and hair ornaments value the sounds they emitted. In the world of silence inside the

---

[18] Reixach regularly shows the Virgin in the richest of brocades. Another example is the cloak of dark gold, edged with a jewelled pattern of pearls and a single ruby (MEV 4665).

Trinitat convent, Sor Isabel makes no mention of the tinkling jewellery. The beauty Sor Isabel describes is visual only, just like the statues and images of the Virgin which the nuns saw around them in the convent church.

The shiny stones and gold accoutrements gleam to signal that the Virgin fulfilled all the norms of beauty of the day. The beautiful jewels suggest the radiant beauty of the Virgin. For it was even less permissible for Sor Isabel than for Santillana to note any of the personal attributes of the Virgin. The embroideries, fabrics, and jewels all serve to emphasize to the nuns that Mary's body, although it was adorned, was not corrupted by anything. The boundaries of the *contemptus mundi* are redrawn.

The decoration of the garments and of the Virgin's body recalls the prophecy of Isaiah about God's provision for his people. The prophet cries out his Magnificat: 'My soul rejoices in my God', a prefiguration of Mary's Annunciation canticle: 'He wraps Israel in a cloak, like a bride adorned in her jewels' (Isaiah 61. 10). Mary, her body prepared through immaculacy, is adorned as the Bride of Christ, and the one who will become Queen of Heaven.

6

The Fabric of Society: Dressing, Undressing, and Gifting in Sor Isabel's Writing

This chapter will address how the fabric of the garments accorded to the Virgin equips her to become Queen. I will set the discussion in the context of how members of the nobility were wont to display their wealth through their garments, since it signalled their rank to observers and, thus, initiated a discourse about the stratification of society. Ronald A. Schwartz contends that demonstration of social hierarchy through clothing is one of its principal, original functions (1979: 27; see also Cordwell & Schwartz 1979). Significantly, Susan L'Engle notes in her study of costume as it appears in legal documents, that 'marriage and its associated nuptials provided another excuse for concocting an elaborate visual scenario' and this included the garments and their part in 'constructing a visual identity' (2002: 138, 141).[1]

In anthropological terms, use of fabric was a way of establishing a 'differentiation from others' on the basis of dress (Roach & Eicher 1979: 9), and this was particularly true in respect of rare fabrics and embellishments such as ermines or jewels. Rarity can also relate to colour, as established in Chapter 4. Fabric, like the clothes it was made up into, acted as a 'visual indicator of social status' (Duits 1999: 73). It can be argued that fabrics are one of the principal constituents of the discourse established by clothing.

In medieval times it was believed that the wearing of clothing was not only an external representation of the inner self but also that, through clothing, the inner self was constructed, because clothing was thought to imprint its characteristics on the wearer (Jones & Stallybrass 2000: 4). Medieval readers would have been skilled in reading the symbols represented by clothing and by how it was embellished and by the fabrics of which it was made. They would have been capable of interpreting Sor Isabel's scenes describing the robing of the Virgin and why she chose to emphasize particular fabrics.

In their chapter 'The Currency of Clothing', Ann Rosalind Jones and Peter Stallybrass examined records of pawnbrokers from Pistoia in Italy,

---

[1] For study of clothing and its retelling of identity, see also Koslin & Snyder 2002.

beginning in the fourteenth century, and they show that in 1417 clothing made up almost 60% of pledges (2000: 30). Clothing was also valuable as a method of payment. Presenting a retainer or courtier with second-hand clothing was an acceptable manner of rewarding him for his services. As Jones and Stallybrass note, 'clothes and jewels were an exchange currency, even for the rich' (29).

In the fourteenth century, clothing was valued as a payment or gift, even when it had been previously worn. Gifts and reminding a patron about them form the subject of a number of Alfonso Álvarez de Villasandino's poems in the *Cancionero de Baena*. The poet is not a wealthy man, although he moves in court circles, and he makes constant requests for gifts from his noble patrons in payment for his poetic services. Many of them are for items of clothing, although he did at different times request other things, such as a mule in order to be able to attend the coronation of Fernando de Antequera, and later a saddle and bridle for the mule he was given (Dutton & González Cuenca 1993: nos 65 and 77). Gifted clothing was normally from the donor's own wardrobe and would have been previously worn by him. Whilst the poet might appear importunate to modern eyes, there was clearly nothing untoward in his reminders to his patrons that they honour their promise to him. For example, Villasandino requests a garment from one of the most important nobles in Castile, Pero López de Ayala, in a poem dated 1407, and makes it clear that he is expecting to receive a hand-me-down: 'Pero en espeçial, señor, me mandastes / –non sé si vos miembra, una vuestra ropa' [But particularly, sir, you promised me / one of your garments, I am not sure you remember it] (Dutton & González Cuenca 1993: no. 102, lines 17–18). In another of his poems, Villasandino reminds Enrique III of Castile that his Christmas gift has still not been delivered and he indicates that several garments would be acceptable:

> Señor lo que vos demando
> es alguna gentil ropa,
> balandrán, galdrapa, opa,
> con que me vaya preçiando. (1993: no. 59, lines 5–8)

> [My lord, what I am requesting from you
> is some high-class clothes
> cape, breeches, and coat,
> so I may look well.]

Villasandino's poems indicate that, in Castile too, gifts of clothing, particularly items that had one previous noble owner, were valued by the recipient and that clothing was a currency for paying for services. Natalie Zemon Davis (2000: 89) points to the way in which 'dons' [gifts] were a mixture of 'wages, pensions, and gifts'. She distinguishes 'dons' from other payments because they are irregular and because they 'bind the officer in his duty in gratitude'.

Sometimes Villasandino specifies that he would prefer not to receive a hand-me-down which had been 'desdoblada' [let down or had the lining removed]:

> Que ya bien saben en toda Castilla
> vuestra gran honra e brío que avedes,
> e bien saben todos que vos non traedes
> ropa ninguna que sea senzilla.
> Por ende, sería a mí grant manzilla,
> si de vos oviesse ropa desdoblada,
> pero más vale algo que no nada. (1993: no. 102, lines 25–31)

> [For your great honour and importance
> are well known in all Castile,
> and everyone knows you do not wear
> any unlined clothing.
> For that reason it would be shameful to me
> if you gave me a well-worn (or let down) garment
> but anything is better than nothing.]

Davis notes how remaking of garments to provide gifts for others was common practice (2000: 51). Such garments could be turned into 'signifying gifts', with women's dresses being remade into cloaks and other items for men to wear.

Villasandino's petitions do not go unremarked by other court poets in the *Cancionero de Baena*. When Villasandino requests some clothes from King Fernando to go to his coronation (1993: no. 66), his request is picked up by Ferrant Manuel de Lando, whose reply is dedicated to the description of the putative gifted garment. Manuel de Lando's tone is gentle, and he parallels the value of the clothing to that of the poetry which Villasandino has delivered:

> Si ropa vos fue mandada
> por este gentil señor,
> creed que será enforrada,
> en peña de grant valor. (1993: no. 67, lines 10–13)

> [If clothing were sent to you
> by that noble Lord,
> be sure it will be lined
> with fur of great value.]

The value of items of clothing in medieval Valencia is borne out by the way they are included in inventories of household goods. In one of these, carried out by the Guild of Cordwainers for a deceased member, items which are unworn and ones which still have wear in them are given particular mention: 'Item altra camisa de llí mijantexa no molt usada' [item another similar linen shirt not very worn], 'Item una altra camisa nova de llí' [item another new linen shirt] (ARV, Gremis, Perg. 72, *Inventari dels béns de Joan Cetina*).

Appeals over clothing were even made to the monarch. Records show that King Joan of Aragon ruled in favour of the Countess of Castro and Denia in 1455 when she wanted to retrieve personal items of clothing, 'robes de vestir' [good dresses], from her chamber, following the death of her husband, Diego Gómez de Sandoval (ARV, Real Justicia, MS 275, fol. 184). His heirs had appropriated all her belongings, even her dresses. The King's decree establishes that the dresses are her personal property, part of her dowry, and that they should not be included within the property bequeathed by the Count to his heirs. The fact that the heirs disputed the ownership of the dresses shows their value. The Guild inventory, the Countess's claim, and Villasandino's poem show that clothing, even when it was second-hand, or even a little threadbare, was still perceived as valuable.

Clothing and jewellery was frequently part of women's dowries. For example, when Blaia Pol married Joan Ferrer in 1498, her parents, Jaume and Antònia, sent a dowry consisting of a 'cofre de roba, vestits i joies' [a chest of clothing, dresses, and jewels], as well as a payment of sixty pounds (BC, Registre 180123, Perg. 235). Similarly, when Aldonça married Berbat Sala in December 1466, her father, Bartomeu Vilar de San Andreu de Vallgorguina presented a chest of clothing, dresses, and jewels to her husband (BC, Registre 18034, Perg. 237).

Villasandino's pleas for garments from his patrons assist in determining what was of value to him. The principal qualities he sought are that the clothes should be 'gentil' and he particularly emphasizes that they should be lined, as befits a nobleman's clothing. In another of petition poems, he claims, in a play on words, that his poverty can be discerned in the garments he wears: 'ya es mi vista doblada / e mi ropa toda senzilla' [now I'm seeing double/lined but my clothes are simple/unlined] (Dutton & González Cuenca 1993: no. 63, lines 17–18). Villasandino's counterpointing of his ageing vision and blurred sight with his unlined clothing, 'doblada' and 'senzilla', reveals how important is the outer display of clothing to life at court, with particular store set on wearing lined clothing.

When Sor Isabel describes the cloak presented to the Virgin Mary by St Michael, she is careful to ensure that its quality corresponds to God's betrothed. The cloak is of magnificent brocade, lined with green damask, a garment far more exceptional than any seen at court: 'lo qual és de un brocat blau de tanta magnificència que jamés reyna ni emperadriu l'à portat ni portarà semblant' [which is of blue brocade of such magnificence that queen nor empress has never nor ever will wear one like it] (fol. 50r; I, 184).

Like the gifted garments Villasandino requests, the Virgin is offered gifts of clothing. Behind the action of soliciting a gift, or being accorded one without asking, of receiving a gift, or exchanging gifts is a whole edifice of cultural relationships. According to Susan Crane, gifting can lead to subordination or alliance, it can stratify parties or bind them up, depending on the nuances of its deployment (2002: 21). Villasandino's petitions for gifts set him in a subordinate role to his patron. In the *Vita Christi*, the clothing and jewellery gifted to the Virgin seem to belong to the narrative scene-setting. However, the marital alliance between God and humanity is cemented through the gifts the Virgin is given. Her reception of them places her in a position of subordination, since there is no reciprocal exchange.

The Virgin's situation mirrors other medieval betrothal stories, such as that of Griselda, who is clothed by her lord for her wedding and then stripped by him when she is cast off (Crane 2002: 29, 34). Crane notes that Griselda's

> reclothing by Walter is [...] a material endorsement. In the first place it is an appropriate sign for their virilocal union – so appropriate that dressing the bride was a traditional responsibility of husbands in fourteenth-century Italy. (2002: 33)

The same material endorsement comes into play in the case of the Virgin. All the clothes and all the jewels she is to wear are chosen by her benefactor, who dresses the bride according to tradition. Her nuptial dressing also represents the way that her will has become obedient to his in her assent to the betrothal. She is to be clothed from head to foot by the generosity of God the Father, which, in medieval terms, signals her obligation. Her re-clothing places her firmly within God's retinue. Accepting clothing from another also implied a transfer of identity from donor to recipient. By accepting the clothing, the Virgin takes on some of the aspects of the donor's nature (Weiner 1992).

The receptivity of Mary in the gifting scene is also to be understood in terms of the representation of the Incarnation in terms of everyday processes Sister Prudence Allen refers to the dynamic process of knitting which is how Julian of Norwich sought to explain the theology of the Incarnation. She uses the analogy to show how Jesus's human nature was connected to the Holy Trinity, and secondly how his soul was knit to his body when he was conceived in his Mother Mary (1997–2002: I, 409). The image of Christ's body being clothed in flesh by Mary was not found only in women's writing but was an oft repeated theological concept (see Chapter 2).

Sor Isabel's concentration on clothing Mary's body in fine fabrics is an outward sign of the invisible inner clothing of God the Son in flesh in her womb. The clothing is sacramental, in that it represents an outward sign of an unseen mystery. It is also eucharistic, because it consists of an outer material substance indicating spiritual reception of the body of Christ. In chapter 35, Sor Isabel already introduced the view that Mary's conception of the Son of God required her body to be attired in a golden dress. For, according to Humility:

> *Consurge, consurge, induere vestimentis glorie tue, quia ecce jam venit plenitudo temporis in quo misit Deus filium suum in terris.* Volent dir: 'Levau, levau, Senyora: vestiu-vos les excel·lents robes de humilitat ab les quals vos acostumau de arrear en les grans solemnitats vostres, en les quals vestidures stà brodada e devisada tota la glòria vostra.'
> (fol. 44; I, 161–2)

> [*Arise, arise, put on garments of your glory, for behold now is come the fullness of time in which God sends his Son to earth,* meaning: 'Arise, arise, Lady, put on the excellent garments of humility which you are accustomed to wear in your great celebrations. These dresses are embroidered and emblazoned with all your glory.']

Sor Isabel expands the Latin text to counterpoint humility and glory. The garments of glory become those of humility.

The use of fine fabric to clothe Mary's body is also prefigured by a number of Old Testament allegories. Sor Isabel most probably had in mind the words of Isaiah, cited in Chapter 5, about the bride and bridegroom, which are echoed in the Magnificat, as she constructs her gifting scene:

> I exult for joy in Yahweh,
> my soul rejoices in my God,
> for he has clothed me in garments of salvation,
> he has wrapped me in a cloak of saving justice,
> like a bridegroom wearing his garland,
> like a bride adorned in her jewels. (Isaiah 61. 10)

She also associates Mary's robing with that of the Princess of Tyre, adorned with jewels and brocade garments, so that the king may 'fall in love with [her] beauty': 'Clothed in brocade, the king's daughter is led within / to the king with the maids of her retinue' (Psalm 45. 15). Sor Isabel's scene at the betrothal of the Virgin incorporates two elements of the psalm, the brocade garments and the presence of the handmaids:

> Ab aquesta vestidura vos contemplava David mirant vostra altesa en sperit, e per ço dix: *Astitit regina a dextris tuis in vestitu deaurato circundata varietate;* volent dir: 'O, Senyor!, e com stà gloriosa aquesta reyna per vostra magestat elegida en mare del unigènit fill vostre, ab la vesti-

dura daurada de aquell tan singular or de profunda humilitat, embellida e circuÿda de totes les virtuts! Aquesta roba, Senyora, és molt pròpria per a la present jornada, car sia certa vostra mercé que ja és venguda la plenitut del temps tan desijat en lo qual lo pare eternal, nostre Senyor Déu, delliberà trametre lo Fill seu en la terra.' (fol. 44; I, 162)

[With those garments David gazed on your Highness in spirit, and for that reason said: *The queen is seated at your right hand in a dress of brocade surrounded by a host*; meaning: 'O Lord and how glorious is that queen chosen as mother of your only son, with a gilded dress of such singular gold of deep humility, embellished and encircled by all the virtues. That dress, Lady, is most appropriate for today, for your Ladyship should be certain that now the longed for fullness of time has come when the eternal father, our Lord God, is minded to send his Son on earth.']

Sor Isabel acknowledges that she is reworking the words of the psalm, but when she associated Mary with special garments to mark the dawn of salvation, she also recalls Ezekiel's prophecy. In order to symbolize Jerusalem's relationship to God through the allegory of a young woman being groomed for love, the prophet reworks Psalm 45. His description of the lady includes how she puts on embroidered dresses, fine leather shoes, and a cloak of silk, as well as jewels, bracelets, and a beautiful diadem (Ezekiel 16. 9–14): 'You were loaded with gold and silver and dressed in linen, silk, and brocade'. The text from Ezekiel continues with a declaration about the lady's perfection:

> You grew more and more beautiful and you rose to be queen. The fame of your beauty spread through the nations, since it was perfect, because I had clothed you with my own splendour – declares the Lord Yahweh.
> (Ezekiel 16. 13–14)

However, unlike Mary, Jerusalem betrays the trust of her Lord and becomes a whore. Mary, in her association with the Second Adam, contributes to the New Creation and does not betray God's trust.

There are therefore a number of occasions on which Old Testament texts inspire Sor Isabel. The Virgin is presented with garments of brocade, twice with brocade cloaks. Her attendant ladies, who personify aspects of her personality, are also clothed in brocade:

> Misericòrdia se era vestida de brocat carmesí, per mostrar la gran fervor de amor que portava. E Pietat portava la roba sua de brocat vert, per mostrar la gran sperança ab què anava de obtenir la sua demanda.
> (fol. 17r; I, 282)

> [Pity was dressed in crimson brocade to show the great fervour of love she bore. And Piety wore her dress of green brocade to show the great hope she had of obtaining what she demanded.]

'Domàs', or damask, is mentioned twice, both times as the lining of the cloak. Silk cloth is mentioned only once as a chemise (see Chapter 5). It is also the fabric of preference in the *Vita Christi* when Christ's feet are washed and dried with the hair of Mary Magdalene and wiped with a towel (fol. 120r; II, 105). All the instances in which silk, brocade, or damask are used to clothe the Virgin occur in the scenes following the Annunciation, when her earthly body must be fittingly arrayed for the heavenly alliance she is making.

Brocade and female beauty in the Peninsula

Santillana's *Poem [...] to his Daughters, Praising their Beauty*, discussed in Chapters 4 and 5, also provides evidence of how rich fabrics are used in the description of feminine beauty. Goldberg noted in her study of Martorell's techniques that his interest in describing his characters did not go much beyond depiction of their clothing. Her words about Martorell's description techniques could almost apply to Santillana's daughters:

> Parenthetically, it should be noted that he did not make a similar effort when describing the physical traits of any of these elegant people. Carmesina's portrait is the standard rhetorical praise of a beautiful woman. (1984: 384)

Modern sensibility, to which Goldberg alludes, would require attention to be paid to the person rather than the clothing, but because in the late medieval period the clothes are the person and imprint themselves upon their character, medieval priorities are the opposite of modern ones. Further, Heller shows how, in relation to the *Roman de la Rose*, with conclusions which could be applied to *Tirant*, reliance on dress to establish personification is particularly important: 'Costume, in this instance and others, was cleverly considered a vehicle for the expression of inner nature' (2001: 945).

The pen-portrait of Santillana's daughters dedicates the majority of verses to minute details about their costly headdresses and the fine fabrics they are wearing. The poem, like medieval portraits, is 'as much a record of costly clothing as of their subjects' (Jones & Stallybrass 2000: 32). Of course, since Santillana has clothed the girls from his purse, their costly garments also serve to promote his ability to provide them:

> Ropas traen a sus guisas
> todas fendidas por rayas

do les paresçen sus sayas
forradas de peñas grisas;
de martas e ricas sisas
sus ropas bien asentadas,
de azeituní, quartonadas
de filo de oro brocadas. (Santillana 2003: 103, lines 37–44)

[They each wear clothes as they please,
all slashed
to show their tunics,
lined with grey ermine;
with marten and rich fabrics.
Their dresses are well fitted
with oriental fabric, divided into sections,
brocaded with gold thread.]

The daughters' garments are lined with furs, including ermine and marten of the highest quality, as befits the nobility (see Sousa Congosto 2007: 74). The fabrics they wear include the exotic 'azeituní' from the Arabic word *zaituni*, a fabric from the town of Tseuthung in the Far East. It is a velvet fabric, normally olive green in colour (Astor Landete 1999: 124). Santillana's daughters also wear brocade, in which he specifically mentions the gold thread. The luminosity of the fabric ensures that the daughters are shining and so that they conform to medieval standards of beauty. In the same way, the Virgin in her golden brocades should be seen as physically perfect.

Recent studies of the symbolic meaning of exterior display show that women's luxury dress and the bodies wearing it exist in a 'dynamic relation'. Jane E. Burns contests that dressed-up women are subjects who deploy clothes as an 'important currency of courtly exchange' (2002: 16). Because of the exotic origins of the jewels, silks, and precious metals, their bodies also become cultural crossing places.

Rembrandt Duits discusses the price of gold thread-work in his study of brocade fabrication and possession in fifteenth-century Florence. He examines examples of silk cloth woven with gold threads in Florentine paintings and argues that the higher the thread count the more sumptuous the fabric. Mention of 'filo de oro' [gold thread] immediately sets Santillana's daughters among the highest-ranking nobles. However, Duits's research strikes a cautionary note. One of his main conclusions is that many of the rich fabrics were an invention, even though in Florence, as in Spain, brocades and silks of that calibre were being produced. He indicates that painted gold brocade was aspirational rather than representing a copy of actual fabrics, arguing that display of riches in painted form enhanced the standing of a patron just as much as possessing them in reality (1999: 84). Santillana's daughters might also have been arrayed in literary 'aspirational' fabrics and dress styles. In Spain brocade garments in Moorish style were certainly owned by royal women. Francisco de Sousa Congosto notes the 'saya encordada' [corded gown] of Leonor de Castilla (?-1244). The dress is of Moorish brocade in silk of a greenish hue. It has threads of gold. The dress is decorated with geometric patterns in Moorish style (2007: 76, fig. 18). Perhaps because of the long tradition of producing silks in Moorish Spain, it should be argued that the brocades described were not just aspirational and that a noble grandee of Spain, like Santillana, would have possessed them. In any case the effect on the reader is the same.

The rich fabrics the Virgin wears may have pointed to the fabulous wealth of patrons who commissioned the paintings. However, the Church did possess such cloth, made into copes and other ecclesiastical robes, and it may have been those garments used on high feast days which inspired both the artists' and Sor Isabel's description of the fabrics the Virgin wears.

As noted in Chapter 5, there were sumptuary laws attempting to restrict the use of gold fabrics to the highest echelons of society, in the Kingdom of Aragon as in other parts of Europe. They were passed from the thirteenth century onwards. The first sumptuary law in Valencia was included in the municipal charter. The law of 1383 was passed to restrict the excessive use of gilded or silver fabrics. Townspeople should wear neither brocades nor silks with gold and silver threads. The same law prohibited the use of pearls or precious stones or gold embroidery or any other decoration containing gold, silver, or silk on clothes, ties, shoes, or any other accessory (Astor Landete 1999: 87–8). In the 1498 Cortes, a prohibition was brought in to prevent those of any estate from wearing garments with decoration in silk, gold, or silver. There was a tax on wearing items of clothing made of brocade or silk; neither could silk chamlet, a costly Eastern fabric with a nap, originating from the Arabic word *khamlat* (Little, Fowler, & Poulson 1962: 254), terzanel (heavy, high-quality silk fabric), or taffeta be used in scabbards or on bridles. Silk embroidery, plated, drawn, or spun gold and silver decoration was also forbidden (Astor Landete 1999: 96).

Queen Isabel and King Fernando issued a royal edict in 1494 in an attempt to prevent the wearing of costly imported fabrics:

> Our subjects and native-born have forgotten all respect and exceeded all rule in their gowns (*ropas*) and suits of clothes (*trajes*), and also in their trimmings (*guarniciones*) and horse trappings (*jaeces*) [...], with the result that, in order to satisfy their appetites and conceits many squander their revenues, whilst others sell, pawn, and consume their capital and inheritances and revenues [...] in order to buy brocades, cloths of drawn gold, and embroideries of gold and silver for their own wear and even their horses and mules [...]. There is another universal damage to our kingdom in that commonly these brocades and cloths of drawn gold are brought

hither by foreigners, who take out of our kingdoms the gold and silver they obtained by their sales. [...] Therefore we prohibit and command that in this present year [1494] [...] and in the two following [...] no one shall presume to bring in or introduce into these our kingdoms from outside [woolen] cloths or any pieces whatsoever of brocade, satin, or velvet (*pelo*) or gold or silver cloth. (Anderson 1979: 140)

Sor Isabel is making a statement about the nature of the Virgin when she arrays her in garments with thread-of-gold, but she was not alone in doing so. In the fourteenth and fifteenth centuries, in Valencian art, all aspects of the Virgin's life, from her Annunciation through her lactation and her depiction as the Virgin of Humility to her death, are bedecked in splendour, with the richest of fabrics, and the most precious of jewels depicted. Significantly, humility and brocaded garments are not incompatible.

Valencia has many examples of retables of the Virgin attired in gold brocades of the highest thread counts, and, whether real or imagined, such fabrics had an impact on the public present in Church. The Master of Perea's *Adoration of the Magi* (MBAV 292) (fig. 14) depicts her wearing a splendid brocade cloak in thread-of-gold on black, equivalent in value to the cloth worn by the visiting Magi. Falcó, in his *Triptych of the Virgin and Child* (Fig. 9), and Reixach, among other artists from the Valencian school, depicts the Virgin wearing gold brocade in his *Annunciation*. In a different episode from the life of the Virgin, her Dormition, the Virgin is also attired in gold brocade.[2] Sor Isabel is no different from Valencian artists in depicting rich brocades to mark different moments in the Virgin's life (see Twomey 2007b), but the richest of cloths is reserved in her writing for the preparations for the Coronation of the Virgin:

> E girant-se lo dit sanct Miquel a un àngel que de prop li stava ab un gran bací d'or molt singular en què venia un excel·lentíssim manto, e prenint-lo lo gloriós príncep, presentà·l a la Mare de Déu, dient: 'Sereníssima e ínclita Senyora: sia de vostra mercé abrigar-se aquest manto en aquesta tan excel·lent festa, car és molt propi per a la present jornada, en la qual vostra senyoria se té ha presentat davant lo consistori de la sanctíssima Trinitat per rebre guardó de les penes e dolors que en la mortal vida haveu sostengudes ab invincible paciència. Lo dit manto, Senyora, és de puríssim or, per divinal potència obrat, passant totes les bellees que per enteniment humà se poden pensar. (fol. 309v; III, 350)

---

[2] Master of Perea, MBAV 211, and Falcó, MBAV, 294; see also his *Triptych of the Virgin and Child*, in the Colección Varez Fisa, Madrid, reproduced in Benito Domenech & Gómez Frechina 2009: 202–3; Reixach, MEV 4660 and MBAV 292.

[And St Michael, turning to an angel who was close by him with a huge and very singular gold salver on which there was a most excellent mantle, and, taking it, the glorious prince presented it to the Mother of God, saying: 'Most serene and exceptional Lady: may your Ladyship clothe herself in this mantle on such an excellent feast for it is proper to today, the day when your Ladyship has to present herself before the consistory of the most holy Trinity to receive your reward for the pain and sorrows which in your mortal life you have endured with invincible patience. The mantle is of purest gold, Lady, worked by the hand of God, beyond all the beauties which can be imagined by human understanding.]

As the Virgin is about to be crowned Queen of Heaven, Sor Isabel clothes her in cloth of pure gold. The thread count she envisages is beyond human workmanship, ensuring that Mary is to be clothed in a garment which is so exceptional and valuable as to fit a denizen of heaven. The garment now presented to the Virgin surpasses the silk and brocade ones with which she was presented at the Annunciation. Their exceptional nature, something beyond what human hands can make, is a feature of other medieval stories. For example in the *Roman de la rose ou de Guillaume de Dole*, Queen Lienor's wedding garment is described as worked by fairy hands, and 'not made by human hands' (lines 5350–1, cited in Burns 2009: 97). Although Sor Isabel's context is very different, she draws on the same theme.

In her description of the mantle, Sor Isabel emphasizes its appropriateness for the feast day. The Assumption is one of the five great feasts of the Spanish Church, ranked alongside Christmas, Easter, Pentecost, and the Ascension. By 1452, evidence from Huesca diocese, in the northern part of the Kingdom of Aragon, shows that two Marian feasts were ranked as principal feasts, the Assumption and the Visitation. However, given that all the feasts are listed in order of their date in the calendar with the exception of the Visitation, which is listed out of sequence, it is probable that the Visitation was an addition:

> Redoble mayor es quando se dizen las an[tiphon]as todas ante et post psalmos et las de magnificat et b[e]n[edictu]s tres uegadas et medianos una uegada. E son las que se siguen. Natiuitas d[omi]ni, Epiphania, Resurrectio d[omi]ni, Pentecostes, Ascensio, Corpus, et Transfiguratio d[omi]ni, Assumptio b[ea]te Marie, Uisitatio b[ea]te Marie.]
> (Huesca, Archivo de la Catedral, MS 21, fol. 88r)

> [High fcast day is when antiphons before and after the Psalms, Magnificat, and Benedictus are said three times and ordinary feast days, once. The high feasts are: Christmas, Epiphany, Easter, Pentecost, Ascension, Corpus Christi, the Transfiguration, and the Assumption and Visitation of the Blessed Virgin.]

In the neighbouring diocese of Urgell, the Assumption was also the principal Marian feast. According to the *Consueta urgellense* [Book of Custom and Practice in Urgell] (La Seu d'Urgell, ACSU, MS 2048), the Assumption ranks alongside Christmas, Easter, Pentecost, and Maundy Thursday, as one of the five principal feasts of the Church.

The Vespers offices owned by Ferrante I of Aragon, completed in 1490, the year of Sor Isabel's death, has three of the Marian feasts marked as more important than the others by means of the marginal decoration accorded to each of them. These are the Nativity of the Virgin, the Assumption, and the Visitation.[3]

Given the importance of the Assumption in the Kingdom of Aragon, it is not surprising that Valencia Cathedral possesses vestments specifically for its celebration. The 1418 inventory lists a 'gremial tot de fil d'or' [a knee cloth all of gold thread work], on which is embroidered God's Majesty with the Assumption of the Virgin, and, on each side, six Apostles with their crowns of small pearls and 'pedres sotils' [dainty gemstones] (Sanchis y Sivera 1933: 9). The gremial is a square cloth placed on the knees of a bishop during certain ceremonies (Alcover 1988: VI, 403). Just like the gold cloak, the gremial for the Assumption is of cloth-of-gold: 'molt propi per aquella jornada' [most appropriate for that day].

Clothing in religious writing

I have argued elsewhere that preoccupation with fine garments is not unique to the *Vita Christi*, nor is it even a feminine concern (2007b). Rejection of clothes was an important aspect of the *contemptus mundi* for those with religious beliefs, with both male and female writers expressing particular concerns about their corruptive power. Eiximenis expresses deep unease in his *Dotzè llibre del crestià* in his advice for the king about how a young princess should dress:

> Aparellan-se axí que no's facen guarlanda de lurs cabells engir lo cap, ne porten draps preciosos axí com draps d'aur e velut o perles o pedres precioses ca açò és massa e empatxa molt la oració de la dona que no sia hoÿda per nostre senyor Déu. (1986–88: II, 406)
>
> [Let them dress so that they do not wear their hair like a garland around their head, nor wear precious cloths, like cloth-of-gold and velvet, or pearls or precious stones, for that is fool's clothing and prevents women's prayers from being heard by our Lord God.]

---

[3] Valencia, Biblioteca de l' Universitat, MS 391, fols. 167r, 118r, 96r.

It is his belief that cloth-of-gold, as well as other rich fabrics, prevent the development of spirituality in young women. His anxiety about garments and riches takes its roots in the New Testament in the events surrounding the rich young man who approaches Jesus with questions about eternal life. When told what he must do to enter the kingdom of heaven, the young man turns sadly away (Luke 18. 18–23).

Given this current of writing about female clothing, it is hardly surprising that Sor Isabel's depiction of a cornucopia of garments, brocades, gold work, and jewels provokes the same reaction in the minds of critics more familiar with the male Franciscan viewpoint. I have previously established how St Francis's own rejection of rich garments as well as his knowledge of fine fabrics, because of being the son of a rich cloth merchant, marks the Order (Wolf 2003: 16–18; Twomey 2007b: 124–5).

Yet when the instructions about garments proscribed by the Franciscans are examined, a dual approach is discernible. Whilst St Clare's Rule, approved on 9 August 1253, exhorts the sisters 'que se vistan de vestidos viles' [to put on rough garments] (*Reglas* 1988: 21), it contrasts the poor nature of the nuns' habits, an outward sign of the poverty they have accepted, with 'otras de mayor riqueza y resplandor' that they will possess in heaven.

For Franciscans, riches were still acceptable objects of desire, but the jewels to be desired were only those stored in the heavenly realm. In his discussion of treasures in heaven, Dominic Janes argues that there was an inherent tension between rejection of earthly riches because of their corruptive power and the employment of the symbolism of wealth, as well as the beauty and desirability of gemstones, gold, and silver, to depict heaven. When heaven was shown as a place bedecked with jewels and gold, 'symbolic connection was affirmed between the two. In this way, worldly symbolism which appealed to the hopes of society at large, was appropriated in the promotion of the Christian message' (1998: 84). In fact, the concept of treasure in heaven had already been established in the New Testament, where the city of God is described as adorned with pure gold and bedecked with jewels (Revelation 21. 18).

Rejection of worldly riches also led some Franciscans to hesitate, whether because of their position in society or because they could distribute such riches to the poor. Angela of Foligno is determined to demonstrate poverty, although she is pragmatic, because she is a tertiary, in recognizing that renunciation of belongings is not always possible, especially for those of noble birth. This is particularly so for married tertiaries, whose husbands may not agree:

> Each of us ought to imitate him in his poverty, and perfectly, if we can. Those who cannot do so perfectly, either because they belong to the

nobility or have a family, should at least have a sincere love of poverty and renounce affection for worldly belongings. (1993: 288)

Given the nature of Franciscan writing about the aspiration to riches in heaven, I have argued that the embrace of poverty and the rejection of worldly riches applied to the Virgin only indirectly (Twomey 2007b: 126–30).[4] In Valencian art, painted silks and brocades make important statements about the Virgin's nature. Artists who were commissioned to represent the Virgin Mary set her amid all the attributes of secular queenship, in a symbiotic relationship between the earthly and heavenly realms, since they, and writers like Sor Isabel, used the ceremonial and trappings of earthly wealth and royal power as a referent for the heavenly variety. In many representations of the Virgin in Gothic art, she holds the sceptre and crown, which earthly queens are given at their coronation, and, in Sor Isabel's depiction of the Coronation of the Virgin (fols 309v–305v*bis*; III, 349–60), she is handed a golden cloak, a sceptre, and then she is crowned with a triple crown (see Chapter 8).

Emphasis on the majesty of the Virgin became important from the eleventh century onwards, and artists responded by clothing her in garments which reflected it. However, because the corruptive power of finery was a commonplace, these rich fabrics underline the fact that, as a woman whose flesh is not stirred by sin, her garments do not corrupt as they would others. Fine fabrics also represent the garments of glory, mentioned in Urban's Rule, for which other women must wait, but which Mary is accorded on earth. It is into this triple context that the scenes dedicated to the robing of the Virgin fit in the *Vita Christi*.

Ceremonial robing and the coronation ceremony in the Kingdom of Aragon

The way the Virgin is presented with ceremonial garments in the *Vita Christi* has many elements in common with Aragonese coronation of queens (see Twomey 2007b). The fabrics Sor Isabel describes for the Virgin's mantle and tunic or overdress are silk and brocade, and they recall those used in coronations, although the colours are different. In Aragon, the queen is dressed in white. Sor Isabel shows the Virgin in a crimson tunic, which, as discussed in Chapter 4, has a long tradition in Hispanic art. The garments are closely linked to the ones in the *Vita Christi*, as the Virgin is prepared for her role

---

[4] For further study of medieval and Renaissance links between queens and the Virgin Mary, see Stroll 1997 and King 1985. See also Nelson 1997 for early medieval rites of queen-making.

as Mother of Christ. The queen first puts on a 'camisa romana de llenç' [a linen undergarment, Roman style] (Astor Landete 1999: 101–2). This shift is an undergarment and those for the nobility were frequently made out of linen. On the eve of the ceremony, the queen 'yra vestida de las vestidures blanques e ornaments de cap acostumats, sols que no port garlanda ne corona en lo cap' [is attired in white clothing, and with customary headdress except that she will wear neither garland nor crown on her head] (BNE, MS 959, fol. 100v). Sor Isabel places a gold crown decked with stars on the head of the Virgin, and this marks her out from earthly queens.

On the coronation day, the queen sets out in the same clothes, but after entering the cathedral she robes in the cathedral sanctuary. The garments she wears are ecclesiastical, which, on other occasions, would be worn by deacons. She is robed in a 'camis de drap de seda blancha' [an alb of white silk], and on top of this she wears a 'dalmàtica de vellut blanqua fresada e sembrada de obratges d'or, ab pedres precioses' [a dalmatic of white velvet, bordered and sprinkled with gold work, with precious stones] (BNE, MS 959, fol. 101v). Finally, after the church ceremony concludes, the queen returns to the king's lodgings and puts on a tunic and a cloak. Pere the Ceremonious's ceremonial for the consecration of the kings of Aragon mentions 'cota e mantell de drap' [a tunic and cloth cloak] (BNE, MS 959, fol. 104r), although Astor Landete refers to the material as brocade (1999: 173). The cloth is likely to be cloth-of-gold.

There are literary antecedents for silk undergarments like the chemise of the Virgin. In *Tirant*, the *camisa* [shift], which the eponymous hero takes from Carmesina as a love token to wear in the joust is made of silk (Martorell 1990: I, 272). According to Sor Isabel, the Virgin's shift is 'molt special' and it is made of the same fabric both as Carmesina's, although, as outlined above, both are of the same material as the coronation *camis*, or alb, worn by queens.

There are also some similarities between Sor Isabel's nuptials of the Virgin and the wedding scene of the King of England, described by the eponymous hero in the early part of *Tirant*:

> Lo dia de sanct Joan lo rey se abillà molt bé ab un manto tot brodat de perles moltes groses, forrat de mart gibellins, les calçes de aquella semblant brodadura molt riques, lo gipó de brocat de fil d'argent tirat, no portant res d'or –perquè no era encara cavaller –sinó al cap, que portava una corona d'or molt richa e de gran stima e lo ceptre en la mà.
> (Martorell 1990: I, 66–7)

> [On midsummer's day the King dressed with a mantle embroidered with very large pearls, lined with stoat fur, his breeches with the same embroidery seeming very fine, his doublet of silver thread brocade, for he was wearing nothing of gold, for he was not yet a knight, except on his head,

where he wore a very fine and highly rated crown of gold, and the sceptre in his hand.]

Tirant provides no description of the infanta the night before the wedding:

> La infanta [...] isqué d'un loch qui·s nomena Granug [...], e molt ben abillada posà's dins un castell que portava, tot de fusta, sobre un carro de XII rodes, que tiraven XXXVI cavalls, los més grans e forts que en tota Francia pogueren trobar. (1990–92: I, 69)
>
> [The princess (...) left a place called Greenwich (...), very well dressed, and sat in a castle made of wood on a cart with 12 wheels pulled by 36 horses, the biggest and most powerful that there were in all of France.]

The wedding garments described by Tirant are even more lavishly decorated with precious stones than the ones described in the ceremonial for the kings and queens of Aragon.

Silk, velvet, and brocade would have been important for a Valencian writer, with the silk industry central to the economy in the fifteenth century. Mola mentions that Valencia was known for its silks and that it had kept alive the traditions learned from the Moors. He considers the Spanish industry to have been reinvigorated by the Venetian one (2000: 21). In the latter half of the fifteenth century, the velvet and brocade industry, and the accompanying professions of dying and shearing, were gaining in importance, and the city's silk-making guilds were applying for and being granted their founding charters. Navarro Espinach's numerous studies of the silk industry and its workers indicate that in the period in which Sor Isabel was living and writing in the city, Valencia established itself as an important centre for production. He indicates that the Guild of Silk-Shearers was being formed between 1465 and 1479 (1992: 43). By 1509, when the dispute between the *velluters* [velvet-makers] and the silk-shearers was heard, 'el dit ofici era el major i el de més mestres que cap dels ·ltres oficis' [the guild was the biggest and had more master craftsmen than any other] (Navarro Espinach 1996: 23). He also notes that the guild was in its earliest phase between 1477 and 1519 (1996: 23–49). Sor Isabel's choice of silk fabrics would have corresponded to the rise of the industry in Valencia in her day.

Synergies between ritual dressing of the Virgin with gifted clothing and convent ritual

Sor Isabel's robing of the Virgin recreates coronation ceremonial, since the Virgin, like a queen, is attended by female allegorical figures, who receive the gifts on her behalf and later assist her in putting them on. Both Holly

S. Hurlburt and Astor Landete refer to the three stages of the coronation of consorts. Hurlburt, discussing the Dogaresses of Venice, shows how coronations of consorts had an important role for the women of the court to play, whilst powerful women are absent from other medieval ceremonies (2003: 187–8). Entry to the convent has also been described as a staged process because it involves three stages of decision making: postulancy, novitiate, and profession (Lowe 2003).

I have also shown how ritual undressing, 'despull', is as important as robing and is central to coronation ceremonials (Twomey 2007b). In the *Vita Christi* the Virgin is accorded garments which better reflect her future role. She removes the garments worn at the Annunciation to put on symbolic ones received as a gift from heaven and, at the end of the *Vita Christi*, she is robed again with even more glorious garments on her arrival in heaven.

For the nuns, the ritual dressing in the *Vita* is likely to have evoked the staged process of entry to the Order, but it would also have called to mind the gifted garments the nuns were given for their vestition. Many of the nuns received their robes, particularly their veils, as a gift from wealthy patrons. This establishes a connection between the gift of clothes to the Virgin more fitting to her new station and the stages of vestition, part of the rite of entry.

The rich brocades postulants wore at vestition formed part of their dowry. McKendrick notes how the value of dowries varied according the rank and status of the woman. A dowry was often paid in cash, with 'a "trousseau" or "ajuar", consisting of jewellery, clothes, brocades, silks, and bedclothes' (1987: 199). The cloth in garments worn at a nun's vestition could prove a valuable asset to the convent, because they remained with the entrant as part of her dowry. Remaking of female garments has been mentioned earlier, but women's dresses could also be turned into ecclesiastical robes or altar cloths. Kate Lowe (2003: 234) indicates that a dress of white material (possibly damask) worn by Suor Angela Caterina at her vestition became property of the convent, being remade as an altar cloth, to modern eyes an unusual transfer of clothing from the realm of the secular to the ecclesiastical.

On the day of profession, the nuns were divested of their outer garments and they put on the rough garments which symbolized their gain of more splendid heavenly ones. Like queens, whose coronation marked the consummation of their earlier betrothal, each nun in the convent had also undergone her espousal to Christ in her profession.[5]

---

[5] As part of the present-day passage into the Order, professing sisters have a garland of flowers placed on their head, a ring placed on their finger, a black, rather than white, veil put on their heads, accoutrements which replicate the dressing of a bride and symbolize marriage to Christ. The church is decorated with garlands of flowers as it would be for a wedding. Parallels between rituals of the preparation of the Virgin in the *Vita Christi* and those of a

The new garments the nuns were given underwent a ritual purification with holy water to mark out the new stage in the purification of their bodies and souls. The ritual undressing in the medieval ceremonials includes aspersion of the nun's new habit: 'Aspergantur uestes aqua benedicta dum conditur et spoliatur soror quae recipienda est' [The robes are to be sprinkled with holy water while the sister who is to be received is hidden from view and is undressed] (MS 865, fol. 2r).

Undressing and dressing the new nun is an activity in which all the sisters take part:

> Adeste domine supplicationibus nostris et hanc famulam tuam benedicere digneris quae in sancto nomine tuo habitum religionis dedimus ut te largiente et deuota in ecclesia perficere et ad uitam pervenire mereamur eternam. (BC, MS 865, fol. 5v)
>
> [Come, Lord, with our prayers, and deign to bless this your servant, to whom in your holy name we have given the habit of religion, so that she may generously and devoutly become perfect in the Church and we may merit eternal life.]

Emphasis is placed in the ritual on the giving of clothing: 'quae in sancto nomine tuo habitum religionis dedimus' [to whom in your holy name we have given this habit]. In 'dedimus' [we have given] the whole community not only takes part but, in spite of their provenance from family members or sponsors, takes on the gifting of the robes which will mark the beginning of a new life for the professing sister.

Conclusion

Bynum, with reference to the writings of the nuns at Helfta, argues that critical assessment of the writing of female mystics is no more than partially successful. She notes how both social scientists and religionists have "favored some sort of 'deprivation theory'" (1982: 183). Critical assessment of Sor Isabel's writing has taken the same avenue. Whilst critics have been partially successful in explaining the existence of ritual robing in the *Vita Christi*, their tendency to categorize the *Vita Christi* as writing suitable for women readers has only allowed a limited evaluation of its function. They have focused on its courtly and literary antecedents rather than its religious ones.

For the garments and fabrics, Sor Isabel draws on her experience within the Church, not prior to it, as comparison with Sanchis y Sivera's inventory

---

novice were striking in a recent profession attended in rural Valencia, in Villar del Arzobispo, even at the level of assistance provided by her attendants, the sisters who fix the veil on the head of the nun professing.

of Church vestments in Valencia reveals (1921). The fabrics are the same ones depicted in medieval altarpieces, and are the ones which would have been seen at major feast days in the copes and ceremonial garments worn by the priests who celebrated in the convent. Her robing of the Virgin draws on artistic traditions in Valencia and the Kingdom of Aragon.

In the preparation of the Virgin's body for her role as Mother of the King of Heaven, important truths about her relationship with God are taught through the implications of gifted clothing, as the Virgin is brought within the lineage of heaven. The ritual dressing also foregrounds clothing rituals in which female protagonists are central: the coronation of queens and convent rituals such as vestition. The ritual robing of the Virgin echoes the ritual dressing and undressing of the queens of Aragon to symbolize their union with the king. The Virgin is robed as she becomes one with the King of Heaven.

The events of the ritual robing and undressing, which is equally important, also foreground the nuns' own experience. They enter the convent to become brides of Christ, accepting the gift of new robes from sponsors but also from the hands of their sisters. Their entry to the convent and all its symbolism is placed at the heart of events in the *Vita Christi* in order to ensure that the sisters will gain rich garments in heaven.

7

Shoes, Shoes, Shoes: Stepping out in Style

> How beautiful are your feet in their sandals, O prince's daughter!
> (Song of Songs 7. 2)

Because Sor Isabel associates the Virgin with female figures of the Old Testament, she adorns her with jewels, like the bride of Isaiah, or clothes her in brocade, like the princess in the Psalms. She dresses her in gilded fabrics to suggest she is the Woman of Revelation, robed in the sun. This chapter continues my exploration of Sor Isabel's adornment of the Virgin's immaculate body and how biblical and patristic commentaries on the feet of the Shulamite have their part to play.

Sor Isabel describes six 'parells de tapins, dient los calçàs sa mercé quant per sis staments de persones seria reclamada' [pairs of high-soled shoes, saying her Ladyship should put them on when she was called upon by the six states of persons] (fols 57r *bis*–59r *bis*; I, 208). She allegorizes these fancy shoes, made of brocade, velvet, silver, and gold thread, as she does other garments gifted to the Virgin.

Fashion shoes: their history and what was written about them

Tapins (high-soled shoes or chopines) were worn by fashionable noblewomen in the late medieval period (Fig. 16). They were worn at court and can be seen in effigies of noblewomen, such as the jewel-encrusted pair which peeps out from under the hem of the gown of Isabel de Portugal, Queen of Castile and Leon, in her effigy at Miraflores monastery in Burgos (Anderson 1979: 226–7). Princesses and queens had chopines in their wardrobe and their cost was astonishing. The Infanta Isabel had several pairs and these were made in the year of her wedding (1490), presumably as part of her trousseau:

> She had two *cebtí*-covered pairs made, a green and mulberry colored, embroidered with drawn-gold thread to the weight of about 23 ounces, at a cost, including labor of 17, 865 maravedis, more than three quarters the price of a team of mules. (Anderson 1979: 231)

16. Chopines dating from the fifteenth and sixteenth centuries, Museu Textil i d'Indumentària.

Carmen Bernis notes that the first documentary evidence for chopines was an order for the royal house of Navarre in 1382 (1962: 87). Because of their expense, chopines formed an important element of the dowry of a young woman, to the extent that 'put into chopines' meant to 'marry off a daughter'. Anderson also notes that a gift would be made by Castile on the marriage of a queen or one of the infantas, which was recorded as 'Chopine of the Queen or of the Infanta' (Anderson 1979: 263, n. 587).

A silk exhibition in Barcelona in the 1950s had four pairs of chopines on display, two from Vic and two from Manlleu (*La seda* 1957: 12). Each pair is described as having patterned leather soles as well as highly decorated uppers. Silks and velvets were used for the uppers: 'Par de chapines de corcho forrados de terciopelo granate decorado con líneas en blanco, cerrados por cintas de seda verde; plantillas de cuero labrado' [a pair of chopines with cork soles lined with burgundy velvet decorated with white strips and fastened with laces of green silk; soles of tooled leather]. Five pairs of *tapins* from the sixteenth century are on display in the Museu Textil i d'Indumentària [Textile and Clothing Museum], in Barcelona.

Chopines were thought to have been first used as part of ceremonial dress in Moorish Spain (Cintora 1988: 83; Astor Landete 1999: 248) and were no doubt worn inside the harem, where they may have singled out favoured concubines. Originally given the onomatopoeic name 'patí' or 'kapkap', *tapins* represent the tapping sound made as the wearer walked. Because cork was readily available in many areas of Spain, the fashion for *tapins* became common by the fourteenth century and spread to other parts of Europe. Bernis (1962: figs 60–1, 66, 68–71, 75) shows that a bourgeois woman, a 'doncella de Barcelona' [unmarried girl from Barcelona], a woman from Barcelona, a Castilian woman on her way to church, as well as women out for a walk in Valladolid, all wear chopines. These are less ornate than those of their betters, although often decorated with patterns ingrained on the cork. Iris Brooke (1972) repeats the mistaken assumption that they were a Venetian invention. Anderson, writing a few years after her, made the confident assertion that this popular notion had been dispelled (1979: 232).

Brooke accurately evaluates how Spanish footwear fashions were adopted in Tudor England during Philip II's period of residence at the English court. When Philip left, 'the extravagances and fantasies of the Spanish courtiers remained in vogue. Queen Elizabeth and her ladies indulged in an orgy of fashionable excesses' (Brooke 1972: 44). Elizabeth wears white silk *tapins* in a portrait which shows her astride the globe in order to illustrate her temporal power. Her stance recalls the Virgin's domination of the serpent (London, National Portrait Gallery, 2561).[1]

Tapins, otherwise known as 'korked shoes', were being denigrated in England by the time Philip Stubbes, a Puritan, wrote his diatribe of 1583, *Anatomy of the Abuses in England*, against those features of the life of his day responsible for present degeneracy:

> Wherto they have korked shoes, prisnets, pantoffles and slippers, some of black velvet, some of white, some of green, and some of yellow; some of Spanish leather, and some of English lether, stitched with silk and embroidered with gold and silver all over the foote, with other gewgaws innumerable. All of which, if I should endeuoure my selfe to express I might with more facilitie number the sands of the Sea, the Starres in the skye, or the grasse upon the Earth so infinit and innumerable be their abuses. For weare I neuer soe experte an Arimethetician or Matematician, I weare neuer capable of the halfe of them, the deuille brochethe soe many new fashions every day. (1877–82: I, 76–7)

Stubbes rails against all styles of ladies' shoes, but particularly disapproves of those of foreign origin, such as the 'korked' shoes and French 'pantoffles'.[2] His diatribe indicates that the shoes could be made either of velvet or of leather, and he describes a variety of colours. He pays attention to the leather, which was often Spanish. Gems and embroidery, either in silver or gold thread, are used to decorate them. For Stubbes, they come with a baggage of disrepute and are part of the devil's armoury of trickery.

In the fifteenth century in Spain, *tapins* were mentioned in a number of other literary works. According to Joan Roís de Corella, who is describing the footwear of the Goddess Venus in his *Visió del Judici de Paris* [Vision of the Judgement of Paris]:

---

[1] The portrait, by Marcus Gheeraerts the Younger (1561/62–1636), depicts Elizabeth standing with her feet on Oxford.

[2] In her study of moralizing works and sermonizing against fashionable attire, Roze Hentschell briefly summarizes Stubbes's 'outrage over pride in apparel' (2009: 575–6).

> y eren los tapins de l'exçellssa Reyna, de çetí carmesi, en estrany artifiçi brodats de vns trossos de caramida, dels quals naxien brots verts de florida artemissa, les fulles esmaltades de blaves lletres, que, distintament deyen: '*Venç gran amor paraules, erbes hi pedres.*'
>
> (cited in Astor Landete 1999: 249)
>
> [And the shoes of the noble queen were of crimson satin, with strange artifice, embroidered with slivers of lodestone, from whence there sprang green shoots of flowering mugwort, the leaves enamelled with blue letters, which each said: Great love conquers words, herbs, and stones.]

Although these chopines seem to have been embellished by his imagination, extant examples of chopines show that their decoration could combine embroidery, floral or leaf patterns, and enamels.[3] Those in the silk exhibition included a sixteenth-century pair with embroidered leaves, listed in the catalogue as follows: 'chapines de corcho forrados de terciopelo labrado con hojas estilizadas en seda ocre y gris-pizarra, cerrados por cintas de seda azul; plantillas de cuero labrado y dorado' [cork chopines with uppers of velvet worked with stylized leaves in ochre and slate-grey silk; fastened with blue silk ties; soles of tooled, gilded leather] (*La seda* 1957: 22). Silk satin was an accepted fabric for shoes, and, according to Alcover, a reinforced type of silk was regularly used to make the *tapins* known as *tapineta*. It was 'teixit de seda amb trama de cotó, molt apropiat per a tapins o sabates' [a silk fabric with cotton thread, most suited for chopines or plain shoes] (1988: X, 147). Florence Lewis May notes that velvet was used for their manufacture too (1957: 215).

Astor Landete does not refer to any other embroidered *tapins* in the writing of Roís de Corella, although he dresses each of the goddesses in them. Those of Pallas are deep purple and embroidered with thistles in flower: 'y en los tapins de setí morat, estauen brodades florits espinosos abriojos' [and on the chopines of dark purple were embroidered prickly thistles in flower] (Roís de Corella 1913: 293) and those of Juno are decorated with flames.

Increasing a woman's height was a key feature of *tapins* (Astor Landete 1999: 247). For that reason Eiximenis, writing over two centuries earlier than Stubbes, uses them to symbolize the sins of vanity and pride in his *Segon del crestià* [Second Book on the Christian]:

> Après diu que tot l'àls és en ella falsia, car diu que si la guardes als peus, tostemps porta tapins, si pot, que la facen pus alta; no poseu lo peu pla perquè vaya pus falagueramente e pus airosa.
>
> (cited in Astor Landete 1999: 247)

---

[3] Seventeenth-century shoes in the Museu del Calçat [Museum of Footwear], Barcelona, show that embroidery of leaves and flowers continued in vogue. Hand decoration was still the principal technique, with factory embroidery taking over only in the nineteenth century.

[Then he says that everything else about her is false, for he says that if you look at her feet, she always wears high-soled shoes, as they made her taller; she never put her foot down flat so as to walk more delightfully or daintily.]

They raised the wearer high off the ground, having thick cork soles, approximately four inches high, sandwiched between two leather soles. Increased height prevented their skirts from trailing in the mud. Solomon, in an attempt to convince the narrator that marriage should be forgotten, advises taking away some of the false adornments that women have, such as dresses and make-up. If a woman's chopines are stripped off her, there is nothing left of value: 'fora'ls tapins, mira que tins' [with her shoes off, see what you have'] (Roig 1978: 149).

In Stubbes's, Roig's, and the Archpriest's diatribes against women's fashions, wearing high-heeled shoes is thought to contribute to humanity's downfall, with a similar note struck by Eiximenis in his *Lo libre de les dones* [Book of Ladies], written in 1390 or 1391 (1981: xv). He describes the unserviceable *tapins* which unmarried ladies wear. Either he, or his copyist, has called them 'patins' [sliding shoes]: 'e als peus ab patins que no ·ls serveys sinó a empatxar lur andar' (1981: 42–3) [and on their feet, with fancy corked shoes, which only serve to hobble their gait]. Eiximenis follows this by describing the ills likely to ensue when women adorn themselves and display such vanity (44–50). He warns, for example, that such women will not be able to give alms properly, thus endangering both their own and their husbands' souls.

Eiximenis does not make it clear whether he believes that ornamentation of the female body will be detrimental, making women concentrate on the earthly rather than the heavenly realm, or whether he thinks that the effects of uncontrolled purchasing will have an economic impact on family income, which will be wrongly expended, with husbands ruined by trying to provide for fripperies. Given the price of the most elegant *tapins*, it is probable that Eiximenis is referring to the high maintenance cost of wives who deck themselves out in *tapins*. Such costs reduce the amount of alms which can be given to the Church, impacting on the spiritual welfare of both the woman and her husband. Finally, he makes the detrimental spiritual effect explicit, commenting that their prayers will not be heard:

> Pens encara la dona, diu aquest, que si molt és entesa en aytals coses, no pora fer grans almoynes, de què reema sos peccats ne de son marit. Pens encara quin sacrilegi és que ab aytals malediccions vingua a la esgleya a fedar e a ensutzar lo loch de Déu [...]. Cert bé pot pensar que ses oraciones non seran exoïdes: més li valria de molt que jamés no anàs a la esgleya que no anar-hi ab tanta offença de Déu. (1981: 46)

[Think then that the lady, if she is very involved in such things, cannot give much in the way of alms, to redeem her sins and those of her husband. Think then what a sacrilege it is for her to come to church in such cursed attire to foul it and soil it. (…) For she may well think that her prayers will be vain and it would be better for her not to go to church than to go, causing such offence to God.]

As well as the economic and spiritual impact of *tapins*, they contribute to determining a woman's body as a locus for all that is foul. Such sinfulness corrupts everything with which it comes into contact, even the sacred space of the church building.

Tapins also had a physical impact because they could be used as a weapon against men. Cantavella discusses a *tenso* that includes a warning by Gabriel Móguer that Majorcan women, who have been maligned by Gabriel Ferruç, are ready to bludgeon him to death with a shoe (Cantavella 1994: 222–3, n. 12, citing Riquer). The same thing happens to Martínez de Toledo's crow. After he has maligned women throughout the *Corbacho* [The Crow], in the epilogue women get their own back by beating him with their shoes:

> La segunda, quel pie me puso en la garganta […] que la lengua sacar me hazía un palmo; las otras no pude devisar, quel golpe de los chapines me cerraba la vista […]. Congoxado de tormento, sudando, desperté e pensé que en poder de crueles señoras me avía fallado. (1985: 281)
>
> [The second, with her foot on my throat (…), forced my tongue out by about six inches; I could not see the others for the blow with corked shoes caused my eyes to be closed. (…) Badly bruised with such torture, sweating, I awoke and thought I had fallen into the hands of most cruel ladies.]

Ryan Giles sees elements of performativity in the scene in which the crow is brought low and deplumed by a band of women for its harsh criticism of their sex.[4] Both the Catalan *tenso* and the *Corbacho* reveal that attacks with chopines were standard fare. In the *Tesoro de la lengua* [Treasury of the Language], Sebastián de Covarrubias y Horozco defines *chapinazo* as 'el golpe que da la mujer con el chapín, que cuando toman cólera suelen descalzarse y vengar con él sus injurias' [the blow a woman gives with her corked shoe. For, when rage takes hold, women usually take off their shoes and avenge their wrongs with them]. He traces the *chapinazo* [blow with a chopine] back to Juvenal's sixth satire (2006: 517).

---

[4] Ryan Giles, 'Hanging Bells on the Cat: Charivari and the Theatrics of the *Arcipreste de Talavera o Corbacho*', paper presented at the 44th Congress on International Medieval Studies, University of Western Michigan, Kalamazoo, 7–10 May 2009.

Tapins in Valencia

Chopines were being made in Valencia throughout the fifteenth and sixteenth centuries, and although the city was not in one of the major cork-producing regions, 'the capital city was long famous for its platform shoes […]. Dozens of pairs made in that city were procured for Queen Isabel's daughters' (Anderson 1979: 234). Records from the Guild of *Tapiners* [chopine-makers] indicate that the guild was already of high status in the city in 1421, when its leaders asked members to approve new statutes on ceremonial and emblems.[5] There were *tapiners* working in the city and also a street named after them in the Parish of Santa Catalina, behind the cathedral, in the heart of the old town (Valencia, ARV, Clero, Pergaminos, 2506).

Two different guilds made shoes in fifteenth-century Valencia, the *sabaters* [cordwainers] and the chopine-makers, and they were locked in litigation over their respective privileges for almost one hundred years.[6] The records of the dispute provide precise details about *tapins*, because each guild had to specify how their work differed. The difference between silk shoes and silk *tapins* had become blurred, and each guild was making shoes proper to the other. The Guild of Cordwainers tried to argue that the *tapiners* were only permitted to make ladies' shoes of mock gold leather, whilst they were permitted to make any leather shoe, including *tapins*. Anderson believes there are no records of textiles associated with these shoes (1979: 232), but in 1513, Ausiàs Mançanera, *tapiner*, is recorded as bringing a pair of satin shoes to be examined as evidence, whilst the Guild of Cordwainers presented three or four pairs of *tapins*.

> axi mateix preten e afferma lo dit offiçi de çabaters que los dits tapiners no poden fer sino tapins de oripell para dones e que los altres tapins de cuyro axi de homens com de dones fon del dit offiçi de çabaters e propri peculiar e de aquells com tota obra de cuyro sia e pertanyga al dit offiçi de çabaters. (ARV, Real Cancilleria, Perg. 719, fol. 2v)
>
> [similarly, the aforementioned Guild of Cordwainers claims and affirms that the aforementioned *tapiners* can only make shoes of gilded leather for ladies and that other leather *tapins*, as well as *tapins* for men, are proper

---

[5] The ceremonials include the right for members of the guild to process with white candles carried on the anniversary of the foundation of the guild or at funerals of guild members. Candles were to be studded with the nails of St Peter with the same emblem picked out on the pall over the coffin. Two *andadors* [processional members] from the guild were permitted to wear blue cloaks also decorated with the emblem of St Peter (see Castillo & Martínez 1999: 108–9).

[6] For a transcription, see Gual Camarena 1952. Luis Tramoyeres Blasco provides an overview of the legal wrangling between shoemakers and leather-makers, as well as chopine-makers (1889: 297–308).

to the said Guild of Cordwainers, and are particular to them, belonging to them as any leather footwear belongs to the aforementioned Guild of Cordwainers.]

The *tapiners* were unimpressed with the claims of the cordwainers and, in a declaration in 1487, they upheld their right to make all kinds of shoes:

al dit offiçi es permés de poder fer totes çabates de dona que de home axí de oripell com de cuiro pintades o no pintades, adzurades o no adzurades, e qualseuol tapins així de home com de dona axí de oripell com de cuyro. (Perg. 719, fols 3v–4r)

[the aforementioned guild is permitted to make all types of ladies' and mens' shoes, whether of gilded fabric or of leather, whether painted or not, whether dyed blue or not, and any chopines, whether for man or woman, of gilded leather or of leather.]

Despite the way that moralists rage against the fine shoes worn by women, the respective claims of the two guilds reveal that *tapins* were worn by both men and women. This detail has been forgotten, probably because of their presence in misogynist texts. In the entry for *chapines* the *Enciclopedia universal ilustrada* claims they are an 'especie de chanclo que usaban las mujeres solamente' [a type of sandal used by women].[7] Similarly, Joan Corominas and José A. Pascual define them as women's shoes (1980–91: II, 330).

In a further attempt to claim the fabrication of all leather footwear for their own members, the cordwainers list the types of shoe that the *tapiners* are forbidden to make:

los dits tapiners qui de present son e pertemps seran no puxen fer ni obrar çabates algunes de home ni de dona; de nenguna natura cabates de dona de oripell adzurades e pintades ab que no sien florejades ni puga fer borzeguins ni antepares stivals ni altres coses de sien de cuyro tocans e pertinyents aldit offiçi de çabaters. (Perg. 719, fol. 8r–v)

[the aforementioned *tapiners*, whether at present or in the future, can neither make nor work on any kind of shoe for men or women. Neither any type of ladies' shoes, whether of gilded leather, dyed blue, or painted, nor can they be flowery. Neither can they make ladies' Moorish boots, nor summer shoes, nor anything else made of leather, for these pertain to and are proper to the aforesaid Guild of the Cordwainers.]

---

[7] The *Enciclopedia* (1928–29: 1557) has a photograph of ladies' *tapins* from the Museu Episcopal de Vic. They are no longer part of the museum's patrimony.

From this attempt to stop the *tapiners* from making decorated shoes, it is apparent that both guilds could claim to be making them.

The final settlement of the dispute provides detail about the height of *tapins*, and how it varied. Following the concordat, the powerful Guild of Cordwainers was within its right to make *tapins* with soles of less than two inches in height, whilst the *tapiners* could make all those which were higher. There was therefore likely to be sufficient market for *tapins* higher than two inches for the *tapiners* to agree to the settlement:

> lo tapí de home sia comú als dits dos offiçis e que aquells dits tapins de home puxen esser fets axí per tapiners com per çabaters e per quant la çabata tapí de dona e no de hombre es mixta car pertany al un offiçi e al altre som concordats que aquella puxa esser feta e obrada axi per lo offiçi dels tapiners com dels çabaters sens encorriment de pena alguna haja de seruir per a dona saluo que les que seran obrades per çabaters no puxen ésser de maior altaria de dos sens la sola. (Perg. 719, fols 8v–9r)

> [men's chopines are to be common to both guilds and those chopines for men can be made either by *tapiners* or cordwainers and, since ladies' chopines are made by both guilds, for they belong to both guilds, we are agreed that they can be made and worked for ladies, by either the Guild of *Tapiners* or the Guild of Cordwainers without any penalty, except that the ones made by cordwainers cannot be higher than two fingers without counting the sole.]

The guild concordat reveals that fancy silk footwear was a lucrative market, which each group of litigants was willing to try to protect by purchasing expensive legal advice. When the dispute was settled, the cordwainers had legitimately appropriated a sector of the *tapiners*' market, whilst the *tapiners* did not make similar gains in the cordwainers' market.

There was another section of the *tapins* market, however, which was not in dispute because it was less lucrative. From the records of the Puritat convent, it is known that the sisters regularly purchased *tapins*. Since it is unlikely that the nuns purchased other than simple and practical footwear, these records show that *tapins*, given a bad name in literary works, could also be serviceable and essential to everyday wear. They were purchased, for example, for both Sister Angela Lançol and for Sister Tolsana: 'hun parell de tapins pera sor Tolsana sinc sous i mig' [a pair of *tapins* for Sister Tolsana at five-and-a-half *sous*] (ARV, Clero, Libro 946, fol. 89v). A folio later, both shoes and *tapins* are itemized: 'sis parels de sabates i hun parel de tapins és tot dotze *sous*' [six pairs of shoes and a pair of *tapins* coming to a total of twelve *sous*] (fol. 90v). When shoes are purchased for Sister Jofrena, these are much cheaper than *tapins*: 'un parel de sabates de sor Jofrena hun sou i mig' [a pair of shoes for Sister Jofrena at one-and-a-half *sous*] (fol. 94r).

A late-fifteenth-century *caixa sepulchral* [tomb] from the Monestir de

17. Tomb of Beatriu Cornell.

Santa Maria de Sixena [Convent of St Mary of Sixena] in Monegres in Huesca province, shows the figure of Beatriu Cornell, prioress of the convent, wearing what appear to be chopines under her habit (MLDC 128) (Fig. 17). The high-soled shoes selected for the prioress to wear in death shows that such footwear was not considered exceptional for cloistered women in Sor Isabel's period.

Representation of the Virgin's and other ladies' shoes in art

Sor Isabel's decision to dress the Virgin in brocade garments had antecedents in Valencian and Aragonese altarpieces. When the Virgin is shod in fancy footwear, which other Franciscans, like Eiximenis, had decried as likely to lead to damnation, it might be assumed that she again copies art. Trens includes a very short paragraph on the shoes of the Virgin, in which he notes the tendency to follow fashion. In most retables, however, female footwear is not visible, since artists discreetly cover ladies' feet to preserve their modesty. Trens also indicates that the Virgin is never depicted without shoes, which he interprets as a sign of 'pudor' [modesty] and 'recato' [demureness] (1947: 639).

Where the Virgin's shoes are visible, there is often no more than a glimpse of a plain black toe, peeping out from beneath elaborately decorated cloaks and dresses. These are often seen in representations of the Virgin standing on the moon, where attention is on her feet.[8]

---

[8] In a panel of the *Retaule de la Mare de Déu Apocalíptica i Sant Vicenç Ferrer amb dos donants* [Apocalyptic Mother of God and St Vincent Ferrer with Two Donors] (MNAC

It is only rarely in pre-sixteenth-century retables that the Virgin wears different colours of shoe. In the period slightly later than Sor Isabel's Nicolau Borràs (1530–1610), in an altarpiece from the Monastery of St Jerome in Cotalba (MBAV 433), shows her in brown round-toed shoes with thin soles. The style is more rustic than courtly. The Virgin also wears a brown rustic style in the Florentine-inspired Virgin of Montserrat.[9] Pere Sarrià (active in Barcelona 1357–1405 / 8) allows the toe of a red pointed shoe (MNAC 3950) to be seen in his *Verge amb àngels* [Virgin Surrounded by Angels]. The *Retaule dels Goigs de la Verge* [Altarpiece of the Joys of the Virgin] (Fig. 18) allows a glimpse of *tapins* to be seen as the Virgin ascends surrounded by angels. By the sixteenth century the Virgin's shoes are more visible and occasionally may be silk shoes. In the *Retaule de Santa Maria del Roser* [Retable of St Mary of the Rosary] from the first third of the sixteenth century, the Virgin wears round-toed silk shoes with extremely high soles (MLDC 94) (Fig. 19).

Shoes depicted on other female saints are also relatively rare and the black pointed style is favoured. For example, in the painting of the *Abraçada a la Porta Daurada* [Kiss at the Golden Gate] (MNAC 64033) by the Master of Retascón (documented 1410–25), St Anne wears black pointed shoes. There is, however, usually more variety in depicting the shoes of female saints. Reixach depicts St Ursula in the central panel of his *Retaule de Santa Ursula i les onze mil verges* [Retable of St Ursula and the Eleven Thousand Virgins], with pointed gold shoes under her red dress and gold brocade cloak (MNAC 15927). More striking are the silver shoes which St Anne wears in the *Retablo de la Purísima Concepción* [Retable of the Most Pure Conception], originally in the Puritat convent (MBAV 287) (Fig. 20). They have thick silver soles and plum-coloured toes. They are a slip-on shoe, designed to protect other shoes, such as *borseguís* [Moorish-style leather boots], worn under them. They are similar to the *tapins* in the Barcelona Textile and Clothing Museum (Fig. 16). Joachim wears a similar pair of brown ones. In his case, the shoes are fully visible and are backless. Another pair of overshoes, this time worn with typical fifteenth-century shoes with long pointed

---

114749), in the *Verge amb quatre àngels* [Virgin with Four Angels] by Pere Garcia de Benavarri, an artist documented in Catalonia and Aragon (1445–83), and in the *Mare de Déu de la Llet* [Virgin Breastfeeding the Child Jesus] (MNAC 015849) by Gonçal Perís Sarrià, one or both black pointed shoes are visible. Both the Master of Sent Coloma de Queralt, in his panel of the *Visitation* (MNAC 4351), and Bonant Zaortiga (active in Zaragoza 1403–1446) in his *Mare de Déu de la Misericòrdia* [Mother of God of Mercy] (MNAC 3945), show the Virgin with black pointed shoes. Joan de Borgonya, an artist from Strasbourg, documented in Valencia from 1503 († Barcelona 1526), depicts a more elaborate black shoe decorated with red, with a broad band fastening (MNAC 5690; *Guia* 2008: 151).

[9] This retable was shown in the Golden Age of Valencian Art exhibition, no. 62 (on loan from Museo de Santa Cruz, Toledo); see Benito Domenech & Gómez Frechina 2009: 216–17.

18. *Retaule dels Goigs de la Verge*.

19. *Retaule de Santa Maria del Roser*.

toes inside them, are those King Solomon wears in a Reixach painting (MBAV 234). Even though most artists emphasize elaborate clothing, depiction of shoes does not follow the same path. It is possible to conclude that fancy shoes were not important in the same way to them or to their patrons.

Biblical shoes and the six *parells de tapins* [pairs of shoes]: Faith, Hope, Charity, and Glory

Wearing shoes, putting them on, or handing shoes to someone else had biblical antecedents. The Old and New Testaments use shoes to symbolize faith in God. At the Passover, those who were saved were the ones who

20. Nicolau Falcó, detail from the panel of St Anne, *Retablo de la Purísma Concepción*.

obeyed the instructions given them by Moses. One aspect of their faith and obedience was to eat the Passover meal with their shoes on: 'Setenament: se devia menjar l'anyell ab los peus calçats, car lo peu calçat va ferm e sens temor' [In seventh place the lamb should be eaten with shoes on for, in shoes, the foot walks firmly and without fear] (fol. 179v; II, 244). With this citation from Exodus, Sor Isabel shows that she associates firm faith with the wearing of shoes. At the moment when, trusting in God, the Virgin receives the Lamb into her body, she, like her forebears, must be wearing shoes. Both are covenants between God and his people when he intervenes to save them, first from oppression in Egypt and then from sin in the Incarnation.

The Virgin's exemplary faith is a central theme in the *Vita Christi*. Faith is the first of the maidens to come and accompany the Virgin following the Incarnation (fol. 38r; I, 141), and before his Passion Christ informs the Virgin that she will be the only one whose faith will be strong enough to enable her to resist despair: 'vós sola restareu constant en la fe' [you are the only one who will remain steadfast in faith] (fol. 170r; II, 209).

Given the close association between shoes and faith, it is significant that the first pair of *tapins* which Sor Isabel selects for the Virgin are silver ones: 'Los uns tapins, Senyora, són tots de argent specialment obrats: aquests, Senyora, calçareu com sereu reclamada per los hòmens qui ·s trobaran en stament de gràcia' [the first shoes, Lady, are of silver all over, finely worked; these, Lady, you will wear when you are called upon by those in a state of grace] (fol. 57v; I, 208). In heraldry, silver represents faith. It is also associated with purity, obedience, gratefulness, and 'firmeza' [determination].

Silver also represents the lily, the flower most often associated with the Virgin's purity, and most often handed to her or present beside her at the Annunciation. The lily, or fleur-de-lys, was a powerful symbol of the Trinity (see Chapter 5; Martí de Riquer 1986: 199). Vicente Castañeda y Alcover interprets silver as belonging to the moon (1923: 76). The moon often circles the Virgin's feet in retables of the Virgin with the Child Jesus at her breast, which emphasize her maternity. Such Madonnas of Humility, according to Williamson, 'combine the Virgin's acceptance of her motherhood, with the sunburst rays of the Apocalyptic Woman and the Virgin-as-Ecclesia, to produce a powerful message about the Virgin's intercessory and salvific potential' (2009: 152). Williamson's reinterpretation of the Madonna of Humility casts light on the part the Virgin was to play in salvation history, which Sor Isabel sought to harness to enhance the moment of the Annunciation.

In heraldry, silver and white are indistinguishable: 'La plata se representa con color blanco' (Castañeda y Alcover 1923: 75). Sor Isabel adorns the Virgin with a pair of white shoes. 'Los altres tapins, Senyora, són de brocat blanch: aquests calçarà vostra senyoria com serà cridada per aquells qui són en lo pas de la mort' [The next shoes, Lady, are of white brocade: these your Ladyship will wear when she is called upon by those on the point of death] (fol. 58r; I, 211). White represents the pure flesh of the Virgin and the flesh which is to become Christ's.

The sixth pair of *tapins* given to the Virgin is blue:

> Los altres tapins, Senyora, són de brocat blau: aquests calçarà vostra mercé quant volrà visitar aquell spital de purgatori hon són aquelles ànimes turmentades per la sentència divina fins sien purgades e fetes dignes de entrar en lo repòs de paraýs. (fol. 58r; I, 211–12)
>
> [The next pair of shoes, Lady, is of blue brocade: these your Ladyship will wear when you wish to visit Purgatory, the great hospital where souls are in torment through God's judgement so being purged and made worthy of entering Paradise and its rest.]

In heraldry, blue represents the heavens, symbolizing justice and qualities like gentleness, mercy, loyalty, and innocence (Castañeda y Alcover 1923: 76). Sor Isabel had already used blue for one of the pairs of gloves to be put on for the alleviation of the ills of those close to death. Those the Virgin touches with the gloves are to be assisted to set their thoughts on heaven:

> E vós, Senyora, vehent los dits malalts axí propinqües a la mort, posarvos eu aquells guants guarnits de blau en les mans vostres, e, tocant-los

> ab molta dolçor, tirant-los a pensar en lo cel e en la gran glòria que aquí speren los verdaders hobedients. (fol. 50r; I, 200)

> [And you, Lady, seeing the sick close to death in that way, you are to put on the gloves adorned with blue, and touching them with great gentleness, lead them to think about heaven and about the great glory which awaits the truly obedient there.]

In devotional allegory, blue is compared to sapphires, which evoke the heavens: 'sapphirus enim similis est sereno celo' [for sapphire is similar to the cloudless sky] (BNE, MS 17674, fol. 11r). Meditating on the sapphire and applying its attributes to the Virgin, the unknown Franciscan author of the *Corona Beatissime Virginis* [Crown of the Blessed Virgin] lauds her for displaying characteristics which liken her to a clear sky: 'tu domina fuisti semper clara et serena, sincera, mundissima et amena. Tu eres semper tota pulcra, tota formosa, tota immaculata, et tota speciosa' [you, Lady, were always bright and serene, sincere, spotless, and pleasing. You are always perfectly beautiful, lovely, without stain, and perfectly splendid] (BNE, MS 17674, fol. 11v). The sapphire's heavenly quality symbolizes perfect sinlessness.

The Virgin is the human being who perfectly displays the second of the three theological virtues, hope (Royo Marín 1997: 275–7). Sor Isabel again draws on heraldic colours in choosing green, for it is the colour of hope, supremely appropriate for those soliciting the Virgin's intervention and for expressing her nature: 'Los altres tapins, Senyora, són de un brocat vert molt singular: aquests calçarà vostra mercé quant serà cridada per aquells qui són en peccat mortal' [The next shoes, Lady, are of very fine green brocade: these your Ladyship will wear when you are called upon by those who are in mortal sin] (fol. 57v; I, 209).

Sor Isabel associates green with hope throughout the *Vita Christi*. Both the green shoes and the green damask lining in the cloak of blue brocade represent hope for sinners (fol. 50r; I, 183). Earlier in the *Vita Christi*, Sor Isabel clothed one of the Virgin's virtuous handmaids, Mercy, in green: 'E Pietat portava la roba sua de brocat vert, per mostrar la gran sperança ab què anava de obtenir la sua demanda' [and Mercy wore her robe of green brocade to show the great hope she had of obtaining her request] (fol. 22v; I, 81).

Hope is the second of the handmaids to attend the Virgin after the Annunciation, when she is associated with the fulfilment of God's promises: 'La segona haurà nom Sperança, aquesta li farà sperar ab gran desig veure complides totes les promissions divines' [the second will be named Hope, for she will make her expect with great longing to see all God's promises fulfilled] (fol. 37r; I, 14). The principal promise is God's covenant with his people, first made in the saving of his chosen race in Noah's Ark, and renewed in the hope of salvation at the birth of the Messiah. The second covenant is the one that the Virgin's response to God will contribute to fulfilling, when she become *Nuestra Señora de la O* [Our Lady of Omega], or *Nuestra Señora de la Esperanza* [Our Lady of Hope or Expecting]. In the Old Testament, the giving of shoes cements a contract (Ruth 4. 7). The gift of the *tapins* is part of a ceremonial cementing of the covenant between earth and heaven.

In Scripture, forgiveness is marked by inviting people to a banquet, by going out to meet the sinner, or by providing new clothing and shoes. For example, in the Parable of the Prodigal Son, the returning sinner has to be clothed by his forgiving father. Sor Isabel consistently shows the Virgin collaborating in the work of redemption. Her version of the parable is recounted as part of the allegorical necklace the Virgin is given, and as the fourth work of mercy, she is commended because she re-clothes the sons of Adam:

> La quarta obra de misericòrdia, ¿qui la ha complida axí perfetament com vostra senyoria? Car, despullat Adam e tots los seus fills de la vestidura de innocència e de tots altres béns, ¿qui·ls ha redreçats e vestits sinó vós, clementíssima Senyora? Car, vehent la nuditat e fretura de cascú de ells, manareu a les vostres donzelles e direu: *Cito proferte stolam primam: et induite illum, et date anulum in manu ejus: et calciamenta in pedibus ejus;* volent dir: Veniu, vós, Caritat: vestiu-lo de aquella vestidura de amor delicatíssima e molt prima; e vós, Fe, dau-li lo anell de vera crehença en la mà sua; e vós, Sperança, calçau-lo de virtuoses obres; perquè, axí arreat, sia plaent al pare eternal, lo qual lo havia avorrit per la nuditat sua.
>
> (fol. 55v; I, 191)

> [Who has complied so perfectly with the fourth work of mercy but your Ladyship? For when Adam and all his sons were stripped of their vestment of innocence and all their other goods, who set them on the right path and dressed them save you, most clement Lady? For seeing the cold and nakedness of each of them, you sent your ladies and said: *Clothe him and place a ring on his hand and shoes on his feet*; meaning: 'Come, Charity, dress him in that most delicate and best clothing of love; and you, Faith, place the ring of right belief on his hand; and you, Hope, put shoes of virtuous works on his feet; and, so dressed, he may be pleasing to the eternal father, who would have turned him away him in his nakedness.']

The prodigal son, who epitomizes the redemption of sinful humanity, returns to his father. His acceptance back into the relationship is symbolized by the robe, the ring on his finger, and the shoes on his feet. Like the Virgin, the prodigal son is completely dependent on his father for both compassion and clothing. In Sor Isabel's reprise of the words of the parable, the Virgin is the one who sends out her ladies to dress the poor and naked sons of Adam. Significantly, it is her handmaid, Hope, who is responsible for providing shoes. When the Virgin now accepts the accoutrements of welcome, clothes, jewels, and shoes, Sor Isabel is also demonstrating that she is human and in need of redemption. She is both able to clothe others and in need of clothing herself.

Hope also provides, later in the *Vita Christi*, the point of contact between Mary and Queen Esther, one of the Old Testament women who prefigure her. According to Mirella Levi d'Ancona, Esther's coronation is a prefiguration of the Virgin's Immaculate Conception (1957: 30), and she, like the Virgin, is a figure of hope:

> E só molt cert que vós, reyna Ester, en mi haveu posat la amor sperança vostra, segons mostràs en vostres angústies e congoxes recorrent a mi en aquelles, e, ab gran confiança, déyeu: *Spem in alio nunqual habui propter in te Deus Israel.* (fol. 230v; III, 47)
>
> [And I am very sure that you, Queen Esther, have set your hope in me, as you showed in your suffering and troubles when you called on me and, with great confidence, said: *I will hope in nothing other than you, O God of Israel.*]

As a model of the theological virtues, the Virgin preaches and teaches hope to the disciples, including St Peter (fols 252v-253r; III, 136–8). She is the only source of hope following the Crucifixion, when the leaders of the nascent Church call upon her in their despair. They expect her to mediate the reception of the Holy Spirit:

> Ajudau-nos, Senyora, car per lo mijà de vostra senyoria havem a rebre aquesta gràcia tan desijada! No·ns façau més sperar, car defallen gràcia tan les forçes nostres per longa sperança! Potent sou, Senyora, en lo cel e en la terra, e acostumat ha vostra senyoria de fer devallar Déu en la terra, com se mostrà en lo gran misteri de la incarnació quant digués: *Ecce ancilla Domini.* (fol. 292v; III, 285)
>
> [Help us, Lady, for through your Ladyship we are to receive that grace for which we long. Do not make us wait any longer, for our strength fails if the wait is long. You are powerful, Lady, in heaven and on earth, and accustomed to bringing God to earth, as is shown in the great mystery of the Incarnation, when you said: *Behold the handmaid of the Lord.*]

The powerful role of the Virgin as mediator between heaven and earth is closely linked to the Incarnation. It is emphasized in the *Vita Christi* by the disciples' dependence on her, even though they are the most important leaders of the early Church. In these scenes, Sor Isabel adapts ideas found in a different form in Eiximenis's *Vida de Jesucrist*. Although Eiximenis did not narrate how the Virgin taught the disciples, he did include it as part of his praise of the Virgin and of the meaning of her name:

Terçament il·luminà et per son lum aprés lo Sanct Sperit endreça la preÿcació et camí dels sancts apòstols e consells lurs e ordinacions generals en la fundació de la sancta religió cristiana et ans que aytals ordinacions o leys publicasen volien esser ajudats aprés per los seus sancts consells et oracions. (BC, MS 299, fol. 62v)

[Thirdly, she shines and by her light, after the Holy Spirit, guides the preaching and way of the holy apostles as well as their counsel and general ruling in the foundation of the holy Church and, before any rules or laws were made public, they wished to be assisted then by her holy counsel and prayers.]

Immediately after the presentation of the green shoes, the Virgin is given a pair of grey velvet ones:

Los altres tapins, Senyora, són de vellut burell, tots brodats de mantes de murta; aquests calçarà vostra senyoria com negociarà en les fahenes àrdues de natura humana, car a vostra mercé han a recórrer tots los temptats e tribulats en la present vida. (fol. 57v*bis*; I, 210)

[The next pair, Lady, are of dull grey velvet, embroidered with clusters of myrtle. These your Ladyship will wear when she is mediating in the arduous tasks for human nature, for it is to your Highness that all those tempted and in trouble must have recourse in the present life.]

The grey *tapins* are embroidered with myrtle. The embroidered myrtle leaves are similar to those in Roís de Corella's literary descriptions. Because of their Moorish origin, embroidery with items from nature was frequent, such as leaves or flowers (see note 3 above). Like the herb *agnus castus* examined in Chapter 5, myrtle was thought to be a plant with properties to cure women's ailments: 'Medicorum arborem aptam scribunt mulierum necessitatibus plurimis' [Moreover medical texts prescribe this tree as good for many female complaints] (St Isidore, XVII, 7, *De propriis nominibus arborum*, 1993–4, II, 350, 49 [St Isidore 2006: 346]). Myrtle was being used in the fourteenth century for medical purposes and is found in a recipe for a wash to cure *mal de mort*: 'lauament de cames per o mal dessut dit [*mal de mort*], item flor de carmoni, fuylls de mirta, e flor de romani' [for a wash for the above sickness, take flower of wild rose, myrtle leaves, and rosemary flower] (BC, MS 864, fol. 43v).[10]

According to St Isidore the etymology of myrtle associates it with the sea: 'Myrtus a mare dicta, eo quod magis litorea arbor sit' [Myrtle is named from the sea because it is by preference a shore tree] (St Isidore 2006: 346). The

---

[10] 'Romani' is a regional name for *romero* [rosemary] (Estevan Gómez 2010: 220). 'Carmoni' has been translated as 'wild rose' by analogy with *carmín* [rose pink] (*DRAE* 1992: I, 416).

word 'a mare' links it to bitterness and makes it appropriate to decorate the shoes which equip the Virgin for helping those beset by trials and tribulations. Its association with the sea, 'a mare', also links it to Maria, and one of her titles, *stella maris*.

In modern-day Spain, myrtle decorates the floats in the Holy Week processions and carpets the ground at Corpus Christi. In the Majorcan municipal processions, celebrating the Estandart d'Aragó, the ground is covered with myrtle and rushes. Records of the procession are found in the thirteenth century.[11] In Valencia, myrtle was also used in civic processions. In 1423, at the entry of King Alfons the Magnanimous, the councillors requested residents to clean up their homes and to strew the streets with myrtle and other scented herbs:

> E per ço los dits molts honorables Justicies e Jurats preguen, insisten e requiren a tots e sengles habitants en los carrers e partides desus specifficades que, cascun en lurs enfronts, facen fer nets lurs enfronts e per al jorn de la entrada del dit senyor Rey empalien e ornen de draps de raç e altres bells draps les parets de lurs halberchs e enfronts, e les carrerres enramen de murta, junch, bova e altres verdejants e specioses erbes lo mils que fer poren. (Carreres Zacarès 1997: 118)

> [And for that reason the honourable town councillors and dignitaries require, request, and insist of each and every inhabitant in the streets and areas specified above that each one tidy their house front and, on the day of the entry of His Majesty the King, decorate the walls of their houses and adorn them with velvet and other beautiful cloths and strew the streets with myrtle, rushes, bulrushes, and other greenery and scented herbs, to the best of their ability.]

Expiración García Sánchez indicates that the multiple purposes of aromatic plants, including myrtle, meant they were planted in the *munà* [royal estates] of Moorish Spain (2008: 207–8, 227). It is extremely likely that in the gardens of Valencia, such as the one next to the convent, myrtle would have grown.

The final pair of shoes is of pure gold thread, like the brocade used to clothe the Virgin for her Coronation in heaven (see Chapter 6): 'Los altres tapins, Senyora, són de or tirat, singularment obrats: aquests estojarà vostra altesa per a la derrera jornada, quant haurà a fer aquell gran camí de la terra al Cel' [The last pair, Lady are of drawn gold, daintily worked. With these will Your Highness be shod on the last day, when you will have to make the great journey from earth to Heaven] (fol. 58r *bis*; I, 213). In heraldry, gold is associated with the sun. It symbolizes fire and is the colour of love

---

[11] Gabriel Llompart, 'La festa de l'Estandart [d'Aragó] en Mallorca (ss. XIII–XV)', <http://ife.dpz.es/recursos/publicaciones/10/59/1llompart.pdf>.

(Castañeda y Alcover 1923: 75), the third and greatest of the theological virtues.

The Virgin is held up throughout the *Vita Christi* as the perfect example of Christian charity. Charity is the third of the maidens to come and reside with the Virgin after her conception. Charity 'la ençendrà tant en la amor de Déu e de sos prohïsmes, que contínuament treballarà en reconciliar nostre Senyor Déu ab natura humana' (fol. 3v; I, 14–15) [will inflame her so much in the love of God and of her neighbour that she will forever work to reconcile our Lord God with human nature].

Sor Isabel demonstrates her awareness of gold's pre-eminence by using it to clothe Charity, 'la pus preminent de totes' and 'la pus amada de ses donzelles' [the most important of all her handmaids, the best loved of all her ladies] (fol. 69v; I, 252):

> La vestidura sua era tota d'or molt singular, sembrada de infinides pedres preçioses; car en ella se han a engastar totes les obres meritòries, per a ésser a Déu plaents e gracioses. (fol. 26v; I, 100)

> [Her garments were all of very special gold, sprinkled with innumerable precious stones, for in her is set every worthy work, so as to be pleasing and gracious to God.]

As the Virgin takes her place among the host of heaven at her Coronation, it is the best of all the theological virtues, charity, which equips her for glorification and to receive the three gold crowns.

The Virgin's contribution to salvation history is exemplified by the beauty of her feet. They show how she was faithful to God, how she placed her hope in him, and how she loved him. The outpouring of praise for the Shulamite's feet also influences Sor Isabel. Many medieval commentators on the Song of Songs apply to the Virgin 'quam pulchri sunt gressus tui in calceamentis, filia principis' [how beautiful are your feet in their sandals, o prince's daughter] (Song of Songs 7. 2), but most significantly Ubertino da Casale cites the verse in his praise of the Virgin glorified, which he links to the moon under her feet. For Ubertino, her feet on the moon imply her treading the path of poverty, as well as the way in which her steps are directed towards God:

> quia multi per dignitatis gradum accedentes ad deum ab ipso recedunt per uite demeritum: hanc lunam habuit uirgo sub pedibus per perfectam gratiam: calcando per uoluntariam paupertatem: unde omnis culpa cecidit sub pedibus uirginis: quia per cincta fuit uirtute ad bellum. O quam pulchri sunt gressus tui in calciamentis filia principis. (Ubertino 1961: 405)

> [for many approaching God through their level of dignity fall back by the lack of merit of their life. The Virgin had this moon beneath her feet

through perfect grace; stepped on through voluntary poverty; for all sin falls under the feet of the Virgin: for she was girded with virtue for battle. O how beautiful are your feet in their sandals, o prince's daughter.]

Alain de l'Isle expounds a number of qualities of the Virgin which stem from the praise of the Shulamite's feet:

> Gressus tui, gloriosa Virgo, sunt nobilitas, virginitas, fecunditas, nobilitas generis, integritas carnis et mentis, fecunditas prolis. Calceamenta sunt affectus, effectus, profectus, excessus; affectus in meditationibus, effectus in operationisbus; profectus in desideriis, excessus in gaudiis.
> (Alanus de Insulis 1844–64: 210, col. 97)

[Your steps, glorious Virgin, are nobility, virginity, fecundity, nobility of character, wholeness in both body and spirit, fruitfulness in your offspring. Your footwear is affects, effects, profession, and expression; affects in meditations, effects in works, profession in what you long for, and expression in joys.]

Sor Isabel, like other medieval theologians, cites Song of Songs 7. 2. Her commentary on it concludes the scene of the gift of the *tapins*:

> *Quam pulcri sunt gressus tui in caltiamentis Filia Principis;* volent dir: 'O, senyora princessa, filla ý sposa del gran príncep Déu eternal! ý quant vos fa bell veure passejar ab aqueixos tapins resplandents de inmortalitat! Tots, Senyora, ab gran alegria seguiran vostra senyoria, obeint lo per ella manat com a reyna ý senyora nostra' (fols 58v–59r; I, 213)

[*How beautiful are your feet, in their sandals, o daughter of the prince*, meaning: 'O Lady, princess, daughter, and spouse of the great Prince, God of all the ages. And how beautiful are your feet in those chopines, or fancy shoes, glittering with immortality! All, Lady, with great joy, are to follow your Ladyship, obeying what you, Lady, command as our Queen and Lady.']

'Calceamenta' is translated by Sor Isabel as *tapins*. Before she is cast as an inveterate fashion-follower, it is worth noting that other medieval writers use *tapí* to translate biblical verses about sandals. In his rebuke of Tirant for taking a favour from Agnes de Berry, Martorell echoes Luke 3. 16: 'I am not fit to undo the strap of his sandal', using 'tapí esquerre' [left chopine]:

> car tu saps bé que no est digne ne mereixedor de possehir cosa alguna que sia de una tan alta e tan virtuosa senyora com aquella, per quant lo teu stat, linatge e condició no és suficient per a descalçar-li lo tapí esquerre.
> (Martorell 1990: I, 100; 2008: 266)[12]

---

[12] According to Hauf, 'sembla que provinent del registre religiós' [they seem to come from the religious register] (Martorell 2008: 270, n. 2).

[for you are fully aware that you are not worthy of possessing anything at all from such a noble and virtuous lady, when your lineage, state, and condition are not high enough for you to take off her left sandal.]

It is also worth noting that, in her commentary on Pygmalion's dressing of the statue in the *Roman de la Rose*, Heller argues that 'choosing not to give a woman sturdy footwear is a way of circumscribing her movements, limiting her to areas where her feet and person will not be defiled' (2000: 6). It is possible also speculate that Sor Isabel chose *tapins* because they were traditionally worn for church or because they did not allow women to undertake much walking, thus enclosing them more in the private sphere.

Some Conception liturgies employ 'quam pulcri sunt gressus tui, filia principis', first, because it echoes Song of Songs 4. 7, 'Tota pulchra es, et macula non est in te', and also because the emphasis on female feet alludes to the crushing of the head of the serpent by the woman in the *proto-evangelium* prophecy. The crushing of the serpent was seen as a figure of the Annunciation but gradually was applied to the Immaculate Conception of the Virgin, which prepared for it.[13] Allusion to the *proto-evangelium* can already be seen clearly in Rupert of Deutz's commentary on beautiful female feet. He combines the feet of the princess beloved of King David with the action of crushing the serpent, undertaken by the woman (Genesis 3. 15): 'Tu autem o filia principis, bene calceata, caput serpentis contrivisti' [For you, o prince's daughter, well shod, crushed the head of the serpent] (1844–64: 168, col. 941). The *proto-evangelium* prophecy about the crushing of the serpent, which marks the end of the battle between good and evil, is one of the most common immaculist signifiers in the late fifteenth century (Twomey 2008: 73–103).

Sor Isabel may also have been influenced by another Old Testament battle between good and evil in which a woman's feet have a part to play, that between Judith and Holofernes. Judith prepares her body, as the Virgin does, by putting sandals on her feet:

> And she washed her body, and anointed herself with the best ointment, and plaited the hair of her head, and put a bonnet upon her head, and clothed herself with the garments of her gladness, and put sandals on her feet, and took her bracelets, and lilies, and earlets, and rings, and adorned herself with all her ornaments. (Judith 10. 3)

Judith's preparations show that her feet are part of the beautification she

---

[13] An *Annunciation* retable from the Kingdom of Aragon depicts the Virgin crushing the serpent (MNAC 56721), linking the Incarnation, the *proto-evangelium*, and the feet of the Virgin. It may or may not also allude to the Immaculate Conception.

must undertake to ready her for meeting Holofernes. Judith prefigures the Virgin in the way she conquered sin, and her special garments and sandals must also have suggested the scenes of adornment of the Virgin.

Many verses from the Psalms and from the Song of Songs are used in Leonardo Nogarola's Conception office, such as 'Tota pulchra es', which is the opening antiphon at first vespers.[14] 'Quam pulchri sunt gressus' [How beautiful are your feet in their sandals] is used as the antiphon before the Magnificat at first vespers (BC, MS 1043, fol. 13r). It is repeated at matins on the octave of the Immaculate Conception (fol. 21r). There can be no doubt that Sor Isabel used the allusion to the Virgin's beautiful feet as an immaculist signifier and the beautification of the Virgin's feet in her sandals was probably suggested to her by repetition of the office.

Honouring the feet of the Virgin no doubt also drew on knowledge of miraculous shoes with healing powers which were venerated in various parts of Europe. The Virgin's shoe was venerated at Soissons, and two miracles about its healing powers are included in Gautier de Coincy's *Les Miracles de Nostre Dame* [Miracles of Our Lady]: 'que dou sant soller Nostre Dame / ne devoit mais douter nule ame' [for no-one ought to doubt the holy slipper of Our Lady] (1970: 207, lines 150–1). Sor Isabel was more likely to know of the Virgin's 'santa sandalia' [holy sandal] gifted to the Praemonstratensian monastery of Santa Maria de Bellpuig in the Kingdom of Aragon. The sandal was reputed to have been given to the monastery by Ermengol IV, Count of Urgell. Fernando el Católico, Sor Isabel's kinsman, knew about the sandal, as he enabled the formation of the Cofradía de la Santa Sandalia [Brotherhood of the Holy Sandal] in 1474 (Corredera Gutiérrez 1997: 54). The sandal is mentioned in passing by Jaime Caresmar (1977: 50), who, whilst recording the different altars in the Church, mentions that the second altar on the left is that of the Virgin of the Conception with the Holy Sandal.

The fine clothing Sor Isabel includes to mark the Annunciation has a significance which has not been previously discerned. In other parts of Europe, particularly the Low Countries, it is known that religious women used the rosary to pray for the Virgin's adornment. Anne Margreet W. As-Vijvers studies a particular and little-known form of the rosary, supported by legend:

> According to a medieval Marian legend, three sisters who lived together in devotion set themselves to prepare Our Lady 'a fine mantle, with a gown and undergarment, and with other precious "jewels", like a headdress, and shoes, and the other things one wears'. From St Stephen's day (26 December) onwards they worked on the manufacture of these clothes by reciting 150 Ave Maria prayers every day – fifty for each garment –

---

[14] See Twomey 2008 for a study of the development of the theme of the Virgin's beauty to signify her Immaculate Conception.

and fifteen Pater Nosters for the decorative accessories. (2007: 41, citing Cornelis de Vooys).

The period of preparation of the garments in the legend corresponds to the cycle of the liturgical year which links the Incarnation and the Annunciation on 25 March. The sisters prayed into place a series of garments which corresponds exactly to those in the *Vita Christi*, the mantle, undergarments (the chemise), gown (the *gonella*), the shoes, the jewels, and the crown.

As-Vijvers insists that the 'iuweelen' for which the devout sisters pray in the legend could be interpreted as 'precious things' (2007: 41, n. 1). It is strange that it is the jewels at which she baulks, whilst she does not attempt to reinterpret any of the other adornments. Sor Isabel's adornment of the Virgin in the *Vita Christi* shows that some medieval women certainly interpreted the jewels as pearls or other necklaces.

The presence of the garments, and the shoes, to adorn the body of the Virgin in the *Vita Christi* shows that Sor Isabel was aware of the practice of saying the rosary to adorn the Virgin. As on many other occasions, she does not directly exhort her reader to pray the rosary and pray the adornment of the Virgin, but she leaves the legend and the practice to subtly underpin her narrative and encourage her nuns in their devotion.

Conclusion

The gift of six pairs of high-heeled silk shoes to mark the Annunciation is one of the most striking scenes in the *Vita Christi*. Shoes were, and are still, a principal means of adorning the female body, with the multiple pairs owned by the rich and famous a mark of their wealth. They are also a means of differentiating their owners from ordinary women.

The shoes presented to the Virgin had been accorded a bad press by male writers, and were thought to portend the downfall of humanity because of the sin of female vanity they encapsulated. In reality, they were not worn solely by high-ranking women. Men also had *tapins*, as the dispute between the guilds shows. They were also worn, presumably in plainer styles, inside the convent.

It could be that Sor Isabel wished to redress the misogynist currents coursing through the Kingdom in her day by deliberately reversing the significance of the *tapins*. Those worn by the Virgin were not to mark her proud nature but rather to symbolize the opposite, her supreme humility. Nor were they capable of turning the Virgin from God, in the way that moralists like Eiximenis, and later Stubbes, believed they would, because she remained the model of piety.

Putting on shoes had biblical precedents, which Sor Isabel sought to evoke.

They beautified the Virgin's feet, evoking those of the beloved Shulamite from the Song of Songs, whose feet, praised by the Lover, prefigured hers. The shoes made them fit for veneration by the hosts of heaven and earth, which were about to pay homage to her. The *tapins* enable her to become the supreme consort, the perfect exemplar of faith, hope, and charity, first for the disciples and then for all Christians, even its male leaders and pontiff.

Finally, the adornment of the Virgin with beautiful garments and with fine shoes recalls a Marian legend associated with the rosary, an important and developing practice in the late Middle Ages. Rosary devotions are examined further in the next chapter.

For Sor Isabel, the embellishment of every part of the Virgin's body was paramount. From the tips of her toes to her crowned head, she is the epitome of the princess of the royal house of Israel, a fitting consort of the King of Heaven.

8

The Crown of Twelve Stars and Franciscan Rosary Devotion

> Surge mea sponsa so swete in sygte
> And so thy sone in sete full shene
> [...] Veni coronaberis
> (BL, Cotton MS Caligula A. II, fol. 107v)

In post-Tridentine paintings of the Immaculate Conception, such as those of Esteban Murillo (1617–82), the Virgin descends to earth on the upturned moon with twelve stars encircling her head. The twelve stars have become so familiar that no representation of Mary Immaculate seems complete without them. In the late fifteenth and early sixteenth centuries, however, representation of the Immaculate Conception was evolving and the twelve stars had not yet become irrevocably part of it. In this chapter, I examine Sor Isabel's crown of twelve stars, comparing it with other contemporary literary and devotional crowns.

The *stellarium*, or twelve-star crown, is based on the vision in Revelation 12 .1: 'Now a great sign appeared in heaven: a woman, robed with the sun, standing on the moon, and on her head a crown of twelve stars'. The *stellarium*, consisting of twelve meditations on the privileges of the Virgin, was 'popular in the seventeenth century' (Stratton 1994: 122), and was one of two beadroll devotions favoured by the Franciscans. The second was a crown of roses or 'Seraphic crown', which consisted of seven mysteries, repeated nine times, to symbolize the sixty-three years of the Virgin's life (Stratton 1994: 124).[1]

The Dominicans favoured a third beadroll prayer, the rosary as known today. Legend holds that St Dominic of Guzmán developed the rosary. However, *Ave* prayers developed in the tenth century, and prayers using beads were common. The development of the rosary as a series of meditations on the life of Christ was promoted by two Carthusians, Adolf of Essen (†1439) and Dominic of Prussia (1380–1460), in *Our Lady Mary's Rose Garden*. The new devotion spread into reformed Benedictine convents

---

[1] The pearl necklace in Villena's version (fol. 50v; I, 185) has sixty-two pearls to represent the years of the Virgin's life.

under the aegis of Johannes Rode (†1439). Subsequently, a confraternity of the rosary was established by Alan of Rupa (1428–75), a Dominican, and by Jakob Sprenger. The confraternity, with handbooks dating from 1438, promised myriad benefits to its devotees (Winston-Allen 2005: 1–3; 118–27; Rubin 2009: 332–8).

Ave prayers were known in Spain before the mid fifteenth century. A vernacular version by Fernán Pérez de Guzmán with 150 stanzas is present in many fifteenth-century poetry collections.[2] He retired to his estates after 1432, which is when he wrote his religious poetry.

Suzanne L. Stratton outlines how the fate of the *stellarium* was linked to that of the Immaculate Conception and to rivalry between the Franciscan and Dominican Orders. In 1640, a decree forbidding it to be recited was passed by the Dominican-dominated Holy Office (1994: 122–137; 130). *Stellarium* confraternities were to be disbanded and, thereafter, the Dominican rosary took precedence. Nevertheless, the *stellarium* persisted in popular piety and was only removed from the list of permitted prayers in 1938 (Stratton 1994: 163, n. 13).

Studies of the rosary rarely compare it to the *stellarium* (Thurston 1912: 189; Paschini 1954: 1350; Winston-Allen 2005). Eithne Wilkins acknowledges that the number of prayers was not fixed until after the 1470s (1969: 26–7; 40–1), although she makes no mention of the *stellarium*.[3] Stratton has dedicated a chapter of *The Immaculate Conception in Spanish Art* to its history, and Rubin acknowledges the presence of the *stellarium* among rosary devotions, in reference to the writing of Pelbart van Themeswar (2009: 336–7).

Stellarium devotion was well established in Spain by the mid seventeenth century. Hipólito Sancho de Sopranis describes a procession in Cadiz with fifteen people participating (1954), twelve of whom represent the twelve stars and the others the three paternosters. For this reason, Stratton (1994: 135–6) places Cadiz at the centre of devotion to the 'Rosario concepcionista' [rosary dedicated to the Immaculate Conception].

In early-sixteenth-century paintings the Virgin is crowned sometimes with roses and at other times with stars, and both are connected to patrons keen to demonstrate their devotion to either the circlet of roses or the *stellarium*. Stratton believes it likely that Murillo's painting of *Santa Ana y la Virgen* [St Anne and the Virgin] (Prado, PO968), in which the Virgin is crowned with roses by two cherubs, stems from his patron's support for the

---

[2] Fernán Pérez's *Ave María trobada* follows the life of Christ. See Dutton 1990–91: VII, 11, for a list of the manuscript witnesses containing this poem (ID0103).

[3] Both Wilkins and Anne Winston-Allen (2005) limit their discussion of Christian prayer-bidding to the rosary because of their respective emphasis on the rose garden and the rose. For a study of prayer-bidding and the crown of stars, see Wely 1941.

Franciscan crown of roses. However, evidence from literary works shows that the crown of stars was already known as a Marian devotion in the late fourteenth century. Eiximenis refers to it as one of the devotions he commends to young women in his *Lo libre de les dones* [Book of Ladies]: 'O dir-li la sua santa devota vida, qui foren LXII anys, o lo *canticum gradum* per los XV graus del temple, o los set goigs o la sua corona, qui fo de XII esteles' [Either retell her holy life, which was 62 years, or the *canticum gradum* for the fifteen steps of the temple, or the Seven Joys, or her crown, which was of twelve stars] (1981: 40).

The Virgin crowned

A crown adorned with twelve stars or light-emitting jewels is presented to the Virgin at the Incarnation and the Assumption in the *Vita Christi*. Both are among the red-letter Marian feasts across the Peninsula. In the rubric to the chapter for the first coronation, Sor Isabel emphasizes its allegorical meaning:

> De la excel·lent e singular corona de dotze murons o esteles, ço és les XII dignitats sues, e ab VII fermalls, ço és los VII dons del Sanct Sperit, presentada a la mare de Déu per lo Princep Miquel. (fol. 59r; I, 214)
>
> [On the excellent and singular crown with twelve finials, or stars, that is to say her twelve dignities, and with seven jewels, which are the seven gifts of the Holy Spirit.]

The performance of investiture equips the Virgin for queenship, at the significant moment at which humanity and divinity are fused in the locus of her body. According to Jones and Stallybrass, 'it is through the investiture, through the putting on of a crown and of coronation robes – that the monarch becomes a monarch' (2000: 2). The investiture in the *Vita Christi* takes on greater significance because the crown is gifted. Crane's view that 'distributions [of gifts] [...] share a presumption that the personal device draws its significance from being integral to the giver, yet also that its significance can be dispersed outward to those who receive the device' (2002: 19) means that the Virgin's crown endows her with 'el poder y la potestad reales, la *auctoritas*' [royal power and authority] (Cea Gutiérrez 2001: 12).

The Annunciation crown is of purest gold: 'Ella, Senyora, és de or molt puríssim obrada maravellosament, la qual té dotze murons, e sobre cascú de aquells replandeix una stela de singular claredat significant les vostres excel·lències e dignitats' [The crown, Lady, is of purest gold marvellously worked, and it has twelve finials, and on each of them shines a star of singular brightness, signifying your excellences and dignities] (fol. 59r; I,

214). The crown is decorated with seven jewels, which Sor Isabel interprets as the seven gifts of the Holy Spirit.

Sor Isabel's allegorical crown mirrors those in use in Christian coronations. Crowns are normally 'de materiales preciosos: oro, plata, gemas' [of costly materials: gold, silver, and jewels] (Cea Gutiérrez 2001: 14). Sor Isabel's concentration on the crown's intricacy of design and its gold tracery – 'marvellously worked' – could have been influenced by the fact that the Valencians were renowned gold- and silversmiths, making a number of pieces of jewellery for royal patrons in the fifteenth century (Sanchis y Sivera 1922: 4).[4]

Sor Isabel also had knowledge of medieval royal crowns to inspire her, some of which she would have seen at court before entering the convent. Hispanic crowns were generally of an intricate design. Isabel la Católica's displays a riotous mix of symbolic flora, including pomegranates to represent the Kingdom of Granada (Granada Cathedral Chapel) (Schamm 1960: fig. 3). Intricate gold tracery is also a feature of an earlier royal crown, that of Beatriz (1202–35), wife of Fernando the Holy (1198?–1252). The crown of Jaume I, in the portrait thought to be of him by Jaume Mateu (Valencia 1402–52), is decorated with pearls (MNAC 9774; *Guia* 2008: 97).

Dominic Janes points to how gold is used frequently in biblical and exegetical writing to symbolize moral purity. He contends that 'the primary significance of gold was its glorious burning brilliance' which could be associated with the 'flaming of *caritas* within a body'; for Gregory the Great, gold was held up as the 'symbol of the values of the City of God: "gold is dimmed when a holy life is corrupted by earthly deeds"'.[5] Janes also notes that gold was associated with godhead to illustrate what was '*best*', citing Justus of Urgell, who asserts that 'just as there is nothing similar to God among metals so nothing in Creation is comparable to the Creator' (1998: 75–7).

In his *Elucidatio Cantica Canticarum* [Elucidation of the Song of Songs], commenting on *manus illius tornatiles aureae*, Alain de l'Isle associates gold with divine wisdom: '*Manus*, inquam, *aureae*, id est divina sapientiae repletae' [His hands of gold, that is, full of divine wisdom] (Alanus de Insulis 1844–64: col. 89). For Bernard of Clairvaux likewise, gold 'denotes the splendour of Divinity, and the wisdom which is from above' (Mabillon 1889–96: IV, 257). Gold's association with supreme holiness meant it was

---

[4] See also Ibarra y Folgado 1919 for a study of metalwork guilds from the thirteenth century onwards. For a study of Valencian silversmithing and a history of the guild, see Igual Úbeda 1956.

[5] On the significance of gold in heraldry see also Chapter 7. Despite the interpretation of gold as representing charity in heraldry, Sor Isabel used crimson to symbolize it (see Chapter 4).

appropriate to designate the Virgin's perfection and sanctity. It is a frequent comparator for the Virgin in Marian poetry, and Gautier de Coincy provides an example of how it can be used in wordplay on 'fin' [pure/end], afiné [purified/refined], and 'finement' [end/purely]:

> Douce dame, sanz finement
> Servir te doit on finement.
> Com ors ies afinée.
> Les tiens afines com or fin
> Et si leur donns a la fin
> Joie qui n'iert finée. (cited in Daniel E. O'Sullivan 2005: 123)
>
> [Sweet lady, without end
> One should serve you purely.
> You are as pure as gold
> You purify your own like pure gold
> And give them at the end
> Never-ending joy.]

In the *Corona Beatissime Virginis*, because of the similarity between *virgo* [virgin] and *virga* [rod], the Virgin is symbolized by the rod of gold: 'Tu es virga aurea omni sanctitate ornata, per aurum tua sanctitas designatur' [you are the rod of gold adorned with all holiness, by gold is your holiness designated] and the unknown author continues: 'nam sicut aurum omnia metallorum excellit nobilitatis et valore sic tue sanctitatis dignitas superat omnium sanctorum in merita et omnium prerogativas angelorum' [for just as gold is better than every metal in nobility and value so the worth of your holiness is higher than the merit of every saint and the prerogatives of all the angels] (BNE, MS 17674, fol. 12v).

Gold is frequently used in immaculist writing as means of promoting the pure origins of the Virgin. Jaume Roig compares the Virgin to 'ver or sens lliga' [true gold without trace metals] (1978: 159). He follows numerous medieval authors who associated pure gold with the purity of the Virgin (Twomey 2008: 146–7). As I have shown, the metaphor of pure gold was first used by the early apologists for the Immaculate Conception in the twelfth century, particularly Pseudo-Peter Comestor and Pseudo-Peter the Cantor (Lamy 2000: 131; Twomey 2008: 127). Both of these theologians compared Mary's pure flesh, necessary for the Incarnation, to a vein of gold, which stretched from the time of Adam and Eve to the time of her conception. Lluís Cathalà contrasts base metals with a eulogy of gold, the purest:

> Dels quals lo més pur bell or se nomena,
> qui té de valer més alta la cima,

> hi resta perfet sens ombra neguna
> d'aquell fonament que scuredat mostra.
>   (cited in Ferrando Francés 1983: 479, lines 52–5)

> [Of (metals) the purest is called beautiful gold,
> which has the highest value,
> and remains perfect without any shadow
> of that flux which shows forth dark traces.]

Cathalà is drawing on a reference to Job 23. 10: 'Let him test me in the crucible, I shall come out pure gold.' Because gold is 'lo més pur' [the purest] in the category of metals, he is able to show that the Virgin, the subject of his poem, is purest of all through her immaculate origins in the category of women.

Miquel Miralles, another fifteenth-century Valencian, constructs a creation image, which contrasts the purity of gold with the roughness of the rocks where it is found:

> Lo sol molt clar, per excel·lent noblea,
> creà ·ls metayls y és d'argentviu la pasta,
> y en aspres lochs l'or més perfet conrea,
> lo qual, com hix, trau tanta gentilea
> que l'aspretat no l'altera ni ·l guasta.
>   (cited in Ferrando Francés 1983: 454, lines 13–17)

> [The clear sun, by excellent nobility
> creates metals with quicksilver for flux,
> and the purest gold is found in inhospitable places
> which as it arises, brings such noble worth
> that the rough surroundings cannot rust or spoil it.]

Gold's association with the sun, or the heavens, and its location amid rough rocks makes it a useful symbol for the Virgin's immaculate nature. The pure flesh of the Virgin was conceived amid sinful nature, just as gold is found amid other substances.

Miralles draws on alchemy for his analogy between the Virgin and gold. It was believed that the sun was the origin of metals. When the alchemist mixes gold, the purest of metals, with quicksilver, he aims to create potable gold, believed at the time to be a cure for every ill. Gold's medicinal properties are suggestive when it becomes a symbol of a Virgin who assented to the Incarnation to save or salve humanity.

Gold has other important characteristics which make it an apt figure for the Virgin. Gold, unlike other metals, cannot rust: 'l'aspretat no l'altera ni ·l guasta' [the rough surroundings cannot rust or spoil it] (line 17). Rust is often used as a metaphor for sin. Miralles wishes to illustrate the Immaculate Conception with an analogy from nature but, unlike Eadmer's chestnut, to which it is comparable, Miralles chooses one with its origins in Scripture: 'the rocks have veins of sapphire, and their dust contains gold' (Job 28. 6).

Gold's shining properties are incorporated into the response at third night prayer in Juan de Segovia's office for the Conception of the Virgin: 'Auctor mortis diabolus ab exordio genus viciauit humanum: sed aurum fulgens reperitur in luto' [The author of death, the devil, from the beginning damaged the human race. But shining gold is visible in the dirt] (*Breviarium gerundense*, Girona, ACG, MS 125, fol. 6v; Ricossa 1994: 135). The response immediately follows an allusion to Eadmer's *De conceptione B. Mariae Virginis* (1844–64) in the preceding lesson.

Rocks and gold symbolized the Immaculate Conception in both art and literature in the late fifteenth century, and could do so alone or in combination. A well-known illustration of Job 28. 6 is by Leonardo da Vinci (1452–1519). It is the basis for his painting of the *Vierge des Rochers* (Louvre, 777) and the *Virgin of the Rocks* (National Gallery, 1093) (Fig. 21) to illustrate the Virgin's immaculate nature.[6] In the panel, the Virgin, together with John the Baptist, the Christ Child, and an angel, is seated on rocks in a wild and rugged landscape. All were pure beings, the first two having been cleansed in the womb from original sin, and they are symbolically sited in the rocky landscape to recall their genealogy. Both the date and the patronage of Leonardo are significant. The date of the Virgin of the Rocks (1483–5) belongs to the period immediately after Pope Sixtus IV approved the office of the Immaculate Conception, and is part of a surge of interest in celebrating it in both art and literature. Both paintings were commissioned by the Milanese Confraternity of the Immaculate Conception for their oratory in San Francesco. They were possibly dissatisfied with the first version, presently in the Louvre, and commissioned the second version of the subject.

Bartolomé Bermejo y Osona's (Barcelona, 1440–1500) image of the Virgin of Montserrat could also be interpreted as a Virgin of the Rocks, given the fervent devotion to the Immaculate Conception in Catalonia. The panel for the altar in the cathedral of Acqui Terme shows the Virgin seated at the foot of the rocky outcrop at the door of the monastery. It was commissioned in 1485 by a merchant, Francesco della Chiesa. The positioning of the Virgin by the artist, and the date of the panel suggest that contemporary viewers would recall the Virgin prefigured by pure gold among the rocks.

---

[6] The web pages of the National Gallery in London indicate that the subject of the painting is not the Immaculate Conception (www.nationalgallery.org.uk). However, given that gold among rocks was always an immaculist signifier in the fifteenth century, Leonardo was simply presenting the Old Testament prefiguration of the Immaculate Virgin in pictorial form for his patrons.

21. Leonardo da Vinci, *Virgin of the Rocks*.

In the mid sixteenth century the fusion of the Virgin of Montserrat and the Immaculate Conception did occur and can be found in a *Retaule de la Inmaculada* [Retable of the Immaculate Virgin] from the Monestir of Santa Maria de Sixena in Monegres, Huesca (MLDC 53), of which the central panel is the Immaculate Conception represented by the Virgin of Montserrat.

The presence of the image of gold in Catalan immaculist literature makes it likely that Juan de Segovia's office, written in 1440 to mark the declaration of the Council of Basle in favour of the new doctrine, was known in Valencia (Twomey 2008: 127). There are copies of Nogarola's office in almost every diocese in the Peninsula, indicating that, when the Pope accorded it indulgences, it quickly replaced Juan de Segovia's.

Sor Isabel's choice of purest gold for the crown could echo the liturgical and the scriptural references to gold among the rocks. It was also likely to reflect the tradition of the *aurea* or gold crown, which was symbolic of the 'state of beatitude' of the saints, which Thomas Aquinas defined as the joy the blessed soul experiences in seeing God (Hall & Uhr 1978: 249). For this reason, the gold crown was particularly appropriate for the Virgin when she received Christ in her womb, and also most fitting for her when she saw God in heaven, according to *aurea* tradition. Émile Mâle argues that tradition was a fundamental element in religious art, which restricted artistic creativity (1908: 15), and evidence suggests that this is what happened to early depictions of the *stellarium*.

Many depictions of the Virgin Immaculate, such as the woodcut which decorates the *Bréviaire à l'usage de Rome* (1502), reproduced in Maurice Vloberg's study of the Immaculate Conception in iconography (1958: 478, fig. 10), show her wearing a gold crown. Gold so perfectly encapsulated how the Virgin could be conceived without sin, although she was from sinful stock, that it prevented any representation of the crown as one of stars. Sor Isabel combines gold with stars to represent the Virgin's twelve dignities, a tradition originated by St Bernard, incorporated into praise of the Virgin by Eiximenis (BC, MS 299, fols 37v–38v), and pointing to the *stellarium* which was being developed by the Franciscans.

Gold crowns in combination with stars are present in both immaculist and non-immaculist contexts. A crown of gold decorated with the twelve stars is found at the frontispiece of the *Pomerium sermonum de beata virgine vel stellarium coronae beatae virginis* (Pelbart van Themeswar 1502), one of the earliest *stellarium* devotions. In the less sophisticated woodcut in the *Bréviaire à l'usage de Rome*, mentioned above, the Virgin's gold crown has twelve stars above it (Vloberg 1958: 478, fig. 10).

The combination crown proved durable. In a Valencian painting dating from the sixteenth century, Abdón Castañeda (1580–1629) depicts a solid gold crown on the *Virgin of the Angels* (MBAV 3860) (Fig. 22). At the central point, the crown has a single star, and twelve other stars decorate the halo. The central

22. Abdón Castañeda, *Virgen de los Ángeles*.

star could be the star of Jacob or the star of the morning, both of which also prefigure the Immaculate Virgin (see Twomey 2005).[7]

---

[7] A few late medieval Coronation miniatures incorporate vestiges of astral symbolism. A French book of hours of the Virgin (BL, Add. MS 27698) sets a Coronation miniature among the Joys of the Virgin. In it, although a plain gold crown (fol. 12v) is held by both Christ and God over the Virgin's head, the clouds are parting, with golden light shining, and stars are visible at very edge of the frame where the gold turns ruddy. The stars do not yet crown the Virgin. Another possible antecedent to a crown of stars faces the Saturday office in a Flemish book of hours (BC, MS 1852, fol. 77v). Mary is depicted on a throne with the Child on her knee. Her aureole has long rays, as in later crowns of stars. The Virgin has an upturned moon

In Valencian art there are a number of representations of the Virgin crowned with stars, mostly in scenes associated with the birth narrative, and Sor Isabel could have been familiar with some of the earlier ones before her entry to the convent. The Master of Artès in his *Retablo de la Natividad* [Retable of the Nativity] (Colección Juan Abellat, Madrid) depicts the Virgin with a halo rimmed with stars at the end of long rays. The Virgin's halo has thirteen stars, whilst St Joseph's halo has none. The Master of Perea in a retable of the *Adoration of the Magi* (Valencia, private collection) depicts the Virgin with a halo rimmed with eleven stars, illuminated by the star of Bethlehem, which shines over the Virgin and child. Another representation of the same theme (MBAV 292) by the same artist (see fig. 14) shows the Virgin's halo fringed with fifteen stars, with an additional star just above the others on the edge of the halo.

Images of the Breastfeeding Virgin, or the Virgin of Humility, also often include the moon and stars from the Apocalypse. Nicolau Falcó's triptych of the *Virgen de la Leche* [Virgin with Child Jesus at the Breast], has a beautiful centre panel in which the Virgin is encircled by the upturned moon (Colección Várez Fisa, Madrid).[8] Her halo has thirteen stars on its rim and her deep-blue cloak is patterned with gold stars. The folds of the red-and-gold brocade cloth which frames the two principal figures are held by two angels, so that they radiate out from the figure of the Virgin to create the illusion of rays of the sun. In the two lateral panels, angels hold a phylactery with the words 'Sancta Maria de Puritate Conceptionis' [Holy Mary of the Pure Conception]. Thought to date from 1500, this is one of the earliest associations of the Apocalyptic Virgin with the Immaculate Conception in either Castile or Aragon, since it contains a reference to it on the phylactery.

Triple crowns

The gold crown presented to the Virgin following her Assumption, close to the end of the *Vita Christi* (fols 310r–305r *bis*; III, 354–60), is a triple crown. In their study of the *aurea* and the *fructus*, Edwin Hall and Horst Uhr discuss the mistaken interpretations which art historians have set on the triple crown which St Elizabeth of Thuringia holds in the panel by Jan van Eyck in the Frick Collection, New York (Fig. 23). These crowns are 'usually said to symbolize Elizabeth's royal birth, her austere piety, and her chastity in marriage'. Hall and Uhr believe they should be interpreted with

---

at her feet. Spanish fifteenth-century depictions of the Virgin crowned with twelve stars, are believed to depict the Virgin of Humility (Stratton 1994: 122; Williamson 2009).

[8] All these retables can be seen in the Golden Age of Valencian Art catalogue, nos 49, 52, 54, and 55 (Benito Domenech & Gómez Frechina 2009: 192–203).

23. Jan van Eyck and workshop, *Virgin and Child with Saints and Donor*.

reference to the sermon 'Corona aurea super caput eius' [A gold crown upon her head], in which the theologian Josse Clichtove (1472–1543) discusses St Elizabeth's triple crown. Clichtove develops the symbolism of the gems and crowns as Elizabeth's 'triple reward of the thirtyfold, sixtyfold, and a hundredfold fruits for her holiness as wife, widow, and virgin' (Hall & Uhr 1978: 252).[9] It is probably also significant that the triple crown is present in a painting in which St Elizabeth gazes at the Virgin and Child, where the Virgin is depicted as both Virgin and Mother.

In the *Vita Christi*, the three crowns are presented in turn by each member of the Trinity. The first of the three crowns is gold, adorned with twelve carbuncles, and presented by God the Father:

> Preniu, mare mia molt cara, aquesta corona, la qual vos tramet la majestat del meu Pare, qui la us tenia fabricada e preparada, per la sua gran potència, ans que lo món fos creat, per-a strenar-la-us en esta jornada.
>
> (fol. 311r; III, 355)

---

[9] See also fig. 2 in the same article for a reproduction of St Elizabeth holding the triple crown from Van Eyck's panel.

[Take, my dearest mother, this crown given to you by the majesty of my Father, who had it made and prepared for you, by his great power, before the world was created, so that you could first wear it on this day].

The presentation of the first of the crowns honours the way God selected the Virgin for her role in salvation. In its emphasis on the Virgin's creation before the Fall, it corresponds to one of the principal signifiers of the Immaculate Conception in the late fifteenth century, the creation of Wisdom: 'from eternity, in the beginning, he created me, / and for eternity I shall remain' (Ecclesiasticus 24. 9) or 'Yahweh created me, first fruits of his fashioning [...] / From everlasting I was firmly set, / from the beginning, before the earth came into being' (Proverbs 8. 22–3). Through 'ans que el món fos creat' [before the world was created], Sor Isabel echoes two of the readings most often used in Conception offices.[10] She also points to the way that Mary's body incorruptible has just been lifted direct into heaven.

The twelve carbuncles that adorn it are like stars, which dispel the darkness of sin: 'carbunculus enim tenebras illustrat, splendore occulis intuentis iubet' [for the carbuncle illumines the darkness, with brilliance it directs the eyes of those who look on it]. Medieval lapidaries held that the carbuncle, a fiery red stone, sometimes equated to a ruby, at others to a garnet, was a light-emitting gem, capable of illuminating the way for those who looked upon it: 'Ningunas tinieblas pueden en tal manera extinguir o amatar la fulgente luz de aquesta, que ella, resplandesçiente, no ponga llamas enlos ojos delos que la miran' [No darkness can thus extinguish or cut off its brilliant light, without its gleaming light setting the eyes of those who look upon it aflame] (fifteenth-century Spanish translation of Marbode's *Lapidary*, Volmöller 1880, cited in Nunemaker 1938: 66).

The second crown, given by Christ, also employs number symbolism relating to the period of his life on earth, both the number of years and hours. In its emphasis on the humanity of Christ, the crown is decorated with myrtle leaves to emphasize the tribulations through which the Virgin has passed. Myrtle is a plant with healing properties (Touwaide 2008: 85) and eminently suited to symbolize the Crucifixion and its victory over sin and death. Myrtle also decorated one of the pairs of the Virgin's *tapins* (see Chapter 7).

---

[10] See Twomey 2008: 179–81 and Boss 2007: 221; and for the image of Mater Sapientiae see Boss 2007: 169–70. Ecclesiasticus 24. 9 is used in the *Breviarium secundum ecclesiae barcinonensis* (Vic, Arxiu Episcopal, MS 83) at none. Proverbs 8. 22 is used more frequently in Conception offices. See, for example, Toledo, Archivo Capitular, MSS 33.6, 33.7, 33.9; Girona, Arxiu de la Catedral, MS 125; Abadia de Montserrat, MS 51; La Seu d'Urgell, Arxiu Capitular, incunable 147; Segovia, Archivo de la Catedral, MS B272. For a discussion of how the creation of the Virgin is an important means of signifying the Immaculate Conception in Hispanic literatures, see Twomey 2008: 175–215.

The third crown is given by the Holy Spirit and represents how the Virgin is crowned as his bride. This is the point which brings the Coronation of the Virgin closest to the *Arbor* of Ubertino da Casale. Ubertino refers fleetingly to the triple Coronation of the Virgin, 'sic tripliciter coronatur ut infra dicitur' [so she was crowned three times as is said below] (1961: 398), which is later fleshed out as 'tripliciter invitatur', and as 'triplex conditio eleuationis' [triple state of elevation] (1961: 402). His triple crowning, triple invitation, and triple elevation of the Virgin may have influenced Sor Isabel's three crowns. Ubertino's crowning of the Virgin by God is described in few words, 'et posuit corona regni super caput suum' [and he placed the crown of the kingdom on her head] (1961: 398), though the crown has two aspects. It is both 'diadema spei' [diadem of hope] and 'corona gloriae' [crown of glory]. The three elevations are that of the rod of Aaron (Exodus 14), of the ark (Numbers 10), and of the voice of the Lord from the 'heart of the tempest' (Job 38).

Although Ubertino has the Virgin crowned only at the Assumption, it is a crowning with nuptial significance: 'et ipsam secum cum triumpho uictorie et iubilo nuptialis leticie in eternum palatium introducentem' [and she being brought with him into the eternal palace with triumph in their victory and joy in their wedding bliss] (1961: 403).

The Virgin is crowned with twelve stars in Roís de Corella's version of Ludolph of Saxony's *Vita Christi*: 'fon encara aquesta excelsa assumpció per sant Johán en Apocalipsi en figures notada quand descriu aquella admirable dona vestida de sol e davall los peus la luna y en lo cap de dotze steles resplandent corona' [that sublime Assumption was described by St John in the Apocalypse in prefigurations when he described that admirable Lady dressed in the sun, with the moon beneath her feet, and on her head a shining crown of twelve stars] (1495: 127).

Ludolph's twelve-star crown also has two different layers of number symbolism in Roís de Corella's translation: 'Los dotze steles de la sua resplandent corona son dotze excel·lents dignitats que circuhida la tenen y encara los dotze apòstols que en la sua alegra mort tots se trobaren' [The twelve stars on her shining crown are twelve excellent dignities which cluster around her and then the twelve apostles, who were all present at her happy death] (1495: 127).

Sor Isabel's number symbolism is detailed and relates to the final stage of the Virgin's life, the fifty days she spent on earth between the Resurrection and Pentecost, represented by flaming rubies, whilst 140 pearls symbolize each of the tongues of flame which descended on the Virgin and the disciples at Pentecost.

The triple Coronation of the Virgin was represented in art from the late fourteenth century. The Master of Sixena, probably Pere Sarrià, depicts the Coronation of the Virgin with three crowns in his retable *La Mare de Déu* [Mother of .

24. Vicenç Castelló, *Coronación de la Virgen*.

God] (MNAC 15916). The triple Coronation was still being represented in the sixteenth century. A Valencian artist, Vicenç Castelló (1586–1636), shows each person of the Trinity holding a gold crown to place on the head of the Virgin (MBAV 464) (Fig. 24).

In late-fifteenth-century art, the most regularly depicted triple crowns are papal ones. Roderic d'Osona (active in Valencia 1440–1518) depicts *San Pere entronitzat* [St Peter on the Papal Throne] wearing a mitre with three crowns (MNAC 15816). Similarly, Pedro Berruguete (Paredes de Nava, 1450–1505) shows St Gregory wearing a triple-crowned mitre in his *Sant Gregori Papa* [St Gregory, Pope] (MNAC 113233). A triptych of *St John the Baptist, St Fabian, and St Sebastian* by Miguel Ximénez (documented in Zaragoza between 1462 and 1505) has St Fabian wearing a triple-crowned mitre (MNAC 15858). Michael Sittow, painter to Isabel la Católica, depicted God the Father with a triple-crowned mitre at the Coronation of the Virgin in his *Couronnement de la Vierge par les anges en présence de la Trinité* (Louvre 1966–11) (Fig. 25). In Sittow's panel, part of a polyptych for the Queen painted mostly by Juan de Flandes (1460–1519), the Virgin kneels before the thrones of Christ and God the Father. The angels place a single gold crown on the Virgin's head.

After the Resurrection of Christ, Sor Isabel calls the Virgin Mary 'papessa': 'Car vós, Senyora, sou la gran papessa a qui Nostre Senyor ha comanat los grans tresors seus e de la església' [For you, Lady, are the great pope, to whom Our Lord has commended his great treasures and those of his Church] (fol. 262r; III, 172). With these words from St Michael, the Virgin is placed at the forefront of the nascent Church, with equivalent status to Peter, the first pope. Cristina Papa cites these words as part of her title in an article in which she comments on Sor Isabel's reinstatement of a female genealogy, as well as on the role of women within the Church: 'il riconoscimento della superiorità di Maria rispetto a tutti gli altri esseri creati era infatti l'unico appiglio per la rivendicazione di un rulo attivo del genere femminile all'interno della comunità ecclesiastica' [recognizing the superiority of Mary in comparison to all other created beings was, in fact, the only way to claim an active role for women within the ecclesiastical community] (1994: 219). Disappointingly, she does not comment directly on 'papessa'. Given the association of the triple crown with papal authority, it is likely that Sor Isabel is enabling the authority it symbolizes to accrue to the Virgin.[11]

---

[11] See the early representations of Maria Regina and the papal symbolism they incorporate in Stroll 1997.

25. Michael Sittow, *Couronnement de la Vierge par les anges en présence de la Trinité*.

Mary's Coronation and the Immaculate Conception in art

In the late fifteenth century Mary's Coronation, as an act of glorification, had become a regular element in altarpieces dedicated to the Joys of the Virgin. By the seventeenth century, Alonso Cano painted a Coronation of the Virgin with a crown of stars.

The Coronation of the Virgin features in a number of fifteenth-century books of hours but there is no evidence of an image like Cano's. The Virgin is crowned with a gold crown and not one of stars. In a Flemish book of hours (BC, MS 1852), the Coronation miniature (fol. 136v) is placed immediately before the Office of the Virgin Mary for Advent, which connects it to the Incarnation. Christ has his hand on the gold crown he is placing on her head. A typical Hispanic depiction of the Coronation involves all the members of the Trinity, in a manner similar to Villena's description of the triple crown (Réau 1955–59: II, ii, 623). The Coronation miniature in the Breviary of Isabel la Católica depicts the Virgin kneeling, whilst a golden crown with elongated finials, each decorated with a swirl of points in gold, is placed on her head. Both Christ and God the Father hold the crown, whilst the Spirit in the form of a dove descends above them (see Backhouse 1993: 7).

Réau distinguishes five principal types of Coronation of the Virgin. He takes the *Coronation* by Pere Nicolau, now in the Cleveland Museum, as typical. Réau follows Mâle's view that the coronation of the Virgin originated in France in the twelfth century (1955–59: II, ii, 622). His view that: 'l'assomption et le couronnement sont souvent superposés ou même fondues sur le même retable ou sur la même toile' [the Assumption and the Coronation are often superimposed or even fused on the same retable or tapestry] (623). His conclusion is very different from that of Levi d'Ancona, for whom Old Testament coronations prefigure the Immaculate Conception.

Gold crowns in the Old Testament

The golden crown gifted to Mary in the *Vita Christi* echoes Old Testament coronation scenes, such as the crowning of Esther (Esther 2. 17) by King Ahasuerus. The enthronement of Bathsheba by her son, King Solomon, is another prefiguration of the coronation of the Virgin (I Kings 2. 19) (see Mâle 1908: 243; Levi d'Ancona 1957: 31). It may perhaps be significant, given Mâle and Réau's views, that a *Coronation of the Virgin* miniature in the Flemish book of hours discussed above is immediately followed by one of Bathsheba, bathing under the gaze of King David (BC, MS 1852, fol. 13r).

Discussing the miniatures in the *Biblia pauperum*, in which she considers the *Coronation of Esther* and that of Bathsheba, Levi d'Ancona argues that all thirteenth- and fourteenth-century depictions of Old Testament coronations were associated with the Immaculate Conception (1957: 28–32). Depiction of the Immaculate Conception in the thirteenth and fourteenth centuries is infrequent in the Peninsula.[12] However, in breviaries prior to or contemporary with Sor Isabel, the Feast of the Immaculate Conception, where it is illustrated, is illustrated by the meeting of the Virgin's parents at the Golden Gate, or by the Elsinus miracle, both of which were used in different Peninsular dioceses for the readings for the feast.[13]

Another important crowning, that of the beloved from the Song of Songs, was used as the *capitulum* or short scripture in many Marian offices: 'Veni coronaberis' [Come and you will be crowned] (see the Jerusalem Bible: 'Come, my promised bride'). In the north of the Kingdom of Aragon the verse is used as part of the reading for compline and Mass at the Virgin's Nativity (*Breviarium urgellense*, La Seu d'Urgell, ACSU, Incunable 147, p. 272r).[14] At Lleida, with its strength of devotion to the pregnant Virgin, 'Veni coronaberis' is the lesson at none on the Feast of the Expectation, celebrated on 18 December (*Breviario de Rodà*, Arxiu Capitular, MS Rc-0026, fol. 440v).

Although many commentators have associated the Coronation with the Virgin's Assumption into heaven, Sor Isabel includes crowning as part of the preparation for the Incarnation. The link between the Coronation and the Incarnation derives from the Song of Songs verse (3. 11) about Solomon's coronation at the hand of his mother, interpreted by many medieval theologians, such as Peter Comestor, as a prefiguration of the action of Mary at the Incarnation: 'Egredemini filiae Sion et videte regem salomonem in diademate, quo coronavit eum hodie mater sua' [Daughters of Sion, come and see King Solomon wearing the diadem with which his mother crowned him today] (*PL* 198, col. 1774). Commenting upon the Annunciation, he adds, 'in hac ergo die Dominicae conceptionis, christus homo hoc diademate coronatus est in utero

---

[12] For example, there is a rarely a miniature illustrating the first letter of the Conception office in Hispanic breviaries or those used in the Peninsula. One breviary of Italian origin illustrates the Conception with a miniature of Abbot Elsinus in the boat crossing to England (BNE, MS Vitr. 21-6, fol. 447r). The Assumption and Nativity are more frequently illustrated, as they were considered the most important Marian feasts.

[13] The meeting at the Golden Gate is illustrated in an early sixteenth-century missal from northern Aragon (La Seu d'Urgell, ACSU, *Missale secundum consuetudinem romanum noviter impressum*, 1502, fol. 146r).

[14] Nativity offices were frequently used for the Conception feast, as I have shown elsewhere (2008). Most of the manuscripts are from northern Aragon, from the Pyrenees area of the Diocese of Lleida, from Girona, or from Urgell. See, for example, the Urgell Missal (La Seu d'Urgell, Arxiu del Ajuntament, MS s/n, fol. 270v); three Girona Missals (ADG, MS 7, fol. 57v; MS 8, fol. 129r; MS 9, fol. 225r); a Missal according to the Vic Rite (Vic, Arxiu Episcopal, MS 69, fol. 81r). However, the same reading is found at the Nativity in the Cistercian monastery of San Cugat in Barcelona (Arxiu de la Corona d'Aragó, MS SC 14, fol. 416r).

matris [...] per hoc autem, quod dicitur eum coronasse mater sua' [on this day of the Conception of the Lord, Christ the man has been crowned in the womb of his mother (...) through this, it is said that his mother crowned him] (col. 1775).

Perhaps even more significant than the Old Testament antecedents is one from the writings of St Clare, which might have been in Sor Isabel's mind as she crowned the Virgin:

> Whose love is more tender
> Whose courtesy more gracious
> In whose embrace you are already caught up
> Who has adorned your breast with precious stones, and has
>   placed priceless pearls in your ears
> And has surrounded you with sparkling gems
> As though blossoms of springtime
> And placed on your head a golden crown
> As a sign to all of your holiness. (1982: 191)

Clare's words, addressed to Agnes of Prague, may well have been read aloud in the Santa Trinitat. Mariteresa Fumagalli Beonio-Brocchieri (1994), commenting on this passage, mentions its focus on the physical and material beauty of the body and its ornaments. Clare's words resonate in two ways for the convent reader. First, how much more than Agnes of Prague was the Virgin fit to be crowned with a golden crown, a sign of her holiness. Secondly, the crowning of the virgin Agnes was one to which all Poor Clares aspired, and, therefore, it again connects the narrative with their own heritage.

The gold crown with stars and fifteenth-century numerical prayer devotions

St Bernard's *Sermon for the Octave of the Assumption* (1844–64: 183, cols 429–48), as Hauf indicated (1987), provided a template for the development of *corona* devotions. St Bernard grouped the twelve stars into three different categories:

> For we can discover in Mary three kinds of prerogatives, which I will call the prerogatives of heaven, the prerogatives of the flesh, and the prerogatives of the heart. And, if now these three constellations be multiplied by four, as each containing three stars, we shall have perhaps the twelve stars which make the diadem of our glorious queen resplendent beyond all others. (1984: 214)

Sor Isabel's crown with its twelve stars and seven jewels incorporates the two different Franciscan number devotions, although twelve is predominant because it provides the structure of the entire episode. Its combination of stars and jewels approximates it to other vestigial fifteenth-century numerical devotions.

Jewels, celestial bodies, and flowers are a feature of a fifteenth-century Spanish devotional crown, the *Corona Beatissime Virginis* (BNE, MS 17674), which is copied alongside prayers and devotions to the Virgin. The *Corona* takes as its starting point a crown of gold 'ut aurum excessit omnia genera metallorum' [for gold is superior to all other types of metal] (fol. 1r), and although it does not have twelve stars, it is decorated with twelve light-emitting jewels: 'duodecim lapidibus insignatam'. The stones include topaz, lapis lazuli, jasper, sapphire, agate, chalcedony, amethyst, carbuncle, chrysolite (topaz), and beryl. The devotion also includes six flowers: rose, lily, crocus, violet, heliotrope, and camomile. There are, in addition, six heavenly bodies: the sun, the moon, and various constellations, including Orion, the Bear, and star of the sea. The *Corona* was attributed to St Ildephonse of Toledo (*PL* 96, cols 233–318; see Castro 1973: 603). Its number devotion is based on a double twelve, which explains why it is of interest to the Franciscans, who copied and possibly authored the devotion. Like Sor Isabel's, embedded within the double twelve is another significant number: seven. There are seven stars and seven virtues. Seven is given the following interpretation:

> septem stellis fuisti decorata cum septem virtutibus fuisti adornata. Tu enim fuisti solidata per fidem, amore inflamata per caritatem, eleuata per spem, per temperanciam fuisti sobria et modesta, per fortitudine uigorata, per iustiticiam equalissima, per prudenciam dissertissima.
> (BNE, MS 17674, fol. 2r)
>
> [you were decorated with seven stars, adorned with seven virtues. For you were grounded through faith, most inflamed with love through charity, elevated through hope, modest and dignified through temperance, strengthened through fortitude, even-handed through justice, and able to discern through prudence.]

The first meditation in the *Corona* is topaz, for it is held to be more splendid than any other stone in the crown. This is because Mary is believed to be 'omnes angelos superas excellentia' [above all angels in perfections]. This statement is followed by a series of examples: 'Quis studiosior in leccione [...] Quis subtilior in contemplacione' (fol. 3r) [Who is more studious in reading? Who is more subtle in contemplation?]. The round shape of the topaz becomes a symbol of how the Virgin is without beginning and end: 'est autem lutanium corpus spericum at rotundum clarum et lucidum pulcrum et graciosum quam omnia sanctissima valde tibi conveniunt' [and this topaz is spherical and round in shape. It is clear and bright, beautiful and noble, for everything holy is appropriate to you] (fol. 4r). For a Franciscan, the topaz meditation points to her immaculate beginning and her assumption into heaven and, throughout the *Corona* meditation, the unknown author displays his belief that the Virgin is like a gemstone, more beautiful than those decorating the crown.

Hauf, discussing Sor Isabel's crown meditation, believes that its 'contenido resultaba mucho más fácil de entender, dado el natural interés de las monjas, en general procedentes de familias de la aristocracia, habían sentido y posiblemente sentían, por las galas y aderezos' [content was simpler to understand, given the natural interest that the nuns, in general from aristocratic backgrounds, had felt, and possibly still felt, for beautiful dresses and adornments] (1987: 114). The Franciscan *Corona* with its jewel meditations shows that Sor Isabel, rather than adhering to an aristocratic tradition, is following a Franciscan one. It is probable that both the meditative *Corona* and Sor Isabel's are examples of Hispanic *stellaria*.

There is evidence of the twelve-star *corona* in Franciscan literary works from other parts of the Peninsula. Fray Ambrosio Montesino, a Castilian poet (1444?–1514?) whose devotion to the Virgin Mary and her Immaculate Conception is attested in many of his *coplas* [verses], dedicates one of the poems in his *cancionero* [book of poems] to the twelve-star crown: 'A las doze estrellas de la corona de la reyna del cielo hizo fray ambrosio las doze coplas que se siguen' [Fray Ambrosio composed the twelve stanzas which follow to the twelve stars in the crown of the Queen of Heaven] (Dutton 1990–91: V, 107a). Each stanza of the *coplas* focuses on a different aspect of the Virgin's life or nature. In the first stanza, Montesino sets out her role as Mother of the Redeemer, and associates her participation in the redemptive process with the Fall 'triaca de la manzana' [remedy for the Fall] (see Montesino 1987: 134, line 4). The second stanza focuses on Mary's purity, and links this to the Trinity's intervention on her behalf. She is pre-elect before the Fall, 'eleta' (line 12). The stanza points to the sacrality of the Virgin Mother, as temple of the Trinity, an image which is used in connection with the Immaculate Conception by Sor Isabel.

Amidst a litany of titles and images of Mary, Montesino includes those of two sacred objects: reliquary of virginity and 'incensario' [thurible] which purifies all that come into contact with it. He equates Mary with the image of the Tree of Jesse, focusing on the fruit Mary will bear, which pays the tribute for sin. Next, he uses a litany of metaphors all of which contrast the Virgin with sin, 'de nuestras tinieblas lumbre' [light for our darkness] (line 45), and provides a series of remedies which the Virgin offers to sinful humanity, such as 'llave de nuestra cadena' [key to our chains] (line 47).

In the seventh stanza he offers another litany relying on three Old Testament prefigurations of the Virgin Birth, where Mary is ark of the covenant (Numbers 10. 33), the burning bush (Exodus 3. 2), and then gateway to heaven, 'quicial y puerta' (Ezekiel 8. 3) (Montesino 1987: 135, line 79). The gateway in Ezekiel's vision and that of the 'camino' [pathway] to heaven (line 74) contrast Mary with Eve.

Montesino uses the Song of Songs to give substance to the relationship between God and Mary. He, like Sor Isabel, emphasizes Mary's role as Bride of Christ by means of her 'desposorio' [betrothal] (1987: 134, line 86). The Virgin's queenship and her perpetual virginity are associated in the penultimate stanza. The final stanza of the poem provides a coda to the whole, as it is a plea for the Virgin to be present at the author's death, 'si no estó contigo / y tú allí no estás conmigo, / ¿con que cara la daré?' [if I am not with you and you are not with me, how will I face it?] (1987: 135, lines 118–20).

Whilst Montesino's poetic litany has internal coherence, and could well be a *stellarium,* the *Aureola monacorum* or *Corona de los monjes* [Monk's Circlet], dating from the fourteenth century according to Dutton (1990–91), has less. Its rubric identifies it as a *corona*, and this, together with its subject matter and Franciscan authorship, may at first sight suggest it is another *stellarium.*

The poem begins with the preparation of the Virgin Mary for the moment of the Annunciation: 'dios te fizo con mesura' [God made you with nobility] (1990–91: II, 239a, line 5), linking it to the reason why Mary's flesh should be pure: 'de gracia & virtud bastada / & de la tu carne pura / fue su persona formada' [knit by grace and virtue and by your pure flesh, was his person formed] (lines 6–8). Next, the poet addresses the holy birth of the Virgin, foretold by prophets, 'de profetas anunçiada' (line 17), and illustrates the role of the Virgin through a series of Old Testament prefigurations, which are either sacred vessels or sacred spaces, 'arca de noe obrada' [well-worked ark of Noah] (line 19), 'de dauid torre bastida / e de salamon cambrera' [strong tower of David and Solomon's chamber] (lines 23–4), or which recall the action of God in salvation history, 'de gese verga florida' [blooming Rod of Jesse] (line 21), '& de jacob escalera' [and Ladder of Jacob] (l. 22), 'paloma que con verdor / es venida' [dove which flew up with a green branch] (lines 27–8). Some of verses are Song of Songs prefigurations: 'pozo de aguas corri- entes' [wellspring of flowing waters] (line 45), 'Lirio entre spinas nado' [Lily sprung up among thorns] (line 46). Both the well and the lily among thorns became symbols of the Immaculate Conception in the early sixteenth century (Vloberg 1958: 478; Twomey 2008: 160–73). One of the stanzas draws on popular etymology of the name Maria: 'de las mares marinera' [sailor of the seas] (line 36). This *Corona* ends with a plea to the Virgin to intercede with her Son on behalf of the sinful author 'pues que tanta es tu grandeza / en los çielos como creo' [since I believe your greatness in the heavens is so great] (lines 53–4). The title seems to signal that it is a *corona* devotion but, in this case, *corona* means nothing more than a collection of ideas.

Coronation of the Virgin and the novitiate

Crowning was part of the nuns' entry to the novitiate, and each nun, on reading of the Virgin being crowned, would have recalled her own important day of entry. The *Orden y ceremonial en el qual con la brevedad possible se da Dotrina, forma y modo como se ha de dar el habito de la aprobacion y profession y velo a las religiosas de Nuestra Madre Santa Clara* [Order and Book of Ceremonies where a very short outline of instruction, manner, and method of giving the habit of entry and profession and the veil to Poor Clare nuns is given] begins the ceremony of the reception of new novices into the Order with an antiphon:

> Iesu corona virginum
> Quem mater illa concipit
> Que sola virgo parturit
> Hec vota clemens accipe
> Qui pergeris inter lilia
> Septis choreis virginum
> Sponsus decus gloria
> Sponsisque reddens premia. (BC, MS 452, fol. 7r)

> [Jesus, crown of Virgins
> your mother conceived you
> and alone a virgin bore you
> You rest among the lilies
> With seven choirs of virgins.
> Accept this sweet vow,
> Worthy bridegroom in glory
> presenting prizes to the encircling choirs
> of virgins and brides.]

Although it would be satisfying to affirm that the Coronation of Mary recalled the antiphon at the start of the ceremony, the instructions in this seventeenth-century manuscript indicate that the antiphon has replaced the *Veni Creator*: 'y de ninguna manera se cante el Veni Creator porque asi lo advierten los ceremoniales antiguos' [and the *Veni Creator* should not be sung under any circumstances, as the old books of ceremeonies indicate] (fol. 6v). A fifteenth-century Poor Clare ritual confirms this with an instruction that the sisters sing the *Veni Creator* (BC, MS 865, fol. 4r). In the seventeenth-century book of ceremonies, just before the novice is taken to the grille which separates the choir from the nave, the nuns intone: 'Veni sponsa christi accipe coronam quam tibi Dominus preparauit in eternum' [Come, bride of Christ, take the crown which Christ has prepared for you in eternity] (MS 482, fol. 8r). It is unlikely that this antiphon was used in earlier rites of entry, but even in older ones the presentation of the veil is linked to heavenly nuptials: 'ut quando ad perpetuam sanctorum remunerationem uenerit cum prudentibus uirginibus et ipsa preparata te perducente ad perpetue felicitatis nupcias intrare mereatur' [as when you come to the perpetual remuneration of the saints with the prudent virgins and you will be prepared and be worthy of entry to the wedding celebration of perpetual happiness] (MS 865, fol. 10r-v). Both rites have echoes of the Song of Songs in 'Veni sponsa' [Come, bride] and the 'Sponsus decus' [Worthy bridegroom], and this imagery is maintained in modern professions: 'Accipe signum Christe in capite [...] ut uxor eius efficiaris, et si in eo permanseris, in perpetuum coronaberis' [Receive the sign of Christ on your head that you may be his wife and if you remain in that state, be crowned for all eternity] (see Warner 1985: 128). The presentation of the crown to the Virgin, the presentation of crowns or garlands to brides, and their mirror image in convent ceremonial is an indication of how the crowning of the Virgin relates to the nuns' own experience, reinforcing its value and power.

Conclusion

In this chapter I have blended study of a number of Franciscan twelve-star devotions in literature and art, using them to illuminate Sor Isabel's. Old Testament prefigurations of the Virgin crowned, in miniature and patristic thinking, explain the powerful tradition of the gold crown. Gold, one of the Old Testament figures most used by commentators to provide biblical support for the Immaculate Conception, was the preferred substance to crown the Virgin for medieval writers and artists. A gold crown had too much significance to allow it to be superseded by one of twelve stars. In Sor Isabel's description of the crown of the Virgin, as in other representations of *stellaria*, such as Pelbart van Themeswar's, or early-sixteenth-century ones, the gold crown and the crown of stars were superimposed.

In previous chapters, I have shown how Sor Isabel weaves Franciscan traditions into her *Vita*. Her use of the *stellarium* offers another example of her technique. With the gift of the crown to the Virgin, Sor Isabel provides her nuns with an allegory of a theological truth. If it is through the putting on of a crown that the Virgin becomes Queen, a member of God's household, and a bride, it is a crowning that the Fathers of the Church have celebrated as a mutual one. The Song of Songs celebrates the crowning of Solomon by his mother, but 'Veni coronaberis' is also a call to the bride to prepare for her wedding by putting the wedding garland on her head. The Virgin crowns Christ in her womb and the Trinity honours her with crown upon crown.

9

Literary Liturgy:
Sor Isabel's Processions and Prayers

Devotion to the Franciscan *corona* is one of a series of elements in the *Vita Christi* which are testimony to Sor Isabel's approach to meditation. Her emphasis on robing (see Chapter 5) and her coronation scene (see Chapter 8) both evoke the vestition and symbolic crowning of novices as brides of Christ in their profession. Other dramatic scenes in the *Vita Christi*, already discussed, are embedded in the routine of convent life. Among them is the liturgical sequence of the elevation of the Host, for the nuns their principal point of contact with the world outside.

Entry to the convent is another performative activity in which the whole community engages, as the fifteenth-century *Ritual per a l'ús de un convent de clarisses* [Poor Clare Book of Rites] (BC, MS 865) shows. The role of the whole community and of the actions they perform is even more apparent in a seventeenth-century version of the profession ceremony (BC, MS 452), in which the physical space of the convent becomes a setting for dramatic movements. Robing takes place at the door of the enclosed space occupied by the nuns, and thus marks the transition from one life to another. As part of passage into the religious life, the novice then publicly embraces Christ. Because of the embrace, the 'Santo Christo' is likely to be a figure of Christ or a crucifix; it could also be the Host displayed in a monstrance:

> Aqui se advierte que para auer de recibir á la que viene á la religion sagrada á de estar toda la comunidad junta a la puerta en dos choros; y con este orden se llegará la que lleua el Santo Christo. Al humbral de dicha puerta con las Ceraforarias y tambien alli junto á de llegar la madre Abadesa y puestas todas las Religiosas en orden luego se arrodillará la que á de tomar el habito al humbral de la puerta haziendo reverencia al Santo Christo, cuya hecha luego se volverá a la mano del Guardian, o confessor que la lleva, y con breuedad se despidirá de los deudos, y despedida se uoluerá axí hazia el Santo Christo, y arrodillada con mucha humildad se abraçará con él. (MS 452, fol. 7v)

> [Here it is to be noted that, because of having to receive the new nun, all the community has to be assembled beside the door in two groups; and, when they are so assembled, the nun carrying the Holy Christ arrives. At

the door, with the candle-bearers, the abbess, and all the nuns positioning themselves in rank order, the postulant will kneel at the door, reverencing the Holy Christ, then she will return to the side of the Guardian or confessor who has accompanied her, briefly say goodbye to her relatives, and then turn back to the Holy Christ and, kneeling with great humility, she will embrace him.]

Although the fifteenth-century ritual does not refer to the embrace, there are several moments of obeisance. The first is after vestition, when the novice is to kneel before the altar 'induta nouicia et genuflecta ante altare' [once the novice has been dressed and has genuflected before the altar] and, at the close of the ceremony, she is again to prostrate herself before the altar (MS 865, fol. 5r–v).

In the *Vita Christi*, once the Virgin has received the Infant Christ in her womb, each of the allegorical ladies bends the knee and worships. This scene recalls convent ceremonial as well as, or instead of, court ceremonial. Villena's celebration of the Incarnation can be read as a parallel to the reverence for the body of Christ present on the Cross or on the altar in the profession ceremony:

> vengueren les dites donzelles ab gran reverència davant la Senyora, e, ficant lo genoll en terra, adoraren lo seu gloriós ventre, dient a sa senyoria: 'O, excel·lent Senyora, que ara que us trobau Mare de Déu poden los miserables recórrer a vostra mercé dient ab gran confiança: *O gloriosa spes nostra, tuo filio nos comenda, tu nos sibi representa, quia in te dulcis Maria speramus ut nos deffendas in eternum;* volent dir: 'O, gloriosa esperança nostra! Comanau-nos, Senyora, al vostre excel·lent fill que·ns guart e·ns defena; presentau-nos, Senyora, a la clemència sua; feu que ·ns accepte la servitut sua; car en vós, dolça senyora Maria, speram que·ns defendreu de tot perill eternalment.' (fol. 48r; I, 177)

> [the damsels came before the Lady and, with great reverence, bending the knee in full homage, they adored her glorious belly, saying to her Ladyship: 'O excellent Lady, now that you are Mother of God, every poor creature can turn with great confidence to your Ladyship, saying: *O glorious hope for us, you represent us, for in you, sweet Mary, do we hope that you may defend us for ever*; meaning: 'Our glorious hope! Commend us, Lady, to your excellent Son who guards and defends us; present us, Lady, to his mercy; as his handmaids, make us acceptable to him; for, in you, sweet Lady Mary, is our hope that you will defend us from all danger for ever.']

Of course, the obeisance at entry to the convent was not the only moment when nuns genuflected. For example, there might have been daily genuflection before the statue of the Virgin, before the altar, or homage before the monstrance.

Similarly, when the Virgin receives all the order and ranks of heaven and earth after the Incarnation (chs 49–60; fols 59v-69v; I, 216–51), it indubitably recalls court ceremonial but may also recall convent salutations. In the seventeenth-century novitiate ceremony, once novices had been received into the Order, they proceeded to approach each of the sisters in order of seniority. This is likely to have been the custom in Sor Isabel's day, although the fifteenth-century book of ceremonies does not refer to it. As the nuns read the presentation of the potentates, angels, and Adam and Eve, the representatives of humanity, to the Virgin, they would have transposed the descriptions to their own experience and to the convent reception of new entrants.

The celebrations held in Poor Clare convents to mark vestition or profession were elaborate, as evidence from Italy shows. Such important events in the convent calendar involved feasting, and it could be speculated that singing, or perhaps even dancing, may have played a part. Evidence from Le Vergini convent in Venice reveals that money was paid to a confraternity to provide trumpets and pipes for a feast day (Lowe 2003: 253). Music and dance for feast days were known in Peninsular convents (see Cátedra 2005: 362). For that reason, it is probable that the festivities described to mark the Incarnation in the *Vita Christi* had something in common with entry to the convent:

> E la Senyora, que singularment ama los hobedients, féu tanta festa de aquests gloriosos prínceps, e se alegrà tant de la sua venguda, que a tots fon manifest ésser per sa senyoria molt amats e estimats e favorits, acceptant-los sa altesa per familiars servidors a ella molt cars. E no solament volgué que una de les sues reals donzelles dançàs ab lo capità principal, ans manà a les tres pus amades que·s leven ensemps e que dancen e ballen e canten ab aquell príncep hobedient e ab los seus seguidors, car dignes són de tota honor e glòria. E los noms de les dites donzelles són: Hobediència, Virginitat e Pobrea; les quals, molt alegres, se levaren a dançar ab aquells sancts àngels, concordant ab ells en totes coses, e ells no menys ab elles, coneixent clarament que tots segueixen una intenció, ço és, de hobeir lo creador e seguir la voluntat sua. E, après lo dançar e ballar, cantaren les tres dites donzelles ab tanta armonia e dolçor.
>
> (fols 61v–62r; I, 224)

> [And the Lady, who loved the obedient above all others, put on a great celebration for those glorious princes, and was so happy at their arrival that she made it clear to all they were loved, esteemed, and favoured. And she did not only wish her royal damsels to dance with the most important of the captains but she ordered her three most beloved ladies to dance, step out, and sing with the obedient prince and with his followers, for they are worthy of all honour and glory. The names of the three damsels are Obedience, Virginity, and Poverty. These three, with great joy, arose to dance with those holy angels, keeping step with them in everything. They did the

same with the damsels, clearly acknowledging that all followed a single intent: to obey the creator and follow his will. And, after dancing and stepping out, the three damsels sang with great sweetness and harmony.]

In Chapter 6, I referred to the importance of entry to the convent and its parallels with coronation ritual undressings, both being all-female ceremonies. There is another all-female ritual evoked in the *Vita Christi*, one with more personal significance for Isabel de Villena. Janet L. Nelson indicates that medieval rituals for the coronation of queens adapted the prayers for electing abbesses (1997: 309–10). Lowe illustrates, albeit in a Venetian context, how election of abbesses contained rituals which evoked those of popes (2003: 240), such as the voting process and the enthronement of the successful candidate. As noted earlier, the 1513 edition of the *Vita Christi* is illustrated with an image of Sor Isabel enthroned, surrounded by her nuns, teaching authoritatively (fol. 232v). Lowe also refers to the bestowal of a ring on the chosen candidate and to depictions of abbesses in which they are shown holding a crozier, the religious equivalent of the sceptre held by queens (2001: 419–20). She notes the investiture of new abbesses with the keys of the convent, a topaz ring, and a crozier (2003: 240). John Moorman records that in one of the Valencian Poor Clare convents, that of Santa Isabel or St Elizabeth, later renamed the Puritat, the abbess had had the right to carry a crozier since 1351 (1983: 679). There are also a number of medieval paintings of St Clare holding a crozier. The *Retaule d'Advocació Franciscana* [Retable of Franciscan Calling] by Lluís Borrassà (active in Girona and Barcelona, 1360–1425), commissioned for the convent of Poor Clares in Vic, depicts her crowned with a gold crown, holding a book, her Rule, and bearing a crozier (MEV 714–19) (Fig. 26).[1] Vicente Cadenas y Vicent notes that a crozier could be incorporated into an abbess's coat of arms (1994: 70) and Isabel's coat of arms in the 1497 edition incorporates both the knotted Franciscan cord and the crozier. In the ritual installation of the Virgin as Mother of God, after receiving new garments, jewels, gloves, shoes, and the crown, she takes her place on the throne, just as the newly installed abbess would have done, once she had received her ring and staff of office.

Entry to the convent and popular medieval devotions

The story of the holy infant Virgin dedicating her life to God and symbolically leaving her mother and father to live at the temple became associated with a particular set of prayers in the Middle Ages, the *Canticum gradum*

---

[1] Lezlie Knox (2008: 185) comments on Sister Dorotea Broccardi's choice of the staff in her representation of Clare, instead of the lily which female saints often hold.

26. Lluís Borrassà, *Retaule d'Advocació Franciscana*.

[Song of the Ascent].² The story of the Virgin's arrival at the temple is part of the Nativity of the Virgin in Jacobus de Voragine's *Golden Legend* (1993: II, 152).³ The prayer model based on it is frequently included in medieval collections of devotions.

Caterina Vigri (1413–63), abbess of the Poor Clares in Bologna, wrote a treatise entitled the *Quindici gradi della perfezione* [Fifteen Steps of Perfection] for her nuns (Knox 2008: 167). Caterina's *Quindici gradi* is divided

---

² Examples of the *Canticum gradum* with slightly different titles are found in many dioceses. See, for example, the Lleida *Santoral* with its *Liber gradus* (Arxiu de la Catedral, MS 27) and the *Opera spiritualia* with its *Canticum gradum* (BNM, MS 9533).

³ New Testament apocryphal stories, including the birth of the Virgin, are collected in Wilhelm Schneemelcher's translation (2001).

into three parts, each representing a different stage of religious life: *incipientes, proficientes, perfecti* [beginner level, proficiency, and perfection]. Caterina's purpose is similar to that of many other medieval women writers who took seriously the injunction to pass on their experience in spirituality to the nuns in their charge.

Eiximenis begins his 'quinze excel·lents virtuts' [fifteen excellent virtues] of the Virgin, which is part of the tenth dignity of her crown, with the theological virtues, Faith, Hope, and Charity, writing:

> Aquest pujament estech senyal de que la Gloriosa auria quinze excel·lents virtuts per les quals pujaria al sobiran grau virtual sobre tota altra pura creatura. E diu que les quinze virtuts serien aquestes, ço és, fe, sperança e caritat, prudència, temprança, fortalea, justícia, penitència, virginitat, humilitat, paciència, obediència, pietat, puritat, devota oració contemplativa per excés. (*Vida de Jesucrist*, BC, MS 299, fol. 87r)

> [That climb was a sign that the Glorious Lady would have fifteen excellent virtues to the highest degree of virtue above any other creature and the fifteen virtues are the following: faith, hope, charity, prudence, temperance, determination, justice, penitence, virginity, humility, patience, obedience, piety, purity and devout contemplative prayer.]

Hauf discusses the similarities between Eiximenis's and Sor Isabel's versions of the ascent of the Virgin to the temple, indicating that hers converts a well-known legend into 'una especie de guión teatral o cinematográfico destinado a representarse mentalmente en la imaginación de las monjas' [a kind of theatre or film script to be played out in the imagination of the nuns] (1987: 108). Whilst some of the virtues Sor Isabel includes in the scene of the Virgin's ascent to the temple are the same as those in Eiximenis's *Vita Christi*, and his description of the ascent 'pudo servir de estímulo a Sor Isabel para organizar "una correlación sistemática" novelada, imaginando que éstan forman un cortejo de hermosas doncellas en torno a la Virgen niña' [it could have served as a trigger to Sor Isabel to set out a 'correlation step by step' written as a story. She imagined that these (virtues) formed a coterie of lovely ladies around the little Virgin] (1987:108). They are, however, as Hauf points out, not ladies in the Virgin's household, nor does the order in which they are placed correspond at all.

The tradition of associating virtues with the Virgin's ascent is not just a Valencian one, as it is present also in John of Caulibus's *MVC*. Although there the Virgin's entry to the temple is accompanied not by the *Canticum gradum* but by seven prayers, there is one prayer which includes a supplication for four virtues. These are humility, patience, kind-heartedness, and gentleness (1997: 16).

Like other medieval number devotions, the *Canticum gradum* varied from region to region. The *Liber gradus* [Book of Steps] (Lleida, Arxiu de la Catedral, MS 27), a devotion used in the north-west of the Kingdom of Aragon, is a thirty-step (twice fifteen) enumeration of virtues. Like Sor Isabel's and Eiximenis's it begins with the theological virtues but it also includes good works, such as visiting the sick and visiting holy places.

Sor Isabel's fifteen steps are, like the fifteen Psalms of the *Canticum gradum*, divided into three groups, each marked by specific prayers. Each group, with its attendant virtues, could easily be mapped on to the stages of contemplation. Sor Isabel begins, like Eiximenis, with the theological virtues, Faith, Hope, and Charity. These are the ones that initiate religious life. She then adds those virtues that draw their practitioner into the religious life: Poverty and Piety. Prayers at the first stage, or after the first five steps, are for human nature.

In the second stage of her steps to perfection, Sor Isabel has the Virgin accompanied by qualities which enable both her and the Poor Clares to continue with their chosen way of life: Constancy, Patience, Prudence, Kind-Heartedness, and Mercy. Prayers in the middle stage of the ascent are for the redemption of the human race (fol. 11r; I, 37).

At the final stage of the ascent Sor Isabel includes qualities such as Devoutness, Diligence in Virtue, and Sweetness of Contemplation, which properly belong to the contemplative life. They are blended with two elements of the Poor Clare Rule: Humility and Virginity. Virginity is the final step in the devotion and it encapsulates the central element of each nun's vocation which permits espousal of Christ, the ultimate goal of each of his brides.

The *Canticum gradum* was thought to be a devotion proper to young unmarried women, as Eiximenis shows when he commends it to them, together with other number devotions, in his *Lo libre de les dones*: 'O dir-li la sua santa devota vida, qui foren LXII anys, o lo *canticum gradum* per los XV graus del temple, o los set goigs o la sua corona, qui fo de XII steles' [Either retell her holy life, which was 62 years, or the *canticum gradum* for the 15 steps of the temple, or the seven joys, or her crown, which was of 12 stars] (1981: 40). There can be no doubt that Sor Isabel also believed that similar number devotions which she embeds in her *Vita Christi* were suitable for the young women in her charge.

Sor Isabel's fifteen steps of the *Canticum gradum* includes short meditations and excerpts from the Psalms, both of which could be used for meditation by her nuns. Given Eiximenis's commendation and his importance in Franciscan circles in Valencia, it is more than likely that the *Canticum gradum* meditation was recommended in standard form for use in the convent. This scene in the *Vita Christi* with its use of the *Canticum gradum* dovetails with the nuns' own devotional life.

Again it is to be reiterated that any exhortation to contemplation is subsumed within Sor Isabel's narrative. Unlike some other contemplative

27. Throne of Prioress Blanca of Aragon and Anjou.

Vitae Christi or partial versions of them, such as the anonymous *Contemplació de la passió* (Hauf 1982), she neither sets the narrative within the framework of devotions to be used at the hours, nor does she step aside from the narrative to periodically exhort the reader to contemplate.

Entry to the convent was the beginning of a spiritual journey for the nuns. It was a step-by-step journey, marked by processions similar to those which accompanied the Virgin's entry to the Temple. Anabel Thomas cites from the *Chronicle of San Giorgio, Lucca*, which provides a contemporary Poor Clare commentary on the way in which parents or relatives would accompany a young woman at her entry to the convent:

> The novice should come without pomp, accompanied simply by her mother [...]. The novice should approach the altar where the confessor will celebrate Mass for the nuns. She should be accompanied by her mother and by several of her relatives [...] and afterwards she is accompanied and introduced by the confessor into the monastery, with great tenderness on the part of her parents because they know they will never see her again in this world [...] and so she will stay under the tutelage of the teacher of the novices until it is time to take the veil. (Thomas 2003: 254)

Such all-female processions were part of convent life, as an evocative depiction of the prioress and her nuns from Monegres in Huesca shows. The prioress's throne from the convent of Santa Maria de Sixera depicts the prioress behind a processional drape with the sister to her right holding a censer (MLDC 19) (Fig. 27). The throne was made for Blanca of Aragon and Anjou, daughter of King Jaume the Just (1267–1327), who was prioress between 1321 and 1347. The processional drape is similar to those used by other artists in processions where bishops are present, such as the retable from the church of Sant Miquel in Montmagastre, Noguera, in the Crown of Aragon, mentioned in Chapter 4, in which a red processional cloth is held in front of the bishop who carries the monstrance (see fig. 7).

The ritual of entry of a young woman in the company of her mother and perhaps, as the text later adds, of other female relatives, is not dissimilar to the Virgin's arrival at the temple. The Italian *Chronicle of San Giorgio* underlines the impact that reading the chapters dedicated to the Virgin's entry to the convent would have had on the nuns in Sor Isabel's charge. It would recall their day of entry, with its rituals, obeisance, and official salutation. It would also recall their farewell to family members and the 'great tenderness' of their mother's presence.

The Virgin as doctor of spirituality

Later in the *Vita Christi* the Virgin becomes a spiritual model of a different order. After the Ascension and Christ's departure for heaven, Sor Isabel positions the Virgin at the heart of the incipient Church. This is not merely the case of a female author promoting a female character to a starring role, since it is has some similarities with other *Vitae Christi*. In John of Caulibus's *MVC* Mary stands among the disciples on the Mount of Olives and she speaks before the others, although her position in the group is not mentioned:

> Then the Lord Jesus began to be lifted above them and to ascend on his own power. His mother and the others fell prostrate and our Lady entreated: 'My blessed Son, please be mindful of me!'
> (John of Caulibus 2000: 320)

In Roís de Corella's translation of Ludolph's *Vita Christi* the Virgin is also present at the Ascension: 'Vengueren donchs los onze e altres dexebles al Mont de los Olives acompanyant la senyora verge mare' [the eleven and the other disciples came to the Mount of Olives, accompanying the Lady Virgin Mother] (1998: 111r). The Virgin's authoritative presence and her active contribution to faith are far more developed in Sor Isabel's version.

Eiximenis writes two different versions of the Ascension, one in which only the apostles are mentioned, and a chapter entitled 'Una exclamació a la gloria de la santa ascenció' [An Exclamation to the Glory of the Holy

Ascension], in which he has the Virgin fall at the feet of her Son, embracing him prior to his departure for heaven:

> o si veeses aquella dolça mare per subirana amor caure als seus peus abraçant-lo ab subiranes làgremes e reverència; ne nengú podia entendre que se deyen abdós sinó que tots los qui u veyen, per sobres de pietat que avien de aquella santa mare, ploraven agrament.
> (*Vida de Jesucrist*, BC, MS 460, fol. 253v)

> [oh, if you saw that sweet mother in her great love fall at his feet, embracing him with great many tears and reverence; for none could grasp what they both said, for those who saw it, through the great pity they had for that holy mother, were crying bitter tears.]

In Eiximenis's *Vida de Jesucrist* it is the Virgin who embraces Christ, whilst in Sor Isabel's it is Christ who kneels at the feet of his Mother, the exact inverse of the embrace in the *Vida de Jesucrist*. It provides an important way of discerning the value Sor Isabel placed on maternal authority.

The same thing occurs with regard to Pentecost. In the *Legenda aurea*, Mary is not mentioned as present at Pentecost. Voragine describes the tongues of flame on the apostles' heads only, discoursing at length on the nature of the Spirit and without mentioning the Virgin's presence: 'on the day of Pentecost, as the Holy Scripture in the Acts of the Apostles indicates, the Spirit came down in the form of tongues of fire on the heads of the Apostles' (1993: I, 299–308). Roís de Corella does mention the Virgin in the *Lo quart del cartoxà*, distinguishing her by name, but she is not given any active part to play in the proceedings. There were 120 members of the nascent Church present and the Virgin was named as being there with the disciples and devout women: 'E axi en aquest cinquante dia devalla lo sant sperit sobrels apostols hi altres dexebles e devotes dones que era quasi cent e vint en nombre amb la verge senyora Marie' [And on that fiftieth day the Holy Spirit came down on the apostles and other disciples and devout ladies who were almost one hundred and twenty in number with the Virgin Lady Mary] (1495: fol. 150v). John of Caulibus does not narrate the Pentecost scene, as his version finishes at the Ascension. Eiximenis, however, does mention the tradition of the Virgin as teacher in a chapter dedicated to what the Virgin did after her Son went to heaven, and his brief outline of the way the Virgin captured her listeners' attention, describing them as 'inflamats e enamorats' [inflamed and deeply moved to love] in listening to her speak, is expanded by Sor Isabel:

> los gents qui la hoyen parlar majorment del seu fill e dels misteris del regne de Déu axí s'en anaven edifficats, e inflamats e enamorats d'ella que jamés ne volgueren altre hoir ne llunyar-se d'ella. (MS 460, fol. 260r)

28. Pere Nicolau, Ascension panel, *Retablo de los Siete Gozos*.

[the people who heard her speak in depth about her Son and of the Mysteries of the Kingdom of God were edified, inflamed, and deeply moved by love for her and never wanted to leave her nor hear any other speak.]

Sor Isabel seems to have taken Eiximenis's brief descriptions of the Virgin's actions as her model for the presence of the Virgin at the Ascension and at Pentecost, combining them with the many representations of the two scenes in medieval art. In these the Virgin is placed at the centre, where she can be considered to symbolize the nascent Church (James Hall 1974: 33, 101). In Ascension panels such as the one in the anonymous Valencian fifteenth-century retable of the *Siete gozos de la Virgen* [Seven Joys of the Virgin] (MBAV 278) (Fig. 28), the Virgin is in the centre of the group of apostles. She looks steadily forward, and is distinguished from the others

29. Artist unknown, Ascension panel, *Retaule dels Goigs de la Verge*.

present by her posture, since the apostles look upward.[4] Pere Nicolau's representation of the Ascension in his *Retablo de los Siete Gozos* (MBAV 2263–9) (Fig. 29) shows the Virgin with St Peter immediately behind her, facing St John.[5]

[4] Another, slightly later, Valencian *Retable of the Seven Joys* (Casa Museu Batlle; see Benito Domenech & Gómez Frechina 2009: 54, pl. 8) depicts the Virgin at the Ascension to the right of the ascending Christ, with St Peter to the left, suggesting an equivalent importance in the two figures.

[5] See also Gonçal Peris Sarrià's *Retablo de los Gozos de la Virgen* [Retable of the Joys of the Virgin] (Palacio Episcopal, Cuenca; Benito Domenech & Gómez Frechina 2009: 92–3). The same positioning can be seen in Francesc Solives's *Retaule dedicat a la Mare de Déu* [Retable of the Mother of God] (Tarragona, active in the second half of the fifteenth century) (MEV 848, 885–7; *Guia de les col·leccions* 2007: 147) and also in Reixach's depiction of the *Ascension* (MNAC 50621). Two panels of the *Ascension* from another part of the Kingdom of

30. Woodcut of the Ascension, *Vita Christi de la Abbadessa del monestir de les monges de la Trinitat*.

31. Woodcut of the Ascension, *Vita Christi d[e] la Reuerent Abbadessa dela Trinitat corregit ab les cotacions nouame[n]t tretes en los marges*.

There was a different tradition of representation of the Ascension which does not include the Virgin at all. The woodcut which illustrates the Ascension in the 1513 edition of the *Vita Christi* depicts only the Apostles and is a witness to the other tradition (fol. 201r) (Fig. 30). The *Vita Christi* woodcut is evidence, if evidence were needed, that the printer was not illustrating the *Vita Christi*, although he was willing to create dedicated woodcuts for it, such as the one of Isabel enthroned. Rather, the woodcuts of most of the scenes in the book would have been used to illustrate any devotional work depicting the same scene from the Bible.

The Ascension woodcut in the 1527 edition of the *Vita Christi* (Fig. 31), however, places the Virgin at the centre of the group of apostles, following the other tradition. In the woodcut, as in many illustrations of the Ascension, the Virgin adopts a different posture from that of the disciples around her. She gazes forward with her hands clasped in prayer, whilst the disciples look upward, with at least one of them in a posture of amazement. The posture is not dissimilar to the anonymous Valencian retable of the *Seven Joys of the Virgin* already described (fig. 29).

Similarly, artistic representations of the Virgin at Pentecost in the Kingdom of Aragon often seat her on a throne, surrounded by the apostles. Frequently the Holy Spirit in the form of a Dove rests on her head or is descending just above it. In one panel, the Virgin's hands are together in prayer, whilst St Peter raises one hand towards Christ (MBAV 278) (Fig. 32).[6] With minor differences, the position of the Virgin at the centre of the Ascension and Pentecost scenes by artists from Valencia and other parts of the Kingdom show that the centrality accorded to the Virgin both physically and verbally by Sor Isabel was a traditional one.

It was Rupert of Deutz (c. 1075–1129) in his commentary on the Song of Songs who provided Sor Isabel with an authoritative source for her construction of Mary as 'doctoressa'. Rupert converts the Virgin into the prototype of the religious life. Rupert begins a tradition of Mary as '*magistra* of the apostles, and the great prophetess of the prophets, both male and female' (Mulder-Bakker 2004a: 189). He presents her as an informant of the evangelist but also as an author, in the same way many medieval women were, such as Elizabeth of Schönau, who dictated to her brother,

---

Aragon depict the Virgin in the centre of the group of apostles (Hispanic Society of America, A31).

[6] In Reixach's version (MNAC 50621), the apostles look down at their books or towards the Dove, whilst the Virgin sits motionless on her throne. The Master of Sixena's Pentecost panel in his *Retable of the Mother of God* (MNAC 15916) shows the Dove descending above the head of the Virgin and the tongues of flame from the Dove passing from her to the apostles. In a lost *Retable of the Virgin* (formerly Colección Muñoz, Barcelona; see Benito Domenech & Gómez Frechina 2009: 141, pl. 4), the Virgin also mediates the reception of the Holy Spirit by the apostles.

32. Pere Nicolau, Pentecost panel, *Retablo de los Siete Gozos*.

Eckbert (Mulder-Bakker 2004a: 9), or Angela of Foligno, who dictated to her confessor (Mooney 1994). *The Virgin Dictating to St Luke*, depicted by Llorenç Saragossà (documented in Barcelona and Valencia 1360–1406) (MBAV 253) (Fig. 33), shows that the Virgin's role as an author was a topic found in the Kingdom of Aragon. The image provides one explanation why medieval women's dictated spiritual works, although carefully examined, were nevertheless often given the seal of approval within the Church.[7]

Following the Ascension, Sor Isabel depicts a Virgin Mary so far advanced

---

[7] Angela's book begins with the approbation which outlines the trustworthiness of the scribe as well as the seal of approval accorded it by Cardinal-Deacon James of Colonna and eight Franciscan lectors. Biographies of the readers are given; for example, two of them were inquisitors. The book was also read by three other friars, all of good repute. 'None of these saw any sign of false teaching in this book' (Angela of Foligno 1993: 123).

33. Llorenç Saragossà, *Escenas de la vida de San Lucas: San Lucas escribiendo su Evangelio al dictado de la Virgen.*

in comparison to other followers of Christ that she acts as their teacher and spiritual guide. The Virgin directs the apostles' spiritual lives with authority, much as Sor Isabel would have directed the spiritual lives of the nuns, and others outside the convent. She acts as their 'maestressa' [instructor] and blesses them to send them out to begin their work of preaching and teaching. In this she seems to follow a short phrase in Eiximenis's *Vida de Jesucrist*: 'N'es penses que sent Pere ne los altres apòstols faessen negú acte pertanyent a la comunitat, vivent la Gloriosa, sens special consell seu' [Be certain that St Peter and the other apostles did not undertake any act relating to the community, whilst the Virgin was alive, without particular counsel from her] (BC, MS 460, fol. 260v). As on other occasions, Sor Isabel expands a phrase in her source to create new scenes which add greater depth to the Virgin's life.

The Virgin also directs the apostles' spiritual lives. Prayer, as discussed in

Chapter 1, is an important element of the Rule, and for that reason underpins each of the principal Gospel events. After the Ascension, prayer, under the direction of the Virgin, becomes the main focus for the apostles. The Virgin guides them, providing them with model prayers, although this is done in a manner appropriate to a woman, 'ab molt dolçor' [with great sweetness]:

> Amonestava·ls ab molta dolçor que stiguessen contínuament en oració, car per lo mijà de aquella obtendrien lo que demanaven, car als perseverants oradors nunqua misericòrdia e gràcia és denegada per la divinal clemència. E los dits apòstols, ab tota l'altra gent que ab ells era, donant molta fe en les paraules de la Senyora, *erant perseverantes unanimiter in oratione;* car ab gran perseverança ý fervor demanaven al senyor ý mestre seu li plagués trametre lo Spirit Sanct, que promés los havia, e que donàs remey a la dolor sens mesura que ells sentien per la separació de la sua vista. (fol. 291v; III, 281–2)

> [She admonished them with great sweetness that they should constantly engage in prayer, for through it they would obtain what they were requesting, for, to those persevering in prayer, grace and mercy are never denied by divine clemency. And the apostles, and all the others who were with them, putting great faith in the words of Our Lady, *persevered together in prayer*; for with great perseverance and fervour they asked their Lord and Master to send the Holy Spirit on them, which he had promised to send, and that he remedy their sorrow since he had been separated from their sight.]

The Virgin had already had the experience of receiving the Holy Spirit at the time of her conception and now assists the Church to receive the Spirit. In her close reliance on the mediative power of divine grace, the Virgin represents one of the principal means of acquiring spiritual knowledge for a Franciscan, and particularly for a Franciscan woman, which is through divine inspiration. The second means is through academic learning.

Sor Isabel's emphasis on the Virgin's magistral authority recalls a legend of St Clare found as an exemplum in the *Speculum spiritualis*. Knox shows how St Clare acts as 'magister' for the brothers, speaking with discernment and interpreting what has happened for all present (2008: 146–7). In the *Vita Christi* the Virgin's authority in spiritual matters means that the apostles obey her unquestioningly and, at her command, kneel to pray:

> E obeynt los apòstols, e tots los que aquí eren, lo manament de la Senyora e doctoressa sua, ficaren los genols, e cascú féu sa oració ab gran devoció e làgrimes, segons manat los era, sperant ab molta fe e desig veure complit lo que demanaven. (fol. 292r; III, 286)

> [And the apostles, and all who were present, obeying the commandment of the Lady, their doctor, knelt down and each made his prayer with great

devotion and tears, as they were commanded, longing with great hope and faith to see what they had asked for come to pass.]

The Virgin's prayers provide the words which others, directly speaking, the apostles, can use in their prayer for Pentecost. The apostles are addressed, 'cascú de vosaltres' [each of you], but the command can equally apply to the reader. They too are commanded in 'manament', and they obey, 'obeint'. Sor Isabel's prayers, mediated by the character of the Virgin, could also be incorporated into the nuns' private prayer:

> Per ço ara cascú de vosaltres diga ab summa devoció: *Cor mundum crea in me, Deus, et spiritum rectum innova in visceribus meis;* volent dir: Senyor e Déu omnipotent! Creau en mi un cor munde e net e deliure de tota culpa que als ulls de vostra majestat puga offender, e feu-lo habitacle e posada disposta per a rectitut que·m tinga ferm e constant en l'amor e temor vostra! (fol. 291v; III, 285)

> [For this reason, now each of you should say with deep devotion: *Create a clean heart within me, Lord, and renew an upright spirit within me*; meaning: 'Lord and omnipotent God! Create a clean and pure heart within me and deliver me from all sin which in the eyes of your majesty may offend, and make it a dwelling and resting-place that keeps me firm and constant in fear and love of you.']

The Virgin is not just authoritative, she has doctoral authority, for she is 'doctoressa', in an age in which women were excluded from university education. The Virgin's authoritative approach is reminiscent of that of women writers such as the cloistered Constanza de Castilla, who wrote prayers and liturgy for others to say. Sor Isabel, through the *Vita Christi*, takes the mantle of authority to guide her reader, both female and male, about the events in the life of Christ, and to mediate their meditation. Her words of prayer, repeated by the apostles, echo those of the Psalm 51. 10.

Popular devotions and the Virgin

Sor Isabel's technique of adapting words from the Psalms at times goes further. In popular devotion a tradition arose of adapting the words of canticles and psalms, turning them into praise of the Virgin. Sor Isabel's laudatory exclamations about the Virgin and her efforts on behalf on humanity seem to be part of that tradition. For example, the words of two Psalms are transferred from God as their addressee to the Virgin. From Psalm 96.1: 'Cantau, totes les coses creades, a la Senyora nostra cançons novelles; resone la lahor de sa senyoria en la congregació dels justs' [Sing new songs, all created things, to our Lady; let the praise of her Ladyship sound in the assembly of the just] (fol. 48r; I, 177); and the song of triumph of Psalm 97: 'Let the earth rejoice, the many isles be glad' echoed in 'e les illes de la mar e tota la terra, car per lo fruyt del seu ventre tots som reparats' [and, in the isles of the sea and all the earth, for by the fruit of her womb we are all made new]. A few pages later, Sor Isabel echoes the words at the beginning of Psalm 149, applying them to the Virgin:

> *O quam magnificata sunt opera tua, Domina. O quam decoratur tua excelsa gubernatio per misericordiam quam exerces quia per te Reges regnant.* Volent dir: 'O, Senyora! e com són magnífiques e grans les obres vostres! O quant és embellida la excel·lent governació vostra e lo alt regiment per les contínues misericòrdies que feu e exerciu! Car per vós mijà de les donzelles vostres los prínceps e reys regnen virtuosament e són prosperats, e sens vostra mercé nengú no pot plaure a nostre Senyor Déu ne fer nenguna obra virtuosa; per què dignament per tots deveu ésser reclamada, axí per prínceps com per súbdits. (fol. 64r; I, 232)

> [*O how your works are to be magnified, Lady. O how far is your excellent government to be embellished through the mercy you show; for, through you, kings reign*; meaning : 'O Lady! And how magnificent and great are your works! O how far is your excellent government and high rule to be embellished through the continuous mercies you show! For, through you, mediated by your ladies, princes and kings reign virtuously and prosper. Without your mercy, none can please our Lord God nor do any virtuous work; because you should be worthily called upon by all, by princes and by people.']

Devotions which adapt psalms and canticles into Marian prayers are found in various fifteenth-century manuscripts in the Peninsula, such as in the Castilian *Opera spiritualia* (BNE, MS 9533), which contains the Hours of the Cross, the *Canticum gradum*, the *Psalterium beate virginis Marie*, offices for the feastdays of the Virgin, for the liturgical year, and the Penitential Psalms. For example, in an adaptation of Psalm19. 1 in the Office of the Virgin, a psalm of praise to God becomes a celebration of Mary's might and power, showing how all the world, including the heavens above, praise her: 'Celi enarrant gloria[m] tuam uirgo marie' [All heavens declare your glory, Virgin Mary] (fol. 63v). Similarly, the words of Psalm 122 sing her praises: 'Letatus sum in te regina celi' [I have rejoiced in you, Queen of Heaven] (fol. 47v). The Psalm 'Letatus sum' is already associated with the Virgin through being sung at vespers and terce in the Hours of the Virgin.[8]

Devotion to the Hours of the Cross was another key aspect of medieval

---

[8] See, for example, the *Catalan Book of Hours of the Virgin*, BL, Add. MS 18193.

spiritual life. Sor Isabel sets a *planctus*, which follows the events of the Crucifixion, in the Virgin's mouth. Such devotions occur from the thirteenth century onward and relate the Virgin's sufferings to the Passion, with each hour containing a meditation and a prayer based on it for each of the Seven Sorrows: the arrest, the scourging, the condemnation, Crucifixion, death, deposition, and burial' (Woolf 1968: 268–9). The influential *Meditationes vitae Christi* follows the pattern of a meditation for each of the monastic hours, beginning with the arrest of Jesus and then the first stage of the trial at matins (John of Caulibus 1997: 255–89). See also the Valencian *Contemplació de la passió* (Hauf 1982), which follows the same pattern of meditations structured to fit with the monastic hours. In Sor Isabel's convent there is evidence of devotion to the Sorrows of the Virgin. The Santa Trinitat had a fourteenth-century Pietà in alabaster, holding the body of Christ on her knees (Benito Goerlich 1998: 160), which is considered one of its most important sculptures. Sor Isabel does not refer explicitly to the monastic hours and in this her Passion story is different from both John of Caulibus's *MVC* and the *Contemplació de la passió*.

The Office of the Conception and the *Vita Christi*

Since the Immaculate Conception of Mary is at the heart of the *Vita Christi*, underpinning her closeness to God and therefore her prayerfulness and her knowledge, it is appropriate to complete this study of the *Vita Christi* with an acknowledgement of Sor Isabel's debt to its liturgy. It is, after all, the Virgin's perfect nature and the way that she was chosen by God before time which enables devotional psalms to be reconstructed in her honour.

Sor Isabel begins her *Vita Christi* showing the Virgin created by divine foreknowledge. She depicts a short but dramatic scene, set in heaven, in which God the Father reveals his purpose. Sor Isabel appropriates the words of Galations 4. 4–5 about the Incarnation to apply to the conception of the Virgin: 'but when the completion of the time came, God sent his Son, born of a woman, born a subject of the Law, to redeem the subjects of the Law.'

As I showed in my study of the Immaculate Conception in Hispanic literature, Proverbs 8. 22–3 is one of its principal signifiers in the Old Testament, being used as short scripture at vespers the length and breadth of the Peninsula (Twomey 2008: 176). With the words, 'ell l'à vista eternalment e d'ella s'és enamorat' [he saw her from eternity and fell in love with her] (fol. 3r; I, 13), Sor Isabel echoes: 'Dominus possedit me in initio viarum suarum, antequam quidquam faceret a principio. Ab aeterno ordinata sum et ex antiquis antequam terra fieret' [God possessed me in the beginning of his ways, before anything was made at the beginning From everlasting, I was firmly set, from ancient times, before the earth came into being'] (Proverbs 8. 22–3).

Sor Isabel chooses to narrate the conception through retelling the story of the Virgin's childless parents, Anne and Joachim. She relates Joachim's rejection at the temple, and his return to his flocks. She then recounts how an angel announced the birth to each of them and how they met at the Golden Gate. The meeting of Joachim and Anne at the Golden Gate, following their individual angelic annunciations, is the point at which, traditionally, the Virgin was believed to have been conceived (James Hall: 1974, 170; Stratton 1994: 20–8). The stories were propagated in the *Legenda aurea* under the feast day of the Nativity of the Virgin (see Voragine 1993: 152). Artists used the Golden Gate as a frequent way of depicting the Immaculate Conception, even in the early sixteenth century. It is to be found in a woodcut illustrating Nogarola's Conception office in a 1509 missal used in the Diocese of La Seu d'Urgell in the north of the Kingdom.

In the Kingdom of Aragon there are a number of miniatures representing the meeting and embrace of Anne and Joachim at the Golden Gate. In Valencia, the Conception office was also illustrated by an initial miniature of the Golden Gate. The *Vesperal* [Book of Hours for Vespers] of Ferrante I of Aragon (BUV, MS 391, fol. 252r), copied in Naples, is dated 1490, the year of Sor Isabel's death. Joachim and Anne meet at the Gate, with the miniaturist carefully representing the outside of the city walls, the rural setting, and Joachim in rustic clothing. There are not many miniatures illustrating the Feast of the Immaculate Conception, which was considered a minor feast, and this illustration is an indication of the significance that the Golden Gate scene had in the late medieval period.

Interest in the stories from the Apocryphal Gospels did not wane, even when the new Conception offices of Segovia and Nogarola, with their heightened emphasis on Old Testament prefigurations of the Virgin, were adopted after 1440 and 1476, respectively. It is probable that this was because the Golden Gate doubled as a representation of the 'porta clausa' [closed door] of Ezekiel 44. 1–2. In the Kingdom of Navarre the story of Joachim and Anne was regularly used for the readings for the Conception feast, even in the fifteenth century.[9] The best-known Valencian representation of Anne and Joachim is the altarpiece from the convent of the Puritat (MBAV 287) (see fig. 6).[10]

---

[9] Pamplona, Archivo de la Catedral, MS 21, *Breviario de Pamplona*, fol. 280r.

[10] Artists across the Kingdom of Aragon frequently painted the Virgin's parents. The Master of Retascón (c. 1410–25) depicts the *Kiss at the Golden Gate* and the panel strikes a contrast with the *Kiss of Judas* in the facing panel (MNAC 64033 and 64034), marking two key moments in the history of salvation, the first kiss marking the beginning of salvation and the birth of the Virgin, and the second,the betrayal and imprisonment of Christ, leading to the events of the Passion. The *Meeting at the Golden Gate* is also one of the panels in the *Retaule de Santa Anna* [St Anne Altarpiece] (MNAC 64038).

Nogarola's Conception office draws heavily on the Song of Songs for the antiphons and readings. 'Sicut lilium inter spinas' (Song of Songs 2. 2) is the opening antiphon at vespers and compline on the feast day, as well as at first vespers on the octave. Jaume Roig's *Espill* includes this verse in the prologue. Sor Isabel does not use it as part of the conception scenes in the *Vita Christi* but sets the verse in the mouth of Adam, as a eulogy to the Virgin, as she stands at the foot of the Cross:

> *Sicut lilium inter spinas, sic amica mea inter filias*; car axí com lo liri resplandeix entre les spines e stà sens màcula en mig de aquelles, axí la nostra Senyora excel·leix entre totes les dones. E, besant lo pare Adam les mans a aquesta excel·lent Senyora, ab molta dolçor e amor mirava aquella bellea de cara, e contemplava los grans beneficis que de aquella e per ella havia rebut tota natura humana. (fols 231v–232r; III, 55)

> [*Like a lily among thorns, so is my beloved among women*; for just as the lily is replendent among the thorns and is without stain in the midst of them, so Our Lady excels among women. And, Adam, kissing the hands of that excellent Lady, with great sweetness and love gazed on the beauty of her face and contemplated the great benefits which from her and by her all nature had received.]

The perfect Virgin, free from any type of sin, takes her place at the foot of the Cross on which sin is defeated by her Son.

Nogarola's office also uses another verse from the Song of Songs, 4. 7, adapting it: 'Quam pulchra es amica nostra, columba nostra, et macula originalis non est in te' [How beautiful you are, our beloved, our dove, and there is no original blemish in you]. As a true Franciscan and upholder of the Immaculate Conception, Sor Isabel cannot fail to include the verse which became synonymous with the Virgin's immaculacy (Twomey 2008: 173–4):

> Quant més podeu pensar és per mi amada ý estimada aquella mia digníssima mare, de la qual yo he dit, per Salamó: *Tota pulchra es amica mea, et macula non est in te;* car ella és tota bella per excel·lència, e màcula a aquella no·s pot per res acostar! (fol. 230v; III, 46)

> [How much more could it apply to my beloved and esteemed, my most worthy mother, of whom I have said through the mouth of Solomon: *You are wholly beautiful and there is no stain in you*; for she is wholly beautiful in excellence, and no stain can touch her at all!]

Sor Isabel's Christ uses these words as he greets Queen Esther, one of the Old Testament prefigurations of the Virgin. *Tota pulchra es* is used in many Conception offices either as a response or, occasionally, as *capitulum* or short scripture. For example, it is used at sext in the Barcelona office (Vic, Arxiu Episcopal, MS 83), as a response at first night prayer in the Urgell breviary (ACSU, Incunable 147), and it is the antiphon at the Magnificat in Juan de Segovia's office (ACG, MS 125).

I have shown elsewhere how creation in the mind of God is another key way of demonstrating immaculist belief (2008: 195) Pure wax on which the seal of the body of Christ is set is a creation image, as Helen Boreland indicates: 'in a perfect creation, the reflection of the idea in the mind of God shines forth in all its brilliance from the wax' (1981: 323). Among the perfectly created beings are Adam, God's original creation, and the new creation, the Virgin and Christ. Jaume Roig took the concept of preservation from the beginning of time as linchpin of his argument in favour of the Immaculate Conception, combining it with the pure wax on which God's seal is to be set.

> D'aquell'amprempta
> original, cort divinal
> ha preservat e reservat
> aquesta sola. (1978: 156)
>
> [From that original imprint,
> the divine court
> has preserved and reserved
> her alone.]

Sor Isabel also applies the image of seal and wax to Christ's body, imprinted from the pure body of the Virgin Mary:

> Acceptau-lo, Senyora: mostrau a natura humana aquesta antorcha gloriosa, feta de aquella puríssima e molt blancha cera, ço és, de la vostra mundíssima carn, ab aquella excel·lentíssima metxa, ço és, la ànima sagrada, qui novament serà creada, vós consentint, e infusa dins aquell petit cors, e unida ab la persona divina, qui és lo foch antich, que no ha començament ni fi. (fol. 42r; I, 156)
>
> [Accept it, Lady: show to humankind that glorious torch, made of pure, white wax, that is of your most pure flesh, with that most excellent mixture, that is the sacred soul which will be newly created, with your consent, and infused into the tiny body, and united with the person of God, without beginning or end.]

She also applies the metaphor more widely than to signify the purity of Christ and his mother. Pure wax can signify the devout soul of all true believers:

> Lo sagell de aquesta dolça font se emprenta en aquella çera gomada de vera devoció que fa regalar la ànima en què·s troba e aparéxer en ells aquelles armes del rey crucificat, emprentades e pintades per contínua recordació. (fol. 245r; III, 106)

an appropriate way of enhancing the spiritual body and preparing the soul for heaven, although the jewels and enamels she describes are allegorical ones. For Sor Isabel, the adornment of the Virgin, with its Old Testament prefigurations in the dressing of the Princess of Tyre or of wanton Israel, is instigated by God the Father. In this, she follows the tradition of St Clare's writing, where jewels are to be put on in heaven.

Contemporary texts relating to female beauty, both those condemning and those praising it, also assist in interpreting Sor Isabel's desire to dress the Virgin in light-reflecting brocade and silk. The Virgin's beauty is luminous, enhanced by radiant jewels, by enamelled, as well as gold- and silver-embroidered fabrics, and by a crown of gold and stars. Glorious light radiates from her. It should be remembered that, at the third reading in Nogarola's Conception office, the liturgy praises her in similar terms: 'O Maria, tua candoris et decoris forma cui in terris non est equalis' [O Maria, your body is beautiful and bright, and there is none like it in all the world] (BC, MS 1043, fol. 14v). The perfect female body is a beautiful one, without equal in the world, and, in the fifteenth century, it was radiant, white, polished, and gleaming. The Virgin's radiance is celestial, like the sun, moon, and stars which adorned the Woman of Revelation. The *capitulum* at none in Nogarola's office points to the Virgin's purity in the same terms. Her whole nature is enhanced and defined by an overshadowing of clear light: 'claritas enim dei illuminabat illam' [the clear light of God illumined her]. As part of the preparation of her body, like a queen preparing for her coronation, she is clothed in the red tunic with its insignia to create a narrative about a royal bride.

The Virgin's perfect body, uncorrupted by even the most worldly of human finery, is at the heart of Sor Isabel's vision of holiness and female sainthood. She sees adornment as an important element of the preparation of the Virgin to become Christ's Mother, Queen of Heaven. Sor Isabel's adornment of the Virgin is again likely to have been suggested by Nogarola's office and its echo of Revelation (21. 2): 'Vidi immaculatam descendentem de celo sic sponsam ornatam' [I saw the Immaculate One coming down from heaven like a bride adorned] (MS 1043, fol, 18r). The Virgin's body is the holy city, Jerusalem, figure of the Church in the New Testament, constructed and bedecked for union with Christ. The narrative created by the red tunic also centres on suffering and blood. It is both the blood of generation and the blood spilled at the Passion.

Yet Sor Isabel's writing of the perfect female body demonstrates how less perfect bodies were perfectible. Throughout the *Vita Christi*, the body of nuns at work and at prayer, following the Rule, can be glimpsed. For Sor Isabel, observance of the Rule is the key. Through it, she reinforces the nuns' sense of community in order to deepen spiritual growth, and yet there is more. Scriptural resonance, whether in the sandals of the dancing

Shulamite, those put on by the Israelites when they were led out of Egypt, or the brocade dress of the Princess of Tyre of the Psalms, underpins each element of the preparation of the female body. The Santa Trinitat community can identify itself as the Church bedecked for espousal to Christ.

Isabel de Villena was a Poor Clare and her writing was in the Franciscan tradition: her devotion to the Eucharist, as well as to the Immaculate Conception, reveals how she had absorbed the religious traditions which enfolded her. Francis's own devotion to the Eucharist and to the manger as altar lies at the heart of the *Vita Christi*. For Sor Isabel, following in the steps of Francis meant following in those of Christ. It also meant following in those of Mary, the perfect and sinless Virgin, the first among Virgins, and the true example of female religious life. The souls of the nuns were fed through the story of the life of Christ, the true bread, beginning with the conception of his mother. Souls were also fed through eucharistic devotion, seen in the worship of the Child at the manger and of the Virgin as tabernacle. As Sor Isabel writes, the life of Christ and that of the nuns become enmeshed. The events of the *Vita Christi* interweaves the two worlds through observation, through meditation, and through prayer. The sisters of the Santa Trinitat are bystanders, so important to Franciscanism, and observers of the events of the *Vita Christi*. They are also observants of the daily cycle of prayer and work, which follows the liturgical cycle of the life of Christ. This reading of the *Vita Christi*, the book which occupies centre stage in their lives, was a means to their own perfection.

The Virgin is conceived as immaculate from beginning to end of the *Vita Christi*. In the opening chapters, the story of her conception sets the Virgin apart from other human beings, and from other women. At the time of the Annunciation, her immaculate nature enables her to be chosen by God and adorned with garments fittingly decorated for the mother of his Son. Yet, the Mother of God is not set apart from her fellow women. The way Sor Isabel imagines the Virgin's body permits a recognition of the female body able to follow in the steps of the Virgin, to pray using her words, and to reiterate her gestures, particularly her sacramental and eucharistic ones. The life of Christ is enacted day by day in the convent in the reading of the Gospels, in the saying of the office, and in the reading of Sor Isabel's *Vita Christi*. From the pages of the *Vita Christi*, as they were written and read aloud, community life would be shaped. I have shown that such was Sor Isabel's intent.

Her vision of immaculate Mary has also led me to a wider perspective on the craftsmen at work in fifteenth-century Valencian society, of its literary groupings, and of its artists, of its goldsmiths at work on the altars of the town and region, of its silversmiths, of its shoemakers and of its *tapiners*, and of the guilds working within the silk industry, the twisters of silk, and the velvet makers, of its broiderers working on ecclesiastical vestments and altar frontals. I have paid more attention than has previously been given to

Valencian industry in Villena studies. This contextualization of Sor Isabel's cloistered world in the one which existed and worked outside the convent walls is valuable in itself, but it is particularly important because of what it instructs about her approach to writing. She lived cloistered from the world, but she was aware of how Valencian society was changing. New entrants to the convent would have brought information about society, about disputes between groups of craftsmen, about the guild foundations, on changing fashions, as well as on Valencia's literary competitions in honour of the Virgin and other saints. Their secular clothes became part of their dowry to be retained as the convent's patrimony. Contemporary fabrics, jewels, enamels, embroideries, and decorative accessories, as well as contemporary production of shoes and fabrics, provide an insight into the context in which Sor Isabel wrote. Knowledge of Sor Isabel's world helps the modern reader to an understanding of the items she saw from within the confines of the convent and to envisage how she moulded her experience into the magnificent story of Christ and his mother which can still inspire today.

Sor Isabel's descriptive power has often been thought to take literary sources as its antecedents but it is among the embroidered cloths, the dowries of rich fabrics and clothing, altar hangings, brocades and silks employed in the copes and vestments of the clergy, among the art work and depictions of the Virgin clothed in splendour that her inspiration takes its principal source. In other words, she drew on what she saw around her, as well as on the Scriptures she read daily, rather than on the novelesque world of her contemporaries for the rich tapestry of the world she weaves around Christ and his mother.

Mulder-Bakker's description of how medieval female writers approached their task casts some light on how Sor Isabel approached hers:

> women proved to be capable and creative authors, consciously shaping their reading and personal experiences into literary products designed for a specific readership. They were knowledgeable women, well versed in Latin and the Scriptures but they did not follow the academic rules of scholastic debate. They did not quote directly from the Bible and the *auctoritates*. They did not produce a series of arguments pro and con, nor did they construct a scholastic *quaestio*. […] In their view scholastic learning hindered the more direct experience of seeing and knowing. They relied instead on forms of their own. (2004a: 17)

Like other female authors in her period, Sor Isabel was a highly gifted writer. She approached the task consciously shaping and blending all her experience, her reading, and her observation of the world around her into a unique *Vita Christi*. She, like many other female writers in her period, had a deep knowledge of the Scriptures and of the liturgy. She was also well versed in Latin, and able to provide translation of it for those with less knowledge than herself. Like other female writers, she did not need to use university style, and although she may have had many sources and authorities she saw no need to name them. She deftly combined citations and their translation within the narrative, embedding her own commentaries. Most importantly, she created a form of her own, which is unlike any previous *Vita Christi*, although drawing on those versions and, in true medieval style, reworking them. She developed some aspects of the *Vida de Jesucrist* by Eiximenis and of John of Caulibus's *MVC*, which she would have had before her as she worked.

Much of Mulder-Bakker's argument shapes understanding of what Sor Isabel achieves in the *Vita Christi*. Like her fellow Franciscans, she was determined to promote Christ's human side, particularly demonstrated through the relationship with Mary, his immaculate mother, his beloved, prefigured as queen, as bride, and as princess. Unlike others, Sor Isabel embroidered her story with colours, fabrics, practices, devotions, and texts taken from liturgy and from the daily round of readings from Scripture, which she and her nuns had seen, heard, or repeated, and which were imbued with deep meaning for them. She compiled everything into a unique story, constructed very differently from a male-authored one, which provided a magnificent vehicle for meditation and an induction to spirituality.

APPENDIX

Translations of Selected Chapters
from Sor Isabel de Villena's *Vita Christi*

Introductory Preface to the *Vita Christi*

Most high, most powerful, most Christian Queen and Lady:
The illuminating light of devotion which shines within your Majesty has brought to your attention that in this your Convent there is a devout *Vita Christi*, written by the illustrious Lady Elionor, otherwise known as Sister Isabel de Villena, our reverend abbess and mother.

And, in so far as your royal Majesty, inflamed in the love of the great King of Paradise, had written to the general bailiwick of this your Kingdom of Valencia, to be sent a copy of it, I thought to do fitting service to your Majesty, and to have it printed so that it may arrive more promptly to your hands. Because in the deep and sorrowful vale of tears of this miserable world those who with wings of some worldly praise raise themselves fall deeper into the pit of the pains of hell, and those who walk on the lowly paths of simple humility rest on the summit of the city of Paradise, that most virtuous and worthy abbess, my predecessor, with the light of her clear understanding looking upon the perils which worldly praise brings, was so steeped in the depths of humility that she did not wish to put her name to any part of the book. Fearing that her virtuous works, locked away in the archives of humility, might be assailed by the iniquitous hands of vainglory, and because the gleaming torches of the brightness of her most illustrious lineage, her royal relatives, had scattered many deeds of glorious renown to exalt the holy Christian faith, she, most devout mother, wished to sow the labour of her shriven conscience on the white paper of this book. She did so in order that those who read it might gather the fruit of profitable doctrine, asking the great King Jesus to be skipper and pilot of the ship of her understanding, so that she could sail on the great sea of her most fortunate life. And the rays of the bright Sun of Justice, shining through the windows of her radiant intellect, so set her ablaze with ardent charity, that she might long labour to compose this weighty tome and book.

And since, lowly nun, she is to be praised for keeping her name a secret when composing a worthy book like this, I believe I will attain no little merit in the face of God by making the name of such a singular mother public knowledge: Sor Isabel de Villena wrote it, Sor Isabel de Villena composed it, Sor Isabel de Villena with sweet and elegant style set it in order, not only for the devout sisters and daughters of obedience who reside in the enclosed house of this Convent, but for all those who live in this brief, trouble-filled, and transitory life.

I, most serene and Christian lady, send it to your Majesty. In it you will find so many deep and high judgements that you will clearly recognize that the Holy Spirit ruled over the understanding and the pen of the most worthy and reverend mother, who was so moved to the service of your Majesty; her estate and life exalt and bring prosperity to the Santa Trinitat.

From your city of Valencia, on the 29th day of the month of March, 1497,
the humble and prayerful servant of your royal Majesty,
Sor Aldonça de Montsoriu,
unworthy abbess of the Santa Trinitat Convent

Here begins a *Vita Christi* in our own language, so that the simple and those who do not know Latin can come to know and contemplate the life and death of Our Lord and Redeemer, Jesus, Our Beloved, to whom glory and honour be given in all our works, as their Creator and the One who ordained them.

Chapter 1

How the most pure conception of his most holy daughter was announced to St Joachim by an angel

Ecce jam venit plenitudo temporis. For as the fullness of time is come and is upon us, ordained by Our Lord God, when his Majesty was considering engaging in the reparation and salvation of human nature, so, to undertake such an important task, it was necessary for the Merciful One to go down to the land of captivity, where the miserable sons of Adam were imprisoned. And he knew that in all that land there was no decent dwelling for his Highness to rest his head. For that reason, he was pleased to order and ordain that such a dwelling be constructed so as to belong to his Majesty, worked in such an excellent and particular manner that none like it was ever found. This was done to such an extent that those looking on, spellbound by the beauty of the house, were to say: *Non est hic aliud nisi domus Dei*; meaning: Certainly this house is made and built for none other than the majesty of Our Lord God, and no other can stay in it. And across this most holy dwelling will be found a stairway to climb to the heights of the heavenly kingdom, unseen and unknown by men. And so that the house might be completed the divine Lord ordered to come to him a great prince among angels, the chief of staff of his household of the court, and said to him:

'Go, head of my household, *in valle lacrimarum*, and seek out a great builder of houses, Joachim by name, not known or thought worthy by men, rather cast aside and despised as infertile. He is much loved by me and engaged to carry out this particular construction of my dwelling-place. And tell him from me that together with his most holy wife, Anna, he is to build my house, in which I wish to perfectly set the first foundation stone.'

And when the head of his household had been fully informed of the magnificence and beauty of the house that the Lord was ordering them to build, he set off from there promptly to complete his task as ambassador.

He came to earth and found there nothing but *labor et dolor*, for every person dwelt in an array of toil and tribulation. And he looked for the master he was searching for, having a great deal of compassion for those who were captive, and he found him in the barren mountains with the shepherds of his flock. He was speaking to them, in his sorrow and heartfelt pain, about how he was thrown out of the temple for his infertility, for which he was not now expecting any remedy. For he was deciding whether to end his life in that solitary place, far from his wife, Anna, and from all his relations and friends. And the simple shepherds were assisting in mitigating his heartfelt pain.

And the angel prince approached them in human form, and, greeting Joachim, said to him: 'O Lord Joachim, *qui sunt hii sermons quos confertis inter vos et estis tristis?* What are the sorrowful arguments of which you are speaking? For your face is sad, as are the faces of your faithful shepherds, for they are taking your sorrow for their own.' And Joachim, not knowing he was an angel, said, 'O virtuous youth, since you can see in my face that my sorrow is too great to recount, why do you want to cause me so much sorrow in having to narrate the words so many times with my lips? For, in faith, I swear to you, each time my sorrow is renewed. So, in mercy, do not seek to increase my sorrow, since you cannot diminish it. If you are so desirous of feeling my suffering, *interroga eos qui audierunt me*: may it please you to ask my servants here before you, for they have heard from me all the cause of my sorrow, which I am not capable of recounting over again.'

And the angel, wanting to make himself known to him, said: 'O courageous knight, descended from that tribe of Judah, of the true royal line of David, do not faint. *Ego sum angelus Domini, et missus sum ad te loqui*: I am an angel of Our Lord God, sent by his Majesty to speak with you and communicate the great and high marvels he is planning to do on earth. For he desires and commands that you, Lord Joachim, return to your wife whom you left with such great sorrow, and she will conceive and bear you a daughter of such great excellence and dignity *quia nullus dicere possit aliquam ante eam similem ei fuisse nec post eam futuram*: you can be certain, Joachim, my Lord, that none can say that there has ever been anyone like that Lady before in all the wide world, nor that afterwards, in the coming time, will there be found anyone equal to her. *Hec est illa lux quam dixit Deus ut fieret, de qua factus est sol*: she is the light that Our Lord ordered should be made and from it the sun is made; for Our Lord God who is the true Sun of Justice will be born of that Lady, your daughter. He has chosen here from eternity for his temple. Of her can be said in truth: *Hoc est templum Dei magnum et famosum, in quo malleus et ferreum non sunt audita cum hedificaretur*: this is the temple of God, great and famed in its construction. That is to say, that in her conception his Majesty does not wish there to be the sound of hammer blows nor of iron, for that foul and onerous burden of original sin will not be found in her Ladyship, not will any hammer blow of any sin be found in her. For this is the imperial queen and she is not held nor implicated under any common law. Rather Our Lord God said to her: *Non pro te, sed pro omnibus hec lex constituta est*. This means that, as God spoke with that Lady in her new conception: "Do not fear, o my temple, for in everything you descend from the same nature in the lineage of Adam, you will not be included in the law constituted by his sin, rather will you be above it, privileged by my grace in exceptional degree. *Quia ego elegi te*: for I have chosen you as my palace and resting place, and I want you to be the garden of my delights."

'O Joachim, what can be lacking in that Lady, for Our Lord God wants to deliberately create her to be his mother? For, with a mother's dignity, she will acquire all the excellent things that can be passed to a created being, whether angel or human. For when he creates that glorious soul, he will array it in his grace and will adorn it with such noble and singular jewels that in her Ladyship the words of Ecclesiasticus will come true: *Ipse creavit eam in spirito suo, vidit et dinumeravit et monstravit*. He created her in his spirit, meaning that Our Lord God has created that excellent Lady according to his pleasure and will. He alone can count the magnificent things about her, and can measure her exaltation and dignity. *Vere templum es Spiritus Sancti, et palacium Filii Dei; et sponsalis thalamus Patris eterni*: for that Lady is the excellent temple of the Holy Spirit, and the royal palace of the Son of God, and the great bridal chamber of the Eternal Father, about whom Our Lord God said through the mouth of David, *Elevata est magnificencia tua super celos*, meaning that his Majesty was thinking to exalt and magnify her above the nature of the angels.

'And as soon as her glorious soul was created and united to her body, he wanted to dress and array her with his grace to a singular degree. For first he placed an excellent carbuncle on her head, that is the singular and unshakeable Memory of her Ladyship, where the Eternal Father would reside, showing his infinite power in the first chamber, which was so richly appointed by his Majesty. The second chamber, which is her Ladyship's Understanding, will be of such clarity that in the dark night of this world it will shine brightly. Her Understanding goes beyond the cherubim and seraphim in its brightness and excellence of knowledge and it will contemplate the glories and excellent works of God more fully. And it will sense more in these than any other pure creature. In that chamber the Son of God Omnipotent will take up residence, imprinting in it his divine wisdom to a most excellent degree, so that to that chamber it may be said, "O most beloved temple of mine, *dedi tibi cor sapiens et intelligens in tantum ut nullus ante te similes tui fuerit nec post te surrecturus sit*", as the Son of God wishes to say to the newly created Lady: "I have chosen you as a temple for my own use, and I have given you a heart and a memory of such wisdom, and intelligence in such abundance and copiousness, that none has been found similar to you before or after." The third chamber of that divine house will be the Will of that Lady, inflamed with love, and here the Holy Spirit will take his dwelling, displaying his seven gifts in the first doorway, as it is written: *Super quam septem dona Spiritus Sancti plenissime requiesca* , for on that Lady the seven gifts of the Holy Spirit rested in their fullness.

'In these three chambers the Three Persons of God stay and dwell, each in his own chamber, and each together in each, *quia opera Trinitatis non sunt divisa*. And Our Lord God, so that his betrothed should have fitting company according to her rank, wishes for seven ladies of singular excellence to be sought out through the length and breadth of his kingdom. These should serve and accompany her Ladyship in the womb of her mother and throughout her life, and these should be her first ladies of the chamber and the best loved. The name of the first will be Faith: she will make her firm in her belief in the Law and the prophets. The second will be called Hope. She will give her the hope and great longing to see all God's promises fulfilled. The third will have the excellent name Charity. She will set her aflame so greatly in the love of God and of her neighbour that she will constantly work to reconcile Our Lord God with humanity. The fourth will be called holy Humility. This maiden will lead her to esteem and know the singular favours given to her by God. From those graces she will give him constant praise and favours. The fifth will be called Ardent Devotion. This maiden will keep her in constant burning love and with an insatiable desire to pray. The sixth will be called Mercy. This maiden will keep her innermost self open to receive the poor and assist those frozen to the bone with cold. The seventh is named Pity. This maiden will lead her to have compassion for those in tribulation and be swift to help them in their need. So you can see, Lord Joachim, how his Majesty wants your daughter to be. And if any should admire his great Excellency, it should be said to them: *Dominus opus habet,* meaning: the Lord God has need of her to be like this to be his mother. He drew and emblazoned her as he had need and as was pleasing to him.'

And Joachim, having heard these words, was beside himself, both because of his great amazement and also because of his singular joy. And he could not speak for a long while. And when he recovered his strength he said, *Magnus est Deus noster super omnes deos. Quis ergo poterit previdere ut hedificet ei dignam domum. Si celum et celi celorum capere eum non queunt, quantus ego sum ut possim ei hedificare domum*; meaning: 'O angel, Our Lord and God is great and most marvellous above all gods. Who is the one of such great prudence and knowledge to build a worthy house for his Majesty? The heaven and all the heavens cannot hold him. Who am I to build a house for his Highness?' And the angel, replying to him, said: 'O Lord Joachim, do you not remember the words of your ancestor David,

Nisi Dominus hedificavit domum in vanum laboraverunt qui hedificant eam: unless the Lord has a hand in the work, worthless or in vain will be your labour? For his Majesty has said, *Sine me nichil potestis facere* [Without me, you can do nothing]. It is true that it pleases God that, following him, you should be the builder of the house. And you take the credit for having built the temple of God which is much more excellent and cannot be compared to that of Solomon. And you will have this singular prerogative among all the saints, for you will be called father of the Mother of God and for that reason you will be honoured above all others.'

And, hearing this, Joachim threw himself on the ground and adored Our Lord God, thanking him again for the great wonders he had done, saying: 'O infinite wisdom and power without end. For it is fully true what is written, *Quod est impossibile apud homines, hoc est possibile apud Deum*: what seems impossible to men, since it has pleased you, Lord, has become possible and can be done. I was scorned and insulted, and thrown out of the temple with great vituperation for having no children. *Quia non est confusio sperantibus in te*: for those who hope in you with their whole heart cannot be long in confusion. For my ancestor David had truly experienced the sweetness of your mercy when he said, *Secundum multitudinem dolorum meorum in corde meo consolationes tue letificaverunt animam meam*: according to the sorrows borne in patience by those who suffer, you, Lord, give them your consolations in great abundance, as is seen in me through experience. For these, Lord, I am more obliged to you than any other man on earth and I give you infinite thanks for that mercy given to me and all my household.' And seeing the angel wishing to leave, Joachim said to him, 'O glorious prince, if I have found favour with you, do me the mercy of coming to my shelter which is very close to here, and there take food with me'.

The angel replied, 'Joachim, Lord, your charitable wish is acceptable to me and esteemed by me and I give you infinite thanks for your invitation. *Quia cibus meus invisibilis est et potus meus a nullo mortali potest videre* [For my food is invisible and what I drink cannot be seen by any mortal]. So Lord Joachim, do not tarry but haste straight to your lady wife, who is most unhappy in your absence. I will go first to her to console her and tell her that she is to receive you.' When the angel had gone, Joachim told the faithful shepherds about the vision and they said, 'Lord, let us be quickly away and let us obey the command of our Lord God and his angel'. And so they set out and were on the road six days.

Chapter 42

How a human crimson tunic, meaning fervent charity, was presented to the Lady. It was embroidered and embellished with honesty and patience

Another angel approached with a most exceptional gold salver, and St Michael took it and presented it to the Lady with great reverence, saying: 'Most high Lady, this tunic is sent by his Divine Majesty to your Ladyship. It is of an excellent crimson, signifying your ardent charity. It is, Lady, all embroidered and strewn with lilies and *agnus castus*, marvellously worked, showing that your charity is most excellently embellished with examples of purity and chastity. The hem of the tunic is of drawn gold, worked with exceptional enamels in an excellent manner, and in that hem your invincible patience is shown. And on those enamels are painted all the sorrows of your Ladyship, so that each time you lower your eyes and see that hem you may have in mind the great multitude of sorrows that you will have to go through in this life. You will go through these sorrows and will complain so very little that you will only mention them and discuss them with your beloved Son. And you might say, *Effundique in conspectu eius lacrimas meas, et dolorem meum sibi exposui*: for in his presence you will shed many tears, and your sorrow will be manifest to his Majesty.'

And the Lady, taking the tunic with great pleasure, handed it to one of her ladies, called Holy Fortitude, and she was the one who had charge of the Lady's wardrobe.

Chapter 47

How St Michael presented to the Lady six pairs of high-soled shoes, saying that her Ladyship should put them on when she was called upon by the six states of persons

Then there came another angel with a beautiful salver made of coral, decorated with most exceptionally worked gold. On it there were six pairs of high-soled silk shoes. St Michael took it and presented it to her Ladyship, saying: 'Excellent Lady, the majesty of Our Lord God gives these shoes to your Ladyship to wear, for you have to cover a great deal of ground to help human nature in its needs, when you are called upon to do so.

'One pair of silk shoes is of specially worked silver. These you will put on, Lady, when you are called upon by the men who are in a state of grace, for, knowing the weakness of human nature, they will be most certain of not being able to remain in that state without your Ladyship. And for that reason, each one continually calls and cries to you, *Conserva me, domina, quoniam speravi in te*, meaning: "O Lady, preserve me in this glorious state, that I may be firm and constant in grace and love of my Lord and Creator, and deliver me from every offence."

'And your Ladyship, rushing to their aid, will say to them, *Nolite confidere in cordibus vestris: quia qui confidit in corde suo stultus est*: "O my sons in the state of perfection, who possess the grace of Our Lord God, guard yourselves from boastfulness, for there is nothing in the world which can more quickly cause you to fall. Do not trust in the stoutness of your heart, for most certainly I tell you, he who trusts in himself is very rough and ready. Rather, each time you feel in virtuous disposition in yourselves you should say with humility, *Suffitientia nostra ex Deo est*, confessing that whatever there is that is good or whatever grace there is in you, is from God alone, and not from yourselves at all. And so you will stay firm in the grace accorded to you."

'The next pair of silk shoes, Lady, is of most exceptional green brocade. These your Ladyship will wear when you are called upon by those in a state of mortal sin. For those miserable creatures, finding themselves in the deep pit of the wrath of God, will call on your clemency, saying, *Salvum me fac, domina, quoniam intraverunt aque usque ad animam meam*, meaning: "O Lady who art fount of mercy, save and deliver us, for the waters of sin have penetrated our soul and have dulled it, slain it, and separated it from God, and there is no-one to deliver us but you, for you are mother of the judge and can reconcile us with him." And, you, Lady, hearing their cry, will be concerned, and with your shoes will go to them and your Ladyship will give them great hope for what is to come, saying to each, *Spera in Domino et declina a malo et fac bonitatem*, meaning: "O miserable ones who have fallen into the depths of sin, do not despair, rather have great hope in the clemency of our Lord God, who will pity you, and keep away from sin and evil, and do good and virtuous works, and you will be delivered from eternal death."

'The next pair of silk shoes, Lady, is of cinder-grey velvet, all embroidered with sprigs of myrtle. These your Ladyship will wear when you deal with the difficult tasks of human nature, for to your Ladyship turn all those who are tempted and in tribulation in the present life. They say to your Highness, *O tu benedicta super mulieribus, qui angelos vincit in puritate, sanctos superas pietate*; and this means: "O Lady, you are blessed above all the lineage of women, and you are higher than the angels in purity, and you are better than all the saints in piety. Come, Lady, to the aid of the people of Our Lord God, your people, for without you those undergoing tribulations perish and those who are tempted fall into sin." And your Ladyship will respond, saying to each, *Eleva de tenebris affectionem tuam et de sempiternis delitiis refice viscera tua*; meaning: "You who find yourself in travail and danger, know that there is nothing that can help you to not feel or to not think about those trials as to lift your love and affection from the darkness of this world and satiate your heart and inner being and for them to take delight in contemplating and desiring the delight eternal. For only those who heartily despise earthly joy believing there is no need of it will be called blessed in this earthly life. And for that reason it is said, *Felicissimus est ergo plane cui felicitate uti opus non est* [Happy is he for whom to be served by happiness is not his task]. And many, desiring rest and earthly glory, fall into eternal pain, because those who have fallen in the past should lead those in the present time to take care. And for that reason it is written, *Felix quem faciunt aliena pericula cautum* [Happy is he who flees the snares which other fall into]: and so despising the world, you will flee all the ills and temptations it offers."

'The next pair of silk shoes, Lady, is of white brocade. These your Ladyship will wear when you are called by those on the point of death. They call to you as they are in such pain and anxiety, saying, *O tu, pia, potens at potenter Maria, de qua fons est ortus misericordie: deffende nos in prelio ut non pereamus in tremendo iuditio*; meaning: "O Lady, you are merciful and powerful, and the greater your power, the greater is your mercy. Through you, God's mercy flows to us like a living fountain. Defend us, Lady, in the battle at the last, so that we may not perish in the fearful judgement which we expect after death." And, hastening to them in your high silk shoes, your Ladyship will take them back into that final grace which whitens and cleanses their soul, making it safe and joyful on its journey. Your Ladyship will say to them, *Induite vos armaturam Dei ut possitis stare adversus insidias diabolis*, meaning: "O my children, do not be afraid in this narrow way, take up the armour of Our Lord God, which is the blood of my Son, and encircled and armed with it, you will be able to vanquish the snares of the devil, who in this way is trying to make you slip away from God's love and grace, which you have obtained by means of his blood. And after that great victory you will come to the glory of immortal life, where you will rest from your labours."

'The next pair, Lady, is of blue brocade. These your Ladyship will put on when you wish to visit that hospital of Purgatory where all those souls in torment through God's decree are held while they are being purged and made worthy of going into the peace of Paradise. For these souls your Ladyship will be so concerned that you will often do great acts of mercy for them, particularly on your special days and feast days. On those days you will say to the souls in torment, *In nomine meo petite et accipietis, ut gaudium vestrum sit plenum*, meaning: "O souls in torment, ask in my name for remission of your sins on my feast days, with great confidence, for mercy will not be denied to any on those days if they show true devotion and ask in faith; rather be certain your joy will be complete and you will fully and completely see God as you so desire. And as you will be in such peace, you will pray each step of the way for those who remembered you when you were suffering trouble and pain and assisted you with their prayers and supplications. I, your love permitting, will be the special advocate of what your benefactors say, and grant you I will never fail them in their anxieties and needs, for works of mercy please me. This is even more true when those works of mercy are done for you, who are confirmed in the grace and love of my beloved Son." And those souls which cry and ask for your succour and help, Lady, not only on your feastdays but on Saturdays, your holy day, saying, *Inveniat anima nostra lucem misericordie tue et recreet nos tue pacis dulcedo*, meaning: "O clement Lady, may our souls find, feel, and be worthy to see the light of your mercy shine over them, and may we be, Lady, recreated in the sweetness of your peace. For you deliver us from the torment we feel and carry us swiftly to the place of peace and repose. *Quoniam benigna est misericordia tua et pietas tua in omnes qui invocant nomen sanctum tuum*, for gentle and very sweet is your mercy to all those who invoke your holy and glorious name."

'The next shoes, Lady, are of drawn-gold, singularly worked. These your Ladyship will keep for the Last Day, when you will have to take that long road from earth to heaven. For your Ladyship will be called by the three members of the Trinity, *Ascende et coronaberis*, meaning: "Come up to the great city of Paradise, excellent Queen, where you will be crowned with all dignity." On that day, Lady, you will wear the shoes of the resplendent gold of immortality and, shod in them, you will enter inestimable glory the length and breadth of your Kingdom of Paradise. You will go around the holy city to give joy to all its inhabitants. They will contemplate your Ladyship with inestimable joy and will speak the words of Solomon to you, honourable Lady, *Quam pulchri sunt gressi tui in calceamenta, filia principis*, meaning: " O my Lady Princess, daughter and spouse of the great prince, Eternal God, how beautiful you look walking in those chopines resplendent with immortality." All follow your Ladyship with great joy, obeying what your Ladyship commands as Queen and Our Lady.'

And the Lady accepted those beautiful silk shoes and handed them for safekeeping to the lady of the bedchamber, ordering her to have them ready for the times when her Ladyship would have need of them.

Chapter 49

How the Viceroy St Michael presented the Lady with a singular chemise, that is deep internal Piety with decoration of Perseverance

And another angel came with a salver decorated with sweet-smelling amber of singular beauty, and bending the knee before the Lady, it set the salver in the hands of the Viceroy, who opened it and presented it to the Lady, with the words: 'Clement Lady, here you see a very special chemise which Our Lord God is sending to your Ladyship. It is all of singular silk, decorated with marvellous gold work. By this chemise, Lady, is signified your deep internal Piety which is natural to you and close to you. The decoration which embellishes it so excellently is perseverance in your works of charity. On top of this chemise you can put on all your other dresses and it will set them off. This chemise will beautify your person so much that those who serve your Ladyship, contemplating you adorned in the chemise, will say, *Honorate reginam plenam omnium gratiarum et contemplamini cum reverentia sanctissimum vultum suum*: Honour that Lady Queen, full of all grace, and contemplate her holy and merciful face.'

And the Lady accepted the chemise given to her by Our Lord God, and handed it to her trusted lady of the bedchamber.

Chapter 270

How the Lady Captain and Mistress of the Holy Guild, staying behind, instructed them to persevere in devout prayer so that they might worthily receive the Holy Spirit. She beseeched him to come with her most fervent prayer.

The Lady, being in the Upper Room after the Lord had departed, spent those ten days in deep sorrow and very great longing because of his absence. Above all the Lady made a great effort to hide her sorrow, so as not to further torment the sorrowful disciples; for none of them could take any comfort since they were separated from their beloved Lord and Master. For that reason, the most prudent Lady, mindful that he had left her on earth to be their governor and mistress, sought with great love to console them, giving them firm hope that soon they would have a comfort for their sorrow and that her Son would send them the Comforter that he had promised. She charged them with great sweetness that they should constantly be praying, for by that means they would obtain what they demanded. For those who persevere in prayer will never be denied mercy and grace by God's clemency. And the disciples and all the other people who accompanied them gave great credence to the words of the Lady: *Erant perseverantes unanimiter in oratione*. For with great perseverance and fervour they asked their Lord and Master to send them the Holy Spirit which he had promised them, and to provide a remedy for the immeasurable sorrow they felt since he was separated from their sight. And as the days went by so the sorrow of the disconsolate disciples grew.

And since they could no longer bear their sadness, on the ninth day, which was Saturday, at vespers, they came together with many tears and threw themselves at the feet of the excellent Lady, saying, *Inveniamus gratiam quam expectamus apud Deum per te, inventricem gratie et salutis*; meaning: 'Our Lady and our Queen, supplicate the divine majesty for us, that we may find before his Highness the grace for which we hope, and may we have it, Lady, through you, who are inventor of grace and of salvation for all human nature. And that is why, Lady, it is said, *Exulta et lauda omne genus humanum, quare talem dedit tibi mediatricem Dominus Deus tuus*: all humankind should be happy and with great reason, for the Lord Our God has given us such a great and worthy mediatrix. O most clement Lady, if you are general advocate of all, how much more must you be ours, who are servants and disciples of the Lord, your Son, so commended to your Ladyship.'

And the Lady, having heard them, pierced with such pity, wanted to withdraw from them to have recourse to divine goodness to help them. So going into her little cell, she asked the apostles and those who were outside to take their rest and cease crying, for she would be all that night engaged in deep prayer, asking the Lord to quickly and fully console them. And all of them, after receiving the blessing of the Lady, stayed with great faith that through her they might obtain all they desired. And the Lady, shutting herself into that devout retreat, bent her knees with indefatigable love and charity and began to say, *O amor iocundissime et gloriosissime, veni in ortum tuum*; meaning: 'O Holy Spirit, who are most glorious and most joyful love, come into your garden, which is the Church, newly founded by the death and precious blood of my Son. Reinforce its pillars, who are the apostles and disciples of my Son, so that with eagerness they may preach the law of the Gospel and preserve the liberties of the Church, keeping her face firmly set against all her enemies, like a brave knight chosen for the ranks of a defensive force by the great Emperor, all-conquering King and Lord of Heaven and Earth. For at the round table of his supper of love, where they were with him like best-loved chosen knights, and where he consecrated his body to give that jewel without price to them for the first time, wanting it to be consecrated and reserved in his Church in memory of the love that his Majesty had for its knights. Because, Lord, that great love which my Son had for human nature must not be hidden from people but preached with great fervour. And the downcast souls of those disciples of my

Son are lacking such fervour; for even though they are full of love for their Lord and Master, they dare not preach or show forth his marvellous works, unless they be strengthened and receive the infused knowledge beyond all understanding through you, Holy Spirit, for of this you are a most singular master. *O lux beatissima, reple cordis intima tuorum fidelium*: O happy light, may the hearts and innermost beings of these your servants be filled by your Lordship with that holy knowledge and wisdom necessary for them to convert the world, and the power to do great miracles, for it is all required because of the great cruelty and evildoing which is in people's hearts today.' And in these prayers and supplications the excellent Lady spent the whole night, and her prayers were most acceptable to the whole of the Holy Trinity, in whose courts the appeals of her Ladyship were never denied.

And since the clement Lady knew that her prayer had been heard, burning with her usual charity, she went forth with that angelic face and settled in a public place where all could reach her Ladyship.

And when the apostles and Mary Magdalene and the other ladies and all who were in the Upper Room saw her, they ran and threw themselves at her feet, saying, *Domina nostra, quis similis erit tibi? Tua excellencia ostendit Omnipotens suam immensam sapi[enti]am – ne spernas vota invocantium nomen tuum*; meaning: 'O Lady, who is there, or will there be, like you, for in your perfection and courage Almighty God has revealed his immense wisdom? O clement Lady, since the Lord God has made you like this, do not reject the demand of those of us who call on your name with such anxiety and sorrow, in the firm faith that we will be heard and will receive consolation in our desolation. For we cannot any longer support the solitude and sadness we feel because your Son is absent. May that glorious Holy Spirit come, who is of one essence with your Son and his Eternal Father. For he alone can take away from our hearts the great sorrow we feel. Help us, Lady, for through your Ladyship we are to receive that grace which we so long for. Do not make us wait any longer, for our strength is fading because of the long wait. You are powerful, Lady, in heaven and on earth, and you are used to bringing God down to earth, as is shown in the great mystery of the Incarnation when you say: *Ecce ancilla Domini*. And then the majesty of the Son of God was in your womb, dressing in human flesh, he was your Son, taking your nature. O Lady, show then your sweetness and power. Call on our Lord God, the Holy Spirit, who will straightway come down at your call.'

And the Lady, very pleased with the fervour and eagerness that the apostles demonstrated for receiving the Holy Spirit in their souls, warned them that they should prepare themselves worthily to receive that grace, saying, *Nescitis quare corpora vestra sunt templum Spiritus Sancti?* And this means: 'My sons, now you know that your persons are to be temples of the Holy Spirit today, for he will enter your bodies and souls and will dwell there through his grace and love. For this reason, each of you should say with great devotion, *Cor mundum crea in me Deus et spiritum rectum innova in visceribus meis*: "Lord and Almighty God, create in me a clean and pure heart, and deliver me from all sin which might cause offence in your eyes, and make it a room and dwelling fit for your grace and love to take its place. Renew, Lord, in my innermost being, the spirit of rectitude which keeps me firm and constant in your love and fear".' And the apostles and all who were present, obeying the commandment of the Lady, their doctor, knelt down and each made his prayer with great devotion and tears, as they were commanded, longing with great hope and faith to see what they had asked for come to pass.

Chapter 271

How, when the Mother of God was with all the apostles and disciples, the Holy Spirit was sent, filling them with singular gifts. They, so inflamed by the blessing of the Lady, went out to preach the great marvels of the Lord

And when the third hour drew nigh and the Queen and excellent Lady was in the midst of her guild, she rose to her feet with singular prudence and knelt on the ground with deepest humility. With her hands joined in prayer and with eyes turned to heaven, in her angelic voice she said, *Veni Sancti Spiritus, et emitte celitus lucis tue radium*, meaning: 'Come glorious Holy Spirit and send from the heights of heaven the rays of your divine light, that it may illumine and inflame the hearts of all your servants.' Once the voice of her Ladyship was heard in the Court of the Holy Trinity, it was so sweet and so pleasing that her suit was immediately accepted. *Et factus est repente de celo sonus*, for there was a sound of thunder and loud noise, coming down from heaven like a rushing wind, *et replevit totam domum ubi erant sedentes*, and it filled the whole house where they were sitting. They were amazed by the sudden new event, *apparuerunt illis dispertite lingue tamquam ignis; seditque supra singulos eorum*: there were visible to them tongues as of flaming fire, and these settled on each one who was present, and there were men and women there, numbering one hundred and twenty. *Et repleti sunt omnes Spiritu Sancto, et ceperunt loqui variis linguis*: and they were filled with the Holy Spirit, giving them graces and singular gifts, and excellent knowledge and wisdom, and they began to speak every language in a singular manner and were understood by every nation. Eager to preach and tell the Gospel to princes, kings, and lords, they did not fear any earthly power, since divine love had spurred them on and moved them. Dying was for them the glory of serving and magnifying their Lord and Master.

How great was the infinite joy that delighted the soul of the most excellent Lady on that day! More than any of them she felt joys and consolations, which could not be guessed or imagined! How great was the joy of the Lady when she saw the pillars of the Church so firm and strong that they could not fall! And the glorious apostles, with their spirits changed from sorrow to inestimable joy, and from weakness to such great firmness and eagerness that they could no longer bear to be indoors. They approached the Lady with great joy, kissing her Ladyship's hands, asking for her blessing and permission to go and preach the great marvels and excellent deeds of her Son, their Lord, for they could not keep quiet about them. With great pleasure they offered themselves up to death and any travail rather than keeping quiet about the holy doctrine of their Lord and Master. And the Lady with great joy blessed them and rejoicing in the great fervour and eagerness she saw in them, said, *Non formidant mortem tui milites, quia stipendia sua in tua veritate fundantu*, meaning, praising the heavenly work and the sudden change that in those knights and disciples of her Son had been brought about by the grace of the Spirit: 'O Lord, may your courageous knights not fear death, for they are most certain that their recompense and pay is founded in your infallible truth. *O quam lete in morte iustus sperat fixus in tuis promissis*: O eternal goodness, with what joy do your upright servants, in danger of death, wait for the recompense you will give, strong in the belief in your holy promises. These never fail those who serve you with love and fervour. Be with them, Lord, my Son. For, because they are your disciples, they are hated and rejected by the people to whom they wish to preach and convert. Your grace and blessing go with them, Lord.'

And so the Lady, signing them many times with the cross, let them leave to do *signa et prodigia magna in populo*, saying: 'Go, my sons, with my blessing and my Son's, and do great signs and wonders before that infidel people who have put your beloved master to death, and bring them to true belief and take pity on their errors and sins; for truly you recall what the Lord my Son said, when he chose you as apostles, *Faciam vos piscatores hominum*: he wanted to make you fishers of men. Carry out your office with unconquerable devotion, *quia merces vestra copiosa est in celis*: for certainly your work will be very great on earth, and in heaven your reward and recompense will be abundant.' The apostles, drunk with the grace and fervour of the Spirit, went out of the Upper Room with great eagerness to begin preaching the Gospel; and no-one stayed with the Lady except the Beloved Disciple to whom she had been commended by the Lord her Son.

Chapter 289

How the Lord crowned his most holy Mother with three most excellent crowns, given to her by the Holy Trinity as a worthy Empress. To her all the angels and men gave praise, honour, and glory with inestimable joy

And before the Lord and his beloved Mother took their seat on their solemn thrones, his Majesty said to his excellent Mother, *Veni coronaberis*, meaning: 'Come, dearest Mother, and you will be crowned by my hand with three crowns sent by the Holy Trinity, before you depart. My disciples, who have a mortal body and have to remain on earth, may see a part of the glory and excellence which you are to possess in heaven as most worthy Empress and Lady of all.' And the most humble Lady knelt before her Son, the Eternal God. Three angels were sent from the most important princes of Paradise, each one carrying one of the crowns on a salver of gold of singular tracery and beauty. They bent the knee with great reverence before the Lord's Majesty and his Mother and offered them to his Majesty.

The Lord took the first and most excellent crown and set it on the head of the Lady his Mother, saying, *Accipe coronam quam Pater meus preparavit in eternam*, meaning: 'Take, my very dear Mother, this crown, which is sent from his Majesty my Father, who prepared and made it through his great power, before the world was created, and gives it to you for the first time on this day. There are set twelve carbuncles shining brighter than the sun in this fitting crown, showing that you shine more brightly than any other creature in the twelve degrees of singular purity. There are scattered on this crown an immeasurable multitude of pearls of singular roundness and beauty, demonstrating that you have so many excellences and virtues that they cannot be understood or counted except by the one who wished to create you like this, showing the greatness of God's power in you. And there are letters in highly esteemed enamel around the crown, showing your dignity to all who look on it. There is written in these letters, *Sol est, virgo, eclypsim nesciens, sol in celis de terra oriens, sol de celis terram prospitiens, sol peccati nubes demoliens*; meaning, that for all those looking on and contemplating your glory and excellence, you, purest Virgin, are the brightest sun which never goes dim with the great eclipse of original sin, but rather you have always shone unmarked by every sin. You are the sun which, going up from the earth, has shone in heaven. And now that you are rising to heaven, you will cast the rays of your most pure brightness on the earth like a glorious sun and you will illuminate the inhabitants of the earth. And with the burning light of that sun, the clouds of sin will be destroyed and will never return, on behalf of those who invoke and call on you, a bright-shining sun. This is why my Father wants you to bear that title on your excellent crown.'

Once Our Redeemer and Lord had set the crown on the head of his most serene Mother, his Majesty took the second crown, setting it above the first to better embellish it, and said to the most pure Virgin: 'My most holy Mother, you will wear this crown for love of me. On it are set thirty-three diamonds of most singular roundness and beauty for the thirty-three years I spent on earth. You served and accompanied me during those years, so that now it is worthy that the infinite merits which accrue to you for such virtuous works shine on your crown. O most excellent Mother, the work on the crown is a mirror of my wisdom, which I took delight in painting and embellishing. On it are 12,053 enamels of different colours for the number of days which passed between when I took flesh in your womb and when I died. And, because of the great sorrow that you suffered on each of those days, you will have infinite joy without end. This crown is made and woven with myrtle leaves, worked in most singular gold, embellishing your crown all over; and there are 143,733 of them, for exactly this number of hours passed between when you conceived me and the moment when I died on the Cross in your presence; and because your love burned so brightly and so fervently in serving and loving me that you never stopped carrying out services and deeds for me. These services and deeds were so noble and so acceptable to me that they could not be recompensed. Now on this day you will receive the glory and exaltation which you merit for such continued and most fervent works which you carried out time and time again. And you will be praised and magnified eternally without ceasing with sovereign delight by all humanity and all the angels. And for that reason is written around this crown with very clear letters singularly worked: *Te beatam laudare cupiunt omnes sancti, sed non sufficiunt, nam tot laudes tibi convenient*; meaning, Blessed Mother, that all the saints long to praise and bless you, but this is not enough to explain your glory and excellence, for you are worthy of all the praises that can be put into words, O glorious Mother. For that gracious name, Mother, is delight and joy of angels and men, calling them to praise and serve you.'

He crowned the most humble Virgin with two noble crowns and then took the third crown, which was of singular brightness and beauty, and his Majesty said to his excellent Mother: 'My most fervent Mother, this crown is sent to you from the Holy Spirit, as his most worthy bride, so that you can appear crowned with three crowns in the presence of all those who serve you on this your feast day, and that they might know you are the great and most excellent Empress of Heaven and Earth. The crown is set with fifty of the finest burning rubies for the fifty days passed between my Resurrection and the Holy Spirit coming upon your guild, of which you are doctor and guide. During those days your love was exercised in continual prayer asking and desiring the coming of the Spirit to comfort and provide support for my apostles; for this reason that most fervent love shines now on your crown. To better embellish your crown, there are set in it 120 pearls, of most singular whiteness and beauty, for the number of tongues of flame which appeared at that coming of the Holy Spirit and settled on the head of each of those who were in your company. In that way, each of them could be certain that the graces and gifts which the Holy Spirit distributed among all his chosen and beloved, were, O Mother, present in you in very great excellence and singularity. Your soul is so disposed and equipped to receive the gifts of the Holy Spirit that his clemency abounds and overflows, and gives his boundless riches. For you, Mother, are a chest of his treasures and a dwelling-place for his repose and delight and, for that reason, in letters of gold in most beautiful script is written, *Hec est domus fidelis, hoc immortale templum, in quo Spiritus Sanctus requiescat,* so that all who contemplate and look on your most excellent crown may know that you are the most faithful house and temple of immortal memory in which the Holy Spirit reposes and dwells with singular pleasure.'

And when he had crowned the most serene Virgin so nobly, he sat on the throne which had been made ready for his Majesty and he ordered the Lady to sit on his right hand, very close to him, since she was his most beloved Mother. And all the angels and men who were present were amazed by the very great glory and magnificence which they saw in the most excellent Mother of God before she departed. They were certain that she would possess even more when she takes up residence in her own kingdom, and with singular joy they began to sing before her Ladyship: *Letare, Maria virgo, leticia innarrabili in anima et corpore in proprio filio, cum proprio filio, per proprium filium.* This means, 'Rejoice, most merciful Mary, most pure Virgin, with the greatest joy in your body and soul, in your own Son, who prepared so much glory for you, and, Lady, delight with him for you are certain never to forgo his company. How great is the glory and joy which is yours through your own Son, the Lord, *quia hec est omnium letantium pulchrum carmen, omnium regnantium sceptrum rectum, omnium peregrinantium panis vite, et omnium expectantium merces summa*: for this is the lovely and delightful song and true joy of all who rejoice, the sure sceptre of all who reign, the softest bread giving both life and salvation to those pilgrims through this mortal life, and the sovereign pay and sure recompense of all who hope for his mercy. O Lady, may the joy your Highness has as Mother of this most excellent Son pass all understanding. And for that, Lady, you alone feel and taste that sovereign delight and all of us will rejoice in the one who is sufficient for us to know, and, most serene Lady, we will celebrate your joy forever in the glory of Paradise, where your Ladyship will soon take up residence.' When they had finished singing, each came one by one to kiss the hand of the most holy Mother of God. Her Ladyship showed them each her very great love, taking much pleasure in their presence.

WORKS CITED

Aichinger, Wolfram (2003). 'Isabel de Villena: la imaginación disciplinada', in Aichinger et al. 2003: 57–69
——, Marlen Bidwell-Steiner, Judith Bösch, and Eva Cescuti (eds) (2003). *The 'Querelle des femmes' in the Romania: Studies in Honour of Friederike Hassauer* (Vienna: Turia and Kant)
Alanus de Insulis (1844–64). *Elucidatio in Cantica Canticorum*, ed. J.-P. Migne (Paris), *PL* 210, cols 51–110
Alcover, Antoni Maria (1988). *Diccionari català-valencià-balear: inventari lexicogràfic i etimològic de la llengua catalana en totes les seves formes literàries i dialectals, recollides dels documents i textos antics i moderns, i del parlar vivent al Principat de Catalunya, al Regne de València, a les Illes Balears, al Departament Francès dels Pirineus Orientals, a les Valles d'Andorra, al marge oriental d'Aragó i a la ciutat d'Alguer de Sardenya*, 10 vols (Palma de Mallorca: Moll)
Alemany, Rafael, et al. (1996). *Concordança de la Vita Christi de Sor Isabel de Villena*. Concordances dels Clàssics Valencians, I (Alicante: Institut Interuniversitari de Filologia Valenciana and Conselleria de Cultura)
Allen, Sister Prudence (1997–2002). *The Concept of Woman*, 2 vols, I, *The Aristotelian Revolution 750 BC–AD 1250*: II, *The Early Humanist Reformation, 1250–1500* (Grand Rapids, MI: Eerdmans)
Amades, Joan (1982–83). *Costumari català*, 5 vols, 2nd edn, facsimile (Barcelona: Salvat)
Andersen, Elizabeth A. (2000). *The Voices of Mechthild of Magdeburg* (Bern: Peter Lang)
Anderson, Ruth Matilda (1979). *Hispanic Costume 1480–1530* (New York: Hispanic Society)
Angela of Foligno, Blessed (1993). *Complete Works*, trans. Paul Lachance, Classics of Western Spirituality, A Library of the Great Spiritual Masters (Mahwah, NJ: Paulist Press)
Archer, Robert (ed. and trans.) (1992). *Ausiàs March: A Key Anthology*, Anglo-Catalan Society Occasional Publications, 8 (Sheffield: Anglo-Catalan Society)
—— (ed.) (2001). *Misoginia y defensa de las mujeres: antología de textos medievales*, Feminismos, 63 (Madrid: Cátedra and Instituto de la Mujer; Valencia: Universitat de València)

—— (2005). *The Problem of Woman in Late-Medieval Hispanic Literature*, Colección Támesis, Monografías, A214 (Woodbridge: Tamesis)

Armstrong, Regis J., J. A. Wayne Hellmann, and William J. Short (eds). (2001). *Francis of Assisi: Early Documents*, 3 vols (New York: New City Press), I: *The Founder*; III: *The Prophet*

Arnold, Janet (1978). 'The "Coronation" Portrait of Queen Elizabeth I', *The Burlington Magazine*, 120 (908): 727–30

As-Vijvers, Anne Margreet W. (2007). 'Weaving Mary's Chaplet: The Representation of the Rosary in Late Medieval Flemish Manuscript Illumination', in Rudy and Baert 2007: 41–79

Astor Landete, Marisa (1999). *Indumentaria e imagen: Valencia en los siglos XIV y XV*, Colección Estudis (Valencia: Ayuntamiento de Valencia)

Auerbach, Erich (1984). 'Figura', in *Scenes from the Drama of European Literature: Six Essays*, trans. Ralph Mannheim, from 'Figura', *Archivum Romanicum*, 1938: 436–89, with introduction by Paolo Valesio, Theory and History of Literature, 9, 2nd edn (Manchester: Manchester University Press), pp. 11–76

Backhouse, Janet (1993). *The Isabella Breviary* (London: British Library)

Barnett, David (2006). 'The Voice of the Virgin: Accessible Authority in the Visitation Episode of Isabel de Villena's *Vita Christi*', *La Corónica*, 35.1: 23–45

Barney, Stephen A. (1979). *Allegories of History, Allegories of Love* (Hamden, CT: Archon).

Bayless, Martha (2007). 'Clothing, Exposure, and the Depiction of Sin in Passion Iconography', in Rudy and Baert 2007: 289–305

Beck, Egerton (1905). 'Ecclesiastical Dress in Art. Article II: Colour (Part II)', *The Burlington Magazine*, 7: 373–6

Beceiro Pita, Isabel (2003). 'La relación de las mujeres castellanas con la cultura escrita', in *Libro y lectura en la Península Ibérica y América*, ed. Antonio Castillo Gómez (Salamanca: Junta de Castilla y León, Consejería de Cultura y Turismo), pp. 15–52

Benito Domenech, Fernando, and José Gómez Frechina (2009). *La Edad de Oro del arte valenciano: rememoración de un centenario (Museo de Bellas Artes de Valencia, 1 de febrero al 27 de abril 2009)* (Valencia: Generalitat Valenciana)

Benito Goerlich, Daniel (1998). *El real monasterio de la Santísima Trinidad*, Serie Minor: Arquitectura, 48 (Valencia: Generalitat Valenciana and Consell Valencià de Cultura)

Berceo, Gonzalo de (1975). *El duelo de la Virgen; los himnos; los loores de Nuestra Señora; los signos del Juicio Final*, ed. Brian Dutton, Monografías, A18 (London: Tamesis)

Berg Sobré, Judith (1979). 'Eiximenis, Isabel de Villena, and Some Fifteenth Century Illustrations of their Works', *Estudis de llengua, literatura, i cultura catalanes: actes del Primer Col·loqui d'Estudis Catalans a Nord-Amèrica, Urbana, 30 de març - 1 d'abril de 1978*, ed. Albert Porqueras-Mayo, Spurgeon Baldwin and Jaume Martí-Olivella Biblioteca Abat Oliva, 15 (Montserrat: Publicacions de l'Abadia de Montserrat), pp. 303–13

Bergmann, Emilie L. (2002). 'Milking the Poor: Wet-Nursing and the Sexual Economy of Early Modern Spain', in *Marriage and Sexuality in Medieval and Early Modern Iberia*, ed. Eukene Lacarra Lanz, Hispanic Issues, 26 (London: Routledge), pp. 90–114

Bernard of Clairvaux, St (1844–64). *Dominica infra octavam assumptionis BV Mariae*, ed. J.-P. Migne, PL 183, cols 429–48.

—— (1984). *St Bernard's Sermons on the Blessed Virgin Mary, translated by a Priest of Mount Melleray*, trans. Ailbe J. Luddy (Chumleigh: Augustine Publishing)

Bernis, Carmen, (1962). *Indumentaria en tiempos de Carlos V*, Artes y Artistas (Madrid: Instituto Diego Velázquez, CSIC)

—— (1978–79). *Trajes y modas en la España de los Reyes Católicos*, 2 vols (Madrid: Instituto Diego Velázquez, CSIC)

—— (2001). *El traje de los tipos sociales en el Quijote* (Madrid: El Viso)

Black, J. Anderson (1974). *A History of Jewels* (London: Orbis)

Blamires, Alcuin (ed.), with Karen Pratt and C. W. Marx (1992). *Woman Defamed and Woman Defended: An Anthology of Medieval Texts* (Oxford: Clarendon Press)

Blanc, Odile (2002). 'From Battlefield to Court: The Invention of Fashion in the Fourteenth Century', in Koslin and Snyder 2002: 157–72

Boreland, Helen (1981). 'Two Medieval Marian Poets: Aspects of the Work of Gonzalo de Berceo and Ambrosio Montesino' (unpublished Ph.D thesis, University of London)

Borja, José Miguel (2008). *El esplendor de los Borja* (Valencia: Generalitat de València, Conselleria de Cultura i Esport and Biblioteca Valenciana)

Boss, Sarah Jane (2000). *Empress and Handmaid: On Nature and Gender in the Cult of the Virgin Mary* (London: Cassell)

—— (2003). *Mary*, New Century Theology (London: Continuum)

—— (ed.) (2007). *Mary: The Complete Resource* (Oxford: OUP)

Boureau, Alain (1994). 'The Sacrality of One's Own Body in the Middle Ages', in *Corps Mystique, Corps Sacré: Textual Transfigurations of the Body from the Middle Ages to the Seventeenth Century*, ed. Benjamin Semple and Françoise Jaouën, Yale French Studies, 86 (New Haven, CT: Yale University Press), pp. 5–17

Brooke, Iris (1972). *Footwear: A Short History of European and American Shoes* (London: Pitman).

Burns, E. Jane (2002). *Courtly Love Undressed: Reading through Clothes in Medieval French Culture,* Middle Ages Series (Philadelphia, PA: University of Pennsylvania Press)

—— (2009). *Sea of Silk: A Textile Geography of Women's Work in Medieval French Literature* (Philadelphia, PA: University of Philadelphia Press)

Bynum, Caroline Walker (1982). *Jesus as Mother: Studies in the Spirituality of the High Middle Ages* (Berkeley, CA: University of California Press)

—— (1988). *Holy Feast and Holy Fast: The Religious Significance of Food to Medieval Women*, 2nd edn (Berkeley, CA: University of California Press)

—— (1991). *Fragmentation and Redemption: Essays on Gender and the Human Body in Medieval Religion* (New York: Zone)

—— (2007). *Wonderful Blood: Theology and Practice in Late Medieval Northern Germany and Beyond* (Philadelphia, PA: University of Pennsylvania Press)

Cadenas y Vicent, Vicente de (1994). *Fundamentos de heráldica: ciencia del blasón*, 2nd edn, Instituto Salazar y Castro (Madrid: Hidalgía)

Cantavella, Rosanna (1987). 'El debat pro i antifeminista a la literatura catalana' (unpublished Ph.D thesis, Universitat de València)

—— (1992). *Els cards i el llir: una lectura de Jaume Roig*, Assaig, 11 (Barcelona: Quaderns Crema)

—— (1994). 'La crítica de la ornamentación femenina: comentarios sobre un fragmento de *Lo somni*', in *Actas del III Congreso de la Asociación Hispánica de Literatura Medieval (Salamanca, 3 al 6 de octubre de 1989)*, ed. María Isabel Toro Pascua, Biblioteca Española del Siglo XV, 2 vols (Salamanca: Departamento de Literatura Española e Hispanoamericana), I, pp. 219–26

—— (2000). 'Isabel de Villena', in *Breve historia feminista de la literatura española (en lengua catalana, gallega y vasca)*, ed. Iris M. Zavala, VI, *Cultura y diferencia: teoría feminista y cultura contemporánea, pensamiento crítico and pensamiento utópico*, 112 (Barcelona: Antropos), pp. 40–50

—— (2003). 'Debate on Women in *Tirant lo Blanch*', in Aichinger et al. 2003: 45–56

—— (2005). 'Isabel de Villena (1430–1490)', in *Una altra mirada: deu dones i el cristianisme*, ed. Pere Lluís Font (Barcelona: Cruïlla), pp. 139–55

—— (2011). 'Intellectual, Contemplative, Administrator: Isabel de Villena and the Vindication of Women', in *A Companion to Spanish Women's Studies*, ed. Xon de Ros and Geraldine Hazbun, Monografías, A (Woodbridge: Tamesis), pp. 97–1070

——, and Lluïsa Parra (1987). *Protagonistes femenines a la 'Vita Christi'*, Col·lecció Clàssiques Catalanes, 15 (Barcelona: LaSal)

Caresmar, Jaime (1977). *La historia de Santa María de Bellpuig de las Avellanas*, trans. Eduardo Corredera Gutiérrez (Balaguer: Ayuntamiento de Barcelona and Diputación Provincial de Lérida)

Carr, Derek C., and Pedro-Manuel Cátedra (1983). 'Datos para la biografía de Enrique de Villena', *La Corónica*, 11: 293–9

Carreres Zacarés, Salvador (1997). *Ensayo de una bibliografía de Libros de fiestas celebradas en Valencia y su antiguo reino* [Valencia: Hijos de F. Vives

Mora, 1925], repr. in *Alfonso el Magnánimo y el Reino de Valencia* (Valencia: Diputació de València)

Castañeda y Alcover, Vicente (1923). *Arte del blasón: manual de heráldica* (Madrid: Librería General de Victoriano Suárcz)

Castillo, Jaume, and Luis Pablo Martínez (1999). *Els gremis medievals en les fonts oficials: el fons de la Governació del Regne de València en temps d'Alfons el Magnànim (1417–1458)* (Valencia: Institució Alfons el Magnànim and Diputació de València)

Castro, Manuel de (1973). *Manuscritos franciscanos de la Biblioteca Nacional de Madrid* (Madrid: Servicio de Publicaciones del Ministerio de Educación y Ciencia, Secretaría General Técnica)

Català Gorgues, Miguel-Angel (intro.) (1982). *Orfebrería y sedas valencianas: salas de exposiciones del Museo Municipal* (Valencia: Ayuntamiento de Valencia)

Cátedra, Pedro Manuel (1985). 'Algunas obras perdidas de Enrique de Villena con consideraciones sobre su obra y su biblioteca', *Anuario de Filología Española, el Crotalón*, 2: 53–75

—— (2001). *Poesía de pasión en la Edad Media: el 'Cancionero' de Pero Gómez de Ferrol*, Publicaciones del SEMYR, Documenta, 1 (Salamanca: Seminario de Estudios Medievales y Renacentistas)

—— (2005). *Liturgia, poesía y teatro en la Edad Media: estudios sobre prácticas culturales y literarias*, Biblioteca Románica Hispánica, II, Estudios y Ensayos, 444 (Madrid: Gredos).

——, and Derek C. Carr (eds) (2001). *Epistolario de Enrique de Villena*, Papers of the Medieval Hispanic Research Seminar, 33 (London: Department of Hispanic Studies, Queen Mary, University of London)

Cea Gutiérrez, Antonio (2001). 'El cielo como triunfo: los galardones de la palma y la corona en Gonzalo de Berceo', *Revista de Dialectología y Tradiciones Populares*, 56: 5–32

Cingolani, Stefano M. (1998). *Joan Roís de Corella: la importància de dir-se honest*, Sèrie La Unitat, 170 (Valencia: Edicions 3 i 4)

Cintora, Pilar (1988). *Historia del calzado* (Zaragoza: Aguaviva)

Cirlot, Victoria, and Blanca Garí (2008). *La mirada interior: escritoras místicas y visionarias en la Edad Media* (Madrid. Siruela)

Cixous, Hélène, and Catherine Clément (1986). *The Newly Born Woman*, trans. Betsy Wing, Theory and History of Literature, 24 (Minneapolis, MN: University of Minnesota Press)

Clark, Anne L. (2010). 'Elisabeth of Schönau', in Minnis and Voaden 2010: 371–91

Clare of Assisi, St (1982). *Francis and Clare: The Complete Works*, trans. Regis J. Armstrong and Ignatius Brady, with preface by John Vaughn, The Classics of Western Spirituality (London: SPCK)

Coakley, John (2010). Women's Textual Authority and the Collaboration of Clerics', in Minnis and Voaden 2010: 83–104

Conde, Juan Carlos (2006). 'Ensayo bibliográfico sobre la traducción en la Castilla del siglo XV – 1980–2005', *Lemir*, 10, [http://parnaseo.uv.es/Lemir]

Constanza de Castilla (1998). *Book of Devotions / Libro de devociones y oficios*, ed. Constance L. Wilkins, Exeter Hispanic Texts, 52 (Exeter: University of Exeter)

Conway, Charles Abbott (1976). *The Vita Christi of Ludolph of Saxony and Late Medieval Devotion Centred on the Incarnation: A Descriptive Analysis*, Analecta Carthusiana, 34 (Salzburg: Institut für Englische Sprache und Literatur, University of Salzburg)

Cordwell, Justine M., and Ronald A. Schwartz (1979). *The Fabrics of Culture: The Anthropology of Clothing and Adornment* (The Hague: Mouton).

Corominas, Joan, and José A. Pascual (1980–91). *Diccionario crítico etimológico castellano e hispánico*, 6 vols, Biblioteca Románica Hispánica, V, Diccionarios, 7 (Madrid: Gredos)

Corredera Gutiérrez, Eduardo (1997). *Páginas de historia catalana: Santa María de Bellpuig de Les Avellanes* (n.p., Catalunya: Institut de les Germans Maristes de Catalunya)

Cotarelo y Mori, Emilio (1896). *Don Enrique de Villena: su vida y obras* (Madrid: Sucesores de Rivadeneyra)

Courcelles, Dominique de (1997). 'Le Retour en Occident après la perte de l'empire chrétienne d'Orient: un parcours au masculine et au feminine dans *Tirant le Blanc*', in *Actes del Col·loqui Internacional Tirant lo Blanc, 21–22 d'Octubre de 1994: estudis crítics sobre 'Tirant lo Blanc' i el seu context*, ed. Jean-Marie Barberà, Biblioteca Abat Oliba, 182 (Barcelona: Centre Aixois de Recherches Hispaniques, Institut Interuniversitari de Filologia Valenciana, and Abadia de Montserrat), pp. 111–22

—— (2000). 'En mémoire d'elle et en mémoire du sang: la *Vita Christi* de Sor Isabel de Villena, abbesse des clarisses de Valence au XVe siècle', *Journal de la Renaissance*, I: 103–20

Covarrubias y Horozco, Sebastián de (2006). *Tesoro de la lengua castellana o española*, ed. Ignacio Arellano and Rafael Zafra, Biblioteca Aurea Española, 21 (Madrid: Universidad de Navarra and Iberoamericana-Vervuert)

Crane, Susan (2002). *The Performance of Self: Ritual, Clothing and Identity during the Hundred Years' War*, The Middle Ages Series (Philadelphia, PA: University of Pennsylvania Press)

Cross, F.L. (ed.) (1958). *The Oxford Dictionary of the Christian Church* (London: OUP).

Dangler, Jean (1998). 'Motherhood and Pain in Villena's *Vita Christi* and Roig's *Spill*', *La Corónica*, 27.1: 99–113

Davis, Natalie Zemon (2000). *The Gift in Sixteenth-Century France* (Oxford: OUP).

De Fiores, Stefano, and Salvatore Meo (1988). *Nuevo diccionario de mariología,* trans. Alfonso Ortiz García, Eloy Requena Calvo, and José María Corzo, from *Nuovo dizionario di mariologia* (Madrid: Ediciones Paulinas)

Dendle, Peter, and Alain Touwaide (eds) (2008). *Health and Healing from the Medieval Garden* (Woodbridge: The Boydell Press)

Deyermond, Alan (1978). 'The Worm and the Partridge: Reflections on the Poetry of Florencia Pinar', *Mester*, 7: 3–8

—— (1983). 'Spain's First Women Writers', in *Women in Hispanic Literature: Icons and Fallen Idols*, ed. Beth Miller (Berkeley, CA: University of California Press), pp. 27–52

—— (1995). 'Las autoras medievales castellanas a la luz de las últimas investigaciones', in Paredes 1995: I, 31–52

—— (1999). 'El tejido en el texto, el texto tejido: Las *chansons de toile* y poemas análogos', *Estudios Románicos*, 11: 71–104

Donovan, Richard B. (1958). *The Liturgical Drama in Medieval Spain*, Pontifical Institute of Medieval Studies, Studies and Texts, 4 (Toronto: Pontifical Institute of Medieval Studies)

DRAE = *Diccionario de la Real Academia Española* (1999). 21st edn, 2 vols (Madrid: Espasa-Calpe).

Dufresne, Laura Rinaldi (1995–96). 'Christine de Pizan's *Treasure of the City of Ladies*: A Study of Social Dress and Hierarchy', *Women's Art Journal*, 16: 29–34

Duggan, Anne J. (ed.) (1997). *Queens and Queenship in Medieval Europe: Proceedings of a Conference held at King's College, London, April 1995* (Woodbridge: The Boydell Press)

Duits, Rembrandt (1999). 'Figured Riches: The Value of Gold Brocades in Fifteenth-Century Florence', *Journal of the Warburg and Courtauld Institutes*, 62: 60–92

Dutton, Brian (1990–91). *El cancionero del siglo XV, 1370–1520*, 7 vols, Biblioteca Española del Siglo XV, Serie Maior, 1–7 (Salamanca: Diputación de Salamanca)

——-, and Joaquín González Cuenca (eds) (1993). *Cancionero de Juan Alfonso de Baena*, Biblioteca Filológica Hispana, 14 (Madrid: Visor)

Eadmer (1844–64). *Tractatus de conceptione B. Mariae Virginis*, ed. J.-P. Migne (Paris), PL 159, cols 301–18

Ehrenschwendtner, Marie-Luise (1996). 'A Library Collected by and for the Use of Nuns: St Catherine's Convent, Nuremberg', in Smith and Taylor 1996: 123–32

—— (1997). '*Puellae Litteratae*: The Use of the Vernacular in the Dominican Convents of Southern Germany', in *Medieval Women in their Communities*, ed. Diane Watt (Cardiff: University of Wales Press), pp. 49–71

Eiximenis, Francesc (1496). *Primer volumen de Vita Christi de Fray Francesc d'Eiximenis corregida y añadida por el Arçobispo de Granada y hizole imprimir porque es muy provechoso* (Granada: Meynardo Ungut and Johannes de Nuremberga)

—— (1981). *Lo libre de les dones*, ed. Frank Naccarato, revised Curt Wittlin and Antoni Comas, with glossary by August Bover i Font, Edicions Catalanes (Barcelona: Curial)

—— (1985). *Scala Dei: devocionari de la Reina Maria. Edició modernitzada*, ed. Curt Wittlin (Montserrat: Abadia de Montserrat)

—— (1986–88). *Dotzè llibre del crestià*, segona part, ed. Curt Wittlin et al., 2 vols, Col·lecció Obres de Francesc Eiximenis, 3 and 4 (Girona: Col·legi Universitari de Girona and Diputació de Girona)

Ellington, Donna Spivey (2001). *From Sacred Body to Angelic Soul: Understanding Mary in Late Medieval and Early Modern Europe* (Washington, DC: Catholic University of America Press)

Enciclopedia universal ilustrada (1928–29), 70 vols (Bilbao: Espasa-Calpe).

Estevan Gómez, Vicente (2010). *Plantas medicinales de Villar del Arzobispo y su entorno* (Villar del Arzobispo: Ayuntamento de Villar)

Feliks, Jehuda (1983). *Song of Songs: Nature, Epic, and Allegory* (Jerusalem: Israel Society for Biblical Research)

Fenollar, Bernat (1493). *Passi en cobles* (Valencia: Pere Hagenbach & Leonard Hutz?)

Ferrando Badía, Juan (1995). *El histórico reino de Valencia y su organización foral*, Història, Sèrie Minor, 27, 2nd edn (Valencia: Generalitat Valenciana, Consell Valencià de Cultura)

Ferrando Francés, Antoni (1983). *Els certàmens poètics valencians del segle XIV al segle XIX* (València: Institut de Literatura i Estudis Filològics and Institució Alfons el Magnànim)

Fischer, Columban (1932). 'Die *Meditationes Vitae Christi*: ihre handschriftliche Ueberliefung und die Verfasserfrage', *Archivum Franciscanum Historicum*, 25: 3–35

Fleming, John V. (1977). *An Introduction to Franciscan Literature of the Middle Ages* (Chicago, IL: Franciscan Herald Press)

Francis of Assisi, St (1999a). 'Exhortations to the Clergy', in *Francis of Assisi: Early Documents, I: The Saint*, ed. Regis J. Armstrong, et al. (New York: New City Press), pp. 52–3

—— (1999b). 'The Admonitions', in *Francis of Assisi: Early Documents, I: The Saint*, ed. Regis J. Armstrong et al. (New York: New City Press), pp. 128–37

Fumagalli Beonio-Brocchieri, Mariteresa (1994). 'The Feminine Mind in Medieval Mysticism', trans. E. Ann Matter, in Matter and Coakley 1994: 19–33

Fuster, Joan (1975a). 'El món literari de sor Isabel de Villena', in his *Obres completes,* 7 vols, 2nd edn, I: *Llengua, literatura, història*, Clàssics Catalans del segle XX (Barcelona: Edicions 62), pp. 153–74

—— (1975b). 'Jaume Roig i sor Isabel de Villena', in his *Obres completes,* 7 vols, 2nd edn, I: *Llengua, literatura, història*, Clàssics Catalans del segle XX (Barcelona: Edicions 62), pp. 175–210

Galerstein, Carolyn L., with Kathleen McNerney (eds) (1986). *Women Writers of Spain: An Annotated Bio-Bibliographical Guide* (Westport, CT: Greenwood Press)

García de la Herrán, María del Carmen (1995). 'El saber femenino en los claustros: las Borja del convento de Santa Clara de Gandía (siglo XVI)', in Graña Cid 1995: 183–97

García Sánchez, Expiración (2008). 'Gardens and Aesthetics in the Gardens of al-Andalus: Species with Multiple Uses', in Dendle and Touwaide 2008: 205–27

Garcia Sempere, Marinela (ed.) (2002). *Lo passi en cobles (1493): estudi i edició*, Biblioteca Sanchis Guarner, 60 (Alicante: Institut Interuniversitari de Filologia Valenciana)

Gascón Vera, Elena (1979). 'La quema de los libros de don Enrique de Villena: una maniobra política y antisemítica', *BHS,* 56: 317–23

Gautier de Coincy (1970). *Les Miracles de Nostre Dame*, ed. V. Frederic Koenig, 4 vols, Textes Littéraires Français, 176 (Genève: Droz)

Generalitat Valenciana (2007). *Exposició la Llum de les Imatges: Lux Mundi, Xàtiva 2007* (Valencia: Generalitat Valenciana)

Gilbert-Santamaria, Donald (2005). 'Historicizing Vergil: Translation and Exegesis in Enrique de Villena's *Eneida*', *Hispanic Review*, 73–74: 409–30

Giles, Ryan (2009). 'Hanging Bells on the Cat: Charivari and the Theatrics of the *Arcipreste de Talavera o Corbacho*', paper presented at the 44th Congress on International Medieval Studies, University of Western Michigan, Kalamazoo, 7–10 May

Gill, Katherine (1994). 'Women and Religious Literature in the Vernacular, 1300–1500', in Matter and Coakley 1994: 64–104

Goffen, Rona (1986). 'Friar Sixtus IV and the Sixtine Chapel', *Renaissance Quarterly*, 39: 218–62

Goldberg, Harriet (1984). 'Clothing in *Tirant lo Blanc*: Evidence of "Realismo vitalista" or of a New Unreality', *Hispanic Review*, 32: 379–92

Goodman, Anthony (2010). 'Margery Kempe', in Minnis and Voaden 2010: 217–38

Graef, Hilda Charlotte (1963–65). *Mary: A History of Doctrine and Devotion*, 2 vols (London: Sheed & Ward)

Graña Cid, María del Mar (ed.) (1994a). *Las sabias mujeres: educación, saber y autoría (siglos III–XVII), comunicaciones leídas a las IV Jornadas de Historia Medieval de la Asociación Cultural Al-Mudayna*, Colección LAYA, 13 (Madrid: Asociación Cultural Al-Mudayna)

—— (1994b). 'Mujeres y educación en la prereforma castellana: los colegios de doncellas', in Graña Cid 1994a: 117–46

—— (ed.) (1995). *Las sabias mujeres II (siglos III–XVI): homenaje a Lola Luna*, *comunicaciones leídas a las VI Jornadas de Historia Medieval celebradas en la Facultad de Geografía e Historia de la Universidad Complutense de Madrid, los días 9 and 10 de marzo de 1995*, Colección LAYA, 15 (Madrid: Asociación Cultural Al-Mudayna)

Grisé, C. Annette (2002). 'Women's Devotional Reading in Late-Medieval England and the Gendered Reader', *Medium Aevum*, 71: 209–25

Gual Camarena, Miguel (1952). 'Concordia entre los gremios de zapateros y chapineros de Valencia (1486)', *Saitabi: órgano de los Institutos de Investigaciones Históricas 'Roque Chabás' y 'Juan Bautista Muñoz*, 9: 134–44

Guia 2008 = *Guia*, 2nd edn (Barcelona: Museu Nacional d'Art de Catalunya)

Guia de les col·leccions 2007 =. *Guia de les col·leccions*, 2nd edn (Vic: Museu Episcopal de Vic)

Guia i Marin, Josep (1996). *De Martorell a Corella: descobrint l'autor del Tirant lo Blanc*, Ricerca i Pensament, 2 (Catarroja [Barcelona]: Afers)

——, and Curt Wittlin (1999). 'Nine Problem Areas Concerning *Tirant lo Blanc*', in *Tirant lo Blanc*, ed. Arthur Terry (Woodbridge: Tamesis), pp. 109–26

Haliczer, Stephen (2002). *Between Exaltation and Infamy: Female Mystics in the Golden Age of Spain* (Oxford: OUP)

Hall, Edwin, and Horst Uhr (1978). '*Aureola* and *Fructus*: Distinctions of Beatitude in Scholastic Thought and the Meaning of Some Crowns in Early Flemish Painting', *The Art Bulletin*, 60: 249–70

Hall, James (1974). *Dictionary of Subjects and Symbols in Art* (London: John Murray).

Harte, N. B., and K. G. Ponting (eds) (1983). *Cloth and Clothing in Medieval Europe: Essays in Memory of Professor E. M. Carus-Wilson*, Pasold Studies in Textile History, 2 (London: Heinemann)

Hauf i Valls, Albert-Guillem (1978). 'La *Vita Christi* de Fr. Francesc Eiximenis, OFM (1340?-1409), como tratado de cristología para seglares', *Archivum Franciscanum Historicum*, 71: 37–64

—— (ed.) (1982). *Contemplació de la passió de Nostre Senyor Jesucrist* (San Boi de Llobregat: Edicions del Mall)

—— (1987). 'La *Vita Christi* de Sor Isabel de Villena y la tradición de las *Vitae Christi* medievales', in *Studia in honorem Prof. M. de Riquer*, ed. Dámaso Alonso, 4 vols (Barcelona: Quaderns Crema [1987–91]), II, pp. 105–64

—— (1990). *D'Eiximenis a Sor Isabel de Villena: aportació a l'estudi de la nostra cultura medieval*, Biblioteca Sanchis Guarner, 19 (Valencia: Institut de Filologia Valenciana and Publicacions de l'Abadia de Montserrat)

—— (1991). 'Text i context de l'obra de Sor Isabel de Villena', in *Literatura valenciana del segle XV: Joannot Martorell i Sor Isabel de Villena*, ed. G. Colón et al., Sèrie Minor: Literatura, 6 (Valencia: Consell Valencià de Cultura), pp. 91–124

—— (1997). 'Text, pintura, i meditació: el *Speculum animae* atribuït a Sor Isabel de Villena, i la funció empàtica de l'art religiós', *Actes del VII Congrès de l'Associació Hispànica de Literatura Medieval (Castelló de la Plana, 22–26 setembre 1997)*, ed. Santiago Fortuño Llorens and Tomàs Martínez Romero, 4 vols (Castelló de la Plana: Universitat Jaume I), I, pp. 33–59

—— (2004). 'Del sermó oral al sermó escrit: la *Vita Christi* de Fra Francesc Eiximenis com a glossa evangèlica', in *La cultura catalana en projecció de futur: homenatge a Josep Massot i Muntaner*, ed. by Germà Colón, Tomàs Martínez Romero, M. Pilar Perea (Castelló de la Plana: Universitat Jaume I), pp. 253–89

—— (2006). *La Vita Christi de Sor Isabel de Villena (s. XV) como arte de meditar: introducción a una lectura contextualizada* (Valencia: Biblioteca Valenciana, Generalitat Valenciana, Conselleria de Cultura, Educació i Esport)

Hayward, Maria (2007). 'Crimson, Scarlet, Murrey, and Carnation: Red at the Court of Henry VIII', *Textile History*, 38: 135–50.

Heigham, John (1622). *The Life of Ovr Blessed Lord and Saviovr Iesus, Gathered out of the Venerable and Famous Doctor Saint Bonaventure, and out of Diuers Other Rare, Renowned and Catholic Doctors, Newly Composed by Iohn Heigham, and by him also Published for the Greater Comfort and Good of all Godly Persons*, 2nd edn (Douai: St Omers; repr., Menston: Scolar, 1973)

Heller, Sarah-Grace (2000). 'Fashioning a Woman: The Vernacular Pygmalion in the *Roman de la Rose*', *Medievalia et Humanistica*, new series, 27: 1–18

—— (2001). 'Light as Glamour: The Luminescent Ideal of Beauty in the *Roman de la Rose*', *Speculum*, 76: 934–59

Hentschell, Roze (2009). 'Moralizing Apparel in Early Modern London: Sermons, Satire, and Sartorial Display', *Journal of Medieval and Early Modern Studies*, 39.3: 571–95

Herrera, María Teresa (1996). *Diccionario Español de Textos Médicos Antiguos*, 2 vols (Madrid: Arco Libros)

Hildegard of Bingen (1998). *The Letters of Hildegard of Bingen*, trans. Joseph L. Baird and Radd K. Ehrman, 2 vols (Oxford: OUP)

Hinton, David A. (2005). *Gold and Gilt, Pots and Pins: Possessions and People in Medieval Britain*, Medieval History and Archeology (Oxford: OUP)

Hofenk-De Graaff, Judith H. (1983). 'The Chemistry of Red Dyestuffs in Medieval and Early Modern Europe', in Harte and Ponting 1983: 71–79

Huizinga, J. (1924). *The Waning of the Middle Ages: A Study of the Forms of Life, Thought, and Art in France and the Netherlands in the Fourteenth and Fifteenth Centuries*, trans. F. Hopman (London: Edward Arnold)

Hunt, Tony (1981). 'The Song of Songs and Courtly Literature', in *Court and Poet: Selected Proceedings of the Third Congress of The International Courtly Literature Society* (Liverpool 1980), ed. Glyn S. Burgess et al., ARCA, Classical and Medieval Texts, Papers, and Monographs, 5 (Liverpool: Francis Cairns), 189–96

Hurlburt, Holly S. (2003). 'Public Exposure? Consorts and Ritual in Late Medieval Europe: The Example of the Entrance of the Dogaresse of Venice', in *Gendering the Master Narrative*, ed. Mary C. Erler and Maryanne Kowaleski (Ithaca, NY: Cornell University Press), pp. 174–89

Hutton, Lewis Joseph (ed.) (1967). Teresa de Cartagena, *Arboleda de los enfermos. Admiración operum Dey*, Anejos de la *BRAE*, 16 (Madrid: RAE)

Ibarra y Folgado, José María (1919). *Los gremios del metal en Valencia: contribución de los archivos valencianos para un estudio sobre la vida corporativa de los ártifices del metal en Valencia de los siglos XIII al XVIII* (unpublished Ph.D thesis, Universitat de València).

Igual Úbeda, Antonio (1956). *El gremio de plateros: ensayo de una historia de la platería valenciana* (Valencia: Servicio de Estudios Artísticos, Institución Alfonso el Magnánimo, Diputación Provincial de Valencia).

Ildephonse of Toledo, St (attrib.) (1844–64). *Libellus de corona virginis*, ed. J.-P. Migne, *PL* 96, cols 233–318

Isidore of Seville, St (1993–4). *Etimologías: edición bilingüe*, ed. José Oroz Reta and Manuel-A. Marcos Casquero, with introduction by Manuel C. Díaz y Díaz, 2nd edn, 2 vols, Biblioteca de Autores Cristianos, 433 and 434 (Madrid: Biblioteca de Autores Cristianos)

—— (2006). *The Etymologies of St Isidore of Seville*, trans. Stephen A. Barney, W. J. Lewis, J. A. Beach, and Oliver Berghof (Cambridge: CUP)

Janes, Dominic (1998). *God and Gold in Late Antiquity* (Cambridge: CUP)

Jantzen, Grace (1995). 'Cry Out and Write: Mysticism and the Struggle for Authority', in Smith and Taylor 1995: 67–76

Jiménez Hernández, Emiliano (1999). *El cantar de los cantares: resonancias bíblicas*, 2nd edn, Colección Trípode (Baracaldo: Gráfite)

John of Caulibus (1997). *Meditationes vite Christi olim S. Bonauenturo attributae*, ed. Mary Stallings-Taney, Corpus Christianorum, Continuatio Medievalis, 153 (Turnhout: Brepols)

—— (2000). *Meditations on the Life of Christ*, trans. and ed. Francis X. Taney, Anne Miller, and Mary Stallings-Taney (Asheville: Pegasus)

Jones, Ann Rosalind, and Peter Stallybrass (2000). *Renaissance Clothing and the Materials of Memory*, Cambridge Studies in Renaissance Literature and Culture (Cambridge: CUP)

Kerby-Fulton, Kathryn (2010). 'Hildegard of Bingen', in Minnis and Voaden 2010: 344–69

King, John N. (1985). 'The Godly Woman in Elizabethan Iconography', *Renaissance Quarterly*, 38: 41–84

Knox, Lezlie S. (2008). *Creating Clare of Assisi: Female Franciscan Identities in Later Medieval Italy*, The Medieval Franciscans, 5 (Leiden: Brill)

—— (2004). 'What Francis Intended: Gender and the Transmission of Knowledge in the Franciscan Order', in Mulder-Bakker 2004b: 143–61

Koch, Barbara (2010). 'Margaret Ebner', in Minnis and Voaden 2010: 394–410

Koslin, Désirée G., and Janet E. Snyder (eds) (2002). *Encountering Medieval Textiles and Dress: Objects, Texts, Images*, The New Middle Ages Series (New York: Palgrave MacMillan)

La seda (1957). *La seda en la indumentaria: siglos XVI–XIX. Colección Rocamor. Exposición organizada por el Colegio de Arte Mayor de la Seda, 23 septiembre –23 octubre* (Barcelona: Palacio de Comillas)

Labrador, J., C. A. Zorita, and R. S. Di Franco (1994). *Cancionero de poesías varias: manuscrito no. 617 de la Biblioteca Real de Madrid*, 2nd edn, Biblioteca Filológica Hispánica, 18 (Madrid: Visor)

Lamy, Marielle (2000). *L'Immaculée Conception: étapes et enjeux d'une controverse au Moyen Âge (XIIe–XVe siècles)*, Collection des Études Augustiniennes, Série Moyen Âge et Temps Modernes, 35 (Paris: Institut d'Études Augustiniennes)

Lawrance, Jeremy (1985). 'The Spread of Lay Literacy in Late Medieval Castile', *BHS*, 61: 79–94

—— (1986). 'Fifteenth-Century Spanish Vernacular Humanism', in *Medieval and Renaissance Studies in Honour of Robert Brian Tate*, ed. Ian Michael and Richard A. Cardwell (Oxford: Dolphin), pp. 65–79

L'Engle, Susan (2002). 'Ad*dress*ing the Law: Costume as Signifier in Medieval Legal Miniatures', in Koslin and Snyder 2002: 137–53

Levi d'Ancona, Mirella (1957). *The Iconography of the Immaculate Conception in the Middle Ages and Early Renaissance* (New York: College Art Association of America, in conjunction with *Art Bulletin*)

Lewis, C. S. (1936). *The Allegory of Love: A Study in Medieval Tradition* (London: OUP)

—— (1964). *The Discarded Image: An Introduction to Medieval and Renaissance Literature* (Cambridge: CUP)

Little, William, H. W. Fowler, and J. Poulson (eds) (1962). *The Shorter Oxford English Dictionary on Historical Principles,* revised and ed. C. T. Onions, 3rd edn repr. (Oxford: Clarendon Press)

Lloyd-Jones, K. (1989). 'Humanist Debate and the "Translative Dilemma" in Renaissance France', in *Medieval Translators and Their Craft*, ed. Jeanette Beer, Studies in Medieval Culture, 25 (Kalamazoo: Western Michigan University, Medieval Institute Publications), pp. 347–71

López Estrada, Francisco (1986). 'Las mujeres escritoras en la Edad Media castellana', in *La condición de la mujer en la Edad Media. Actas del Coloquio celebrado en la Casa de Velázquez del 5 al 7 de noviembre de 1984 (III Coloquio hispano-francés, Madrid, 1984)*, ed. Yves-René Jonquerne and Alfonso Esteban (Madrid: Universidad Complutense and Casa de Velázquez), pp. 9–38

Lorris, Guillaume de, and Jean de Meun (1973–76). *Le Roman de la Rose*, ed. Félix Lecoy, Les Classiques Françaises du Moyen Âge, 92, 95, and 98 (Paris: Honoré Champion)

Lowe, Kate (2001). 'Elections of Abbesses and Notions of Identity in Fifteenth- and Sixteenth-Century Italy, with Special Reference to Venice', *Renaissance Quarterly*, 54: 389–429

—— (2003). *Nuns' Chronicles and Convent Culture in Renaissance and Counter-Reformation Italy* (Cambridge: CUP)

Luna, Lola (1995). 'Escritoras para una historia literaria', in Graña Cid 1995: 127–33

Mabillon, John (ed. and trans.) (1889–96). *The Life and Works of St Bernard, Abbot of Clairvaux*, rev. Samuel J. Eales, 4 vols (London: John Hodges)

Machado, Ana Maria da Silva (1995). 'O testemunho dos prologos na prosa didáctica, moral e religiosa', in Paredes 1995: III, 131–46

McKendrick, Geraldine (1987). 'The Franciscan Order in Castile c.1440–c.1550' (unpublished Ph.D thesis, University of Edinburgh)

MacKenzie, Donald A. (1922). 'Colour Symbolism', *Folklore*, 33: 136–69

McNerney, Kathleen, and Cristina Enríquez de Salamanca (eds) (1994). *Double Minorities of Spain: A Bio-Bibliographical Guide to Women Writers of the Catalan, Galician, and Basque Countries* (New York: Modern Language Association of America)

Macpherson, Ian (1997). 'Fray Íñigo de Mendoza, Francisco Delicado y dos enigmas salomónicos', in *Actas del VI Congreso Internacional de la Asociación Hispánica de Literatura Medieval (Alcalá de Henares, 12–16 de septiembre de 1995)*, ed. José Manuel Lucía Megías (Alcalá de Henares: Universidad de Alcalá); repr. in Macpherson and MacKay 1998: 205–22

—— (1994). '*Manteniendo la tela*: el erotismo del lenguaje caballeresco-textil en la época de los Reyes Católicos', in *Actas del Primer Congreso Anglo-Hispano* (Madrid: Castalia), I, pp. 25–36; repr. in Macpherson and MacKay 1998: 196–204

——, and Angus MacKay (1998). *Love, Religion, and Politics in Fifteenth-Century Spain*, Medieval Iberian Peninsula: Texts and Studies, 13 (Leiden: Brill)

McSheffrey, Shannon (1995). 'Literacy and the Gender Gap in the Late Middle Ages: Women and Reading in Lollard Communities', in Smith and Taylor 1995: 157–70

Mâle, Emile (1908). *L'Art réligieux de la fin du Moyen Âge en France: étude sur l'iconographie du Moyen Âge et sur ses sources d'inspiration*, 8th edn (Paris: Armand Colin)

Marino, Nancy F. (2006). *Don Juan Pacheco: Wealth and Power in Late Medieval Spain*, Medieval and Renaissance Texts and Studies, 311 (Tempe, AZ: Arizona Center for Medieval and Renaissance Studies)

—— (2008). *Poems for the Royal Weddings 1496–97*, Papers of the Medieval Hispanic Research Seminar, 64 (London: Department of Hispanic Studies, Queen Mary, University of London.

Martínez de Toledo, Alfonso (1959). *Little Sermons on Sin*, trans. Leslie Byrd Simpson (Berkeley, CA: University of California Press)
Martínez de Toledo, Alfonso (1985). *Arcipreste de Talavera o Corbacho*, ed. J. González Muela, 4th edn, Clásicos Castalia, 24 (Madrid: Castalia)
Martíncz Ruiz, Juan (1967). 'La indumentaria de los moriscos según Pérez de Hita y los documentos de la Alhambra', *Cuadernos de la Alhambra*, 3: 55–124
Martínez y Martínez, Francisco (2004). 'El tercer casamiento de Pedro el Ceremonioso', *III Congreso de Historia de la Corona de Aragón: dedicado al período comprendido entre la muerte de Jaime I y la proclamación del Rey Don Fernando de Antequera, julio de 1923*, 2 vols (Valencia: Ajuntament, Delegació de Cultura), pp. 541–77
Martorell, Joannot (and Martí Joan de Galba) (1990). *Tirant lo Blanc*, ed. Albert G. Hauf, with Vicent Josep Escartí, Clàssics Valencians, 7 and 8, 2 vols (Valencia: Conselleria de Cultura, Educació i Ciència de la Generalitat Valenciana)
Martorell, Joannot (and Martí Joan de Galba) (2008). *Tirant lo Blanch*, ed. Albert Hauf, with Anna Isabel Peirats (Valencia: Aldaia)
Matter, E. Ann, and John Coakley (eds) (1994). *Creative Women in Medieval and Early Modern Italy: A Religious and Artistic Renaissance* (Philadelphia, PA: University of Pennylvania Press)
—— (2010). 'Italian Holy Women', in Minnis and Voaden 2010: 529–55
May, Florence Lewis (1957). *Silk Textiles of Spain: Eighth to Fifteenth Century* (New York: Hispanic Society of America)
Mechthild of Magdeburg (1998). *The Flowing Light of the Godhead*, trans. Frank Tobin, Classics of Western Spirituality (Mahwah, NJ: Paulist Press)
Miguel Prendes, Sol (1998). *El espejo y el piélago: la 'Eneida' castellana de Enrique de Villena*, Teatro del Siglo de Oro, Estudios de Literatura, 47 (Kassel: Reichenberger).
Minnis, Alastair, and Rosalyn Voaden (eds) 2010. *Medieval Holy Women in the Christian Tradition c. 1100-c. 1500* (Turnhout: Brepols)
Mola, Luca (2000). *The Silk Industry of Renaissance Venice* (Baltimore, MD: John Hopkins University Press)
Montesino, Fray Ambrosio (1987). *Cancionero de Fray Ambrosio Montesino*, ed. Julio Rodríguez Puértolas (Cuenca: Diputación Provincial)
Mooney, Catherine M. (1994). 'The Authorial Role of Brother A. in the Composition of Angela of Foligno's Revelations', in Matter and Coakley 1994: 34–63
Moorman, John R. H. (1983). *Medieval Franciscan Houses*, Franciscan Institute Publications, History Series, 4 (St Bonaventure, NY: Franciscan Institute, St Bonaventure University)
Morreale, Margarita (1954). 'Un ensayo medieval de exegesis moral: *Los doze trabajos de Hercules* de Enrique de Villena', *Revista de Literatura*, 5: 21–34

Mulder-Bakker, Anneke B. (2004a). '*Maria doctrix:* Anchoritic Women, the Mother of God, and the Transmission of Knowledge', trans. Myra Scholz, in Mulder-Bakker 2004b: 181–99

—— (ed.) (2004b). *Seeing and Knowing: Women and Learning in Medieval Europe 1200–1500*, Medieval Women: Texts and Contexts, 11 (Turnhout: Brepols)

Mulvaney, Beth A. (2005). 'The Beholder as Witness: The "Crib at Grecchio" from the Upper Church of San Francesco, Assisi and Franciscan Influence on Late Medieval Art in Italy', in *The Art of the Franciscan Order in Italy*, ed. William R. Cook, The Medieval Franciscans, 1 (Leiden: Brill), pp. 169–99

Muñoz, Ferran (2002). 'Lectura i contemplació: noves aportacions al voltant del retaule del convent de la Puritat de València', *Afers: fulls de recerca i pensament*, XVII: 57–72

Muñoz Fernández, Ángela (1995). *Acciones e intenciones de mujeres: vida religiosa de las madrileñas (ss. XV–XVI)*, Mujeres en Madrid (Madrid: Dirección General de la Mujer and Horas y Horas)

Munro, John H. (1983). 'The Medieval Scarlet and the Economics of Sartorial Splendour', in Harte and Ponting 1983: 13–70

—— (2007). 'The Anti-Red Shift – To the Dark Side: Colour Changes in Flemish Luxury Woollens, 1300–1550', in Netherton and Owen-Crocker 2007: III, 55–95

Navarro Espinach, Germán (1992). *El despegue de la industria sedera en la Valencia del siglo XV*, Sèrie Minor: Història, 10 (Valencia: Generalitat Valenciana, Consell Valencià de Cultura)

—— (1996). *El col·legi de l'art major de la seda de València*, Sèrie Minor: Història, 38 (Valencia: Generalitat Valenciana, Consell Valencià de Cultura)

—— (1999). *Los orígenes de la sedería valenciana (siglos XV–XVI)*, Colección 'Estudis', 14 (Valencia: Ajuntament de València)

Nelson, Janet L. (1997). 'Early Medieval Rites of Queen-Making and the Shaping of Medieval Queenship', in Duggan 1997: 301–15

Netherton, Robin, and Gale R. Owen-Crocker (eds) 2007. *Medieval Clothing and Textiles*, 3 vols (Woodbridge: The Boydell Press)

Newton, Stella Mary (1980). *Fashion in the Age of the Black Prince: A Study of the Years 1340–1365* (Woodbridge: The Boydell Press)

Nunemaker, J. Horace (1938). 'A Comparison of the Lapidary of Marbode with a Spanish Fifteenth-Century Adaptation', *Speculum*, 13: 62–7

O'Connor, Edward Dennis (ed.) (1958). *The Dogma of the Immaculate Conception: Its History and Significance* (Notre Dame, IN: University of Notre Dame Press)

O'Sullivan, Daniel E. (2005). *Marian Devotion in Thirteenth-Century French Lyric* (Toronto: University of Toronto Press)

Oma Echevarría, Ignacio (1973). *Las monjas concepcionistas: notas históricas sobre la Orden fundada por Beatriz de Silva* (Burgos: Aldecoa)

Papa, Cristina (1994). '"Car vos senyora sou la gran papesa": mariologia e genealogie femminili nella *Vita Christi* di Isabel de Villena', in Graña Cid 1994a: 213–25

Paredes, Juan (ed.) (1995). *Medioevo y literatura. Actas del V Congreso de la Asociación Hispánica de Literatura Medieval (Granada, 27 de septiembre – 1 de octubre de 1993)*, 4 vols (Granada: Universidad de Granada)

Paschini, Pio (1954). 'Rosario', *Enciclopedia Cattolica*, 12 vols (Rome: Sansone), X, pp. 1350–1

Pearson, Hilary (2010). 'Was Teresa de Cartagena an Author?', paper presented at the 21st Colloquium of the Medieval Hispanic Research Seminar, Queen Mary, University of London, 24–25 June

Pelbart van Themeswar (1502). *Pomerium sermonum de beata virgine vel stellarium corona beate virginis* (Lyons: Johannes Cleyn)

Pelikan, Jaroslav (1996). *Mary through the Centuries: Her Place in the History of Culture* (New Haven, CT: Yale University Press)

Penketh, Sandra (1996). 'Women and Books of Hours', in Smith and Taylor 1996: 266–80

Péreç, Jaume (1485). *Expositio super Magnificat* (Valencia: Alfonso Fernández de Córdoba).

Pérez de Guzmán, Fernán (1965). *Generaciones y semblanzas*, ed. R. B. Tate, Colección Támesis, Serie B: Textos, II (London: Tamesis)

Pérez de Tudela y Bueso, María Luisa (1994). 'El convento del monasterio de Santa Clara la Real de Toledo (1247–1993)', in *Las clarisas en España y Portugal: Actas del congreso internacional (Salamanca, 20–25 de septiembre de 1993)*, ed. José María Mayor and María del Mar Graña Cid, Archivos e Historia, 2 vols (Madrid: Junta de Castilla y León, Universidad Pontificia de Salamanca, and Consejería de Cultura y Turismo), I, pp. 485–509

Piera, Montserrat (2003). "Writing, *Auctoritas,* and Canon Formation in Sor Isabel de Villena's *Vita Christi*", *La Corónica*, 32.1: 105–18

Piponnier, Françoise (1970). *Costume et vie sociale: la cour d'Anjou (XIVe–XVe siècles)*, Civilisations et Sociétés, 21 (Paris: Mouton)

Power, Eileen (1975). *Medieval Women,* ed. M. M. Postan (Cambridge: CUP)

Price, Richard M. (1998). '"God is More Weary of Woman than of Man": Reflections on a Text in the *Golden Legend*', in *Gender and Christian Religion: Papers Read at the 1996 Summer Meeting and the 1997 Winter Meeting of the Ecclesiastical History Society*, ed. R. N. Swanson (Oxford: Ecclesiastical History Society), pp. 119–27

Queller, Donald E., and Thomas F. Madden (1993). 'Father of the Bride: Fathers, Daughters, and Dowries in Late Medieval and Renaissance Venice', *Renaissance Quarterly*, 46: 685–711

Raabe, Pamela (1990). *Imitating God: The Allegory of Faith in 'Piers Plowman B'*, (Athens, GA: University of Georgia Press)

Réau, Louis (1955–59). *Iconographie de l'art chrétien*, 3 vols in 6 (Paris: Presses Universitaires de France), II, ii, *Iconographie de la Bible, Nouveau Testament*

Recio, Roxana (1991). Alfonso de Madrigal (El Tostado): la traducción como teoría entre lo medieval y lo renacentista', *La Corónica*, 19: 112–31

—— (1993). 'Las interpolaciones latinas en la *Vita Christi* de Sor Isabel de Villena: ¿traducciones, glosas, o amplificaciones?', *Anuario Medieval*, 5: 126–40

—— (1996). '"Por la orden que major suena": traducción y Enrique de Villena', *La Corónica*, 24.2: 140–53

Reglas (1988). *Reglas y constituciones generales de la orden de las hermanas pobres de Santa Clara* (Rome: Curia General de la Orden de los Frailes Menores, Oficina pro monialibus)

Ricossa, Luca Basilio (1994). *Jean de Ségovie: son office de la Conception, 1439. Étude historique, théologique, littéraire et musicale*, Série 36, Musicologie, 113 (Bern: Publications Universitaires Européennes)

Ríos Lloret, Rosa E. (2003). *Germana de Foix; una mujer, una reina, una corte* (Valencia: Generalitat Valenciana and Biblioteca Valenciana)

——, and Susana Vilaplana Sánchis (2006). *Germana de Foix i la societat cortesana del seu temps* (Valencia: Generalitat Valenciana, Biblioteca Valenciana and Consorci de Museus de la Comunitat Valenciana)

Riquer, Isabel de (1994). 'Los libros de Violante de Bar', in Graña Cid 1994a: 161–73

Riquer, Martín de (1961). 'Don Enrique de Villena en la corte de Martín I', in *Miscelánea en homenaje a Monseñor Higinio Anglés* (Barcelona: CSIC), II, pp. 717–21

—— (1972). *Literatura catalana medieval*, Publicaciones del Museo de Historia de la Ciudad, 25, Delegación de Servicios de la Cultura del Excmo. Ayuntamiento de Barcelona, 4 (Barcelona: Ayuntamiento de Barcelona, Delegación de Cultura)

—— (1986). *Heráldica castellana en tiempos de los Reyes Católicos*, Biblioteca Filológica (Barcelona: Quaderns Crema)

Rivera Garretas, María-Milagros (1990). *Textos y espacios de mujeres (Europa siglos IV–XV)* (Barcelona: Icara)

—— (1994). 'La educación en los tiempos de la vida femenina: *Le Livre des trois vertus* de Christine de Pizan y *Castigos e dotrinas que vn sabio daua a sus hijas*', in Graña Cid 1994a: 107–16

Roach, Mary Ellen, and Joanne Bubolz Eicher (1979). 'The Language of Personal Adornment', in Cordwell and Schwartz, 1979: 7–21

Robertson, Elizabeth (1993). 'Medieval Medical Views of Women and Female Spirituality in the *Ancrene Wisse* and Julian of Norwich's *Showings*', in *Feminist Approaches to the Body in Medieval Literature,* ed. Linda Lomperis and Sarah Stanbury, New Cultural Studies (Philadelphia, PA: University of Pennsylvania Press), pp. 142–67

Roest, Bert (2004). *Franciscan Literature of Religious Instruction before the*

Council of Trent, Studies in the History of Christian Traditions, 117 (Leiden: Brill)

Roig, Jaume (1978). *Espill o Llibre de les dones*, ed. Marina Gustà, Les Millors Obres de la Literatura Catalana, 3 (Barcelona: Edicions 62 and La Caixa)

Roís de Corella, Joan (1495). *Lo quart del cartoxà aromançat per lo reuerent e magnifich mestre Joan Roíç de Corella, caualler e mestre en sacra teologia* (Valencia: Lope de Roqua)

—— (1913). *Obres de J. Roíç de Corella amb una introducció per R. Miquel y Planas segons els manuscrits y primers edicions*, ed. Ramon Miquel i Planas (Barcelona: Miquel-Rius)

—— (1973). *Obres completes*, ed. Jordi Carbonell, Clàssics Albatros, 1 (Valencia: Albatros)

Romero Lucas, Diego (2003). 'La traducción valenciana de las *Meditationes Vitae Christi* del Cartujano Ludolfo de Sajonia: las primeras ediciones valencianas impresas', *Quaderns de Filología: Estudis Literaris*, 8: 299–314

Round, Nicholas G. (1962). 'Renaissance Culture and its Opponents in Fifteenth-Century Castile', *Modern Language Review*, 57: 204–15

—— (1969). 'Five Magicians, or the Uses of Literacy', *Modern Language Review*, 64: 793–805

Royo Marín, Antonio (1997). *La Virgen María: teología y espiritualidad marianas*, 2nd edn (Madrid: Biblioteca de Autores Cristianos)

Rubin, Miri (1991). *Corpus Christi: The Eucharist in Late Medieval Culture* (Cambridge: CUP)

—— (2009). *Mother of God: A History of the Virgin Mary* (New Haven, CT: Yale University Press)

Rudy, Kathryn M., and Barbara Baert (eds), 2007. *Weaving, Veiling, and Dressing: Textiles and their Metaphors in the Late Middle Ages*, Medieval Church Studies, 12 (Turnhout: Brepols), pp. 289–305

Ruiz Casanova, José Francisco (2000). *Aproximación a una historia de la traducción en España*, Lingüística (Madrid: Cátedra)

Rupert of Deutz (1844–64). *In cantica canticorum de incarnatione Domini*, ed. J.-P. Migne, *PL* 168, cols 839–962

Russell, Peter (1985). *Traducciones y traductores en la Península Ibérica (1400–1550)*, Monografies de Quaderns de Traducció e Interpretació, 2 (Bellavista: Escuela de Traductores e Intérpretes, Universidad Autónoma de Barcelona)

Sales, Agustín (1761). *Historia del Real Monasterio de la Santísima Trinidad, religiosas de Santa Clara, de la Regular Observancia, fuera los muros de la ciudad de Valencia, sacada de los originales de su archivo i monumentos coetaneos, con que tambien se ilustran varias familias, i successos del reino, andc; su autor Agustín Sales, presbítero de la Iglesia de San Bartholomé, doctor theologo por la Universidad de Valencia, i cronista de la misma ciudad i reino* (Valencia: Josep Estevan Dolz).

San Pedro, Diego de (1973). *Pasión trobada*, ed. Dorothy Sherman Severin

(Naples: Pubblicazioni della Sezione Romanza dell'Istituto Universitario Orientale)

Sánchez Cantón, F. J. (ed.) (1919). '*El arte de trovar* de Don Enrique de Villena', *Revista de Filología*, 6: 158–80

—— (1950). *Libros, tapices y cuadros que coleccionó Isabel la Católica* (Madrid: CSIC, Instituto Diego Velázquez)

Sanchis y Sivera, José (1921). 'El arte del bordado en Valencia en los siglos XIV y XV: apuntes para su historia', *Revista de Archivos, Bibliotecas y Museos*, 25: 200–23

—— (1922). 'La orfebrería valenciana en la Edad Media', *Revista de Archivos, Bibliotecas y Museos*, 26: 1–17; 235–59; 612–37

—— (1933). *El arte del bordado y de los tapices en Valencia (siglos XIV y XV)* (Valencia: Tipografía Moderna)

Sancho de Sopranis, Hipólito (1954). 'La devoción concepcionista en San Francisco de Cádiz', *Archivo Íbero-Americano*, 14: 207–46

Santiago Lacuesta, Ramón (1979). *La primera versión castellana de 'La Eneida' de Virgilio: los libros I-III traducidos y comentados por Enrique de Villena (1384–1434)*, Anejos del *BRAE*, 38 (Madrid: RAE)

Santillana, Íñigo López de Mendoza, Marqués de (2003). *Poesías completas*, ed. Maxim. P. A. M. Kerkhof and Ángel Gómez Moreno, Clásicos Castalia, 270 (Madrid: Castalia)

Schamm, Percy E. (1960). *Las insignias de la realeza en la Edad Media española*, trans. Luis Vázquez de Parga (Madrid: Instituto de Estudios Políticos)

Scheepsma, Wybren (1995). '"For Hereby I Hope to Rouse Some to Piety": Books of Sisters from Convents and Sister-Houses Associated with the *Devotio Moderna* in the Low Countries', in Smith and Taylor 1995: 27–40

Schmidt, Victor M. (2007). 'Curtains, *Revelatio*, and Pictorial Reality in Late Medieval and Renaissance Italy', in Rudy and Baert 2007: 191–213

Schneemelcher, Wilhelm (ed.) (1991). *New Testament Apocrypha*, ed. R. McL. Wilson, trans. Angus John Brockhurst Higgins, 2nd edn, 2 vols (Cambridge: James Clarke), from the original *Neutestamentliche Apokryphen in deutscher Übersetzung, völlig neubearbeitete Auflage*, ed. Edgar Hennecke (Tübingen: Mohr, 1904)

Schneider, Jane (1978). 'Peacocks and Penguins: The Political Economy of European Cloth and Colours', *American Ethnologist*, 5: 413–47

Schwartz, Ronald A. (1979). 'Uncovering the Secret Vice: Towards an Anthropology of Clothing', in Cordwell and Schwartz 1979: 23–46

Scott, Margaret (1980). *Late Gothic Europe, 1400–1500*, The History of Dress Series (London: Mills and Boon)

Segura Graíño, Cristina (1994). 'Las sabias mujeres de la corte de Isabel la Católica', in Graña Cid 1994a: 175–87

Seidenspinner-Núñez, Dayle (1997). '"But I Suffer not Woman to Teach": Two Women Writers in Late-Medieval Spain', in *Hers Ancient and Modern:*

Women's Writing in Spain and Brazil, ed. Catherine Davies and Jane Whetnall, Manchester Spanish and Portuguese Studies, 6 (Manchester: Department of Spanish and Portuguese, University of Manchester, 1997), pp. 1–14
—— (trans.) (1998). *The Writings of Teresa de Cartagena. Translated with Introduction, Notes and Interpretive Essay*, Library of Medieval Women (Cambridge: D. S. Brewer)
Sheingorn, Pamela (2003). '"The Wise Mother": The Image of St Anne Teaching the Virgin Mary', in *Gendering the Master Narrative: Women and Power in the Middle Ages*, ed. Mary C. Erler and Maryanne Kowaleski (Ithaca, NY: Cornell University Press), pp. 105–34
Shevelow, Kathryn (1989). *Women and Print Culture: The Construction of Femininity in the Early Periodical* (London: Routledge)
Short, William J. (1999). *Poverty and Joy: The Franciscan Tradition*, Traditions of Christian Spirituality Series (London: Darton, Longman, and Todd)
Sigüenza Pelarda, Cristina (2000). *La moda en el vestir en la pintura gótica aragonesa* (Zaragoza: Institución Fernando el Católico, Diputación de Zaragoza)
Silleras-Fernandez, Nuria (2008). *Power, Piety, and Patronage in Late Medieval Queenship: Maria de Luna*, The New Middle Ages (Basingstoke: Palgrave Macmillan)
Smith, Colin (ed.) (1972). *Poema de mío Cid* (Oxford: Clarendon Press)
Smith, Lesley (1996). '*Scriba, Femina*: Medieval Depictions of Women Writing', in Smith and Taylor 1996: 21–44
——, and Jane H. M. Taylor (eds) (1995). *Women, the Book and the Godly: Selected Proceedings of the St Hilda's Conference (St Hilda's College, Oxford, August, 1993)* (Cambridge: D. S. Brewer)
——, and Jane H. M. Taylor (eds) (1996). *Women and the Book: Assessing the Visual Evidence* (London: British Library)
Smith, Paul Julian (1987). 'Writing Women in Golden Age Spain: Saint Teresa and María de Zayas', *Modern Language Notes*, 103: 220–40
Solano, Jesús (1954). 'La Inmaculada en los padres españoles', *Estudios Marianos*, 15: 130–51
Solomon, Michael (1997). *The Literature of Misogyny in Medieval Spain: The 'Arcipreste de Talavera' and the 'Spill'*, Cambridge Studies in Latin American and Iberian Literature, 10 (Cambridge: CUP)
Sousa Congosto, Francisco de (2007). *Introducción a la indumentaria en España* (Madrid: Istmo)
Stratton, Suzanne L. (1994). *The Immaculate Conception in Spanish Art* (Cambridge: CUP).
Stroll, Mary (1997). '*Maria Regina*: Papal Symbol', in Duggan 1997: 173–203
Stubbes, Philip (1877–82). *Anatomy of the Abuses in England in Shakspere's Youth*, ed. Frederick J. Furnivall, The New Shakespeare Society, Series VI, 4, 6, and 12, 2 vols (London: Trübner)

Surtz, Ronald E. (1995). *Writing Women in Late Medieval and Early Modern Spain: The Mothers of Saint Teresa of Avila*, Middle Ages Series (Philadelphia, PA: University of Pennsylvania Press)

—— (2010). 'Iberian Holy Women: A Survey', in Minnis and Voaden 2010: 499–525

Thomas of Celano (1999). 'The Life of St Francis by Thomas of Celano', in *Francis of Assisi: Early Documents*, 3 vols, *Volume I: The Saint*, ed. Regis J. Armstrong et al., 2nd edn (New York: New City Press), pp. 171–308

Thomas, Anabel (2003). *Art and Piety in the Female Religious Communities of Renaissance Italy: Iconography, Space, and the Religious Woman's Perspective* (Cambridge: CUP)

Thurston, Herbert (1912). 'The Rosary', *The Catholic Encyclopaedia*, 18 vols (New York: Robert Appleton), XIII, pp. 184–8

Tillier, Jane Yvonne (1985). 'Passion Poetry in the *Cancioneros*', *BHS*, 62: 65–78

Tormo, E. (1920). 'Orfebrería valenciana de fines del siglo XVI: las cruces procesionales de Játiva y Onteniente', *Boletín de la Sociedad Española de Excursiones*, 28: 193–204

Torres-Alcalá, Antonio (1983). *Don Enrique de Villena: un majo al dintel del Renacimiento* (Madrid: José Porrúa Turanzas)

—— (1984). 'El estoicismo senequista de Don Enrique de Villena', *Bulletin Hispanique*, 86.1–2: 26–38

Touwaide, Alain (2008). 'The Jujube Tree in the Eastern Mediterranean: A Case Study in the Methodology of Textual Archeobotany', in Dendle and Touwaide 2008: 72–100

Tramoyeres Blasco, Luís (1889). *Instituciones gremiales: su orígen y organización en Valencia* (Valencia: Domenech)

Trens, Manuel (1947). *María: iconografía de la Virgen en el arte español* (Madrid: Plus Ultra)

Turner, Jack (2007). *Spice: The History of a Temptation* (London: HarperCollins)

Twomey, Lesley K., (1997). '"Cechs són aquells que tenen lo contrari": Fanatical Condemnation of Opponents of the Immaculate Conception in Fifteenth-Century Valencia', in *Faith and Fanaticism: Religious Fervour in Early Modern Spain*, ed. Lesley K. Twomey (Aldershot: Ashgate), pp. 23–35

—— (2003a). 'Sor Isabel de Villena, her *Vita Christi* and an Example of Gendered Immaculist Writing in the Fifteenth Century', *La Corónica*, 32.1: 89–103

—— (2003b). '*Una qüistión sobre la conçebçión de Santa María*: The *Cancionero de Baena* Debate on the Immaculate Conception', *Hispanic Research Journal*, 4: 99–112

—— (2005). 'Relectura del color rojo: la alegoría en la *Vita Christi* de Isabel de Villena', in *Las metamorfosis de la alegoría: discurso y sociedad en la Península Ibérica desde la Edad Media hasta la Edad Contemporánea*, ed.

Rebeca Sanmartín Bastida and Rosa Vidal Doval (Madrid: Iberoamericana-Vervuert), pp. 189–202

—— (2006). 'On the Scent of Mary: The Power of Perfume in the *Espill*', *Catalan Review*, 20: 337 46

—— (2007a). 'La corona de doce estrellas: devoción y desarrollo', in *Actas del XV Congreso de Hispanistas: 'las dos orillas' (Monterrey, México, 19 24 de julio de 2004)*, 3 vols (Monterrey: Fondo de Cultura Económica, Asociación Internacional de Hispanistas, Tecnológico de Monterrey, and Colegio de México), II, pp. 601 10

—— (2007b). 'Poverty and Richly Decorated Garments: A Re-Evaluation of their Significance in the *Vita Christi* of Isabel de Villena', in Netherton and Owen-Crocker 2007: III, 119 34

—— (2007c). 'María: joya entre joyas', in *Avanzando hacia la igualdad*, ed. Antonia Medina Guerra (Malaga: Diputación de Málaga and Asociación de Estudios Históricos sobre la Mujer), pp. 55–72

—— (2008). *The Serpent and the Rose: The Immaculate Conception and Hispanic Poetry in the Late Medieval Period,* Studies in Medieval and Reformation Traditions, 132 (Leiden: Brill)

—— (forthcoming). '*Manus mee distillaverunt mirram:* The Essence of the Virgin and an Interpretation of Myrrh in the *Vita Christi* of Isabel de Villena', in *Medieval Hispanic Studies in Memory of Alan Deyermond*, ed. Andrew M. Beresford, Louise M. Haywood, and Julian Weiss (in press)

Ubertino da Casale (1961). *Arbor Vitae Crucifixae Jesu*, ed. Charles T. Davis (Turin: Bottega d'Erasmo)

Vela i Aulesa, Carles (2001). 'Les ordinacions de mercaderies encamerades o falsificades: evolució del control municipal sobre la qualitat de les espècies i les drogues (segles XIV–XV)', *Quaderns d'Historia*, 5: 19–45

Vicente Conesa, María Victoria (1997). *Seda, oro y plata en Valencia: Garín 258 años* (Valencia: TRP Comunicación)

Vilanova, Arnau de (1499). *Tratatus de virtutibus herbarum* (Venice: Simon Pope)

Villena, Enrique de (1923). *Arte de trovar*, ed. F. J. Sánchez Cantón (Madrid: Victoriano Suárez)

—— (attrib.) (1983). *Tratado de astrología atribuido a Enrique de Villena*, ed. Pedro M. Cátedra, intro. Julio Samsó, Biblioteca Humanitas de Historia del Pensamiento, Serie: Historia de la Ciencia y de la Técnica (Barcelona: Humanitas)

—— (1989). *Traducción y glosas de la Eneida*, ed. Pedro M. Cátedra, 2 vols, Biblioteca Española del Siglo XV, Serie Básica: 2 and 3 (Salamanca: Diputación de Salamanca)

—— (1994–2000). *Obras completas*, 3 vols, ed. Pedro M. Cátedra, Biblioteca Castro (Madrid: Turner)

—— (2004). *Tratado de fascinación también conocido como ojo fecho o mal de ojo*, ed. Carmen de la Maza (Barcelona: Obelisco)

Villena, Sor Isabel de (1497). *Vita Christi de la Reverent Abbadessa de la Trinitat* (València, Lope de Roqua; repr. facsimile, Valencia: Del Cènia al Segura, 1980; repr. facsimile, Valencia: Biblioteca de València, 2006).

—— (1513). *Vita Christi de la Abbadessa del monestir de les monges de la Trinitat* (Valencia: Jorge Costilla)

—— (1527). *Vita Christi d[e] la Reuerent Abbadessa dela Trinitat corregit ab les cotacions nouame[n]t tretes en los marges* (Barcelona: Carles Amorós)

—— (1916). *Vita Christi compost per Isabel de Villena, abadessa de la Trinitat de Valencia, ara novament publicat segons l'edició de l'any 1497*, ed. Ramón Miquel y Planas, 3 vols, Biblioteca Catalana (Barcelona: Casa Miquel-Rius)

—— (1995). *Vita Christi*. Selection and edition by Albert-Guillem Hauf i Valls, Les Millors Obres de la Literatura Catalana, 115 (Barcelona: Edicions 62 and La Caixa)

—— (2006). *Vita Christi de Sor Isabel de Villena*. Edición facsímil. Estudio introductorio de Albert G. Hauf i Valls (Valencia: Biblioteca Valenciana and Generalitat Valenciana, Conselleria de Cultura)

—— (1992). *Vita Christi: Sor Isabel de Villena*, ed. Josep Almiñana Vallés, 2 vols (Valencia: Ajuntament Regidora d'Acció Cultural)

Vloberg, Maurice (1958). 'The Iconography of the Immaculate Conception', in *The Dogma of the Immaculate Conception*, ed. Edward Dennis O'Connor (Notre Dame, IN: University of Notre Dame Press), pp. 463–512

Volmöller, Karl (1880). *Ein Spanisches Steinbuch* (Heibronn)

Voragine, Jacobus de (1850). *Legenda aurea*, ed. Theodor Grässe (Leipzig: Librariae Arnoldianae)

—— (1993). *The Golden Legend: Readings on the Saints*, trans. William Granger Ryan, 2 vols (Princeton, N.J.: Princeton University Press)

Walsh, John K., and Alan Deyermond (1979). 'Enrique de Villena como poeta y dramaturgo: bosquejo de una polémica frustrada', *Nueva Revista de Filología Hispánica*, 28: 57–85

Warner, Marina (1985). *Alone of All Her Sex: The Myth and Cult of the Virgin Mary* (London: Picador)

Weber, Alison (1993). 'Teresa de Jesús', in *Spanish Women Writers: A Bio-Bibliographical Source Book*, ed. Linda Gould Levine, Ellen Engelson Manson, and Gloria Feiman Waldman (Westport, CT: Greenwood Press), pp. 484–94

Webster, Jill R. (1993). *Els Menorets: The Franciscans in the Realms of Aragon from St Francis to the Black Death*, Pontifical Institute of Medieval Studies, Studies and Texts, 114 (Toronto: Pontifical Institute of Medieval Studies)

Weiner, Annette B. (1992). *Inalienable Possessions: The Paradox of Keeping while Giving* (Berkeley, CA: University of Berkeley Press)

Weiss, Julian (1990). *The Poet's Art: Literary Theory in Castile c. 1400–60*,

Medium Aevum Monographs, New Series, 14 (Oxford: The Society for the Study of Mediaeval Languages and Literature)

Weissberger, Barbara F. (2004). *Isabel Rules: Constructing Queenship, Wielding Power* (Minneapolis, MN: University of Minnesota Press)

—— (2005). 'Invisible Threads in the Tapestry of Sovereignty: Carmentis, Arachne, and Athena in *Jardín de nobles doncellas*', in *'Entra mayo y sale abril': Medieval Spanish Literary and Folklore Studies in Memory of Harriet Goldberg*, ed. Manuel da Costa Fontes and Joseph T. Snow, Hispanic Monographs: Homenajes, 25 (Newark, DE: Juan de la Cuesta), pp. 397–419

Wely, Daniel Van (1941). 'Het Kraansje der Twaalf Sterren in de Geschiedenis van der Rosenkrans', *Colectanea Franciscana Neerlandica*, 6: 1–71

Whalen, George (1995). 'Patronage Engendered: How Goscelin Allayed the Concerns of Nuns' Discriminatory Publics', in Smith and Taylor 1995: 123–36

Whetnall, Jane (1984). '*Lírica femenina* in the Early Manuscript *Cancioneros*', in *What's Past is Prologue. A Collection of Essays in Honour of L. J. Woodward*, ed. Salvador Bacarisse et al. (Edinburgh: Scottish Academic Press), pp. 138–50, 171–75

—— (1992–93). 'Isabel González of the *Cancionero de Baena* and Other Lost Voices', *La Corónica*, 21: 59–82

—— (2006). 'Las transformaciones de Petrarca en cuatro poetas de Cancionero: Santillana, Carvajales, Cartagena, y Florencia Pinar', *Cancionero General*, 4: 81–108

—— (2007). 'Mayor Arias: "¡Ay, mar brava, equiva!"', in *Seis siglos de poesía española escrita por mujeres: pautas poéticas y revisiones críticas*, ed. Dolores Romero López et al. (Bern: Peter Lang), pp. 11–25

Wilkins, Constance L. (1998). 'El devocionario de sor Constanza: otra voz femenina medieval', in Aengus Ward (ed.), *Actas del XII Congreso de la Asociación Internacional de Hispanistas (Birmingham, August 1995)*, 7 vols (Birmingham: Department of Hispanic Studies, University of Birmingham), I, pp. 340–9

—— (2002). 'The Prayerbook of Constanza de Castilla: Reflection of a Liturgical Life', in *Two Generations: A Tribute to Lloyd A. Kasten (1905–1999)*, ed. Francisco Gago Jover (New York: Hispanic Seminary of Medieval Studies), pp. 253–64

Wilkins, Eithne (1969). *The Rose-Garden Game: The Symbolic Background to the European Prayer Beads* (London: Gollancz)

Williamson, Beth (2004). 'Altarpieces, Liturgy, and Devotion', *Speculum*, 79: 341–416

—— (2009). *The Madonna of Humility: Development, Dissemination, and Reception (c.1340–1400)*, Bristol Studies in Medieval Culture (Woodbridge: Boydell Press)

Winston-Allen, Ann (2005). *Stories of the Rose: The Making of the Rosary in he Middle Ages* (University Park, PA: Penn State Press)

Wogan-Browne, Jocelyn (1994). 'Chaste Bodies: Frames and Experiences', in *Framing Medieval Bodies*, ed. Sarah Kay and Miri Rubin (Manchester: Manchester University Press, 1994), pp. 25–41

Wolf, Kenneth Baxter (2003). *The Poverty of Riches: St Francis of Assisi Reconsidered*, Oxford Studies in Historical Theology (Oxford: OUP)

Woolf, Rosemary (1968). *The English Religious Lyric in the Middle Ages* (Oxford: Clarendon Press)

INDEX

Abbess, 12–13, 19, 22, 24–5, 27, 31, 35, 40, 57, 59–60, 75, 96, 102, 117, 205, 207, 208, 229, 236, 237
    Alfani da Perugia, Battista (active fifteenth century), Poor Clare, abbess of Santa Maria de Monteluce, 1
    González de la Fuente, María, Franciscan Third Order, abbess, St Anthony of Padua convent, 59
    Puig, Violant del (†1461), Poor Clare, abbess, Santa Trinitat, 12
    Solsona, Isabel de (†1462), Poor Clare, abbess, Santa Trinitat, 12
    Vigri, Caterina (1413–63), Poor Clare, abbess, 1, 208
    See also Constanza de Castilla; Hildegard of Bingen; Villena, Isabel de
Abstinence, 54, 55, 57
    Self-denial, 54
    See also Fasting; Feasting; Renunciation
Adam, 43, 45–6, 49, 80, 109, 112, 139, 169, 183, 206, 225–6, 237, 239
    See also Eve; Fall; Sin
Adoration, 14, 47–8, 67–9, 74, 82, 84, 121, 123, 131, 143, 189
    See also Agnus Dei; Body, of Christ; Corpus Christi; Host; Pyx; Sacrament; Veneration
Aeneid, *see* Virgil
Agnus castus, *see* Chasteberry
Agnus Dei, 82–3, 116–17
    See also Adoration; Body, of Christ; Corpus Christi; Host; Pyx; Veneration
Alb, *see* Vestment
Alcanyís, Miquel (active 1408–47), painter, 113–14 (Fig. 15)

Retablo de la Santa Cruz, 113–14
Alfani da Perugia, Battista, *see* Abbess
Alfons d'Aragó i Foix (1336–1442), 2
Alfons the Magnanimous (1396–1458), King of Aragon, 3, 6, 172
Allegory, xi, 86–7, 90, 107, 139, 168, 203
    Allegorical ladies, 205
    See also Charity; Chastity; Humility; Piety; Pity; Poverty
Alms, 9, 11, 157–8
Amor hereos, *see* Love
Anne, St, mother of the Virgin, 17, 30–1, 35, 37, 47–8, 66, 104, 163, 166 (Fig. 20), 180, 224
    Annunciation to St Anne and St Joachim, 15, 38, 224
Annunciation, s*ee* Feasts, of the Virgin
    See also Anne, St
Antequera, Fernando de (1380–1416), King of Aragon, 3, 5–6, 134
Aragon, Kingdom of, 2, 3, 6, 43, 56, 63, 66, 68, 79, 94–6, 103, 111, 116–17, 123–4, 142, 145, 147, 152, 163, 175–6, 189, 197, 210, 217–18, 224
    Aragonese, 3, 9, 30, 58, 147, 162
    Crown of Aragon, 3, 69, 212
    King of Aragon, 5, 131, 148–9
    See also Queen
Arbor vite crucifixae Iesus, *see* Ubertino da Casale
Archpriest of Talavera, *see* Martínez de Toledo, Alfonso
Aristotle (384 BC–322 BC), philosopher, 43, 104
Ark, of the Covenant, *see* Covenant
Artès, Master of (active in Valencia 1472–1538), artist, now thought to be Pere Cabanyes, 69, 189
Retablo de la Nativitat, 189

Ascension, 14, 16, 18, 68, 144, 212–18 (Figs 28, 29, 30 and 31), 220, 229
Assumption, *see* Feasts, of the Virgin
Auctoritas, *see* Authority
Authority, 5, 9, 24–7, 31, 34, 92, 119, 181, 194, 213, 219–21, 228–30
  Auctoritas, 7, 181
Azeituní, *see* Velvet

Balaguer, Baltasar Joan, fray, later prior of the Monastery of Valldigna, *certamen* (poetry competition) poet, 103–4
Beauty, 95, 105–6, 112, 125–6, 128–30, 132, 138–41, 146, 173, 176, 198, 225, 230–1, 237–8, 246, 251–3
  See also Body, Female Body
Beloved, *see* Love
Betrothal, *see* Marriage
Birth, of Christ, 13, 15–6, 36, 87, 122
Birth, of the Virgin, 23, 35, 63, 201, 208, 224
  See also Feasts, of the Virgin, Nativity of the Virgin; Forment, Damià, *Naixement de la verge*; Nativity
Black, 81–2, 91–2, 95–6, 99, 121, 143, 150, 155, 162–3
  See also Colour
Blanche of Anjou, *see* Queen
Blazon, 19, 121–3
  Emblazon, 112, 115, 138, 240
  See also Enamel
Blood, 42, 43, 50, 89, 97, 104–7, 117, 231, 244, 247
  See also Body, of Christ
Blue, 81, 83, 85, 97, 99, 100, 116, 123, 136, 156, 159–60, 167–8, 189, 244
  See also Colour
Body, 42–84, 124, 131, 137, 140, 174–5, 182, 198, 231, 239, 251
  Female body, 30, 42–4, 48–51, 54, 62, 109, 113, 115, 157–8, 175, 177, 181, 230–2
  Male body, 42–3
  of Christ, 16, 19, 89, 104, 117, 137–8, 205, 223, 226, 247
  Virgin's body, 45–6, 89, 104, 125, 132, 138, 152, 153, 166, 177–8, 191, 226, 231–2, 253
  See also Blood; Community; Corpus Christi; Eucharist; Host; Milk; Tears; Womb
Border (of garment), 88–9, 92, 96, 109, 111, 122–3, 125, 148
  See also Blazon; *Cortapisa*; Embroider; Enamel; Gem; Jewel
Borja, Alfons de (1378–1458), Bishop of Valencia, 12
Borrassà, Lluís (1360–1425), painter, 207–8 (Fig. 26)
  Retaule d'advocació franciscana, 207–8
Bread, 55–6, 117, 232, 253
  See also Body, of Christ; Eucharist; Food; Host; Sacrament; Tabernacle
Bride, 96–8, 108, 132, 137–8, 147–8, 150, 152–3, 192, 197, 201–4, 210, 231, 234, 252
  See also Bridegroom; Marriage
Bridegroom, 16, 96, 138, 202–3
  See also Bride; Marriage
Brocade, 69, 85–6, 88, 92–3, 96, 98–9, 102, 111, 128–9, 131, 136, 138–44, 146–50, 153, 162–3, 167–8, 172, 189, 231–3, 243–4
  See also Cloth; Damask; Gold, Cloth-of-Gold; Fabric; Silk; Velvet
Broiderer, *see* Guild, of Broiderers
Burial, of Christ, 77–8, 82, 223
  See also Entombment; Mourning; Sepulchre; Shroud; Tomb

Calatrava, Order of, *see* Order, of Calatrava
Calico, *see* Cotton
Cambray, *see* Cotton
Camlet, *see* Silk
Cantar que fizo el Marqués a sus fijas loando la fermosura de ellas, *see* Santillana, Marquís de
Canvas, *see* Cotton
Carbuncle, 41, 190–1, 199, 239, 251
  See also Gem; Jewel
Castañeda, Abdón (1580–1629), painter, 187–88 (Fig. 22)
  Virgen de los Ángeles, 188
Castelló, Vicenç (1586–1636), painter, 193–4 (Fig. 24)
  Coronación de la Virgen, 193
Castile, Kingdom of, 2, 3, 4, 11, 13, 24, 92–3, 98, 123, 134–5, 153–4, 189

Queen of Castile, *see* Queen
Català, Lluís, *certamen* poet, 38, 88–9, 125, 183
Catholic Monarchs, 92, 99, 111
   See also Fernando el Católico; Isabel la Católica;
Cell, 74–5, 247
   See also Cloister; Enclose; Nun
Chalice, 81, 123
   See also Blood; Eucharist
Charity, 27, 88, 103–4, 165, 169, 173, 178, 182, 199, 209–10, 236, 240, 242, 246–8
   See also Allegory, Allegorical ladies
Chasteberry, 113, 115
   Agnus castus, 110–11, 113, 115–16, 117, 118, 131, 171, 242
Chastity, 81, 88, 115, 189, 242
   See also Allegory, Allegorical ladies
Chemise, 85, 89, 99, 109–10, 140, 148, 177, 246
     See also Clothe, Clothing; Dress; Garment, Undergarment; Shift; Tunic; Vestment
Chestnut, *see* Food
Chicken, *see* Food
Cinctorres, Master of (active 1400), painter, 65 (Fig. 4)
   Naixement de la Verge i la Presentació al Temple, 65
Cinnamon, *see* Spices
Circumcision, s*ee* Feasts, of the Virgin, Purification
Cistercian, *see* Order
Clare, St (1194–1253), first abbess of San Damiano, foundress of the Franciscan Second Order, the Poor Clares, 9, 12, 31, 32 (Fig. 3), 52, 59, 198, 207, 208 (Fig. 26), 220, 229, 231
   Office of St Clare, 31
   Rule of St Clare, 26, 29, 31, 55
Clares, Poor, *see* Order, Franciscan, Second Order
Cloak, 69, 71, 81–2, 85, 97, 100, 108, 131–2, 135–6, 138–40, 143, 145, 147–8, 159, 162–3, 168, 189
   See also Clothe, Clothing; Dress; Garment; Mantle; Robe; Vestment
Cloister, 11, 108
   Cloistered, 34, 36, 40, 67, 172, 221, 229, 233

   See also Enclose, Enclosed
Cloth, 61, 63, 65–7, 69, 71, 73, 75–8, 81–3, 91–5, 102, 106, 111, 115, 119, 120, 140–6, 148, 150, 172, 189, 212, 233
   See also Brocade; Cotton; Damask; Fabric; Gold, Cloth-of-gold; Linen; Red, Crimson; Red, Scarlet; Silk; Velvet; Wool
Cloth-of-gold, *see* Gold
Clothe, 20, 69, 89, 92–4, 97, 105–7, 126, 137–40, 144, 153, 168–70, 172–3, 175, 231, 233
   Clothes, xvi 63, 76, 79, 81, 90, 106, 133–7, 140–2, 145, 148, 150, 169, 176, 233
   Clothing, 20, 69, 80, 88–90, 93, 94, 106–109, 112, 118, 122, 126, 133–38, 140, 142, 145–46, 148–52, 154, 163, 165, 169–70, 176, 224, 233
   Hand-me-down, 134–5
   Second-hand, 134, 136
   Re-clothe, 106, 137, 169
Cloves, *see* Spices
Coincy, Gautier de (1177–1236), 89, 176, 183
   Les Miracles de Nostre Dame, 89, 176
Colour, 19, 85, 87–8, 90–99, 102–7, 109, 117–9, 121, 123–4, 131, 133, 141, 147, 155, 163, 168, 172, 234, 252
   See also Black; Blue; Gold; Green; Grey; Red; Purple; Silver; White
Community, 29, 31, 37, 41–2, 44, 55, 59, 61–2, 151, 194, 204, 219, 231–2
   See also Convent
Compassion, 17–8, 24, 40, 49–51, 90, 124–5, 169, 238, 240
   See also Passion; Pietà; Sorrows, of the Virgin
Compline, 197, 225, 228
   See also Hours
Conception, Immaculate, *see* Feasts, of the Virgin
Confession, 34, 74–5
   Confessor, 25, 204–5, 211, 218
   See also Penitence; Prayer
Constanza de Castilla (†1478), prioress, Santo Domingo del Real, Madrid, writer, 23–4, 34, 221
   See also Abbess

Contemplació a Jesús crucificat, see Fenollar, Bernat
Contemplació de la passió de Nostre Senyor Jesucrist, 17–18, 124, 211, 233
Contemplation, 17–18, 24, 26, 35, 48, 51–54, 75, 107, 199, 210, 229
Contemplative, 35, 51, 54, 60, 62, 83, 209–10
  See also Meditation; Prayer
Convent
  Jerusalem, Poor Clare (Valencia), 9
  Puritat, Poor Clare (Valencia), xi, 37, 55, 57, 60–1, 161, 163, 207, 224
    Libro de dades i rebudes (1454 a 1460), 56, 60
  Santa Isabel (St Elizabeth, later the Puritat), Poor Clare (Valencia), 9, 207
  Santa Trinitat, Poor Clare (Valencia), 9, 10 (Fig. 1), 11, 13, 23, 33, 37, 39–41, 45, 55, 58–62, 68, 74, 82–3, 102, 115, 117, 198, 223, 232, 237
Cope, *see* Vestment
Corbacho, see Martínez de Toledo, Alfonso, Arcipreste de Talavera
Cordwainers, *see* Guild, of Cordwainers
Corona Beatissime Virginis, see Crown
Coronation, s*ee* Feasts of the Virgin, Coronation
  See also Crown; Queen, Coronation of queens
Coronet, *see* Crown
Corporal (cloth used at Eucharist), 69, 83
  See also Body, of Christ; Eucharist; Veil
Corpus Christi, 68–9, 82, 144, 172
  See also Agnus Dei; Body, of Christ; Eucharist; Host; Monstrance; Procession; Pyx
Cortapisa (decorative band at cuff or hem), 87–9, 121–2, 125, 131
  See also Blazon; Border; Enamel; Gem; Jewel;
Cotton, 120, 156
  Calico, 76
Cambray, 99, 120, 127–8
  Canvas, 76
  See also Cloth; Fabric; Linen
Court, 2–4, 6, 16, 22, 30, 44, 88, 90, 92, 102, 108–9, 111, 118, 134–6, 150, 153, 155, 182, 205–6, 237, 249

Courtier, 4, 95, 102, 134, 155
Courtly, 5–6, 87, 108–9, 118, 141, 151, 163
Covenant, 45, 166, 168–9, 200
  Ark of, 45, 200
Crimson, *see* Red
Cross, *see* Crucifixion
Crown, xii, 16, 20, 85, 86, 88, 97, 121, 123, 127, 131, 144–5, 147–9, 168, 173, 177–8, 179–204, 207, 209–10, 231, 245, 251–3
  Corona Beatissime Virginis [Crown of the Blessed Virgin], 130–31, 168, 183
  Corona de los monjes, 113, 201
  Coronet, 97
  Crown of roses, 179, 181
  Crown of stars, 179–203
  Triple crown, 16, 147, 189–90, 192, 194, 196
  See also Castelló, Vicenç, *Coronación*; Crown; Diadem; Rosary; *Stellarium*
Crucifixion, 40–1, 78–80, 105–6, 116, 123–4, 170, 191, 223
  Cross, 18, 40–1, 76–7, 79–80, 83–4, 97, 103, 113, 116–17, 123–4, 205, 222, 225, 250, 252
Cuenca, town in Kingdom of Castile, 5–6, 215

Dalmatic, *see* Vestment
Dalmau, Lluís (1428–61), painter, 96
  La Verge dels consellers, 96
Damask, 81, 85, 92, 94, 122, 126, 136, 140, 150
  See also Brocade; Cloth; Fabric; Silk; Velvet
Defunsión de Enrique de Villena, señor doctor e de exçellente ingenio, see Santillana, Marqués de
Deutz, Rupert of (c. 1075–1179), Benedictine theologian and exegete, 175, 217
Diadem, 139, 192, 197–8
  See also Crown
Diamond, 85, 122, 128, 130, 252
  See also Gem; Jewel
Disease, 43, 55
Dispute (between Guilds), 149, 159, 161, 177, 227, 233

INDEX

Candlemakers and Apothecaries, 227
Sabaters and the *Tapiners*, 159–61, 177
Velluters and Silk-Shearers, 149
Doctor, 5, 15, 33, 47–8, 212, 220–1, 249, 252
Doctoressa, 217, 220, 227
Doctrine, 19, 25, 29, 37, 44, 69, 117, 131, 187, 236, 250
See also Doctor
Dogaresse, *see* Venice
Dominic, St (1170–1221), of Guzmán, founder of the Dominican Order, supposed inventor of the rosary, 15, 179
Dormition, *see* Feasts, of the Virgin
Dotzè llibre del crestià, *see* Eiximenis, Francesc
Dowry, 6, 11, 110, 136, 150, 154, 233
See also Gift; Marriage; Nun
Dress, 136–41
  Dressing, 90, 133, 137, 149–52, 175, 207, 231, 248
  Undressing, 133, 150–52, 207
  See also Chemise; Garment; Habit; Nun, Vestition; Robe; Shift; Stripping; Tunic; Dress, Undressing; Stripping; Veil, Veiling; Veil, Unveiling; Vestment

Egg, *see* Food
Egypt, flight to, 47–49, 61, 75–6
Eiximenis, Francesc (1327–35?–1409), Franciscan, theologian, Bishop of Elna, patriarch of Jerusalem, xv, 1, 3, 13, 15–7, 30, 33, 40–1, 44–5, 47–8, 52, 55, 61, 71, 79, 86, 104, 118–19, 125, 145, 156–7, 162, 170, 177, 181, 187, 209–10, 212–4, 219, 229–30, 234
  Dotzè llibre del crestià [Twelfth Book of the Christian], 44, 145
  Lo libre de les dones [Book of Ladies], 157, 181, 210
  Vida de Jesucrist [Life of Christ], 13, 15–7, 40, 46–7, 52, 71, 73, 79, 104, 119, 170, 209, 213, 219, 229, 234
Elizabeth I (1533–1603), Queen of England, 92, 155
Elizabeth of Schönau (1129–65), Benedictine visionary, 34, 217

Elizabeth of Thuringia, St (1207–31), Franciscan, member of Third Order, 189–90
Elizabeth, St, 47, 54
  See also Feasts of the Virgin, Visitation
Embrace, 47, 79, 147, 198, 204–5, 213
  See also Body; Kiss; Touch
Embroider, 19, 88–9, 91, 96, 104, 108–13, 115, 117–18, 120–3, 125, 131, 138–9, 142, 145,148, 153, 155–6, 171, 231, 233–4, 242–3
  Embroidery, 19, 81, 92, 109–10, 112–13, 115–16, 118, 120–2, 129, 131–2, 142, 148, 155–6, 171
  See also Cortapisa; Sew; Shoe; Vestment
Emotion, xv, 18, 42, 49–50, 53
  See also Body, Female body; Spirituality, Female spirituality; Tears
Enamel, 19, 116, 121–4, 126–7, 156, 231, 233, 242, 251–2
  Enamelwork, 122
  See also Blazon; Border; *Cortapisa*
Enclose, 120
  Enclosed, 39, 46, 52, 67, 87, 112, 204, 236
  See also Cloister; Convent; Nun; Order
Enrique II (†1379), King of Castile, 2
Enrique III (1379–1406), King of Castile, 4–5, 134
Enrique of Aragon and Castile, *see* Villena, Enrique de
Entombment, 78, 80–1, 84
  See also Burial, of Christ; Sepulchre; Shroud; Tomb
Ermine, 111, 121, 133, 141
  See also Marten
Eucharist, 19, 52–4, 63, 67–9, 71 (Fig. 8), 74–5, 81, 83, 116–17, 138, 232
  See also Chalice; Corporal; Corpus Christi; Host; Monstrance; Pyx
Eve, 34, 45–6, 49–50, 80, 109, 183, 201, 206
  See also Adam; Fall
Exposición del salmo, 'Quoniam videbo', *see* Villena, Enrique de
Ezekiel, 139, 201, 224

Fabric, 19–20, 90, 93, 95, 109–10, 113, 125–8, 132, 133–52, 153, 156, 160, 231, 233–4
  See also Brocade; Cloth; Cotton; Damask; Gold, Cloth-of-gold; Linen; Red, Crimson; Red, Scarlet; Silk; Velvet; Wool
Falcó, Nicolau (active late fifteenth and early sixteenth centuries, Valencia), painter, 65–6 (Fig. 6), 71–2 (Fig. 9), 99, 101 (Fig. 13), 143, 166 (Fig. 20), 189
  Retablo de la Purísima Concepción, 66, 101, 163, 166
  Tríptico de la Virgen de la Leche, 71–2, 189
Fall, 14, 42, 50, 53, 86, 191, 200
  See also Adam; Eve; Sin
Fasting, 54–6, 75
  See also Abstinence; Feasting; Food
Feasting, 55, 120, 206
  See also Fasting; Food
Feasts, of the Virgin, 12, 15, 36, 37, 55–6, 68–9, 111–12, 144–5, 181, 197, 222, 224–5, 252
  Annunciation, 12, 14–16, 31, 47, 53, 61, 89, 97, 99, 101 (Fig. 13), 109, 112–14 (Fig. 15), 116–17, 122–3, 125, 132, 140, 143–4, 150, 167–8, 175–7, 181, 197, 201, 224, 228
  Assumption, 14–19, 56, 68, 86, 89, 144–5, 181, 189, 192, 196–8, 200, 228–9
  Conception, Immaculate, 19–20, 23, 25, 37–9, 41, 44, 87, 103–4, 112, 131, 170, 175–6, 179–80, 183–5, 187, 189, 191, 196–7, 200–1, 203, 223–6, 232, 188, 192, 194, 196–7, 202, 204
  Coronation, 14, 18, 86, 143, 147–50, 172, 173, 192, 194, 196, 202
    Coronation of kings, 134, 181, 182
    Coronation of queens, 35, 92, 111, 118, 147, 150, 152, 207, 231
      Coronation of Queen Esther, 170, 196
  Dormition, 14, 143
    See also Assumption
  Expectation, 197
    Nuestra Señora de la O, 169
  Nativity, of the Virgin, 15, 31, 63, 64 (Fig. 4), 65 (Fig. 5), 145, 208, 224
  Presentation, 15, 125
    Presentation in the temple, 55, 65 (Fig. 5)
  Purification, 123
    Circumcision, 51
  Visitation, 68, 144–5, 163, 229
    See also Elizabeth, St
Fenollar, Bernat (1438–1516), *certamen* poet, 12, 18, 102
  Contemplació a Jesús crucificat, 18, 124
  Passi en cobles, 12, 79–80, 103
Fernando de Antequera (1380–1416), King of Aragon, 3, 5–6, 134–5
Fernando el Católico (1452–1516), King of Aragon, 95, 120, 142, 176
Ferrante I of Aragon (1492–94), King of Naples, 145, 224
Florence, silk-producing town in Italy, 141
Foix, Germana de (1488–1536), second wife of Fernando el Católico, 95, 120
Foligno, Angela of, Blessed (1248–1309), Umbrian mystic, Third Order Franciscan, 1, 15, 34, 146, 218
Food, 25, 54–6, 115, 241
  Capon, 56
  Chestnut, 56, 185
  Chicken, 56
  Egg, 55–57
  Honey, 57
  Neule, Christmas wafer, 56
  Rice, 55, 57
  Snail, 56
  Turrón (nougat), Christmas sweetmeat, 56
  Walnut, 56
  See also Abstinence; Bread; Fasting; Feasting; Spice
Forment, Damià (active 1499–1540), sculptor, 63–4
  Naixement de la Verge, 64 (Fig. 4)
Francis of Assisi, St (1181–1226), founder of the Franciscan Order, 16, 38, 55, 68, 100, 117, 146
Franciscan, *see* Order

Gandia, town in the Kingdom of Valencia, 2–3, 11–12, 56

Garcia de Benavarre, Pere (active 1450s-1470s), artist, Northern Aragon, 63
Garland, 138, 145, 148, 150, 203
  See also Coronation; Marriage
Garment, 59, 87–90, 94, 96, 105–7, 108–11, 118, 120–2, 125–7, 132, 133–52, 153, 162, 173, 175–8, 207, 232
  Undergarment, 110, 148, 176
  See also Chemise; Dress; Shift
Gem, 127, 145–6, 155, 182, 190–1, 198, 200
  See also Carbuncle; Diamond; Jewel; Pearl; Ruby; Sapphire; Topaz
Gift, 16–17, 20, 85–7, 95, 103, 105–10, 113, 115, 125–6, 131, 133–5, 137–8, 149–54, 169, 174, 176–7, 181–2, 196, 203, 244, 249, 253
  See also Alms; Clothe, Clothing; Dowry; Marriage
Ginger, *see* Spice
Gloss, *see* Translation
Gold, 82–3, 85, 88, 92–4, 96–9, 105–6, 109–12, 119, 121, 126–32, 139, 141–6, 148–9, 155, 159, 163, 172–3, 181–5, 187–90, 194, 196, 198–9, 203, 207, 231, 242, 245–6, 251–3
  Cloth-of-gold, 82, 94, 115, 119, 123, 145–6, 148
  Drawn-gold, 88, 111, 142, 172, 245
  Gold leaf, 94
  Gold plate, 116, 142
  Golden, 88–9, 138, 141, 147, 196, 198
  Spun-gold, 142
  Thread-of-gold, 96, 143
Goldsmiths, *see* Guild, of Goldsmiths
González de la Fuente, María, *see* Abbess
Gospel, 14–15, 22, 31, 62, 82, 87, 109, 220, 232, 247, 249–50
  Apocryphal Gospel, 15, 38, 87, 224
  Gospel of St John, 14
  Gospel of St Luke, 14, 63, 86, 219 (Fig. 33)
  Gospel of St Matthew, 31
  See also Saragossà, Llorenç, *Escenas de la vida de San Lucas: San Lucas escribiendo su Evangelio al dictado de la Virgen*; Scripture
Granada, Kingdom of, 182
  Conquest of, 76

Green, 81, 85, 111, 115, 121–3, 136, 140–2, 153–6, 168, 171, 243
  See also Colour
Gremial, *see* Vestment
Grey, 141, 156, 171, 243
  See also Colour
Guild, xi, 61, 91, 120, 136, 149, 159–61, 177, 182, 227, 232–3, 246, 249
  of Apothecaries, 227
  of Armourers, 120
  of Broiderers (*Bordadores*), 120
  of Candle-makers, 227
  of Cordwainers, 136, 159–61
    of *Sabaters*, 159
  of Goldsmiths, 19, 232
  of Silk-Shearers, 149
  of Silversmiths, 182, 232
  of *Tapiners*, xi, 159–61, 232
  of Velvet-makers, 149, 232
    of *Velluters,* 149

Habit, 11, 93, 146, 151, 162, 202, 204
  See also Nun; Tunic; Veil; Vestment
Hand-me-down, *see* Clothe, Clothing
Headdress, 73–4, 76, 78, 120, 128, 140, 148, 176
  Moorish headdress, 76
  See also Garland; Hood; Veil
Health (spiritual), *see* Salvation
Helfta, town in Germany, site of an important female foundation, 50, 151
Hildegard of Bingen (1098–1179), prioress, foundress of the abbey of St Rupert, Bingen, xv, 1, 24–5
Honey, *see* Food
Hood, 76, 128
  See also Cloak; Headdress; Veil
Host, 67–9, 74–5, 81–3, 116, 204
  Consecration of the Host, 54, 67, 81
  Elevation of the Host, 83, 204
  See also Body, of Christ; Corpus Christi; Eucharist; Monstrance; Pyx
Hours, 18, 30, 37, 48, 52, 97, 125, 211, 222–3
  Book of hours, 99, 188, 196, 222
  of the Virgin, 188, 222
  See also Compline; Matins; None; Terce; Vespers
Humility, 26–7, 46–8, 52, 75, 138–9, 143, 177, 205, 209–10, 228, 236, 240, 243, 249

Humility topos, 24, 26–7, 29
  See also Allegory, Allegorical ladies; Virgin, Madonna or Virgin of Humility
Humours, 50–1, 115
  See also Disease

Ildephonse of Toledo, St (†667), 38, 45, 199
  Pseudo-Ildephonse, 130
  See also Crown, *Corona Beatissime Virginis*
Incarnation, 14, 16–17, 41, 47, 58, 63, 69, 82, 90, 103, 137, 166, 170, 175, 177, 181, 183–4, 196–7, 205–6, 223, 248
Incarnate, 83–4
  See also Body, of Christ; Womb
Isabel de Portugal, *see* Queen, Queen of Castile
Isabel of Castile and Aragon (1472–98) (Infanta), oldest daughter of Isabel la Católica and Fernando el Católico, Queen of Portugal, 153
Isabel la Católica (1451–1504), Queen of Castile, 11, 19, 21, 23, 29–30, 35, 119–20, 142, 159, 182, 194, 196
  See also Queen, Queen of Castile
Isaiah, 105–6, 108, 132, 138, 153
  See Scripture

Jacomart (1411–61), painter, 99–100 (Fig. 12), 113
  Anunciación, 100
Jaume I, the Conqueror (1208–76), King of Aragon, 2, 94, 182
Jaume II, the Just (1267–1327), King of Aragon, 2, 212
Jerusalem, convent, *see* Convent
Jewel, 19, 82, 85, 99, 102, 106, 108–9, 111, 113, 121, 125–7, 129–34, 136–39, 141, 143, 146, 153, 170, 176–7, 181–82, 199–200, 207, 231, 233, 239, 247
Jewellery, xi, 109, 125, 128–32, 136–7, 150, 182, 230
  See also Carbuncle; Diamond; Gem; Pearl; Ruby; Sapphire; Topaz
Joan II (1398–1479), King of Aragon, 3
Joan de Joanes (1505–79, Valencia), painter, 99

John, of Caulibus, 13–14, 35–6, 40, 51–2, 71, 76, 78–9, 209, 212–13, 223, 234
  Meditationes Vitae Christi (*MVC*), 13–14, 35, 40, 51, 71, 73, 78–79, 82, 209, 212, 223. 234
John, St, disciple, 18, 54, 74–5, 81, 123, 192, 215
John the Baptist, St, 47, 123, 185, 194
Joseph, St, 15–16, 47, 49, 61, 189
Joys, of the Virgin, 88–9, 122–3, 125, 163, 174, 181, 188, 196, 210, 214–15, 217
  Retaule dels Goigs de la Verge, 163–4
  See also Crown, *Corona Beatissime Virginis*; Nicolau, Pere, *Retablo de los Siete Gozos*; Rosary; Sorrows, of the Virgin; *Stellarium*
Juan II (1405–54), King of Castile, 3, 6
Juan of Castile (1478–97), prince, second son of Isabel la Católica and Fernando el Católico, 92, 98
Juana of Castile (Juana la Loca) (1479–1555), second daughter of Isabel la Católica and Fernando el Católico, briefly Queen of Aragon and Castile, 99, 110
Julian of Norwich (1342–1416), writer, 1, 43, 137
Juvenal, 158
  Satire, 43, 158

Kempe, Margery (c.1373–1438), mystic, 34, 43
Kiss, 47–8, 163, 224–5, 250, 253
  See also Body; Embrace; Retascón, Master of, *Abraçada a la Porta Daurada*; Touch
Knit, 137, 201
  See also Embroider; Sew; Spin; Weave

Lando, Ferrant Manuel de, poet, 135
Leather, *see* Shoe
Legenda aurea, *see* Voragine, Jacobus de
Leonor de Castilla (?–1244), Queen of England, 142
Libro de dades i rebudes (1454 a 1460), *see* Convent, Puritat
Linen, 77, 81, 111, 128, 136, 139, 148
  See also Cloth; Cotton; Fabric
L'Isle, Alain de (1128–1203), theologian, 5, 55, 174, 182

Liturgy, 1, 24, 37, 39, 124, 204–29, 231, 233–4
 See also Feasts, of the Virgin; Hours
Lo libre de les dones [Book of Ladies], *see* Eiximenis, Francesc
López de Ayala, Pero (1332–1407), poet, statesman, 4–5, 134
 See also Villasandino, Alfonso Álvarez de
López de Mendoza, Íñigo, Marquís de Santillana (1398–1458), 3, 5–7, 95, 129–30, 132, 140–2
 Defunsión de Enrique de Villena, señor doctor e de exçellente ingenio, 5
 See also Villena, Enrique de
Love, 43, 47–8, 55, 87, 107, 115, 118, 138–40, 147–8, 156, 169, 172–3, 198–9, 206, 213–14, 221, 223, 225, 236, 237, 240, 243–50, 252–3
 Amor hereos, 43
 Beloved, 24, 30, 74, 82, 112, 118, 175, 178, 197, 206, 225, 234, 239, 242, 250, 253
 See also Song of Songs
Ludolph of Saxony (1295–1377), writer, 14–8, 38, 77, 80, 192, 212
 Vita Christi, 14, 16–18, 192, 212
Luna, Álvaro de (1390–1453), Constable of Castile, favourite of Juan II, 6

Macip, Vicent (1475–1550), painter, 99
Majorca, Kingdom of, conquered by the Kingdom of Aragon, 56, 158, 172
Manger, 35–6, 47, 67–8, 71, 90, 232
Maniple, *see* Vestment
Mantle, 25, 85, 92, 115, 144, 147–8, 176–7, 221
 See also Cloak
March, Ausiàs (1400–1459), poet, 3
March, Pere, 'el Viejo' (1336–1413), poet, 3
María de Albornoz, *see* Villena, Enrique de
María of Castile (1401–58), Queen of Aragon, 2–3, 11–12, 17, 40, 116, 123
Marriage, 2, 3, 5, 16, 97–8 (Fig. 11), 115, 133, 150, 154, 157, 189
 Betrothal, 109, 113, 131, 137–8, 150, 201, 207
 Nuptials, 108, 131, 133, 148, 203

 Nuptial, 20, 137, 192
 See also Bride; Bridegroom; Dowry; Gift
Marten, 94, 128, 130, 141
 See also Ermine
Martí, the Humane (1356–1409), King of Aragon, 6, 30
Martínez de Toledo, Alfonso (c. 1398–c. 1470), Archpriest of Talavera, writer and moralist, 33, 38, 94, 127–30, 158, 230
 Corbacho, 30, 43, 158
Martorell, Joannot (1413–65?), author, 3, 74, 88, 109–10, 115, 118, 122, 140, 148, 174
 Tirant lo blanc, 3, 73–4, 87, 104, 108–10, 115, 118, 122, 126, 130, 140, 148–9, 174
 See also Princess, Carmesina
Mary Magdalene, St, 15, 17, 22, 30, 51, 104, 140, 227, 248
Master of Calatrava, *see* Order, of Calatrava
Master of Cinctorres, *see* Cinctorres, Master of
Master of Perea, *see* Perea, Master of
Master of Retascón, *see* Retascón, Master of
Mater Dolorosa, *see* Mother, of God
Mater Sapientiae, *see* Mother, of God
Matins, 18, 52, 176, 223
 See Hours
Meditation, 18, 30, 36–7, 41, 51, 85, 131, 174, 179, 199–200, 204, 210, 221, 223, 232, 234
 See also Contemplation; John of Caulibus, *Meditationes*; Ludolph of Saxony, *Vita Christi*; Prayer
Meditationes Vitae Christi (*MVC*), *see* John, of Caulibus
Milk, 42, 50, 105
 See also Blood; Body, Female body; Falcó, Nicolau, *Tríptico de la Virgen de la Leche*; Perís Sarrià, Gonçal, *Mare de Déu de la Llet*; Tears; Virgin
Miralles, Miquel, *certamen* poet, 184–5
Misogyny, 33, 43
 Misogynist, 33, 42–3, 62, 160, 177, 230
Monstrance, 69, 83, 204–5, 212

See also Body, of Christ; Corporal; Corpus Christi; Eucharist; Procession; Veil
Montesino, Ambrosio de, fray (1444?-1514), Franciscan, poet, 200–1
Montserrat, *see* Virgin of
Mother, of God, 38, 43, 65, 85, 144, 162–3, 205, 207, 215, 217, 232, 241, 249, 253
   Mater Dolorosa, 124
   Mater Sapientiae, 31, 191
Mourning, 81–2
   See also Compassion; Entombment; Sepulchre; Sorrows, of the Virgin; Veil
Murillo, Esteban (1617–82), painter, 179–80
Murrey, *see* Red
Myrtle, 171–2, 191, 243, 252
Mystic, 25, 43, 67, 151

Nativity, of Christ, 31, 47, 67–9, 71, 73 (Fig. 10), 77–8, 83, 86, 117, 123, 189
Nativity, of the Virgin, *see* Feasts, of the Virgin
Navarre, Kingdom of, 224
   House of, 154
Neule, *see* Food
Nicolau, Pere (active c. 1390–1408), painter, 99, 113, 196, 214 (Fig. 28), 215, 218 (Fig. 32)
   Retablo de los Siete Gozos, 214–5, 218
Nogarola, Leonardo, liturgist, 37, 39, 45, 106, 112, 176, 187, 224–5, 228–9, 231
   See also Liturgy
None, the ninth hour, 52, 119, 189, 191, 197, 231
   See also Hours
Novice, *see* Nun
Nun
   Novice, 89, 151, 202, 204–6, 211
   Postulant, 150, 205
   Profession, 12, 150, 151, 202–3, 204–6
   Vestition, 150, 152, 204–6, 228
   See also Abbess; Dowry; Habit; Veil; Vocation
Nuptial, *see* Marriage

Order
   Cistercian, 53, 197
   Conceptionist, 55, 58
   Franciscan, xv, xvii, 1–2, 9, 11, 13, 19, 23, 32 (Fig. 3), 35–7, 39, 44, 47, 50–1, 55, 58–9, 63, 68, 82–4, 85, 87, 113, 117, 131, 146–7, 162, 168, 179–181, 187, 199–201, 203, 204, 207, 208 (Fig. 26), 210, 218, 220, 225, 227, 229, 230, 232, 234
      Second Order, 1, 11, 82
         Poor Clares, 1, 3, 9, 11–13, 27, 29, 37, 42, 51–2, 54, 59–60, 89, 198, 202, 204, 206–8, 210–11, 229, 232
      Third Order (Tertiary), 1, 59
   of Calatrava, 5–6
   of Santiago, 6
   Trinitarian, 11–12, 40
Original sin, *see* Sin

Pasión trobada, *see* San Pedro, Diego de
Passi en cobles, *see* Fenollar, Bernat
Passion, of Christ, 12, 14, 16–18, 76, 78, 80, 83, 106, 123–5, 166, 223–4, 231
   See also Compassion; *Contemplació de la passió de Nostre Senyor Jesucrist*; Fenollar, Bernat, *Contemplació a Jesús crucificat*; Fenollar, Bernat, *Passí en cobles*; Pietà; Roís de Corella, Joan, *Lo quart del Cartoxà*; San Pedro, Diego de, *Pasión trobada*
Patron, 9, 11–2, 26, 29, 109, 131, 134, 136–7, 141, 142, 150, 165, 180, 182, 185
   See also María of Castile
Paul, St, writer of Acts of the Apostles and letters to Christian communities, 15, 33, 42–3, 87
Pearl, 85, 88, 94, 96, 106, 121–2, 128–31, 142, 145, 148, 177, 179, 182, 192, 198, 251, 253
   See also Gem; Jewel
Penitence, 50, 55, 209
   See also Confession
Pentecost, 18, 68, 102, 107, 123, 144–5, 192, 213–14, 217–8 (Fig. 32), 221, 229
Pepper, *see* Spices
Pere, the Ceremonious (1319–87), King of Aragon, 94, 148
Perea, Master of, artist (active in Valencia

1490–1510), 99, 102 (Fig. 14), 121, 131, 143, 189
Adoración de los Reyes (MBAV), 102, 131
Adoration of the Magi (private collection), 121, 189
Pereç, Jaume, Bishop of Valencia, 13
Pérez de Guzmán, Fernán (1376–1460?), Lord of Batres, poet, 4–7, 180
Perís Sarrià, Gonçal (1380–1451), artist, Valencia, 69, 71 (Fig. 8), 77–8, 99, 117, 163, 215
Mare de Déu de la Llet, 163
Retablo de los Gozos de la Virgen, 215
Retablo de San Martín, con Santa Úrsula y San Antonio Abad, 69, 71
Verónica de la Virgen, 99
Perseverance, 85, 110, 220, 246–7
Pietà, 53, 124, 223
See also Compassion; Crucifixion; Mourning; Passion, of Christ; Sorrows, of the Virgin
Piety, 9, 18, 63, 85, 140, 177, 180, 189, 209–10, 243, 246
See also Allegory, Allegorical ladies
Pity, 140, 213, 240, 243, 247, 250
See also Allegory, Allegorical ladies
Possessions, 17, 30, 55, 57–8, 82, 116
See also Riches; Wealth
Postulant, see Nun
Poverty, 46, 58, 73, 81, 86, 113, 136, 146–7, 173–4, 206, 210
See also Allegory, Allegorical ladies
Prayer, 16, 24, 31, 39, 46, 48, 52–4, 59–60, 62, 145, 151, 157–8, 171, 176, 179–80, 185, 198–9, 204, 207–10, 217, 219–23, 225, 228–9, 231–2, 237, 245–9, 252
See also Contemplation; Hours; Meditation
Presentation, see Feasts of the Virgin
Princess, 74, 88, 145, 149, 153, 174, 175, 178, 231–2, 234, 245
Carmesina, 87–8, 110, 115, 118, 122, 130, 140, 148
Margaret of Austria (1488–1533), daughter of Emperor Maximilian, 92, 98
Princess of Tyre, 138, 153, 231–2
See also Isabel of Castile; Juana of Castile; Martorell, Joannot, *Tirant lo blanc*;
Procession, 68–9, 82, 116–17, 123, 159, 172, 180, 204, 211–12
See also Corpus Christi; Feasts, of the Virgin; Monstrance
Profession, see Nun
Puig, Violant del, see Abbess
Purification, see Feasts, of the Virgin
Puritat, convent, see Convent
Purple, 92, 95, 104–5, 156
See also Colour; Red
Pyx, 53, 82–3
See also Adoration; Body, of Christ; Corporal; Corpus Christi; Eucharist; Host; Monstrance; Veil; Veneration

Queen, 3, 6, 11–12, 21, 30, 35, 38, 94–5, 110–11, 118, 133, 137, 139, 147–50, 153–4, 156, 174, 198, 203, 207, 231, 234, 239, 245–9
Coronation of queens, 92, 147, 152, 207
Queen of Aragon, 30, 35, 131, 149, 152
Blanche of Anjou (1280–1310), Queen of Aragon, 3
See also María of Castile
Queen of Castile, 131, 153
Isabel de Portugal (1428–96), Queen of Castile and Leon, wife of Juan II, 153
See also Isabel la Católica
Queen of Heaven, 20, 132, 144, 200, 222, 229, 231.
See also Virgin

Read, 5–6, 8–9, 13, 21–41, 44, 62, 79, 85, 88, 107, 124, 198, 206, 230, 232–3, 236
Reader, 8, 21–3, 26, 30–1, 33–4, 36–7, 42, 47, 49, 52, 90, 102, 117–18, 133, 142, 151, 177, 198, 211, 218, 221
Reading, 5–6, 8, 21–41, 13, 17, 44, 60–1, 81, 85–107, 117, 133, 191, 197, 199, 202, 224, 231–4
Red, 3, 63, 66, 69, 81, 85, 89, 91–9, 102–3, 105–7, 110–12, 117, 121, 123, 163, 189, 191, 212, 231

Crimson, 19, 85, 87–8, 90–9, 102–7, 121, 140, 147, 156, 182, 242
  Incarnate, 94
  Murrey, 94
  Scarlet, 19, 88, 92–7, 99–100, 105–6
  Tawny, 94
Redemption, 13–14, 50, 84, 169–70, 210
Reixach, Joan (Valencia, c.1411-c.1484), painter, 77, 99, 131, 143, 163, 165, 215, 217
Renunciation, 57–9, 83, 146
  See also Abstinence; Fasting; Food; Possessions; Riches; Wealth
Resurrection, 16, 68, 192, 194, 252
Retascón, Master of (documented 1410–25), 163
  Abraçada a la Porta Daurada, 163
Revelation, 25, 47, 63
  Woman of Revelation, 87, 179, 231
  See also Scripture; Vision
Rice, *see* Food
Riches, 113, 143, 253
  See also Possessions; Wealth
Ritual, 67–8, 75, 81–2, 84, 90, 112, 149–52, 202, 204–5, 207, 212, 228–9
Robe, 16, 38, 74–5, 95, 97, 97–100, 106, 115, 125, 129, 148, 150–2, 168–9, 179, 181
  Robing, 111, 133, 138, 147, 149–52, 204
  See also Chemise; Clothe, Clothing; Dress; Garment; Habit; Nun, Vestition; Shift; Tunic; Vestment
Roís de Corella, Joan (1433 / 43–1497), poet and translator, xv, 14, 17–8, 77, 79–81, 86, 115, 118, 124, 155–6, 171, 192, 212–3
  (Trans.) *Lo primer del Cartoxà*, 14
  (Trans.) *Lo quart del Cartoxà*, 14, 18, 77, 79, 124, 213
  (Trans.) *Lo segon del Cartoxà*, 14
  (Trans.) *Lo terç del Cartoxà*, 14
  Vida de Santa Anna, 17, 155
  Visió del Judici de Paris [Vision of the Judgement of Paris], 115
Rosary, 20, 124, 129, 163, 176–7, 179–80, 230
  Retaule de Santa María el Roser, 163, 165
  Rupa, Alan of (1428–75), Dominican, founder of the rosary confraternity with Jakob Sprenger, 180
  See also Crown, crown of roses; Crown, crown of stars; *Stellarium*
Ruby, 99, 131, 191
  See also Gem; Jewel
Rupa, Alan of, *see* Rosary

Sabaters, see Guild of *Sabaters*
Sacrament, 16, 48–9, 53, 67, 74–5, 83–4, 96–7, 98 (Fig. 11), 105, 138, 232
  See also Host; Eucharist; Marriage
Saffron, *see* Spices
Salvation, 31, 36, 43–4, 49, 55, 58, 85, 87, 90, 107, 111–12, 116, 131, 138–9, 167–8, 173, 191, 201, 224, 237, 247, 253
  Health (Spiritual), 43
San Pedro, Diego de, 76
  Pasión trobada, 76
Sandals, 153, 160, 173–6, 231
  Santa sandalia, 176
    Cofradía de la Santa Sandalia [Brotherhood of the Holy Sandal], 176
Santa Trinitat, convent, *see* Convent
Santiago, Order of, *see* Order
Santillana, Marquís de, Íñigo López de Mendoza (1398–1458), 3, 5–6, 95, 129–30, 132, 140–2
  Cantar que fizo el Marqués a sus fijas loando la fermosura de ellas, 40, 95, 129
Sapphire, 122, 127–8, 130, 168, 185, 199
  See also Gem; Jewel
Saragossà, Llorenç, (documented in Barcelona and Valencia 1360–1406), painter, 218–19 (Fig. 33)
  Escenas de la vida de San Lucas: San Lucas escribiendo su Evangelio al dictado de la Virgen
  See also Gospel
Satire, *see* Juvenal
Scarlet, *see* Red
Scourging, 76–7, 80, 106, 123, 223
  See also Crucifixion; Passion
Scripture, xv, 9, 14, 29, 34, 46, 87, 107, 117, 169, 185, 197, 213, 223, 225, 233–4
  See also Gospel; Revelation
Second-hand, *see* Clothe, Clothing

Self-denial, *see* Abstinence
Sepulchre, 74, 81, 120
   See also Burial, of Christ,
      Entombment; Shroud; Tomb; Veil
Sew, 126
   Sewing, 52, 119
   See also Embroider, Embroidery
Shame, 79–80, 83, 135
Shift, 78, 109–10, 148
   See also Chemise; Clothe, Clothing;
      Garment, Undergarment
Shirt, 120, 136
   See also Clothe, Clothing; Garment
Shoe, 20, 85, 96, 139, 142, 153–78, 230, 233, 243–5
   Chopines, 153–4 (Fig. 16), 156–62, 173, 245
   Leather (boot, footwear, shoe, sole), 139, 154–60
   Silk shoe, 20, 159, 163, 177, 242–5
   Tapins, 85, 153–61, 163, 165–9, 171–2, 174–5, 177–8, 191
      Chapinazo [blow with a shoe], 158
      Tapineta, heavy silk for making *tapins*, 156
Shroud, 63, 75, 77–8, 80–2
   See also Burial, of Christ;
      Entombment; Sepulchre; Tomb; Veil
Silk, 20, 61, 76, 81, 85, 90–6, 98–9, 109–11, 116–17, 119, 121, 129, 139–42, 144, 147–50, 154–56, 158–9, 161, 163, 177, 231–3, 243–6
   Azeituní, 141
   Camlet, 98–9, 142
   Silk industry, 91, 149, 232
   Taffeta, 142
   Terzanel, 142
   See also Brocade; Cloth; Damask; Fabric; Guild, of Silk-Shearers; Guild, of Silkmakers; Sandal; Shoe, Silk shoe; Velvet
Silkmakers, *see* Guild, of Silkmakers
Silk-Shearers, *see* Guild, of Silk-Shearers
Silver, 82–3, 94, 102, 110, 116–17, 121, 128–30, 139, 142–3, 146, 153, 155, 163, 166–7, 182, 231, 242
   See also Guild, of Silversmiths
Silversmith, *see* Guild, of Silversmiths
Sin, 40, 42, 48–9, 63, 80, 105, 112, 116, 127, 147, 156, 158, 166, 174, 176–7, 184, 187, 191, 200, 221, 225, 230, 239, 243–4, 249, 250–1
   Original, 19, 39, 41, 44, 185, 239, 251
   Sinful, 44, 78, 80, 105–6, 112, 158, 169, 184, 187, 200–1, 227
   Sinfulness, 80, 105–6, 158
Sinless, 80, 116, 132
   Sinlessness, 168
Sinner, 24, 36, 168–9
   See also Penitence; Temptation
Sittow, Michael (or Michiel), (c.1465–1525), court painter to Isabel la Católica, 99, 194–5 (Fig. 25)
Sixtus IV (1414–84), pope, 37, 45, 106, 185
Slashed, 99, 141
   See also Dress; Sleeve
Sleeve, 94, 99, 110, 128
   See also Chemise; Dress; Slashed
Snail, *see* Food
Solsona, Isabel de, *see* Abbess
Song of Songs, 86–7, 112, 131, 173–6, 178, 182, 197, 201, 203, 217, 225, 227–8
   See also Allegory; Scripture
Sorrows, of the Virgin, 89, 121–2, 124–5, 144, 223, 241–2
   Seven Sorrows, 124–5, 223
Soul, 11, 19, 22, 40, 42, 50, 55, 59, 75, 87, 107, 131–32, 137–38, 151, 157, 167, 187, 226–7, 231–2, 239, 243–5, 247–8, 250, 253
   See also Body
Spices, 56, 115
   Cinnamon, 56–7, 128
   Cloves, 56
   Ginger, 56–7
   Pepper, 56–7, 115
   Saffron, 56–7
Spin, 61, 119
   See also Sew, Sewing; Weaving
Spirit, Holy, 27, 39, 41, 46, 50, 86, 103–4, 107, 170–1, 181–2, 192, 196, 213, 217, 220, 236, 239–40, 246–50, 252–3
Spirituality, 1, 53, 68, 146, 209, 212, 223, 234
   Female spirituality, 50, 54
   Franciscan spirituality, 84
   Spiritual, 6, 9, 11, 24, 29, 31, 34, 41, 43, 51, 58, 68, 83, 85, 87, 108,

138, 157–8, 211–12, 218–20, 223, 229, 230–1
Stellarium, 179–80, 187, 201, 203
    See also Crown; Joys; Rosary
Stole, *see* Vestment
Strip, 59, 78–9, 137, 157, 169
    Stripping, 59, 79
Sumptuary law, 129, 142, 230
    See also Clothe, Clothing; Dress

Tabernacle, 38–9, 53, 63, 67, 82, 232
    See also Body, of Christ; Corpus Christi; Eucharist; Host; Veil, Veiling
Tapin, *see* Shoe
Tapiners, *see* Guild, of *Tapiners*
Tapineta, *see* Shoe, *Tapin*
Tawny, *see* Red
Tears, 50–3, 213, 221, 242, 247, 249
    Tears of St Francis, 50–51
    Tears of the Virgin, 50, 53
    Vale of tears, 236
    See also Blood; Body, Female body; Compassion; Milk; Pietà; Sorrows, of the Virgin
Temple, 15–6, 38–41, 44–6, 48, 52, 54, 57, 65, 119, 181, 200, 207–12, 224, 238–9, 241, 248, 253
Temptation, 42, 244
    See also Sin
Terce, the third hour, 52, 119, 222
    See Hours
Teresa de Cartagena (1415?–35), nun, writer, 23–5, 27
Teresa of Avila, St (1515–82), foundress of the Discalced Carmelite Order, mystic, 1, 2, 22
Tertiary, member of the Third Order, *see* Order, Third Order
Terzanel, *see* Silk
Thomas of Celano, Franciscan, writer, 36
Thread, gold, *see* Gold
Tirant lo blanc, *see* Martorell, Joannot
Toledo, town in the Kingdom of Castile, 55, 60, 163, 191, 199
Tomb, 11, 15, 18, 78, 81, 161, 162 (Fig. 17)
    See also Burial, of Christ; Entombment; Sepulchre; Shroud
Topaz, 199–200, 207
    See also Gem, Jewel

Tordesillas, town in the Kingdom of Castile, 12
Tortosa, town in the Kingdom of Aragon, 65
Touch, 35, 46, 51, 74, 85, 167–8
    See also Body, Female body; Embrace; Kiss; Touch
Translation, 7–8, 13–14, 25, 29–30, 38, 77, 89, 113, 191–2, 212, 233, 235
    Gloss, 8, 25
Trinitarian, Order, *see* Order
Tunic, 85–9, 92–4, 97–9, 103–5, 107, 110–11, 113, 115, 117–18, 121, 141, 147–8, 231, 242
    See also Chemise; Clothe; Dress; Garment; Shift
Turrón, *see* Food

Ubertino da Casale, 16, 71, 76–7, 79, 86, 173, 192
    Arbor vite crucifixae Iesus, 16, 73, 86, 192
Undergarment, *see* Garment
Undressing, *see* Dress
Unveiling, *see* Veil
Urban IV (†1264), pope, 59, 68
    Rule of Urban IV, 59, 147

Valencia, city of, 9, 68, 237
    Kingdom of Valencia, 96, 123, 236
Veil, 11, 63–84, 120, 128, 150–1, 202, 211
    Unveiling, 82–3
    Veiling, 63, 78, 81–4
Velluters, *see* Guild, of Velvet-makers
Velvet, 59, 81, 90–1, 95–6, 99, 111–2, 141, 143, 145, 148–9, 153–6, 171–2, 232, 243
    Azeituní, 141
    See also Brocade; Cloth; Silk
Veneration, 53, 63, 67–8, 75, 82, 89, 178
    See also Adoration; *Agnus Dei*; Body, of Christ; Corpus Christi; Host; Monstrance; Pyx; Sacrament
Venice, town noted for its silk industry, 91, 149, 155
    Dogaresse of Venice, 150
Vespers, 39, 52, 59, 112, 176, 222–5, 247
    See also Hours
Vestition, *see* Nun

Vestment, 22, 81, 96, 102, 107, 111–2, 118, 121, 123, 145, 152, 169, 232–3
  Alb, 148
  Cope, 96, 111–12, 123, 142, 152, 233
  Dalmatic, 81, 110–11, 148
  Gremial, 81, 145
  Maniple, 81
  Stole, 78, 81
  See also Brocade; Damask; Silk
Vida de Jesucrist, *see* Eiximenis, Francesc
Vida de Santa Anna, *see* Roís de Corella, Joan
Vigri, Caterina, *see* Abbess
Villasandino, Alfonso Álvarez de, poet, 134–7
  Petiçión que fizo a Pero López de Ayala
Villena, Elionor de, baptismal name of Sor Isabel, 2–6, 27, 58, 236
Villena, Enrique de (1384–1434), 2–9
  Albornoz, María de, wife of Enrique de Villena, 4
  Arte cisoria, 7
  Arte de consolaçion, 7
  Arte de trovar, 8
  Dotzè llibre del crestià, 33, 44, 145
  Doce trabajos de Hércules, 7
  Dotze treballs de Hèrcules, 7
  Exposición del salmo 'Quoniam videbo', 9
  Scala Dei, 30
  Tratado de astrología, 7
  Tratado de la fascinación o de aojamiento, 7
  Tratado de la lepra, 7
Villena, Marqués de, *see* Villena, Enrique de
Vinci, Leonardo de (1452–1519), painter, 185
  Vierge des Rochers, 185
  Virgin of the Rocks, 185–6
Virgil, poet, 5, 8
  Aeneid, 8
Virgin
  Madonna or Virgin, of Humility, 143, 189
  Virgin, of Montserrat, 121, 163, 185, 187

See also Feasts, of the Virgin, Expectation, *Nuestra Señora de la O*; Mother of God, Mater Dolorosa; Mother of God, Mater Sapientiae
Visió del Judici de Paris, *see* Roís de Corella, Joan
Vision, 14, 25, 51, 87, 106, 115, 118, 131, 155, 179, 201, 231, 241
  See also Revelation
Visitation, *see* Feasts, of the Virgin
Vita Christi, *see* Ludolph of Saxony
  See also Villena, Isabel de
Vocation, 6, 11, 210
  See also Abbess; Nun
Voragine, Jacobus de, Blessed (1230–1298), Dominican, writer, Archbishop of Genoa, 15, 55, 71, 76–7, 208, 213, 224
  Legenda aurea (Golden Legend), 15, 76, 208, 213, 224

Walnut, *see* Food
Wardrobe, 94, 134, 153, 242
  See also Clothe, Clothing; Dress
Wax, 226–7
  See also Guild, of Candlemakers
Wealth, 6, 58, 111, 131, 133–4, 142, 146–7, 177
Wealthy, 58, 134, 150
  See also Possessions; Riches
Weaving, 52, 61, 119
  Weave, 61, 126
  See also Embroider; Knit; Sew; Spin
White, 3, 63, 66, 76–7, 82, 167, 226, 231, 244, 253
  See also Colour
Womb, 46, 53–4, 67, 69, 79, 89, 104, 107, 115, 117, 138, 185, 187, 198, 203, 205, 222, 240, 248, 252
  See also Body, Female body; Body, of Christ; Holy Spirit; Incarnation
Wool, 91–5, 105, 143
  Flanders wool, 94
  See also Cloth; Fabric; Red, Crimson; Red, Scarlet

Zaragoza, town in Kingdom of Aragon, 117, 163, 194